Trench Warfare under Grant & Lee

CIVIL WAR AMERICA
Gary W. Gallagher, editor

TRENCH WARFARE UNDER GRANT & LEE

Field Fortifications in the Overland Campaign   EARL J. HESS

THE UNIVERSITY OF NORTH CAROLINA PRESS
CHAPEL HILL

© 2007 The University of North Carolina Press
All rights reserved
Designed by Kimberly Bryant
Set in Monotype Garamond and The Serif
by Tseng Information Systems, Inc.
Manufactured in the United States of America

This book was published with the assistance of the
Anniversary Endowment Fund of the University of
North Carolina Press.

∞ The paper in this book meets the guidelines for
permanence and durability of the Committee on
Production Guidelines for Book Longevity of
the Council on Library Resources.

Library of Congress Cataloging-in-Publication Data
Hess, Earl J.
Trench warfare under Grant and Lee : field fortifications in
the Overland Campaign / Earl J. Hess.
p. cm. — (Civil War America)
Includes bibliographical references and index.
ISBN 978-0-8078-3154-0 (cloth : alk. paper)
1. Overland Campaign, Va., 1864. 2. Virginia—
History—Civil War, 1861–1865—Trench warfare.
3. United States—History— Civil War, 1861–1865—Trench
warfare. 4. Fortification, Field—History—19th century.
5. Fortification—Virginia—History—19th century.
6. United States—Defenses—History—19th century.
7. Confederate States of America—Defenses—History.
8. Grant, Ulysses S. (Ulysses Simpson), 1822–1885—Military
leadership. 9. Lee, Robert E. (Robert Edward), 1807–1870—
Military leadership. I. Title.
E476.52.H475 2007
973.7′36—dc22

2007009466

11 10 09 08 07   5 4 3 2 1

For Pratibha *&* Julie, *Three Little Woids*

Contents

Illustrations

Maps

Preface

The Overland campaign from the Wilderness to Cold Harbor in the spring of 1864 involved six weeks of fighting that was unprecedented in American history. The campaign involved three field armies, nearly 200,000 men, and produced 64,000 Union casualties and 36,000 Confederate losses. It resulted from Lt. Gen. Ulysses S. Grant's determination to pursue the most direct line of approach to the Confederate capital, pushing Maj. Gen. George G. Meade's Army of the Potomac on a relentless drive across sixty miles of hostile territory and forcing Gen. Robert E. Lee's Army of Northern Virginia to fight or retreat to the defenses of Richmond. Lee's ability to keep his army in front of Meade's while other Confederate forces fended off Maj. Gen. Benjamin Butler's Army of the James enabled the Confederate government to remain in Richmond as the grand drama unfolded, but Federal troops were within ten miles of the capital at Cold Harbor by early June.[1]

Two tactical features of this campaign stand out: Grant's decision to remain in close contact with Lee's army until it broke, and the widespread use of field fortifications by both armies. The former was a calculated choice, but the origin of the latter was more complicated. Field fortifications were a more common element of Civil War campaigning before the battle of the Wilderness than historians and students of the conflict have realized. They were employed on a sporadic basis in many campaigns of 1861–63 in both the east and the west. The tendency was for combatants to dig in either before an engagement (due often to a commander's decision to remain on the defensive) or immediately after a pitched battle (due often to the soldiers' emotional reaction to the shock of combat). The Peninsula campaign saw widespread use of fieldworks: all of Lee's army dug in right after the battle of Fredericksburg, and both sides dug earthworks during the battle of Chancellorsville. Lee's decision to fortify at Mine Run altered the course of Meade's attempt to attack the Army of Northern Virginia in early December 1863.[2]

The armies were well aware of the value of fieldworks before the battle of the Wilderness, but they had not consistently used them in every campaign. With the exception of the Confederate Warwick Line on the Peninsula, Maj. Gen. Joseph Hooker's fortified bridgehead at Chancellorsville, and Lee's defenses at Mine Run, the fieldworks employed before 1864 tended to be shallow and moderately strong fortifications. Sometimes they were what the postwar generation termed hasty entrenchments, dug hurriedly just before the onset of fighting, sometimes literally under fire. Examples of this type of fieldwork occurred at Gaines Mill and Gettysburg. Moreover, prewar fortification manuals widely recognized that anytime a soldier took cover behind a preexisting terrain feature, such as a building, fence, or roll in the ground, that action constituted a legitimate use of field cover for defensive purposes — it was part of the story of field fortification.[3]

In short, there was no earth-shattering break from tradition when Grant's and Lee's men began to dig in during the Overland campaign. The real difference lay in one of degree — the extent to which the men relied on earthworks, the consistency with which they dug in, and the complexity and strength of the fieldwork systems they constructed. As a whole, American armies tended to dig in more frequently than European armies even before the Civil War. The Overland campaign greatly accentuated that difference.

The history of field fortifications in the Civil War has been neglected by scholars, even though it has long been recognized that these earthworks played a prominent role in the 1864–65 campaigns. The prevailing interpretation is that the widespread use of rifle muskets caused the armies to seek cover more desperately than they had ever done when armed with smoothbore muskets. That interpretation is open to revision. As mentioned earlier, fieldworks were often used during the campaigns of 1861–63, when smoothbores were more common. Soldiers dug in right after the fighting ended at Big Bethel and First Bull Run, to name two battles fought very early in the war, and after Fredericksburg and Gettysburg, to name prominent engagements close to the midpoint of the conflict. Psychologically, they were shocked by the experience of combat and wanted to improve their chances of surviving another contest as long as the enemy remained within striking distance.[4]

The same pattern surfaced at the Wilderness. Only a portion of either army entrenched with light fieldworks on May 5 and 6, the two days of heavy fighting at the Wilderness. No action took place on May 7, yet every unit in both armies dug in, completing two continuous lines of opposing earthworks across that wasted battlefield. If Grant had evacuated the field on the night of May 6, this would not have happened. Grant's decision to move on to Spotsylvania took the reliance on fieldworks to another level of intensity. Here, Lee's army constructed the most impressive trench system of its career to date. Not only did the Confederates dig in automatically when they reached the contested field, but also they dug deeply into the earth, constructed thick parapets with obstructions in front, and built numerous traverses, especially along the line of the Mule Shoe Salient. Some of the works at Spotsylvania, held from May 8–20, were nearly as strong as the semipermanent works that ringed Washington, D.C., and Richmond. This was the trend of the near future, with similarly strong earthworks at North Anna, Cold Harbor, and eventually Petersburg.

Rather than the presence of the rifle musket, it was the presence of the Army of the Potomac that inspired the Confederates to dig in so extensively during the Overland campaign. Grant's policy of continuous contact meant that the armies would be within striking distance of each other, subject to sudden attacks that could best be repelled if the defenders were behind some protection. Lee could not know when Grant would launch another assault, so the men automatically used their entrenching tools whenever they took up a new position. The Federals dug in too for a similar reason, but they also used fieldworks offensively to hold ground close to the Rebel position or to conserve strength on one part of a battlefield while massing an assault formation on another.

Similar developments took place simultaneously in Georgia as Maj. Gen. William T. Sherman led an army group consisting of 100,000 men from Chattanooga toward Atlanta. The defending force, Gen. Joseph E. Johnston's Army of Tennessee, quickly learned the value of fieldworks for defensive purposes. Sherman's men became adept at using fortifications offensively to lodge close to the opposing lines and deliver harassing skirmish fire on the defenders. In both campaigns, soldiers erected headlogs atop the parapet to shield their heads and shoulders as they fired muskets under the raised logs. Such headlogs had first been used at Chancellorsville and Gettysburg by members of the Union Twelfth Corps; the same troops served under Sherman during the Atlanta campaign, where similar headlogs were widely employed. During the course of four months, Sherman drove nearly 100 miles into Georgia and eventually captured Atlanta despite the many lines of strong earthworks the Confederates constructed in his path.[5]

The extensive use of fieldworks in both theaters led many observers to think of siege warfare, and they often used the terminology to describe what was taking place. Journalist William Swinton, for example, referred to the Overland campaign as "a kind of running siege." It is not entirely accurate to refer to Cold Harbor or the Atlanta campaign as sieges, for that term historically referred to an engagement whereby the attacker attempted to capture a fixed objective, such as a city. The besieger tried to achieve that objective by starving the defender out, or by constructing siege approaches above ground in the form of saps or underground in the form of mine galleries. Both the Overland and Atlanta campaigns saw some limited attempts to use siege approaches, most notably the start of a Union mine at Kennesaw Mountain and another at Cold Harbor, but the Federals never relied on starvation or siege approaches to achieve their objectives in either campaign.[6]

Both in Virginia and in Georgia, the campaigns were based on maneuver. Grant and Sherman did not allow themselves to be stymied by Confederate fieldworks, as had happened to Meade at Mine Run. They had plenty of room and a superiority of manpower to move around these defended positions, so that trench stalemate did not develop anywhere along the line of advance in either campaign. A key difference in the conduct of each campaign lay in Grant's insistence on pounding Lee's fortified positions with assaults that always failed to break them, suffering nearly debilitating losses in the process. It is arguable that such pounding was necessary to establish a psychological superiority for the Union army in Virginia, as Grant himself repeatedly argued and as some modern historians have accepted. Sherman did not need to do this, for Federal forces in the west had long before established an advantage in morale over their opponents. He had the opportunity to rely primarily on maneuver to deal with fortified lines, accomplishing his objective with far fewer casualties. As a result, contemporaries and latter-day observers viewed the Atlanta campaign as a model military endeavor while cringing at the Overland campaign as a gory mess. This is unfortunate for Grant's reputation, for he accomplished his goal essentially using the same grand tactics as Sherman and against a stronger, more resilient Confederate army, yet he garnered less credit for generalship.[7]

This book is meant to stand on its own as a study of field fortifications during the Overland campaign, but it also is a continuation of my earlier work, *Field Armies and Fortifications in the Civil War: The Eastern Campaigns, 1861–1864* (Chapel Hill: University of North Carolina Press, 2005). The reader is invited to consult that earlier work for more detail on my methods, sources, and interpretations in dealing with the history of field fortifications during the first three years of the war in the east. The research for this series of books extended over a period of nearly twenty years and has taken me to numerous archives and more than 300 battlefields and fortification sites. I supplement numerous soldier letters, diaries, and memoirs, both published and unpublished, with official reports, map research, examination of historic photographs, and relevant secondary studies of the major battles. A unique source of information was the battlefields of the Overland campaign, portions of which are fairly well preserved. The remnants of field fortifications at the Wilderness, Spotsylvania, North Anna, and Cold Harbor yielded insights into design and construction methods that were unobtainable in the written record. Many of the works at Spotsylvania and a small but important segment of remnants at Cold Harbor are priceless relics of the Civil War that are well protected by the National Park Service. The bits and pieces of remnants associated with the Bermuda Hundred campaign are not so well protected. Many of the maps in this book are the first detailed representations of the fortification remnants on many Overland campaign battlefields. I hope that, after spending many hours in the hot woods sketching their outlines, these maps will intensify public interest in the fortifications and help lead to an increased awareness of the absolute need for battlefield preservation.

I use the term "trench warfare" differently than one would use it for World War I, for the Overland campaign never became bogged down in anything like the matrix of complicated trenches that characterized the Western Front. Trench warfare in the context of the Civil War refers to campaigning that was centered on the presence of significant earthworks. When Grant or Lee made daily decisions about how to use their troops, they were forced to consider the difficulties of dealing with a heavily fortified enemy line. Much of Grant's thinking on the grand tactical level, at least by the time of Spotsylvania, was focused on trying to entice Lee out of his earthworks so he could fight him in the open field. Lee often commented on his desire to meet the enemy in the open as well. Ironically, neither commander fully got his wish at any time during the campaign after May 6.

Another volume will cover the subsequent campaigning around Petersburg, from June 15, 1864, to the end of the war. It will complete the series of three volumes that detail the use of field fortifications in the eastern campaigns of the Civil War.

I would like to thank the staff members of all archives represented in the bibliography for their assistance in making their holdings available to me. Also, Frank A. Boyle kindly shared a transcript of the Thomas A. Smyth Diary in the Delaware Public Archives in Dover.

I also am aware of the great debt I owe to the staff members of the National Park Service who are responsible for taking care of the battlefields of the Overland campaign. The fortification remnants are an irreplaceable historical resource. It is all too easy to forget, as one walks through the quiet landscape, that professionally trained historians, rangers, and security personnel keep a watchful eye on these environments so that anyone from a first-grade pupil to an aging historian can enjoy them in their own way. I have come to deeply appreciate their work.

My sincere thanks go to Pat Brady, David W. Lowe, Gordon C. Rhea, and the two historians who evaluated the manuscript for the University of North Carolina Press for their careful reading and helpful comments.

Finally, my wife Pratibha supports me in ways more varied and important than I can express.

Trench Warfare under Grant & Lee

Engineer Assets in
the Overland Campaign

By the spring of 1864, the commanders of the Army of the Potomac and the Army of Northern Virginia could rely on three years of experience with organizing and using their respective engineer assets. The Federal government entered the war in 1861 with a minuscule cadre of engineer officers and one company of engineer troops. Both were enlarged in the ensuing years. The Confederate government had started the war with nothing but soon created a small corps of engineer officers that was later expanded. The Southerners waited until 1863 to organize engineer troops. One thing both Union and Confederate armies in Virginia had in common was that they tended to be allocated the lion's share of engineering resources available to their respective governments.

FEDERAL ENGINEERS

The U.S. Army Corps of Engineers witnessed a change of leadership just before the start of the Overland campaign. Brig. Gen. Joseph G. Totten, who had led the corps as chief engineer since 1838, died of pneumonia at age seventy-six on April 22, 1864. He was replaced by Richard Delafield, who received a promotion to brigadier general as a result of his new assignment. Delafield, only ten years younger than Totten, was another venerable member of the corps. He had been one of three officers sent by Secretary of War Jefferson Davis to study European military systems during the Crimean War.[1]

Although the corps leadership consisted of elderly men past their prime as field engineers, the Federals had enough young, energetic subalterns to fill the needs of the Army of the Potomac. Of the 86 engineer officers on duty in early 1864, 21 were assigned to the east while only 9 were with Maj. Gen. William T. Sherman's army group in Georgia. The engineer officers with Grant and Meade tended to be young; some of them were fresh out of West Point and thrust into assignments with minimal field experience.[2]

James Chatham Duane, born on June 30, 1824, in Schenectady, New York, served as chief engineer of the Army of the Potomac during the Overland campaign. His father had been a delegate to the Continental Congress, mayor of New York City, and a delegate to the convention that ratified the U.S. Constitution. Duane graduated from West Point in 1848 and was commissioned in the Corps of Engineers. He taught at the academy and commanded the U.S. Army's only engineer company on the Utah expedition against the Mormons in 1857. He led the enlarged U.S. Engineer Battalion during the Peninsula campaign and served as Maj. Gen. George B. McClellan's chief engineer during the Maryland campaign. Transferred south in January 1863, Duane experienced the special problems associated with operating along the Georgia and South Carolina coast until returning to the Army of the Potomac as chief engineer on July 15, just after Gettysburg. He continued in this position until the end of the war, although his rank never caught up with his responsibilities. Promoted to major in July 1863, he never rose higher than a brevet rank as brigadier general before the war ended. After Appomattox, Duane mostly served on lighthouse duty, although he was chief engineer for two years before his retirement in 1888. Duane died in 1897 at age seventy-three.[3]

Grant also had an engineer officer on his U.S. Army headquarters staff during the Overland campaign. Born in 1831 in Massachusetts, Cyrus B. Comstock graduated first in the West Point class of 1855; he served at various coastal forts and taught at the academy before the war. Comstock worked on the defenses of Washington, D.C., was a subordinate engineer officer during the Peninsula campaign, and served as chief engineer of the Army of the Potomac from November 1862 until March 1863. His transfer west brought him into Grant's orbit, and he served for a time as chief engineer of the Army of the Tennessee. When Grant went east in March 1864, he took Comstock along as his senior aide-de-camp. As such, Comstock became one of the more influential advisers of Grant's entourage, at least according to the testimony of other staff officers and commanders. Brig. Gen. John A. Rawlins, Grant's chief of staff, blamed Comstock for the series of often ill-prepared attacks against fortified Confederate positions at Spotsylvania and Cold Harbor. Grant valued Comstock's opinion and sometimes used him as a liaison with his subordinates. Comstock's influence was felt on a far wider scale than the technical issues that normally occupied Duane's time.[4]

Junior engineer officers, such as George L. Gillespie, labored diligently at those technical issues as well. Born at Kingston, Tennessee, in 1841, Gil-

Cyrus Ballou Comstock. (Roger D. Hunt Collection, U.S. Army Military History Institute)

lespie graduated second in his West Point class of 1862 and was assigned to the Army of the Potomac three months later. He was awarded the Medal of Honor for his exploits in carrying a dispatch from Maj. Gen. Philip Sheridan to Meade on May 31, 1864, during the Cold Harbor phase of the Overland campaign. He was captured but escaped, then was nearly captured a second time but managed to reach Meade's headquarters with important information. After the war, Gillespie served for a time as chief of engineers. He also designed the standard version of the Medal of Honor, in use ever since 1904, while serving as assistant chief of staff of the army. Gillespie died in 1913.[5]

James St. Clair Morton was an outstanding engineer who saw service in the Overland campaign. Born in Pennsylvania, he graduated from West Point in 1851 and served at various coastal and river forts. He was chief engineer of the Army of the Ohio (later designated the Army of the Cumberland) from June 1862 until November 1863. Morton commanded the Pioneer Brigade of that army during much of this time as well. Wounded at Chickamauga, he later became an assistant to Chief Engineer Totten in Washington, D.C., then was appointed chief engineer of Maj. Gen. Ambrose E. Burnside's Ninth Corps on May 18, 1864. Morton lacked many of the social graces but was widely respected for his skill, energy, and personal bravery. The latter quality led to his death on June 17, 1864, during the first round of fighting at Petersburg. His loss left a hole on Burnside's staff that was never adequately filled.[6]

These engineer officers not only laid out and supervised the construction of fieldworks, they did a variety of other tasks as well. The demand for maps of the Virginia countryside occupied the topographical talents of many engineer officers. Also, given the paltry number of staff officers assigned to corps and division leaders, engineers often were called on to perform duties unrelated to engineering. They frequently were shifted from one headquarters to another, as needed. In the words of Capt. George H. Mendell, who commanded the U.S. Engineer Battalion, they were "almost constantly employed in reconnaissances, . . . in guiding troops to positions, and performing such other staff duty, as the corps commanders desired."[7]

The engineers assigned to the Army of the James also struggled to meet the challenges of the Overland campaign. Francis U. Farquhar, a Pennsylvanian who graduated from West Point in 1861, served as chief engineer for Maj. Gen. Benjamin F. Butler. He had earlier been an aide-de-camp on Brig. Gen. Samuel P. Heintzelman's staff at First Bull Run, was with McClellan on the Peninsula, and then went south to become chief engineer of the Department of Virginia and North Carolina. He took the field with Butler's Army of the James, but poor health led to his reassignment on May 17, 1864. Farquhar, who was a friend of Lt. Col. Henry Pleasants, the digger of the famous mine at Petersburg, then became chief engineer of the Eighteenth Corps in Butler's army until health problems ended his war career. He taught at West Point during the last months of the conflict and worked on many civic projects after the war. Farquhar died in 1887 at the age of forty-five.[8]

Another engineer serving with the Army of the James was Peter Smith Michie, who had been born in Scotland in 1839. Migrating with his family at age four, Michie attended a high school in Cincinnati, Ohio, and then graduated second in his West Point class of 1863. He was immediately sent to Morris Island, where he worked on the siege approaches to Battery Wagner. Maj. Gen. Quincy A. Gillmore took him along to Virginia, where he later became chief engineer of the Army of the James. Michie taught at West Point after the war until his death in 1901.[9]

The Corps of Topographical Engineers, in existence since 1818, was merged with the Corps of Engineers in 1863. Thus, for the Overland campaign, topographical duties were shared by all engineer officers in the

Francis Ulric Farquhar. (Massachusetts Commandery, Military Order of the Loyal Legion and the U.S. Army Military History Institute)

Army of the Potomac, but Nathaniel Michler took charge of mapping. Born in Pennsylvania, he graduated seventh in the West Point class of 1848 and was commissioned in the Topographical Engineers. Michler quickly made a reputation in mapping, surveying, and geographic exploration. He worked on a number of projects, including the U.S.-Mexico boundary survey, initial efforts to plot a course for a proposed canal across Panama, and reconnaissance forays across Texas. As captain of engineers, he served in the Army of the Ohio and the Cumberland until transferred east in 1863. Michler was captured by Confederate cavalry while making his way to the Army of the Potomac but was soon exchanged. He filled in as chief engineer for Meade in the fall of 1864, when Duane took a sick leave. Michler ended the war with a brevet commission as brigadier general. After the conflict he supervised public buildings in the District of Columbia, among a variety of other duties, and died in 1881 at age fifty-three.[10]

Michler prepared for the Overland campaign by overseeing the compilation of twenty-nine maps, to the scale of one inch per mile, covering the region between Gettysburg, Petersburg, the Chesapeake Bay, and Lexington, Virginia. He combed all available sources, including previous work by army engineers and U.S. Coast Survey maps, for topographical data. Michler's sheets were sent to Washington to be reproduced by photography, lithography, or engraving. In addition to these maps, which were distributed to commanding officers, several other series of previously compiled maps were reproduced for distribution.

Yet, all this preparation was inadequate. Michler soon realized that these maps were not detailed or accurate enough to enable commanders to select defensive positions or prepare marching orders and plan routes of advance. The countryside on which the Overland campaign was played out was "of the worst and most impracticable character—a most difficult one for executing any combined movement." Not even the Confederates had adequately detailed information, for the Federals often saw Rebel mapping parties at work during the campaign. Michler had to do the same, and his assistants anticipated the needs of the army and tried to probe forward as far as possible without getting shot or captured. Michler had two officers assigned to him, plus seven civilians and several enlisted men detailed from the ranks of various regiments. These men provided a constant stream of information that was used to update and correct preexisting maps, resulting in "several editions" of the general map Michler had prepared before the start of the campaign. The members of his crew were very busy from May 4 until the explosion of the Petersburg Mine on

July 30, one and a half months following the close of the Overland campaign. They had already issued 1,200 maps to the Army of the Potomac even before May 4 and supplemented them with an additional 1,600 maps after that date. The men conducted "over 1,300 miles of actual surveys" to produce these maps.[11]

Col. Theodore Lyman, an astute member of Meade's staff, found these maps to be less than all that was needed by the army, even though he realized the enormous effort expended to make them. The maps were "printed in true congressional style on wretched spongy paper, which wore out after being carried a few days in the pocket." After the war, Lyman compared them with a map produced by army engineers in 1867 to the scale of three inches to the mile. Compiled in peacetime, with opportunities for careful study and in a scale that allowed for greater detail, Lyman found these newer maps to be far more accurate in the configuration of streams and in the location of specific points of interest. Michler's wartime maps were accurate only in a general way—"in the distances and directions of the chief points." Smaller but significant points, such as Todd's Tavern and the house of S. Alsop, were as much as one and a quarter miles off their true location. The configuration of many roads was so far off as to be "quite wild." Lyman spared no words when he wrote that the "effect of such a map was, of course, utterly to bewilder and discourage the officers who used it, and who spent precious time in trying to understand the incomprehensible."[12]

Michler's men could do a much better job on maps depicting battlefields of the immediate past. After the armies moved south of the North Anna River, Duane instructed Michler to thoroughly map the battlefield there. Lt. Charles W. Howell led three assistants in surveying the ground over the course of three days. Men detailed from the 1st Massachusetts Cavalry held flags and tapes to aid the survey, and protected the party from possible guerrilla attacks. This map, later published in the atlas to accompany the War Department's publication of official reports and dispatches, is detailed and relatively accurate.[13]

The contingent of engineer officers serving with the Army of the Potomac was huge compared to that serving under Sherman in the west, but actually it was barely large enough to handle the many and varied tasks of the army. The Army of the Potomac had more engineer troops than any other Union field army. The U.S. Engineer Battalion consisted of four companies—one predating the outbreak of war and the other three organized after Fort Sumter. By 1864, the Volunteer Engineer Brigade con-

Members of Company B, U.S. Engineer Battalion, August 1864. (Library of Congress)

sisted only of the 50th New York Engineers. Both units had served consistently with the Army of the Potomac since before the Peninsula campaign. The 15th New York Engineers also belonged to the Volunteer Brigade, but it was on detached duty at the Engineer Depot in Washington, D.C. Butler's Army of the James had the services of eight companies of the 1st New York Engineers under Col. Edward W. Serrell during the Bermuda Hundred campaign. The other four companies remained in the Department of the South, stationed primarily at Hilton Head, Folly Island, and Morris Island. Butler also used a company of the 13th Massachusetts Heavy Artillery to manage his pontoon train.[14]

Both the U.S. Engineer Battalion and the Volunteer Engineer Brigade were commanded by regular engineers, Capt. George H. Mendell and Brig. Gen. Henry W. Benham respectively. Benham also was on detached duty at the Engineer Depot, allowing Lt. Col. Ira Spaulding, who commanded the 50th New York Engineers, to report directly to Duane. Born in Oneida, New York, Spaulding was already forty-six years old when the Overland campaign began. "He knew nothing of military matters when he joined the Regiment," recalled Wesley Brainerd, a friend and fellow officer, "and served devoid of any ambition except to perform well the

duties of Captain." Spaulding was a strong but unassuming personality, "one of the wiry kind that could stand a great amount of fatigue and thrive under it." He had no difficulty transferring his skill as a civil engineer to the military realm. Spaulding was promoted major in November 1862 and lieutenant colonel in June 1863; he ended the war as brevet colonel. Though his health broke after the war, he worked for a time as chief engineer of the Northern Pacific Railroad but died in 1875 of heart disease.[15]

Spaulding's friend, Wesley Brainerd, was born in Rome, New York, in 1832. He received an academy education and worked as a draftsman for the Norris Locomotive Works in Philadelphia. Moving to Rome as a businessman before the war, Brainerd recruited a company for the 50th New York Engineers and rose to the rank of colonel by the end of the war. He even led the Volunteer Engineer Brigade for a time in February 1865. After the war, Brainerd worked in the lumber business at Chicago, where he helped to fight the great fire of 1871. Later he entered the iron smelting business and got involved in mining operations in Colorado. Brainerd died in 1910.[16]

Rather than keep the 50th New York Engineers intact, Duane divided it into four battalions for the Overland campaign. Three of those battalions had three companies each, while the fourth, designated as a reserve, contained two companies. The regiment's twelfth company was on detached duty at the Engineer Depot in Washington. Thirteen to fourteen pontoons were assigned to each of the first three battalions, and twenty-four pontoons were given to the reserve battalion. Each of the first three battalions was then assigned to a corps: Maj. Brainerd's 1st Battalion to the Second Corps, Maj. Edmund O. Beers's 2nd Battalion to the Sixth Corps, and Capt. James H. McDonald's 3rd Battalion to the Fifth Corps. They performed engineer duties and took charge of the entrenching tools in their respective corps. If any of the battalions needed additional help or pontoons, their commanders could draw on the reserve battalion, which Ira Spaulding personally directed. This arrangement did not include the small regular engineer battalion. Mendell detached his companies to serve with individual corps only on an as-needed basis and usually for just a day or two.[17]

The Ninth Corps was not assigned a battalion because it was not part of the Army of the Potomac when the Overland campaign began. Ambrose Burnside outranked Meade and had commanded the army in late 1862, so he was allowed to report directly to Grant. This changed when the Ninth Corps was fully incorporated into the army structure on May 24. Even then, Burnside received no engineer troops, so James St. Clair Morton created his own. He devised a plan, approved by Burnside, for each division commander to designate "an old and reliable regiment" for engineer duty. The change was welcomed in some of the units thus assigned. George Washington Whitman liked the idea when his 51st New York received the order to take up the spade. "[W]e are not expected to take much part in the fighting," he reported to his mother, "but as our folks drive the enemy, or take a new position we go to work and fortify it."[18]

But Morton's scheme was impractical because it was only a halfway measure. The regiments were caught in the cracks that separated areas of command. Their leaders had to report to their brigade commanders as well as to Morton, and both officers placed demands on them. "Interference with his engineers was resented by Major Morton," noted the historians of the 35th Massachusetts, the designated engineer regiment for the

First Division, and deciding which commander to obey "was sometimes a vexatious question." No one approved of brigading the four regiments together under Morton's sole command, for the Ninth Corps divisions were sadly understrength; the parent brigades could not afford to lose an entire regiment. As a result, the designated units had to fight as well as dig.[19]

While Burnside's engineer regiments muddled through their double duty, the Volunteer Engineer Brigade was busy with a variety of tasks during the Overland campaign. Its members constructed wharves, using barges and pontoons, to build up Belle Plain as a supply depot for Meade's army. They dug trenches and even served in them as infantry in rare times of emergency. They corduroyed civilian roads, built bridges of all kinds, and cut military roads through wooded and hilly terrain. All told, the engineers of the Army of the Potomac constructed thirty-eight bridges during the Overland campaign, making a total length of 6,458 feet. The 17th Michigan began duty as the designated engineer regiment of the Third Division, Ninth Corps, by "burying dead horses, making roads, and assisting at working batteries" on May 18. The regiment spent some time digging trenches at the North Anna and Cold Harbor, and even acted as provost guard and as skirmishers for a few days at the latter place, but it spent more time working on transportation facilities. The vast majority of work on the extensive field fortifications of the Overland campaign was done by infantry troops. According to the clerk who recorded events in Company B, 50th New York Engineers, the "greater part of labor performed during the campaign has been on roads and bridges."[20]

In addition to the regular and volunteer engineer troops, Meade's army had a detail of pioneers attached to each brigade. These were men detached from the ranks, but they were never trained as engineer troops. Their job was to facilitate the movement of infantrymen by repairing roads and bridges, bury the dead, help construct trenches and latrines, and do any other jobs of manual labor needed by their brigades. At least one commander reported that his pioneers dug a trench at the Wilderness. Brig. Gen. George W. Getty, commander of the Second Division of the Sixth Corps, praised his pioneer officer Lieutenant Cole, who "constantly kept his pioneers close up" at the Wilderness and later "placed them in the front line and did good service until the close of the battle." In February 1864 Meade imposed a uniform organization on the pioneer detachments. He ordered each brigade commander to create one if they had not already done so, consisting of a lieutenant, three noncommissioned officers, and enough privates to equal 2 percent of the effective strength of the brigade. When the brigade pioneers assembled on the division level, a captain was to be detailed to command them. Brigade quartermasters had instructions to issue axes to half of the privates in the pioneer detachments, shovels to one-third of them, and picks to one-sixth. The pioneers retained their arms but pack mules carried their tools.[21]

CONFEDERATE ENGINEERS

Brig. Gen. Edward Porter Alexander, a superb artillery officer in the First Corps of Robert E. Lee's army, was jealous of the size and quality of Meade's engineer assets. They were worth the equivalent of a corps to Grant's demanding operations in the spring of 1864, Alexander thought. He went on to criticize Lee's engineer component, mostly because of a shortage of equipment rather than the quality of the Confederate personnel. A shortage of spades there may have been, but Lee's engineers helped the Army of Northern Virginia survive nearly a year of Grant's incessant hammering.[22]

The Confederates lagged behind their opponents in developing engineer resources for the first half of the war but were beginning to catch up by 1864. Most of the credit belonged to Jeremy F. Gilmer, who became chief engineer on September 25, 1862. Until then, the Engineer Bureau had been headed by a succession of temporary administrators. Gilmer had graduated fifth in his West Point class and had served in the U.S. Army Corps of Engineers and in the Mexican War. He had been Gen. Albert S. Johnston's chief engineer at Shiloh and Lee's chief engineer for a short time in the summer of 1862. Under Gilmer, the Confederate Corps of Engineers grew into a substantial institution. By 1864, the regular engineer officers numbered 120 with a provisional corps of 100 officers to supplement them. In June 1863 Gilmer had issued orders that spelled out the duties and responsibilities of engineer officers in the field. The government fully recognized his value to the corps by giving him a commission as major general later that year. President Jefferson Davis even authorized Gilmer's leave of absence from the bureau to help Gen. G. T. Beauregard defend Charleston, South Carolina, where Gilmer acted both as an engineer and as second in command of the Department of South Carolina, Georgia, and Florida. This ten-month-long tour apparently satisfied Gilmer's long-held desire for field duty. He returned to his administrative work in Richmond by the summer of 1864.[23]

In the field, it was not easy to find the right people for important jobs. Lee needed a new chief engineer for the Army of Northern Virginia in March 1864, just before the opening of the Overland campaign. He proposed his oldest son, Brig. Gen. George Washington Custis Lee, as a replacement for Lt. Col. William Proctor Smith. The younger Lee had graduated first in his West Point class and had ample experience as an engineer before and during the war, but most of his work had taken place well behind the lines or in the dusty offices of Richmond. Col. Alfred L. Rives, temporarily heading the bureau in Gilmer's absence, recommended Maj. Gen. Martin Luther Smith instead. Smith was appointed on April 6, 1864.[24]

Born in Danby, New York, Smith had graduated from West Point in 1842 and received a commission as a topographical engineer. He later married a woman from Athens, Georgia, and served in the Mexican War. When the Civil War broke out, Smith chose to support the South. He became a major in the Corps of Engineers but soon accepted the colonelcy of a Louisiana infantry unit. Smith rose in the volunteer ranks to major general by November 1862, yet he often performed engineer duties. He worked on the defenses of New Orleans and Vicksburg and was among those Confederates captured by Grant when Vicksburg surrendered on July 4, 1863.[25]

Smith was a superb field engineer, tireless in his work and possessing a good eye for terrain. He had a rectangular flag with a dark red background and white letters that spelled out "Chief Engineer. A.N.V." On May 3, just before the opening of the campaign, Smith outlined the duties of field engineers in Lee's army. These included the need to sketch the terrain at all times, noting distances, the location of streams, the condition of crossings for infantry and wheeled vehicles, and the availability of campsites and good defensive positions. When close to the enemy, engineer officers had to locate their position, noting weak and strong points, and see to it that defending units connected their flanks properly. Smith wanted his subordinates to make weekly reports of their activities as well as write formal reports after every major battle.[26]

Near the end of the Overland campaign, just after the June 3 attack on Lee's lines at Cold Harbor, Smith apologized to a friend for not writing more often. The press of business was very heavy, and he often had to spend the night separated from his headquarters wagon. Moreover, "bivouacking supperless under a tree or a bush, not to mention an occasional march or duty occupying the whole night," made for a stressful existence. Yet Smith was certainly the best chief engineer Lee had during the war, and he served at a time when the Army of Northern Virginia was entering the most intense phase of its use of field fortifications.[27]

Even though the Confederates were fighting on home territory, their engineers devoted a lot of energy to mapmaking. Alfred L. Rives, who continued to run the Engineer Bureau during Gilmer's absence, promoted the use of photography to reproduce copies of existing maps. He reproduced prints of a general map of eastern Virginia and of another map depicting the vicinity of Richmond. Jedediah Hotchkiss, a topographer attached to the Second Corps of Lee's army, sketched new maps of the Wilderness, Spotsylvania, North Anna, and Cold Harbor battlefields soon after those engagements ended. He also copied preexisting maps when there was no time to send them off to Richmond for photoreproduction. In addition to his topographical duties, Hotchkiss often helped to select, design, and supervise the construction of fieldworks.[28]

The Confederates were slower in organizing engineer troops than the Federals. The process began in May 1863, based on a proposal submitted by Gilmer several months earlier, and proceeded in fits and starts. Organizers encountered many roadblocks as they tried to recruit men from the ranks. Division commanders offered little help, reluctant to lose valuable manpower. In the wake of his heavy losses at Gettysburg, Lee agreed with them and suspended organizing efforts. Secretary of War James A. Seddon worked out a deal with Lee, promising to funnel enough conscripts to his army to compensate for the loss of men. Eventually the Confederate government organized all or parts of four regiments of engineer troops, all part of the Provisional Army of the Confederate States (and thus enlisted as regulars serving for the duration of the war). The 1st Confederate Engineers served entirely with Lee's army and was the only engineer unit Lee had at his disposal during the Overland campaign. Two companies of the 2nd Confederate Engineers, organized in the fall of 1864, saw service with the Army of Northern Virginia. The other companies of the 2nd were stationed at various posts along the Atlantic and Gulf coasts. Most companies of the 3rd Confederate Engineers served in the Army of Tennessee, while the 4th Confederate Engineers operated in the Trans-Mississippi.[29]

The 1st Confederate Engineers supplied "a want long felt by our army," asserted Lt. Col. William W. Blackford. "A better disciplined or finer body of men were not to be found in Lee's army." They performed a variety of tasks, including building bridges, large and small. The regiment engaged in earthwork construction but also held sections of trenches now and then as needed, and thus the men always kept their muskets handy. In addition, they helped to guard supply lines and unload stores when necessary.[30]

The regiment included some exceptionally good officers, all handpicked and most with some prior engineer experience. Col. Thomas M. R. Talcott was the son of Andrew Talcott, chief engineer of the Virginia Forces, the state army commanded by Lee in 1861. The younger Talcott had worked as a railroad engineer before the war and also served in the Virginia Forces. When the state army was disbanded late in 1861, he became an artillery officer and served on Lee's staff as an aide.[31]

As early as July 25, 1863, Gilmer recommended that Thomas Talcott be promoted to lieutenant colonel and put in charge of organizing the first regiment of engineers. The twenty-five-year-old officer threw his heart into the work, searching for innovative ways to fill the ranks because division leaders continued to balk at the idea of losing their men. He proposed that the large pioneer corps of five divisions in the Army of Northern Virginia be reduced to the average size of the pioneer corps in the other, smaller, divisions and the surplus men be transferred to his regiment. Lee quickly turned down this idea. As a result, the 1st Confederate Engineers received a lot of conscripts rather than veteran infantrymen. As soon as individual companies completed their organization, they were put to work. Company F performed pontoon duty with Lee's army during the Mine Run campaign in November–December 1863. Company D began working on the Interior Line of the Richmond defenses in mid-January 1864. A Union cavalry raid on the capital sparked fears for the security of Yankee prisoners held on Belle Isle in the James River, and Company A, C, and G were sent to guard the prisoners as soon as the companies were organized. These men performed their thankless guard duty from February 7 to March 10 before Talcott pried them away with the argument that he needed to train and drill his companies to prepare them for the spring campaign. He finished the organization of the regiment by April 1, gaining promotion to colonel, while William W. Blackford became its lieutenant colonel. Blackford had started the war as a cavalry lieutenant with no prior engineer experience but later accepted a commission as captain of engineers. He was assigned to Maj. Gen. J. E. B. Stuart's staff until appointed to the 1st Confederate Engineers and became a good field engineer by learning on the job.[32]

This lone regiment was a meager engineer asset for the Army of Northern Virginia, which fielded 159 infantry regiments at the start of the Overland campaign. Meade's Army of the Potomac had only one regular engineer battalion and one volunteer engineer regiment even though it fielded 228 infantry regiments in early May 1864. The pioneer companies of Lee's army helped the engineers to a limited degree. These companies had been in existence since early 1863 and consisted of men detailed from the ranks. They closely supported the infantry in noncombat roles. At the start of the Overland campaign, Lee had a pioneer company for each division of his army. These units repaired roads, dug trenches and latrines, and buried the dead after major engagements. Talcott proposed that free blacks be impressed to fill up the pioneer companies, but James A. Seddon pointed out that they could be legally enrolled for only six months and were more sorely needed to work on semipermanent defenses around Richmond.[33]

All of these Union and Confederate engineer assets—the professionally trained officers, the troops with specialized skills, and the pioneers working as common but experienced laborers—were essential to the operations of both armies in the Overland campaign. Their duties were only partially oriented around field fortifications. Lt. Henry Herbert Harris of Company C, 1st Confederate Engineers, kept a faithful record of his unit's activities during the campaign. From May 5 to June 18, it spent eighteen days repairing or building bridges, seven days working on fortifications, and two days holding the trenches as infantry. The other days were spent in miscellaneous duties. In short, 40 percent of the regiment's time was devoted to bridge work and only 15 percent of it on fortifying. When constructing fieldworks, the engineer officers laid out defensive lines and the engineer troops helped to build some of the more complex aspects of those lines, such as embrasures for artillery positions and large redoubts. But the infantry did most of the labor on field fortifications during the Overland campaign. This combination of technical expertise and brute strength produced the most sophisticated and impressive field fortifications yet seen in American history.[34]

ENGINEERS AS INFANTRY COMMANDERS

The Army of the Potomac, Army of the James, and Army of Northern Virginia had a number of prewar engineer officers serving in high positions of command. Meade and his chief of staff, Maj. Gen. Andrew A. Humphreys, had been topographical engineers. Two of the four corps commanders in the Army of the Potomac, Maj. Gen. Gouverneur K. Warren and Maj. Gen. Horatio G. Wright, had been engineers. Burnside's chief of staff, Maj. Gen. John G. Parke, also had been a topographical engineer before the war. In the Army of the James, both corps commanders, Maj. Gen. William F. Smith and Maj. Gen. Quincy A. Gillmore, had been engineers. Butler's right-hand man, Brig. Gen. Godfrey Weitzel, also had served in the prewar corps. He commanded a division in the Eighteenth Corps before being assigned to act as Butler's chief engineer. On the Confederate side, Lee had been an engineer and so had Gen. G. T. Beauregard, commander of the Department of Southern Virginia and North Carolina.[35]

The engineers who served in high positions of command in the Union forces failed to show much aggressiveness in handling large formations in the field. Meade's caution had already been demonstrated in the Mine Run campaign the previous winter, and Warren and Wright were competent but uninspiring leaders. Smith and Gillmore proved dismally inadequate to the opportunities presented to the Army of the James during the Bermuda Hundred campaign. Only Lee and Beauregard were aggressive, risk-taking commanders. There is no surprise inherent in the number of engineers who held high-level positions in the three armies, for the entire prewar military structure was heavily weighted in favor of the U.S. Army Corps of Engineers, which operated West Point and received the top graduates of that institution into its ranks. Moreover, it must be pointed out that Confederate fortunes seemed to call for more risk taking than was necessary on the Union side in the spring of 1864. Also, there is no evidence that the engineers who commanded corps and armies initiated the trend toward a more heavy reliance on field fortifications in the Overland campaign. In fact, the only corps commander who ordered his men to dig in early in the campaign was Maj. Gen. Winfield S. Hancock, who had not been an engineer before the war.[36]

GEOGRAPHY

The Overland campaign began and ended along the seam that joins the Atlantic Coastal Plain and the Piedmont. The former was lifted up from the seabed and moved westward by the movement of the earth's plates over millions of years. Constituting 25 percent of Virginia's land and averaging 100 miles wide, the Coastal Plain has a mixture of sand and clay. The rivers drain east-southeast in this part of Virginia, crossing from the Piedmont to the Coastal Plain. The seam is marked by the Fall Line, the presence of exposed rock in the streambed that creates rapids or falls. These rapids hindered boat traffic upstream from the Tidewater to the upper reaches of those rivers and gave an economic advantage to the towns and cities planted at the Fall Line. Fredericksburg, Richmond, and Petersburg owed their early growth to this geographic factor.

When roaming the countryside from the Rapidan and Rappahannock to the James, one can hardly tell that he or she has crossed from the Piedmont to the Atlantic Coastal Plain. The elevation ranges from a high of about 350 feet above sea level at the Wilderness to as low as 100 feet at Cold Harbor. The ground retains its flat appearance and the mix of pine and hardwood trees remains constant, although softwood trees tend to predominate. The weather is hot and sultry as spring gives way to summer. During the Overland campaign, the rivers of eastern Virginia posed obstacles that were overcome by an army equipped with pontoons and skilled engineers. The sixty-mile route over which Grant intended to travel was covered with dense forests and thickets, but it also had a network of usable roads and was close enough to available water routes to give Union supply officers some logistical choices.[37]

The Wilderness

Ulysses S. Grant wanted the Army of the Potomac to advance along the shortest line possible across the disputed ground that separated the Rapidan River from the Confederate capital. Benjamin Butler's Army of the James would cooperate with this movement by advancing toward Richmond from the southeast, aiming to cut between the capital and the important rail center of Petersburg nearly thirty miles to the south. The two armies could either compel Robert E. Lee to retreat sixty miles to protect Richmond or force him to be the target of a pincers movement from the north and south. If Meade tied the Rebel army down, Butler might capture either Richmond or Petersburg. Any of these possibilities could shorten the war by many months.

Grant made his personal role in this contest very clear. "I shall aim to fight Lee between here and Richmond if he will stand," he informed Butler. Grant spelled out Meade's responsibility in an equally clear manner. "Lee's army will be your objective point. Wherever Lee goes there you will go also." If the Army of Northern Virginia could not be shattered in open battle anywhere north of the capital, Grant intended to push it into the Richmond defenses and lay siege to the city.[1]

Neither Grant nor any of his subordinates could gauge the true difficulties of executing this bare outline of a strategic plan. Over and above the size, strength, and morale of Lee's army, no one predicted the extensive use of field fortifications that was soon to develop in the Virginia campaign. Grant gave a passing thought to the Richmond fortifications when he initiated plans to assemble a siege train to reduce the city. But it probably would have surprised everyone in all three field armies if they had been told in late April that the Overland campaign would see a virtual explosion in the use of fieldworks. Within a week after the start of the campaign, Lee's army was digging field fortifications at Spotsylvania that would rival the defenses of Richmond and Washington in their strength and complexity. Far from crushing Lee in open battle, and almost as far from easily driving him into the capital city, Grant encountered a major tactical problem of the Overland campaign: how to pry the Army of Northern Virginia from one trench stronghold after another in the long, bloody march south. Trench warfare settled into the countryside of northern Virginia even before Grant could think of using his siege train against the walls of Richmond.

Grant crossed the Rapidan River on May 4 with 120,000 men. He wanted to flank Lee's 65,000 veterans out of their entrenched position near Mine Run and thus steered the army through the tangled landscape of the Wilderness. Grant hoped to move through this uninviting terrain before battle was offered, but Lee struck as soon as possible. He sent Lt. Gen. Richard S. Ewell's Second Corps eastward along Orange Turnpike while Lt. Gen. A. P. Hill's Third Corps advanced to the south along a parallel route, Orange Plank Road. Both corps approached the right flank of Grant's line of march. Lt. Gen. James Longstreet's First Corps had a longer distance to travel from its winter camps near Gordonsville and would follow Hill's men. When they realized that Lee was offering battle, Grant and Meade assumed a defensive posture across the Wilderness from the Rapidan to Shady Grove Church, facing west. Both commanders planned to use this position as a jumping-off point to launch an attack of their own, hoping to meet Lee west of the Wilderness.[2]

This tangle of scrub and second-growth forest had already seen one Union defeat, the battle of Chancellorsville exactly a year before. Much had taken place in the meanwhile, particularly the brilliant Union victory at Gettysburg, but the Wilderness still held few delights for the soldiers of the Army of the Potomac. It was a relatively small area, about fourteen miles east to west and eight miles north to south. The trees had been harvested for more than 100 years to provide fuel for iron smelting furnaces. Most of the vegetation was now second- or third-growth pine trees and black oak, but the mixture included dogwood, hazel, evergreen, and chestnut. Most important for the soldiers, the Wilderness had a thick layer of underbrush and saplings that presented a royal obstacle to movement of any kind. The land was generally level, as the Wilderness lay at the junction of the Coastal Plain and the Piedmont. It was cut into by ravines and small runs that generally had wide, gentle slopes. On the center of the developing Union line, however, bluffs up to ninety feet tall bordered some sections of Wilderness Run.[3]

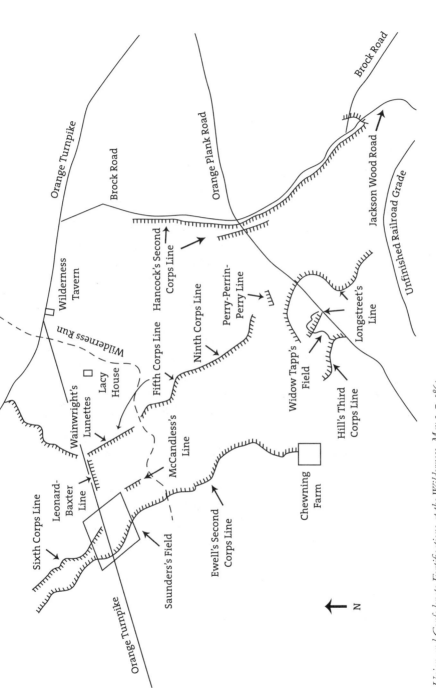

Union and Confederate Fortifications at the Wilderness, May 5–7, 1864

MAY 5

From the start of the Wilderness battle, portions of both Union and Confederate armies tended to rely heavily on earthworks while other units barely paid attention to them. Brig. Gen. Charles Griffin's division of Gouverneur K. Warren's Fifth Corps took position on the Orange Turnpike just west of the clearing around the Lacy House. Griffin's men threw together a log breastwork and dug a trench behind it, piling the earth on top. They also cut down trees in front of the line to clear a field of fire and create a tangled slashing to trip up an attacker. While Griffin waited for more divisions to extend his right and left, Ewell's Confederate column reached the western edge of Saunders's Field, two and a half miles west of Griffin, and began to dig in. The Confederates had the advantage of a slight rise and a wide, open field in their front. Ewell not only enhanced the natural strength of his position with "Slight works" but also bolstered it with thirteen guns. The opposing sides in this northern axis of battle entrenched even before the first shot was fired.[4]

It took all morning for Warren to assemble his men and prepare to advance. Three divisions went into line with another in reserve, while a division from the Sixth Corps was on its way to extend Warren's Line to the north. It appears that all the Fifth Corps units dug in. The old Iron Brigade, now in Brig. Gen. James S. Wadsworth's division, used its available axes to cut trees and brush while the spades were put to use in digging a shallow trench. Griffin's division started the action along Orange Turnpike by advancing across the open terrain of Saunders's Field at noon. In spirited fighting the attack was bloodily repulsed, but Brig. Gen. Joseph J. Bartlett's brigade achieved a limited success. Bartlett advanced along the southern edge of the field and managed to cross the fortifications, driving back Brig. Gen. John M. Jones's Virginia brigade. In a scenario that would become all too familiar in the coming weeks, Bartlett was unsupported on either flank. He could not maintain or exploit his limited penetration of Ewell's position and had to retire. Thus far, the Confederates were mostly content to wait behind their earthworks and shoot down the attacking Federals. But farther to Griffin's left, Brig. Gen. John B. Gordon's Georgia brigade and Brig. Gen. Junius Daniel's North Carolina brigade counterattacked into the open ground around Higgerson's House from their entrenched positions and helped to repulse Warren's left wing. The spewing musketry and artillery set fire to the Confederate works in a few places, and the blaze spread out onto the open field south of Orange Turnpike.[5]

The initial advance of the Fifth Corps was decisively turned back all

Ewell's Line at Saunders's Field, north of Orange Turnpike, Wilderness. The photographer probably stood in the roadbed of Orange Turnpike and looked north. Note how the log and post revetment is propped up with diagonal supports. (Massachusetts Commandery, Military Order of the Loyal Legion and the U.S. Army Military History Institute)

along the front. Warren's men fell back to the Lacy House clearing, with Griffin resuming his earlier spot in the earthworks. Warren had two fresh brigades left, under Col. Samuel H. Leonard and Brig. Gen. Henry Baxter. They took position along Orange Turnpike, facing south, while the rest of the corps continued to face west. Finally, Maj. Gen. Horatio G. Wright's division of the Sixth Corps arrived on the field at 3:00 P.M. Wright resumed the Union offensive by striking Ewell's Line north of Saunders's Field. Even though his division extended farther north than did Ewell's corps, a series of counterattacks by two Confederate brigades stalled Wright's advance. By 4:00 P.M., the fighting along Orange Turnpike shuddered to a halt.[6]

As the fighting rolled back and forth along Orange Turnpike, a separate battle developed along Orange Plank Road. A. P. Hill pushed Maj. Gen. Henry Heth's division eastward, delayed long enough by Federal cavalry

Ewell's Line at Saunders's Field, south of Orange Turnpike, Wilderness. This photograph depicts the forward and rear line; the number 43 seems to be located on the parapet of a gun emplacement. (Massachusetts Commandery, Military Order of the Loyal Legion and the U.S. Army Military History Institute)

so that Meade could rush Brig. Gen. George W. Getty's division of the Sixth Corps to the junction of Plank Road and Brock Road. Getty secured this key intersection just before Heth arrived, and Maj. Gen. Winfield S. Hancock's Second Corps was headed for the same spot. Hancock had marched to Chancellorsville after crossing the Rapidan River on May 4.

Confederate parapet at Saunders's Field, Wilderness. Most of the dirt has washed away from this parapet made of earth and logs. (Massachusetts Commandery, Military Order of the Loyal Legion and the U.S. Army Military History Institute)

He then redirected his line of advance westward, by way of Todd's Tavern, when Grant and Meade formed a line facing west.[7]

By mid-afternoon of May 5, Hancock's lead unit took post to Getty's left near the junction. He immediately ordered his division commanders to fortify on the west side of Brock Road. Hancock described the work as "a substantial line . . . of earth and logs the whole length of my line of battle." Lt. Col. Michael W. Burns of the 73rd New York referred to it as "a breast-work hastily constructed of such material as was at hand, such as logs, brush, & c." The left end was refused across Brock Road to the east,

Edwin Forbes's sketch of Second Corps constructing Brock Road Line, Wilderness. Note the thick growth of small saplings interspersed with older trees. (Library of Congress)

to protect the left flank. The men cut as much timber and brush as possible in front of the line. A drawing by field artist Edwin Forbes depicts the vegetation as small saplings, with a few older and larger trees interspersed. The cut saplings and trees made a good revetment for the hastily thrown-up parapet.[8]

Meade urged Hancock and Getty to advance, and they were ready to do so by 4:15 P.M. Two Second Corps divisions under Maj. Gen. David B. Birney and Brig. Gen. Gershom Mott cooperated with Getty in this attack, making a total of 17,000 men advancing against Heth's 6,500. Some Confederate units had fashioned slight breastworks of hastily piled logs, but Heth's line was largely unfortified. This was essentially an open field fight, at least as far as one could be had in this matted thicket. The overwhelming Federal superiority in numbers came to naught, as Heth's men put up a tough defensive fight and all three Union divisions attacked without coordinating their efforts. Getty, Birney, and Mott could not push the Confederates back.

Lee sent Maj. Gen. Cadmus M. Wilcox's division of Hill's corps to help Heth. Wilcox was too late to aid in stopping the Union advance, but he suggested a counterattack. The two Rebel divisions moved out at 5:30 P.M. and soon realized how difficult it was to attack in this tangled environment. The three Union divisions had no difficulty blunting the advance.

By now, army headquarters was well aware of Hill's advanced position, about a mile farther east than Ewell's, and Grant wanted Warren to shift some of his Fifth Corps units southward to attack Hill's left. Wadsworth's division and a part of Brig. Gen. John C. Robinson's division managed to claw their way through the brush so as to be only 100 feet from Hill's pickets by dusk, but there was no time left to deliver what might have been a crushing blow that day.[9]

Hancock's earthworks along the Brock Road failed to play a role in the fighting on May 5, except to serve as a fallback position in case of trouble. Both sides chose to engage on essentially unfortified ground along the Orange Plank Road, closing in for a sustained firefight that littered the woods with casualties but resulted in nothing more than a tactical stalemate.

A final round of fighting took place that evening on the extreme northern end of the battle line, north of Orange Turnpike. Brig. Gen. James B. Ricketts's division of the Sixth Corps arrived on the field by late afternoon. After spending some time taking position, Ricketts sent Brig. Gen. Truman Seymour's brigade in an attempt to get around Ewell's left flank. Unfortunately for Seymour's troops, Ewell had already extended his line by deploying Brig. Gen. John Pegram's brigade. Pegram's Virginians were told to entrench. "Our regiment had never up to this time, to my knowledge, fought behind breastworks," recalled William W. Smith of the 49th Virginia. His comrades did not take it seriously. They expected "to be called on, as usual, to jump those made by the enemy," so they simply made "a pretense of obeying the order, rolling together what dead logs lay convenient and filling in with loose stones and rails readily accessible."[10]

This negligence was very short-sighted, for Meade issued orders for attacks all along the front of the Fifth and Sixth Corps that evening. The only serious effort to advance was launched by Seymour, who drove unexpectedly into Pegram's waiting and poorly fortified brigade. The two units engaged in a fierce battle that continued until 10:00 P.M., when Seymour broke it off to recover from heavy casualties.[11]

Pegram's men had an immediate change of opinion about the value of field fortifications. As soon as the Federals retired, they threw their heart into converting a meager breastwork into a substantial earthwork, similar to the one that protected the rest of Ewell's corps. William W. Smith now marveled at how his comrades "set to work . . . with axes and other implements." Capt. Samuel D. Buck directed his men of the 13th Virginia as they worked "like beavers. . . . Dead trees were rolled together and soon every man and officer was busy throwing up dirt on the logs with tin plates, hands and in every way possible." In only one hour, Pegram's brigade constructed a strong earthwork in its front.[12]

Darkness put an end to a day of confused maneuver, stubborn fighting, and stalemate for the Federals. While Grant wanted Warren and Maj. Gen. John Sedgwick of the Sixth Corps to renew their efforts along Orange Turnpike the next day, he pinned his hopes on a promising setup along Orange Plank Road. If Hancock and Getty could advance west at the same time that Wadsworth and Robinson continued to advance south, Hill could be crushed. To facilitate this plan, Grant moved two divisions of Ambrose Burnside's Ninth Corps to fill the gap between the two wings of Meade's army. If all went well, five Union divisions would press Ewell's three divisions, while seven more divisions could overwhelm Heth and Wilcox.

Lee also wanted to take the offensive on May 6. Longstreet was not yet on the battlefield, but he promised to have his veterans along Orange Plank Road to help Hill by dawn. Lee therefore instructed Ewell to attack early on May 6 to draw Federal attention from Orange Plank Road. Nevertheless, Ewell's men strengthened their works on the night of May 5. Seymour reported that "the cutting and felling of trees was continual" along the Confederate line. Unfortunately for Heth and Wilcox, no one did anything to straighten out the confusion in Hill's corps. When Heth asked the corps commander how he should realign his men, Hill simply told him to let the boys rest and wait for Longstreet to relieve them.[13]

MAY 6

The Federals struck first early on the morning of May 6. Hancock, Getty, Wadsworth, and Robinson coordinated their movements well enough so that they came close to crushing Heth and Wilcox. Not only were Hill's units not aligned properly, but also most of them had not bothered to fortify their positions. Early that morning Wilcox had sent out his pioneers to slash timber in front of his division, but they were fired on by the advancing Federals. Brig. Gen. Alfred M. Scales's North Carolina brigade, on Hill's far right, had made slight works, but it retreated quickly from them because the Tar Heels were outflanked. Only Brig. Gen. John R. Cooke's North Carolina brigade of Heth's division had decent earthworks, and it held its ground longer than any other unit. Cooke also had some artillery on his line, and an open field fronted his position. Brig. Gen. James C. Rice's brigade of Wadsworth's division tried to push Cooke out

Confederate works near Saunders's Field. The photographer located this view on Ewell's left, between Orange Turnpike and Spotswood House. It looks south, toward the Confederate right. (Massachusetts Commandery, Military Order of the Loyal Legion and the U.S. Army Military History Institute)

of the way and was soundly repulsed. Soon after, with Hill's position collapsing, Cooke also withdrew. Even though some of Hill's units tried to toss together crude breastworks under fire, it was far too late to make a difference.

As the Confederates retreated in a confused mass, the pursuing Yankees were slowed by the tangled vegetation. They had managed to maintain cohesion and coordination between the divisions only long enough to push Hill from his position; now all that broke down. Birney's and Wadsworth's divisions collided in the woods, and confusion reigned almost as supremely among the Unionists as among the Confederates. This offered a few precious minutes for Hill's men to scamper westward. Lee's "composure was shattered" as he watched his veterans run from the jaws of a Yankee trap, and still the head of Longstreet's corps was nowhere in sight.[14]

A line of twelve guns under Lt. Col. William T. Poague was all that stood in the way of the advancing Federals. They were in the east edge of Widow Tapp's Field, on the north side of Orange Plank Road. Poague told his men "to pile up rails, logs, etc., at each gun for protection from bullets." Then he opened fire as soon as he could see Hancock's vanguard through the forest. His guns were unsupported by infantry, but the Federals hesitated and regrouped.[15]

At this critical moment, Longstreet finally arrived and deployed the head of his column. He threw his corps into the fight brigade by brigade, as they came up, forcing the Federals on the defensive. Col. Lewis A. Grant's Vermont brigade of Getty's division took shelter behind works that a unit of Hill's corps had dug sometime on May 5. The entrenchment was no more than "two irregular lines of old logs and decayed timber" on "a slightly elevated or rolling position," but the Vermonters repulsed several attacks before falling back. The 12th New Jersey and 14th Connecticut of Col. Samuel S. Carroll's Second Corps brigade also found a breastwork built by the Confederates and used it to make a determined stand. By 8:00 A.M., Longstreet's piecemeal offensive ground to a halt east of Widow Tapp's Field, but he saved both Hill's corps and Lee's army.[16]

Longstreet broke the stalemate along Orange Plank Road when he organized a renewal of his attack, making effective use of an unfinished railroad grade. Unlike Thomas J. "Stonewall" Jackson at Second Manassas and Warren at Bristoe Station, Longstreet did not use it as a fortification but as a cleared avenue of approach in this tangled environment. Designed to connect Fredericksburg with Orange Court House, the grade paralleled the Plank Road a quarter mile south. Only the right-of-way had

Confederate works near Orange Plank Road, Wilderness. The man is probably standing in front of this log and earth parapet, as the shallow depression he occupies does not seem deep enough to have produced the dirt on the parapet. If so, the view looks south. (Massachusetts Commandery, Military Order of the Loyal Legion and the U.S. Army Military History Institute)

Another view of Confederate works at Orange Plank Road. Some of the planks are visible in the roadbed. (Massachusetts Commandery, Military Order of the Loyal Legion and the U.S. Army Military History Institute)

been cleared and cuts and fills had been made; there were no rails or crossties. Lee's chief engineer, Martin L. Smith, discovered its usefulness as a way to flank Hancock's left.

Longstreet sent four of his brigades, guided by staff officer G. Moxley Sorrel, along the railroad. They appeared at Hancock's left about 1:00 P.M. as other Confederate units attacked his front. The Federals pulled back rather quickly, before Sorrel's column became firmly engaged. Longstreet personally led Brig. Gen. Micah Jenkins's South Carolina brigade along Orange Plank Road in an effort to capture the intersection with Brock Road. Elements of Sorrel's flanking column mistakenly fired on Jenkins, killed the brigade leader, and seriously wounded Longstreet. This greatly delayed the Confederate follow-up to Hancock's withdrawal.[17]

Nevertheless, the fighting was far from over. North of Plank Road, Maj. Gen. Charles W. Field's Confederate division pressed Wadsworth, who lost his cool and ordered the 20th Massachusetts to counterattack alone. The Massachusetts veterans had a good defensive position behind log works that Hill's men had constructed, but they reluctantly followed Wadsworth as he led them into a cauldron of Rebel fire. The regiment lost one-third of its number, and Wadsworth was mortally wounded. Field also took shelter behind a log breastwork for a short time.[18]

The Union force that had come so close to crushing Hill withdrew to the fieldworks along Brock Road. Grant tried to bring the Ninth Corps into play between the two Federal wings, but Burnside moved with caution because of the rugged terrain facing his corps. He held one division in reserve and sent another to reinforce Hancock. Burnside pushed Brig. Gen. Robert B. Potter's division and Col. John F. Hartranft's brigade of Brig. Gen. Orlando B. Willcox's division southward to find Longstreet's left flank. They made contact with a Florida brigade under Brig. Gen. Edward A. Perry, an Alabama brigade under Col. William F. Perry, and another Alabama brigade under Brig. Gen. Abner Perrin behind crude breastworks north of Plank Road. According to one report, some corpses also were part of the breastworks, which faced northeast. The Federals advanced and managed to capture a portion of the Confederate works, but a counterattack drove them back. Burnside added another brigade to his line and resumed the advance. He nearly broke Perry's Alabamians, but three additional brigades from Longstreet's and Hill's corps arrived in time to restore the Confederate position.[19]

This ended any threat to the Confederate left flank along Orange Plank Road as Lee and Brig. Gen. Richard H. Anderson, Longstreet's successor, worked to untangle the Confederate units. This gave the Federals time to settle into position along the Brock Road. Whereas some Union survivors of the Wilderness called the Brock Road Line "a first rate line of works," others characterized it as "extremely light." The cleared area in front was comparatively shallow, and the parapet was only chest high. Hancock had twelve guns parked in available open spaces at the junction of Plank and Brock roads. In addition, a man in Jenkins's brigade noted that many white oak saplings in front of the line had been so badly scarred by bullets that they had bent over, forming an effective abatis.[20]

Lee pushed his men forward against this position at 4:15 P.M., but the advance stalled when the men came within sight of the line. Estimates place the Rebels at a distance of 30 to 100 yards from the Yankees when the defenders began to deliver a heavy volume of lead through the woods. It is true that not all Federals fired well. Some of the green soldiers crouched too low behind the parapet and pointed their muskets into the air before pulling the trigger. But Lee's attack was broken up well short of the line by the Federals who did fire properly. Also, the thicket itself made it difficult to mass troops and push them onto the works. As Gordon C. Rhea has put it, the "Wilderness checked Lee much as it had earlier thwarted the Federals."[21]

Hancock's men probably would have held the Confederates at arm's length for the rest of the day if not for an unforeseen development. Just as the works on Ewell's Line had caught fire the day before, so did Hancock's Brock Road Line. Samuel Clear of the 116th Pennsylvania thought it was caused by burning cartridge paper from the Union musketry. The logs in the breastwork caught fire because the Yankees did not have time to cover them completely with dirt. The flames spread "for many hundred paces to the right and left," as Hancock reported. The westerly wind blew the smoke and flames "directly into the faces of the men," preventing them from firing and forcing many to abandon the defenses. At one point on the line, a pile of canister with powder charges attached caught fire and exploded, "severely" burning five gunners of the 6th Maine Battery.[22]

As portions of Mott's division gave way, Jenkins's South Carolinians moved into the gap and planted their colors on the smoldering works. The flags drew a barrage of artillery fire from the guns Hancock had collected near the intersection of Orange Plank and Brock roads. The Federals also mounted an immediate counterattack. Col. John R. Brooke's brigade of the Second Corps advanced from the south and Col. Daniel Leasure's brigade of the Ninth Corps came from the northeast. With the line restored, the Federals "pulled down the works each side of the fire and built around it," recalled Josiah Fitch Murphey of the 20th Massachusetts. Then they "let the fire burn itself out." While they waited, the Federals stayed back a few yards to escape the smoke. As Lee pulled back and dusk cooled the evening, the fierceness of this last attack was demonstrated by the bodies of seventeen Rebels that lay in front of a single company of the 20th Indiana. That evening, Hancock made certain that his command was well protected by improved fieldworks. "Line well built," he reported to army headquarters at 7:15 P.M. "I have just been around there. The pits are well filled and the men well prepared."[23]

To the north, the fighting along Orange Turnpike did not see such dramatic near misses as the drama that unfolded along the Plank Road on May 6. Ewell's men had constructed abatis in front of their works the night before. Col. Charles S. Wainwright, Warren's artillery chief, was busy entrenching thirty-four guns that morning. He placed them in a line south of the turnpike where the woods were "comparatively thin, . . . and much [of it] was cut by the men to make breastworks."[24]

The Sixth Corps was supposed to attack at 5:00 A.M. on May 6, but Ewell advanced fifteen minutes before that time. His units made no headway, resulting in a continuation of the tactical stalemate, but they forced a delay in the offensive planned by both the Fifth and Sixth Corps. With lots of pressure from Meade to move ahead, Sedgwick sent Seymour's brigade in another attempt to turn Ewell's left.[25]

Seymour again struck Pegram's brigade. "The men enjoyed the novelty of fighting behind breastworks immensely," reported William W. Smith. During lulls in the fighting—Seymour apparently advanced five times—some of the Rebels taunted their enemy. "'Come on. Walk up, gentlemen. If you can't come, send on your wooly-heads.'" This was a crude reference to reports that African American troops were with the Army of the Potomac. Smith remembered that his comrades were absolutely gleeful at the ease with which they shot down the Yankees from behind their works. "'Say, boys, isn't this the mos'est fun for the leas'est money?'" He later claimed that "a general spirit of hilarity prevailed" behind the parapet. Ord. Sgt. Buck Thompson became so excited that he forgot a basic tenet of trench warfare. Thompson stood tall to reload and was instantly hit in the throat.[26]

Seymour's attacks accomplished nothing except to increase the casualty list of the Sixth Corps. By 10:35 A.M., Meade acknowledged that nothing more could be done along Orange Turnpike and ordered Warren and Sedgwick to "throw up defensive works to enable you to hold your position with the fewest possible number of men." He wanted the two corps commanders to report how many troops they could spare to attack the left flank of the Confederates facing Hancock. Meade correctly saw fieldworks as a way to enable his army to shift the offensive to another part of the battlefield.[27]

More Confederate works near Saunders's Field. The log revetment is discernible, and there appears to be no trench. (Library of Congress)

Warren and Sedgwick readily responded to Meade's order. Earlier that morning Warren had used both the 50th New York Engineers and the U.S. Engineer Battalion as infantrymen. Griffin distributed ammunition to the 1,042 men in the New York regiment and sent them into the trenches south of the turnpike. The regular engineers had been given notice the evening before that they might be shoved into battle and took position on the morning of May 6 with fifty rounds of ammunition directly behind Ricketts's division just north of the turnpike. In light of Meade's order, Warren called for entrenching tools and put the regular engineers to work on the new line. Duane sent Nathaniel Michler to Sixth Corps headquarters to help.[28]

Meade warned the two corps leaders that if they wanted to locate the line to the rear of their present position, they had better strengthen their skirmish line to keep the Rebels from suspecting a move to another part of the battlefield. Sedgwick assured Meade that neither he nor Warren intended to fall back an inch as work proceeded rapidly on both corps fronts. Wright issued a directive to his brigade commanders in the First Division, Sixth Corps, to dig in on their forward position, "making any slight changes in the position of the lines that may be necessary to secure proper ground." They had to wait until entrenching tools arrived, meanwhile organizing work details big enough to get the job done quickly but small enough so as not to weaken the line. The circular even recommended what kind of fieldwork to build. "Probably most readily constructed will be breast-works of timber." Wright ordered that the pioneer companies help the infantrymen dig. Sgt. James M. Snook of the 50th New York Engineers brought three wagonloads of entrenching tools to Sedgwick by 1:30 P.M., after a three-mile trip that took him almost two hours. He distributed 400 tools, getting receipts from responsible officers, and then waited twenty rods behind the line as the men worked. Some of Sedgwick's troops still did not have adequate numbers of shovels. The 6th Maryland in Seymour's brigade had to wait until the 122nd New York of Shaler's brigade had finished its fieldwork and then borrowed its tools. The New Yorkers even helped the men from Maryland dig in before the tools were passed to yet another regiment.[29]

Soon Sedgwick was able to report that his "breast heights" were nearly finished, except in places where the men were too close to the enemy. Michler rode along the entire Sixth Corps Line, inspecting the work and offering advice where necessary. After that, he prepared a sketch map to send to army headquarters.[30]

Neither Warren nor Sedgwick gave up any of their troops to help Hancock after the Confederates launched a final attack late in the afternoon. It was put into motion on the report that Sedgwick's right flank was unprotected. Gordon's Georgia brigade was moved to Ewell's far left so as to hit the Federal flank squarely from the north. Two other units would help. Brig. Gen. Robert G. Johnston's North Carolina brigade was ordered to make a wide swing around the Union flank behind Gordon and strike the Sixth Corps rear. Pegram's Virginians would have to give up their well-used fieldworks and attack the front of Seymour's battered unit. If successful, the well-planned assault might engulf Sedgwick's right wing.

Seymour's battered brigade had received some help in the form of Brig. Gen. Alexander Shaler's brigade, which mingled its regiments with Seymour's. The two units erected earthworks that faced only westward. No one tried to explain why neither commander thought of refusing the flank and digging earthworks that faced north. This neglect contributed to the collapse of the Sixth Corps flank and nearly spelled a larger disaster for all of Sedgwick's units. Gordon conducted his short flank movement well, and the position of Seymour-Shaler quickly fell apart. A stream of running Yankees began to flow southward. James Snook almost lost empty tool wagons; "3 minutes after we left rebs were on the Spot," he later confided to his diary. Fortunately for the Sixth Corps, Brig. Gen. Thomas H. Neill realized what was happening in time to refuse his brigade's right flank and hold. Gordon was stopped in his tracks, and his brigade was the only arm of the three-pronged Confederate offensive that came into serious contact with the Yankees. Both Pegram's and Johnston's attacks failed as much because of the tangled woods as Union resistance. In fact, most of Johnston's Tar Heels lost their way in the growing darkness and failed to find any Federals at all.[31]

Gordon held a good portion of Sedgwick's fortified line when the battle ended. On examining the captured works in the dim light, Isaac G. Bradwell of the 31st Georgia was astonished by what he saw. The fieldwork was "made of dirt, logs, dead men, blankets, and every object that could be picked up. The dead presented a ghastly appearance with limbs extended out from among the logs and rubbish." The presence of corpses in these Sixth Corps works was later confirmed by another Rebel, Joseph McMurran of Walker's Stonewall Brigade, who also noted improvised sandbags made by wrapping blankets and rubber ponchos around balls of dirt.[32]

The Confederate assault nearly isolated the U.S. Engineer Battalion. After twelve hours of idly holding a line behind Ricketts's division, the engineers received tools at 4:30 P.M. and began to build traverses at the far right of the Fifth Corps line that paralleled the Turnpike and faced south. Gordon caused so much confusion and readjusting of the Sixth Corps position that the Fifth Corps units also refused their flank, effectively abandoning the engineers who did not know what was going on due to the thick vegetation. They had almost finished the traverses before realizing that they were between the opposing armies without weapons. In fact, some Fifth Corps units began to fire on them until an officer in one of the regular infantry units of that corps recognized the group. The engineers hastened back to the trench they had held all day to drop the tools and retrieve their guns. Company C was sent out on the skirmish line while the rest of the battalion supported a nearby battery, but no one came under more fire.[33]

Gordon's attack had been a close call. Lt. Col. Ira Spaulding's 50th New York Engineers was one of several units rushed to the north side of Orange Turnpike in response to this emergency, but it was not engaged. Only one man in the regiment was wounded by a shell fragment that day.[34]

The battle of the Wilderness came to an end after two days of bitter fighting. Many units continued to dig in on the evening of May 6, and Grant made sure that Warren understood he wanted the Fifth Corps line to be well fortified by dawn. Any units that had not already done so began to entrench on May 7, even though no fighting took place. Grant urged Burnside to fortify a slight hill on the Ninth Corps sector on May 7. By the end of the day, both armies were entrenched along the entire length of their lines. The 50th New York Engineers and the U.S. Engineer Battalion constructed twelve corduroy bridges across Wilderness Run, a small and sluggish stream that bisected the battlefield behind the Fifth Corps. Warren told Spaulding to keep his New Yorkers ready to go into action as infantry if the need arose, but he assured the lieutenant colonel that he would not call on him except "in case of absolute necessity, as the Government could not afford to lose the services of our men as engineer soldiers."[35]

TERRAIN AND TACTICS

The most impressive feature on the Wilderness battlefield was the vegetation through which the long lines of earthworks wended their way. It has long been held that the tangled trees, saplings, and brush of the Wilderness represented a marvelous opportunity for Lee to compensate for the disparity of numbers between his army and Meade's force. Confederate staff officer Charles S. Venable later recalled that Lee was happy to catch Grant moving through this area. It was obvious that the new Union commander had learned nothing from Maj. Gen. Joseph Hooker's defeat at Chancellorsville the year before and was willing "to throw away to some extent the immense advantage which his great superiority in numbers in every arm of the service gave him." Some Union observers noted the same point. Brig. Gen. John Gibbon, who commanded the Second Division of Hancock's Second Corps, told his family that "a small force is almost as good as a large one" in a place like the Wilderness. The vegetation was so dense that artillery could hardly be used, a fact confirmed by the report of Union medical officers who noted that wounds inflicted by musketry accounted for a higher-than-normal proportion of overall casualties at the Wilderness. Historians have also accepted Venable's interpretation about the advantages to be gained by meeting Grant in this matted environment.[36]

Yet there is every reason to question this long-held tenet. Gibbon himself, in the same letter from which the above quote was taken, went on to explain that the "whole country is a dense tangled jungle, thro which no line can march & see 50 paces." The terrain was such "that no very decided result is easily attained by either side. It is literally fighting in the dark for the possession of certain roads." Gibbon was right. The terrain of the Wilderness was just as much an impediment to Lee's ability to bring his troops to bear on Grant as vice versa. It was a mistake to use Chancellorsville as a model, for Hooker lost that battle because of a sudden and unexpected breakdown of self-confidence. Chancellorsville was a Union defeat because of a lack of effective leadership, not because it was fought in the vegetation of the Wilderness.[37]

In the woods, neither side was able to win a decisive advantage over the other. Whether conducted by Union or Confederate units, advances through the thicket always were brought up short as soon as firing began, and the advance quickly became a static firefight at short range. Only when operating in the few open areas were the Confederates able to achieve some tactical advantages. Counterattacking across Widow Tapp's Field, the brigades of Longstreet's corps were able to blunt Hancock's advance on the morning of May 6, only to stall once they had pushed the Yankees deep into the woods east of the field. G. Moxley Sorrel led an effective turning movement along the unfinished railroad grade, which enabled four Confederate brigades to move into a position where they could outflank Hancock. But as soon as the Rebels left the grade and entered the woods, their progress stalled. On the evening of May 6, a very promising attack by Gordon, Johnston, and Pegram was nullified by the difficulties of moving even one brigade at a time through the vegetation. Only Gordon was able to strike his intended target, chasing away one small Union brigade and another one that had been battered by useless frontal attacks on a fortified position. The next Federal brigade, Neill's, quickly ended Gordon's drive.

One of Lee's most potent weapons was the unexpected, smartly executed flank attack, and the terrain of the Wilderness made it difficult for him to use it. Stonewall Jackson had conducted his flanking movement at Chancellorsville on May 2, 1863, by moving along a series of roads and taking advantage of Hooker's indecision, as well as of Maj. Gen. Oliver O. Howard's lack of a properly refused and fortified line for his Eleventh Corps. Only one of those ingredients was offered Lee at the Wilderness, the open avenue of the unfinished railroad grade along Orange Plank Road on May 6, but Hancock was too wary to be caught and extricated his men in time. As J. F. J. Caldwell of Brig. Gen. Samuel McGowan's South Carolina brigade put it, the Wilderness was an advantage to the Confederates only if they remained stationary. If they had to move at all, they quickly lost all opportunity to keep the men well in hand. Lee's offensive tactics were muffled by his choice of battlefield.[38]

Casualties were horrendous. Meade lost 17,666, or 17 percent of his large army, while Lee lost about 11,000 men. In addition to the human toll, the relentless musketry tore up the vegetation like a machine. Chap. A. M. Stewart of the 102nd Pennsylvania marveled at how it "peeled, scarred and pierced" the saplings and small trees all the way from the ground up to ten feet high on the larger trees. The vegetation was literally cut down by rifle fire "as though a hundred axe-men had been at" work. Stewart found one small tree that had at least fifty bullet marks on its trunk.[39]

Neither army used field fortifications uniformly during the fighting of May 5 and 6. Edward Hagerman suggests that Lee failed to order entrenchments dug before and during the fighting because he wanted to entice Grant to attack him, or because he wanted to retain the option of taking the offensive. These were perfectly valid reasons for not fortifying, but Hill deserves criticism for failing to order Heth and Wilcox to dig in on the night of May 5. Their lack of protection and the jumbled nature of their line nearly led to a disaster on the morning of May 6.[40]

"The woods were filled with fallen trees of moderate size," reported Charles W. Trueheart of the 8th Alabama, "which formed admirable material for the rapid construction of breastworks." When Rebel units got the order to work, it was remarkable how quickly they could throw together some sort of protection, using bayonets or knives to loosen the soil and scooping it up with tin plates, pieces of bark, or their bare hands.[41]

The fighting on May 5 and 6 falls into the pattern of the past, not the future. A similar level of reliance on hasty fortifications can be seen throughout most of the Chancellorsville campaign. Judging from available evidence, the works constructed during both engagements were comparatively simple and of modest height and strength. The exception to that rule was Hooker's fortified bridgehead, constructed late in the Chancellorsville campaign to protect his line of retreat across the Rapidan River. It was a heavy fieldwork of commanding strength. Nothing on that level of construction was built at the Wilderness.

During the fighting on May 5–6, 1864, Ewell made very good use of fieldworks. His line was well placed before an open field, and he ordered the men to dig in even before the first shot was fired. Ewell used the works primarily for defensive purposes. Only occasionally did brigade-sized counterattacks sally forth to gain a temporary local advantage over attacking Federal units. This fortified line was also the launching point for Gordon's strike on the evening of May 6, a significant offensive designed to mangle and roll up Meade's right flank. Federal fieldworks north and south of Orange Turnpike were meant to serve offensive as well as defensive purposes. They protected the Federal position on the right wing but were often evacuated in order to launch offensive strikes at Ewell.

Hill ignored the use of fieldworks. Only sporadically did a few of his brigades take it upon themselves to throw together crude breastworks. Hancock, on the other hand, demonstrated a newfound respect for field fortifications. Like Warren and Ewell, his first act on reaching the battle-field on May 5 was to dig in. The Brock Road Line proved its worth as a defensive-offensive feature. From it, Hancock launched his ineffective advance on May 5 and his very effective attack on May 6. This line saved the Federals from a near disaster in the afternoon, when Lee personally directed a heavy attack against it.

Typical of the pattern set in 1862 and 1863, more digging took place right after the fighting stopped at the Wilderness than during the battle itself. All units of both armies dug in on May 7, and the existing earth-works were strengthened and made more formidable. The old pattern, exhibited from the battle of Big Bethel on, was to let fortifications play a marginal role before and during the fighting, but to eagerly dig in after the men had smelled powder and become sudden converts to the doctrine of trench warfare.

In the past, of course, that conversion usually was of short duration. Fredericksburg offers a good example of this pattern. The battle of December 13, 1862, saw a marginal use of fieldworks. Lee's artillery was dug in, but only a handful of infantry units built breastworks, dug trenches, or used the famous stone wall at the foot of Marye's Heights as cover. Lee fortified his entire line only after the battle ended. Yet he fought the next engagement at Chancellorsville on a different field with a strident offensive spirit and won a brilliant victory. His men went into the battle of Gettysburg disdainful, once again, of the use of field fortifications. If Grant had retreated from the Wilderness on May 8 instead of moving on toward Spotsylvania, the same pattern might have played out. But faced with continuous confrontation by an aggressive leader like Grant, Lee's men finally accepted the need for fieldworks on a continuing basis from Spotsylvania on to the end of the war. Lee's army launched far fewer attacks during the rest of the Overland campaign. Instead, beginning at Spotsylvania, his men happily dug in as much as possible before and during a battle and contented themselves with shooting down any Yankees who ventured near.

Trench warfare—the reliance on field fortifications as a matter of course—pivoted on the experience of battle in the Wilderness and settled in during the Spotsylvania phase of the Overland campaign. While Lee's army relied on fieldworks more obviously than Meade's, the Federals also accepted their value. The only difference was that Grant never intended to give up the offensive, and he believed that constant advances were needed to keep Lee off balance so the Rebel commander could not duplicate the surprise attacks that had ruined the reputations of previous eastern generals. "If any opportunity presents [it]self for pitching into a part of Lee's Army," Grant told Meade on May 5, "do so without giving time for [di]sposition." Comments like this one, and the bloody results of Grant's hammer blows during the Overland campaign, have led many historians to conclude that he lacked the artfulness necessary to coordinate large maneuvers on the battlefield. The common image is that he defeated Lee, eventually and at horrendous cost, by sheer weight of resources rather than by superior strategy or tactics.[42]

But this image of Grant is flawed. His performance in the Vicksburg campaign should disabuse anyone of the notion that Grant was incapable of planning and executing strategic moves that gained objectives at minimal cost in life. His opening move of the Overland campaign turned Lee's fortified position along the Rapidan and forced the Army of Northern Virginia to fight outside of prepared fortifications. Although Grant mostly reacted to Lee's challenges on May 5, he took the initiative on May 6 and prepared an attack by Hancock that nearly crushed a good portion of Lee's army. On the level of grand tactics as well as strategy, Lee had finally met a worthy opponent.[43]

◢ Spotsylvania, May 8–11

Grant decided on the morning of May 7 to disengage at the Wilderness and move on to the strategic crossroads at Spotsylvania Court House. The move began at 8:30 P.M., with the Fifth Corps in the lead and the Sixth Corps following. Lee guessed Grant's intention to sidestep his right and started Richard H. Anderson's First Corps at 10:00 P.M. Delays caused by Gouverneur K. Warren's caution and Confederate cavalry beset the Union advance. As a result, Anderson reached Laurel Hill, an open area at the junction of Brock Road and Old Courthouse Road northwest of Spotsylvania, only minutes before Warren. The Confederates hastily entrenched with logs and fence rails.

The battle of Spotsylvania began at 8:30 on the morning of May 8 with Fifth Corps attacks on this fortified line. Both sides committed units as they arrived on the battlefield. Warren's uncoordinated assaults were repulsed, and his men dug in on the opposite side of the open area at the edge of Spindle Field. Already the Confederates were building stronger fieldworks than those used at the Wilderness, with headlogs placed atop the parapet and raised by blocks to form fire slits. This was an innovation first used by both armies in 1863. The Federals employed such headlogs at Chancellorsville and Gettysburg, while the Confederates used them at Mine Run.[1]

George G. Meade extended Warren's line to the left as the Sixth Corps came up on the evening of May 8. There was brisk skirmishing as the Federals sought to find and turn Anderson's right flank, but Richard S. Ewell's Second Corps arrived in time to block all attempts. Meade ordered John Sedgwick to dig in as evening turned into night. Winfield S. Hancock's Second Corps remained at Todd's Tavern all of May 8. Situated at the junction of Brock Road and Catharpin Road, where the former angled southeastward toward Spotsylvania Court House, Hancock guarded the most direct road linking the Wilderness battlefield with the developing fight at

Laurel Hill, Spotsylvania. Taken one and a half years after the war, from the Confederate position, looking north across Spindle Field toward the Federal line. (Massachusetts Commandery, Military Order of the Loyal Legion and the U.S. Army Military History Institute)

Spotsylvania. He also guarded Meade's rear as the army commander sought to concentrate his forces at Spotsylvania. Upon arriving at Todd's Tavern early on the morning of May 8, Hancock ordered his division leaders "to intrench their lines, to slash the timber in their front, and to obstruct the road leading toward the enemy."[2]

Ewell dug in on the night of May 8, and his corps constructed what would soon become the most famous earthwork of the Overland campaign. Configured as a gigantic bulge protruding northward, it was known as the Mule Shoe Salient. This part of Lee's line was controversial from the start, for salients tended to be notorious liabilities. Vulnerable to cross fire and assault from several directions, the Mule Shoe was one of the largest and most pronounced bulges in any fortified line of the Civil War.

Maj. Gen. Edward Johnson's division of Ewell's Corps constructed the Mule Shoe Salient. Capt. William W. Old, Johnson's aide-de-camp, directed the placement of the line in the darkness, without lights or local guides. Old followed a slight rise of ground to deny the Federals an opportunity to use it for artillery positions. This forced him to adopt the curving bulge. The presence of Union pickets at the nearby Landrum House compelled Old to deflect the line southward to complete the salient. Old seems to have been in charge of this project, for Ewell's engineers did not object to his work.

At dawn on May 9, the Confederates could clearly see the defects of the line. The salient formed a three-sided pen that could trap thousands of Rebel troops. It was too late to alter it, however, for the Federals had all day to maneuver and attack. Lee's chief engineer, Martin L. Smith, recognized the need to deny the rise of ground to the enemy and argued that the salient could be held if packed with artillery. Lee was not so sure. He consulted with Ewell, who assured him the place was tenable.[3]

The salient was quite large—1,800 yards wide at the base and 1,320 yards deep from the base to the tip. Two civilian structures stood inside its perimeter. The salient was 1,160 yards wide at the McCoull House, which was 390 yards south of the tip. The Harrison House stood 560 yards south of McCoull's and 370 yards north of the base. A second line was constructed across the width of the salient between the two houses and held by John B. Gordon's division. Edward Porter Alexander, commander of Anderson's artillery, estimated that the salient added two miles to the Confederate line.[4]

Alexander considered the salient "a great mistake," an opinion echoed by many of Ewell's troops. Officers and men alike complained about it

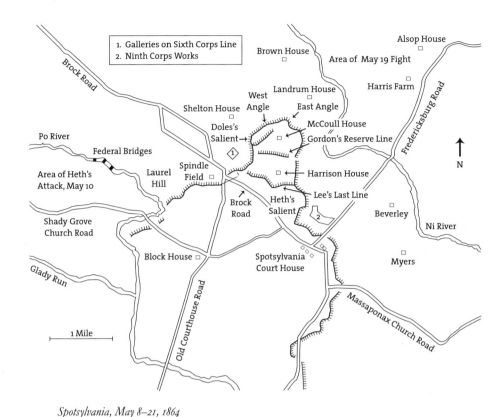

Spotsylvania, May 8–21, 1864

even as they dug during the night of May 8–9. Johnson's Rebels had few tools but worked diligently to make the fieldwork as strong as possible in order to compensate for its deficiencies. They cut down oak trees and piled the trunks to form the base of the parapet. The Confederates accomplished a great deal in one night and continued to improve the work for the next three days. Brig. Gen. James A. Walker, commander of the Stonewall Brigade, later described the salient as "one of the very best lines of temporary fieldworks I ever saw." He refused to blame Old or the engineers, arguing that the "force of circumstances dictated" the placement of the line. Artillery officer Thomas H. Carter, however, called it an "unfortunate work" and "a wretchedly defective line." Carter thought the Confederates kept it only because of the labor expended on its construction and because of "the belief that our troops, entrenched, could never be driven out."[5]

May 9 was mostly a day of maneuver and positioning. Grant sent the Ninth Corps to explore the possibilities of outflanking Ewell's right as Hancock shifted most of his Second Corps from Todd's Tavern to attempt to turn Lee's left. He kept Brig. Gen. Gershom Mott's division behind to guard the Tavern area, aided by earthworks built that day under the supervision of Company D, U.S. Engineer Battalion. Ambrose Burnside crossed the Ni River but stopped well short of the Confederate flank, while Hancock crossed the Po River and advanced to the Block House by evening. His further progress was stopped by Brig. Gen. William Mahone's division of Hill's corps, which arrived on the other side of the Po by 7:00 P.M. The river flows generally north to south, but its course loops considerably eastward in this locality. Thus Hancock was forced to cross it twice in his effort to drive to the southeast and enter Lee's rear. While Lee had little, as yet, to worry about from Burnside, he saw an opportunity to strike a blow at Hancock, who was separated from the rest of Meade's army by the Po River. On the night of May 9, Heth's division marched from Spotsylvania Court House to attack Hancock from the south. It would take all night and part of the next day for Heth to get into position.[6]

The Sixth Corps began May 9 by strengthening its fortifications. Later in the day, a Confederate sharpshooter at Laurel Hill shot its beloved commander. Sedgwick died instantly and was replaced by Horatio G. Wright, who would lead the corps for the remainder of the war. For other units on this expanding battlefield there was a lot of work to be done. Brig. Gen. John Bratton's South Carolina brigade of Maj. Gen. Charles W. Field's division took up a position west of Old Court House Road at Laurel Hill and made "a little breast-work of logs and rails." His left regiment, positioned in the woods, pulled together fallen trees to make its fieldwork. Cadmus M. Wilcox's division was assigned the task of guarding Lee's right against Burnside's tentative approach. Brig. Gen. Samuel McGowan's South Carolina brigade, one of Wilcox's units, built a line of works east of the courthouse using fence rails as the base of the parapet. Poague's artillery battalion took position 400 yards east of the courthouse behind works already started by another unit. His gunners labored to improve them. "This was our *first experience* in an entrenched position," he later recalled, discounting the hastily formed breastwork his men had thrown up at Widow Tapp's Field on May 6. Inside the salient, Brig. Gen. Cullen A. Battle's Alabama brigade helped to improve Gordon's Reserve Line. The 6th Alabama had only two spades, so most of the men used bayonets, hatchets, cups, "and whatever else we [could] find."[7]

Similar work was done on the Federal side, for the lengthening blue line was fortified as soon as it was formed. The companies of the U.S. Engineer Battalion were sent to various parts of the line wherever help was needed

Confederate line at Laurel Hill. This view depicts a line of sharpened stakes (inclined palisades) made of small trees in front of the Confederate position. (Library of Congress)

in strengthening the entrenchments. Many Yankees noticed the dramatic difference in terrain. The dense thicket of the Wilderness was behind them and the landscape around Spotsylvania was more open, with numerous farms and cleared spaces. Yet the patches of woods could be nearly as thick as the Wilderness, and the rolls and ridges were a bit more pronounced. There were "some magnificent forest trees" on the Sixth Corps front. Milton Myers of the 110th Ohio identified white oak, black oak, hickory, and blooming dogwoods. Small trees were in plentiful supply and were cut to make abatis. Officers reprimanded two men of Myers's regiment for cutting a big oak in front of the line, as it would "unmask our position."[8]

MAY 10

Grant continued to look for a way to flank or drive Lee out of his fortifications on the morning of May 10. The Fifth Corps demonstrated against the Laurel Hill line but could find no weakness. Neither could Hancock find a good place to cross the Po on Mahone's front. Receiving reports that

Lee was shifting more troops to confront Hancock, Grant withdrew most of the Second Corps while leaving one division south of the Po as bait to lure the Confederates into an advance. The other two divisions were to join Warren for a combined attack at Laurel Hill, to be directed by Hancock. In cooperation with this assault, the Sixth Corps was scheduled to attack the west side of the salient and Burnside would try to find a way to approach Lee's right. Grant issued orders on the morning of May 10 and set 5:00 P.M. as the launching time for the assaults.[9]

While Hancock withdrew David B. Birney and John Gibbon across the Po River, Brig. Gen. Francis C. Barlow repositioned his division to draw the Rebels. He deployed his four brigades facing south along Shady Grove Church Road, extending westward from the Block House crossing of the Po. All four brigades dug in along the south edge of the road. Hancock had worked out a phased withdrawal plan for Barlow's command, to be put into effect when the Rebels began to advance. The two brigades on the right, led by Col. Paul Frank and Col. John R. Brooke, were to pull back to the north side of Shady Grove Church Road and dig in 100 yards to the rear of their former position. The other two brigades, led by Col. Thomas A. Smyth and Col. Nelson A. Miles, were then to fall back to a slight rise and make "hastily a light line of breastworks of rails and such other materials as they could collect on the ground" to protect two pontoon bridges and one wooden bridge across the Po. Then Frank and Brooke were to cross the river, to be followed by Smyth and Miles.[10]

Barlow's withdrawal did not work this neatly. Heth deployed south of Shady Grove Church Road, opposite Frank and Brooke, as Barlow set his retreat in motion. Heth ordered his men forward at 2:30 P.M., and they easily took the line south of the road against minimal resistance by the Federals. Reforming at the works, the Confederates moved on and grappled hand to hand with Frank and Brooke. The fighting set the works on fire, and the blaze soon spread to the thick woods north of the Union line. While this battle raged, Smyth's brigade quickly threw up a breastwork to cover the crossing, but Miles was forced to ford the river farther downstream.

Soon enough, the hard-pressed troops under Frank and Brooke broke off their fight and retreated. Brooke's men got to the crossing, but Frank's had to ford farther upstream. A collection of guns that Hancock had earlier accumulated north of the Po played a crucial role in stopping Heth's Rebels as they continued to advance toward the crossing, giving Smyth time to pull back over the river. Heth repositioned his victorious division along Shady Grove Church Road at 5:00 P.M. as Mahone crossed the river to align to his right. Both divisions reworked the Federal entrenchments to face north.[11]

It had been a very close call for Barlow. The rest of the Second Corps had been taken out of this trap south and west of the Po River in time, but it had been a mistake to leave one division as bait for Lee. Barlow was only lightly entrenched—time was in short supply and no one intended that he offer a prolonged resistance to Heth's advance. The light works along Shady Grove Church Road probably were no more than shallow trenches and small parapets, weaker than the Second Corps works along Brock Road at the Wilderness, and Frank and Brooke were outnumbered as well. Excited by the combat raging south of the Po, Capt. Charles N. Turnbull took it upon himself to lead the U.S. Engineer Battalion toward the scene of action and volunteered to help hold back Heth's men. His offer was not accepted, but it earned him a reprimand from George H. Mendell and James Chatham Duane. Corp. Gilbert Thompson admitted that "it would be very poor policy indeed" to expose the engineers needlessly to enemy fire, "although I am ready & willing to do my best when the pinch comes."[12]

Heth's assault delayed and disrupted plans for the combined Second Corps–Fifth Corps attack at Laurel Hill. Hancock, who was to lead it, returned to help extricate Barlow's division from the cul-de-sac south of the Po River. Meanwhile, Warren got permission from Meade to begin the attack without him. He sent his corps, with Gibbon on the right as support, into a futile advance against Field's division between the Po River and Old Courthouse Road at 4:00 P.M. Warren allowed Charles Griffin's division and one of Gibbon's brigades to drop out of the attack.

The Confederates had already made their position at Laurel Hill too formidable to be taken by storm. Not only did they have a strong earthwork, but also an expansive open field offered an ideal killing zone. Abatis fronted the works, and in places patches of woods stretched all the way to the Rebel line, shielding the Confederates. When Hancock arrived on the scene at 5:30 P.M., Warren and Gibbon were still attacking to no avail. Hancock saw the "densely wooded hill" that Gibbon had to contend with, "rendered more difficult and hazardous by a heavy growth of low cedar trees, most of them dead, whose long, bayonet-like branches interlaced and pointing in all directions presented an almost impassable barrier to the advance of our lines." This obstacle was a natural slashing, conveniently placed by nature in front of Field's line. None of Warren's and Gib-

Another view of Confederate works at Laurel Hill. The same man appears here as in the previous view. This photograph depicts a line of abatis immediately in front of the Confederate works, and the pile of logs in the foreground was accumulated by local residents who were scavenging timber from the Confederate entrenchments. (Massachusetts Commandery, Military Order of the Loyal Legion and the U.S. Army Military History Institute)

bon's advances came close to penetrating this strong position. They were broken up by heavy and accurate fire, by the trees, or by the reluctance of men and officers to risk their lives in an obviously futile enterprise. Only a handful of Yankees made it to the Rebel works, and they were easily taken prisoner.[13]

Despite these difficulties, Grant wanted Hancock to continue applying pressure at Laurel Hill as a diversion for Col. Emory Upton's attack on the west face of the salient. By the time Hancock finished organizing his effort and set out at 7:00 P.M., it was too late to help Upton. This second attack of the day mostly repeated the earlier attempt, with Fifth Corps units and some Second Corps outfits making little more than a pretense of attacking. The only serious effort was mounted by Brig. Gen. J. H. Hobart Ward's brigade of Birney's division, which Hancock committed because it was relatively fresh. Ward managed to get his men into a section of Field's trench on the far Confederate left, held by Brig. Gen. John Gregg's Texas and Arkansas brigade. Gregg's Line bulged forward in a semicircle, creating a mini-salient. Some of Ward's men crawled through the tangled trees and caught Gregg by surprise, but they had to give up their foothold as no Federals came to support them. The key to Ward's minor success was that he pushed his men as quickly as possible, without pause, to the objective. The key to his failure was lack of help to exploit his gains.

Over on the Union left, Burnside advanced against Wilcox's Rebel division, which barred the way to Spotsylvania Court House. The Confederates had constructed log breastworks near Fredericksburg Road, the main transportation artery east of the courthouse. This was enough to cause Burnside's lead division, under Brig. Gen. Orlando B. Willcox, to stop a quarter of a mile from the courthouse and dig in. Willcox was dangerously extended, so Grant instructed Burnside to pull him back a mile, advance Brig. Gen. Robert B. Potter's division to join him, and form a uniform line from which a further advance might be made. Willcox secured his final position of the day with "fence-rail breast-works along the whole line." He reported to Burnside that he was "[w]ell intrenched" and felt "perfectly easy" about his situation. On the Confederate side, Heth's division reinforced Wilcox, taking any opportunity to capture the road junction at the courthouse out of Burnside's tentative reach.[14]

UPTON'S ATTACK, MAY 10

Whereas the attacks at Laurel Hill had been poorly coordinated and directed against a position already tested in previous action, the Sixth Corps

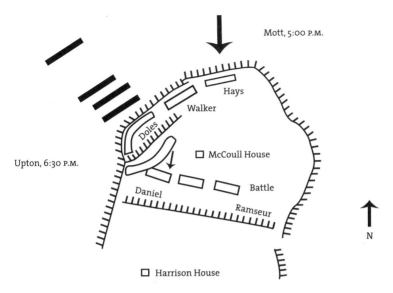

Mott, 5:00 P.M.

Hays

Walker

Doles

McCoull House

Upton, 6:30 P.M.

Battle

Daniel

Ramseur

N

Harrison House

Upton's Attack on Doles's Salient, May 10, 1864

assault on the west side of the Mule Shoe Salient was well planned and brilliantly executed, at least up to a point. It also aimed at a yet unchallenged part of Lee's line. Emory Upton was chosen to lead the attack after much consultation between Grant, Meade, Wright, and division leader Brig. Gen. David A. Russell. Upton was allowed to handpick his units, and he chose twelve regiments from four brigades—a total of 5,000 men.

One of Meade's engineer officers, Lt. Ranald S. Mackenzie, helped Russell select the spot to be attacked. It was a shallow bulge halfway along the west side of the salient held by Brig. Gen. George Doles's Georgia brigade and therefore known as Doles's Salient. Two hundred yards of open ground lay before the line, but a thick woods west of that field provided a perfect place for Upton to mass his troops. Also, Doles had no skirmish line in front of his position because the Federals were too close. A secondary line lay 100 yards behind Doles. It was short, just long enough for one brigade, and its left end was connected to the main line by an extension of the parapet. This meant that the area encompassed by the salient was open only to the Confederate right. If Upton broke through the forward line, he would find himself in a pen, forced to break through another line or wriggle his way through the sole opening. Presumably neither Russell nor Mackenzie saw this secondary line, although Russell had a clear enough view of Doles's forward line to see that the Rebel works were "very carefully finished, high as a man's head & loopholes at top," as he told staff officer Oliver Wendell Holmes Jr. Upton later reported on the headlogs, abatis, and numerous traverses that graced Doles's fortification. In addition, Gordon's Reserve Line ended a couple of hundred yards south of Doles's Salient. Even if the Federals broke out of the pen at Doles's position, they would be compartmentalized in the northern half of the larger salient. The tactical problem was harder than any Federal commander realized, and the possibilities for a decisive breakthrough more limited as well.[15]

Upton prepared carefully for the attack. He showed each regimental commander the ground to be crossed and explained what was expected of him. His command deployed into four lines of three regiments each. The first line was to penetrate the works without firing a shot and then go right to widen the breach. The second line was to stop inside the works and fire ahead at any Rebels who appeared, supported by the third line. The fourth was to stay in the woods and act as a reserve.

Mott's division of the Second Corps was supposed to support Upton's left flank. Mott had marched his command from Todd's Tavern on the evening of May 9 to the Brown House, four-fifths of a mile from the tip of the Mule Shoe Salient. His job initially was to cover the gap between the Sixth and Ninth Corps. That was an impossible task with his available manpower. Then Mott received orders to help Upton, but he was not informed that the attack scheduled for 5:00 P.M. had to be postponed. He dutifully advanced at 5:00 P.M. with only 1,500 men, for the rest of his small division was stretched out in a long picket line trying to cover the expanse of wooded ground toward Burnside's right. This pitiful advance hit the Confederate line far to the left of Upton's intended attack, near the tip of the Mule Shoe Salient, at a section held by Brig. Gen. Harry T. Hays's Louisiana brigade, and was easily repulsed. Mott's effort to support Upton was a failure due to inadequate resources and neglect on the part of higher commanders and their staffs. Moreover, he was too far away from Upton to effectively cooperate with him.[16]

After a half-hour bombardment by three Union batteries, Upton launched his attack at 6:35 P.M. It was nearing dusk, but the handpicked regiments moved swiftly across the open ground and broke through the line almost before the Confederates knew what was happening. Once again, as with Ward's brigade at Laurel Hill, a speedy crossing of the killing field greatly facilitated success. For a while, the first Union line was stalled at Doles's works. The Georgians crouched behind the parapet with bayonets fixed, "ready to impale the first who should leap over," as Upton dramatically put it. While some intrepid Federals jumped up on the parapet and were shot down, others "held their pieces at arms length and fired downward." Some Yankees tossed their bayoneted muskets across the parapet into the Confederate trench. As more Federals managed to cross the embankment, numbers began to tell, and soon Doles's position fell apart. Upton's men, "like a resistless wave," captured Doles himself, over a thousand prisoners, several flags, and Smith's battery of Lt. Col. Robert A. Hardaway's battalion.[17]

Other Rebel units, however, responded swiftly to this rupture. Brig. Gen. Junius Daniel's North Carolina brigade held the short secondary work 100 yards behind Doles. His left, which joined the forward line at Doles's left flank, held firm, but Daniel refused his right wing so that most of the secondary line was abandoned. This opened up the pen, but it strengthened the main line to the south of Upton's breakthrough. Daniel gave up a local advantage to prevent a wider rupture of the defenses that protected the Mule Shoe Salient. There was a risk in this, because Gordon had earlier evacuated his secondary line across the salient to act as a reserve farther to the left where an attack was expected. In short, both Confederate trench lines south of Upton's break were empty. Cullen A. Battle's and Stephen D. Ramseur's brigades came up from the south to reinforce Daniel's makeshift position in the open. They held firmly against all of Upton's efforts to widen the breach to his right.

This completed phase one of the Rebel effort to contain Upton. Phase two was offensive in nature. Brig. Gen. Robert D. Johnston's North Carolina brigade came from a point farther to the left to counterattack, aiming for another point north of the breach. Walker's Stonewall Brigade did likewise, supported by Brig. Gen. George H. Steuart's North Carolina and Virginia brigade. The latter rushed from the far right of Ewell's Second Corps line, across the width of the Mule Shoe Salient, to advance to the left of Walker's brigade. Col. Clement A. Evans's Georgia brigade also advanced on the southeast side of the breach.

These movements essentially created a wall around the break on all sides. Upton not only was stalled but also outnumbered. His men fell back to the outside of the captured works, allowing the Confederates to reenter the pen and free Doles and many other prisoners. The battery also was reclaimed. Upton's tantalizing success evaporated quickly, and the fight was over by 7:30 P.M.

Upton's carefully crafted attack was highly successful in opening a hole in the Confederate position, but the necessary second step—to widen and exploit—was never taken. Daniel's quick response to the breakthrough prevented Upton from opening the breach wider, and the absence of Mott allowed the Confederates to reposition a few of the brigades packed in the Mule Shoe Salient to restore the line. Upton's fourth line gamely went forward to help, but the men were too few in number. The Federals lost 1,000 men in this fight while the Confederate casualties totaled 1,300 troops.[18]

Ewell's veterans performed well in defending the Mule Shoe Salient. Perhaps they compensated for the weaknesses inherent in the salient position with a heightened sense of alertness and keen determination to hold their segment of Lee's line regardless of its deficiencies. But Lee was understandably troubled by the affair. He issued detailed instructions to Ewell on minor tactical matters, a rare departure from habit for him. Ewell was to do everything to get ready for more attacks. "I wish General Rodes to rectify his line and improve its defenses, especially that part which seemed so easily overcome this afternoon," he lectured Ewell. "If no flanking arrangement[,] a ditch had better be dug on the outside, and an abatis made in front." There is, however, no indication that these suggestions were carried out. Digging a ditch outside the parapet only 200 yards from Union skirmishers, even at night, was not worth the risk.[19]

The fighting on May 10 cost Grant 4,100 men. It resulted in the avoidance of a near disaster to Barlow's division on the right, paltry gains by Burnside on the left, useless slaughter in the Second and Fifth Corps at Laurel Hill, and a brief success by Upton that was not taken advantage of due to inept planning for support troops. Grant deserved much of the blame for these failures. He impulsively set operations into motion with inadequate reconnaissance to see where the Rebels were weak. The biggest effort of the day took place at Laurel Hill, the strongest segment of Lee's line. Except for Upton's part of the program, assault preparation was meager and uncoordinated. The attempt by Mott to help Upton, despite the insurmountable difficulties he faced, was the worst operational failure of the day.[20]

MAY 11

The work of entrenching continued on the night of May 10. Hill's Corps extended Lee's line to the right of Ewell to form a continuous trench from Laurel Hill to Fredericksburg Road. Marcus B. Toney helped to dig another bulge, called Heth's Salient, just south of the Mule Shoe Salient. It was a minor protrusion in comparison and would prove resilient against attacks in the coming days. The work on Heth's Salient was done on a dark night in dense woods. The engineers who laid it out shouted to each other to coordinate their efforts, a tactic made possible by the absence of Federal units nearby. Toney and his comrades used bayonets and tin plates to throw up a defensible work by morning. The trench was over five feet deep, and pine logs topped the parapet. A constant drizzle all day on May 11 muddied the newly dug trench and made the men miserable.[21]

McGowan's South Carolina brigade began a typical feature of trench warfare, keeping one-third of its men awake all night and rousing the rest at 3:00 A.M. to guard against a possible dawn attack. Such vigilance was justified, for the campaign was far from over. If the Federals came, however, they could expect resilient soldiers behind strong earthworks. "We now have good breastworks," crowed Col. Bryan Grimes of the 4th North Carolina in Ramseur's brigade, "and will slay them worse than ever."[22]

That evening, an interesting discussion of Grant's handling of the campaign took place between Lee and several of his subordinates. A. P. Hill and others had gathered at Heth's headquarters, a church in the village of Spotsylvania, for some business. Many present criticized Grant for wasting his manpower on fruitless attacks against their strong fortifications, but Lee disagreed. "'Gentlemen, I think that General Grant has managed his affairs remarkably well up to the present time.'" As the group continued to debate Grant's generalship, Hill boasted that he wanted the Yankees to "'continue to attack our breastworks; we can stand that very well.'" Lee again disagreed by voicing his greatest fear. "'This army cannot stand a siege,'" he stated, "'we must end this business on the battlefield, not in a fortified place.'" Yet that evening Lee mistakenly read Grant's movements as an indication that he planned to break contact and retreat to Fredericksburg. Lee told Heth that he wanted to go on the offensive if the Federals withdrew northward.[23]

Lee's reading of Grant's intentions broke down on the evening of May 11. Instead of retreating to Fredericksburg, the Union movements that night portended another attack. Meade had begun the day by asking his corps commanders "to determine what further works, if any, are necessary to reduce the number of men holding them to the lowest number possible" so as to spare troops for another attack. While Wright felt secure enough with his present works to send 6,000 men, Warren wanted his division leaders to cut trees "well out to the front" of the Fifth Corps line before he could spare any troops.[24]

Grant was encouraged by Upton's partial success on May 10 and decided by mid-afternoon on May 11 to duplicate it on a much more massive scale.

Instead of trying to figure out how to use support troops to widen the initial breach, Grant simply decided to mass thousands of men in the first strike force. The entire Second Corps, some 20,000 men, would smash into the tip of the Mule Shoe Salient from a staging area near the Brown House, where Mott's division was still stationed. The Fifth Corps was to hold Lee's left in place at Laurel Hill, while the Ninth Corps was to hit the east side of the salient and the Sixth Corps would be ready to help wherever needed.

It was a complex plan, and Grant did not allow much opportunity to prepare it. He insisted that Hancock strike at dawn on May 12. As trusted members of his staff went to tell Burnside of his part in the program, Grant decided they should scout the Rebel lines on their way back to headquarters. Cyrus B. Comstock, Orville E. Babcock, and three of Hancock's aides started back too late to see much before dusk, and drizzly rain further impeded their ability to reconnoiter. Mott, whose division had held this area for some time, had little to offer in the way of intelligence. As a result, so few details of the battlefield were known that Hancock used a compass to determine his line of advance. Everyone knew that "a large white house"—McCoull's—was located inside the Rebel salient; someone took a bearing on it from the Brown House before dark and marked the direction. One of Mott's officers drew a crude map of the area on the wall of the Brown House to help orient Second Corps staff.[25]

Hancock's men started from Laurel Hill at 10:00 P.M. on May 11, moving behind the Sixth Corps on their way to the Brown House. George H. Mendell led the way along muddy lanes. The head of the column reached the staging area at 12:30 A.M., but it was nearly dawn before the massive attack force completed its formation on and near the Brown property. Barlow deployed in an open field while Birney assembled in woods to his right. Mott was to go in behind Birney, and Gibbon was to act as a reserve.[26]

Barlow was not pleased with the prospects. Hancock could give him no detailed information about the terrain, the conditions of the Rebel works, or the strength of the units behind them. The only thing Barlow could do was mass his division in a tight formation so as to get as many men into the works as fast as possible. He wanted "to charge through Hell itself," in the words of his staff officer, Lt. John D. Black, and Hancock consented to his wishes. Barlow placed his twenty-three regiments in "a solid square," with Miles and Brooke in front and Smyth and Col. Hiram R. Brown (who relieved Frank after he was arrested for drunkenness on May 10) forming the second line. Spaces between regiments and between brigades were reduced to effect a more compact formation. Barlow, depressed at the thought of what would happen in such an uncertain venture, considered his attack a forlorn hope. His only chance was to get into the salient quickly and capture the Rebel artillery before the guns could tear the packed mass apart.[27]

Hancock issued orders for his pioneers to carry their tools in the attack and dig defensive works inside the captured Confederate position. He made arrangements for three wagons loaded with entrenching tools to be available for general distribution to infantry units as needed. Hancock was thinking of his pioneers playing a role similar to that of modern combat engineers.

Denied sleep, the men of the Second Corps finally completed their preparations at 4:00 A.M. on May 12. A light drizzle continued to fall. For Birney's waiting soldiers, standing in formation under the pine trees to Barlow's right, it was a wet, chilly dawn. Their teeth chattered as rain dripped onto their soaked clothing from the overhanging tree branches, and a heavy mist obscured what lay ahead.[28]

Barlow could have prepared his division with a lighter heart had he known the state of readiness among the troops defending the salient. While the Federals prepared to attack, Lee prepared to evacuate the bulge and pursue. Convinced from Union movements that Grant intended to fall back to Fredericksburg, he ordered the thirty guns packed in the salient withdrawn under cover of darkness and prepared to do the same with Johnson's 4,500 infantrymen as soon as possible after dawn. The Confederate artillery, which Barlow feared could rip his mass formation to shreds, would not be a problem.

The order to prepare the artillery for moving forward was general, but Alexander decided to keep the First Corps guns at Laurel Hill in their positions all night. By mounting ammunition chests and cutting numerous roads to the rear, he could draw them out of the works quickly. Brig. Gen. Armistead L. Long, artillery chief of the Second Corps, could not afford to do this. The configuration of the salient restricted his movement to one path and made the process of withdrawal much more difficult. Long began pulling out just before dusk of May 11. Only some guns in Rodes's sector on the western shoulder of the salient were left in place. They could be withdrawn faster, and, mindful of Upton's attack on May 10, this area seemed a possible target for future Yankee strikes. But the tip and the east side of the salient were shorn of artillery support.[29]

By 1:00 A.M., muffled noises could be heard by the Rebel pickets. Suspicion gave way to concern that an attack was in preparation. Johnson pleaded with Ewell to return the guns. Ewell forwarded the request to Lee, who approved it, but staff delays caused the order to filter down to battalion commanders no sooner than twenty minutes before dawn. Two battalions were in the process of returning to their positions when Hancock unleashed his men.[30]

The works that formed the salient, however, were exceptionally strong, "more like a fort than the usual field breastworks," thought Capt. Edward C. Jackson of the 125th New York in Barlow's division. Another Federal, Mason Whiting Tyler of the 37th Massachusetts in Neill's division of the Sixth Corps, termed them "as well built and as scientifically laid out as any extemporized earthworks I ever saw."[31]

The parapet was well fitted with headlogs raised by blocks to provide a fire slit for Johnson's troops. There was a gradual slope on the outside of the parapet before it straightened to form a steep slope to the ground. There was no ditch in front, but the Confederates had expended enormous energy in building dozens of traverses behind the parapet. Traverses and parapet alike were three to four feet thick and well revetted with logs and posts. The traverses were placed about forty feet apart and usually were twenty feet long, according to a staff officer in the Stonewall Brigade. Often the Confederates also enclosed the rear of the bays formed by these traverses. George Clark of Brig. Gen. Abner Perrin's Alabama brigade later claimed that the bays and traverses offered "little or no protection" in the heavy and close range fire to come on May 12. A photograph of the works near the West Angle, taken soon after the war, shows the traverses to have been a foot or more higher than a man's head. To a degree, Clark's assertion was true, but the protection afforded was significant enough to enable the Rebels to hold sections of the work for hours.[32]

The ground in front of the line offered advantages for both sides. On some sectors—in front of Ramseur and Doles, for example—there was cleared ground for only 200 yards. The Stonewall Brigade had a greater area of open ground in its front, and Walker placed his skirmishers in the woods' edge. Farther to the right, the cleared land extended as much as 800 yards in front of the works. Here Confederate skirmishers were placed 200 yards inside the woods. The forest generally helped the Federals, especially where it came close to the formidable earthworks. Just as with Upton, the woods shielded Hancock's formations and helped to make it possible for the Second Corps to achieve a dramatic surprise.[33]

While the fortifications themselves were impressive, the position was not. The slight elevation that the works occupied was not necessarily important to the Confederates, and the ravine that lay north of the salient was deep enough to create quite a bit of dead space as close as fifty yards from the Confederate fortifications. The numerous high traverses were necessary because of the bulge, which exposed defending troops to enfilade fire, and there was anything but an ideal killing ground in front of the works. The Mule Shoe Salient was, in a real sense, an engineering mistake from the standpoint of terrain and troop position.

4. The Mule Shoe Salient at Spotsylvania, May 12

After a few hours of hasty preparation, one of the most impressive and costly days of fighting in American history began under a dark and rainy sky on the morning of May 12. Hancock's attack was scheduled to begin at 4:30 A.M., but the clouds postponed daylight a while. He waited five minutes and gave the order to go in. A juggernaut began to roll toward the tip of the Mule Shoe Salient. David B. Birney's and Gershom Mott's divisions, forming the right wing, moved through the woods and across a shallow swamp to enter open ground fronting the Stonewall Brigade and Col. William Monaghan's Louisiana brigade to its right. James A. Walker's skirmishers, posted on a slight ridge, were easily swept away. The Federal formation surged across the open ground, over a ravine with "a small water course" that angled across its path, and on to the works.

Hancock's left wing, Francis C. Barlow's division in front followed by John Gibbon, moved forward across the open fields of the Brown and Landrum farms, 400 yards wide and "extending up to the enemy's works." Barlow's left cleared the Landrum House, then his division crossed the ravine and closed in on a section of the line held by Col. William Witcher's Virginia brigade and George H. Steuart's North Carolina and Virginia brigade. Witcher's left held the East Angle. To his right, Steuart continued to occupy the right end of Ewell's Line, barely stretched out to cover the east side of the salient. Barlow's extreme right just lapped around the East Angle.[1]

For several minutes into the attack, the Second Corps maintained its formation very well, "as if on parade," thought William H. Green of the 17th Maine. The Federals broke into a run close to the Confederate line, "rolled out a tremendous cheer," and tore at the obstructions to clear paths. John R. Brooke's brigade of Barlow's division crawled through fifty yards of thick abatis at the tip of the salient. Brooke's pioneers, deployed "at intervals" in his front, helped the infantrymen pull it apart to let their

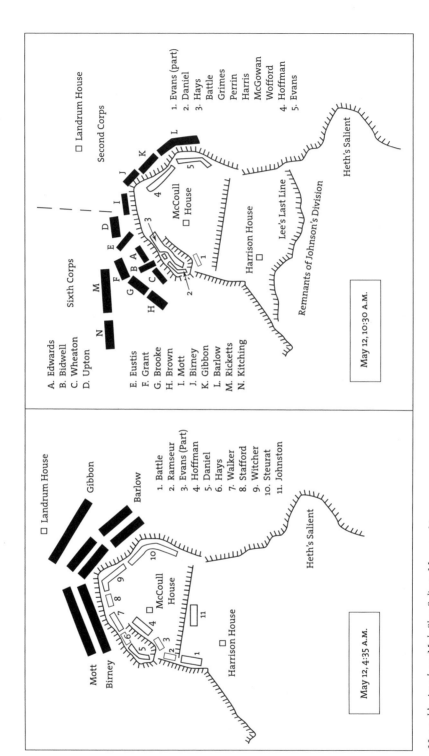

□ Landrum House

□ Landrum House

Gibbon

Second Corps

Barlow

Sixth Corps

1. Evans (part)
2. Daniel
   Battle
   Grimes
   Perrin
   Harris
   McGowan
   Wofford
3. Hays
4. Hoffman
5. Evans

1. Battle
2. Ramseur
3. Evans (Part)
4. Hoffman
5. Daniel
6. Hays
7. Walker
8. Stafford
9. Witcher
10. Steurat
11. Johnston

A. Edwards
B. Bidwell
C. Wheaton
D. Upton

E. Eustis
F. Grant
G. Brooke
H. Brown
I. Mott
J. Birney
K. Gibbon
L. Barlow
M. Ricketts
N. Kitching

Mott
Birney

McCoull
House

McCoull
House

□

□

Harrison House
□

Harrison House
□

Lee's Last Line

Remnants of Johnson's Division

Heth's Salient

Heth's Salient

May 12, 10:30 A.M.

May 12, 4:35 A.M.

Hancock's Attack on Mule Shoe Salient, May 12, 1864

comrades through. On other parts of Barlow's front, "some were cutting" as others were "pulling and lifting limbs to one side, and at every opening thus made a stream of men would rush through." A short line of inclined palisades fronted one section of the work. George D. Bowen of the 12th New Jersey and a fellow captain pulled out one pale to create an opening big enough for their men to squeeze through.[2]

Hancock's neat formations began to unravel as soon as his men passed the obstructions. Clambering over the rugged parapet broke the ranks apart far more than did the obstructions. For the moment, it did not matter. Hancock's corps engulfed the tip of the salient and most of the Confederates in it like a gigantic fish swallowing bait on the end of a line. There was a brief period of intense hand-to-hand fighting as the Federals "went to work with bayonets and clubbed muskets." The Rebels were powerless to stop the Yankees. Many of their rifle muskets were dampened by the drizzle and would not work. Percussion caps popped without igniting the charge, and there was no artillery support to compensate for the problem. Only one gun managed to get into position and fire one round. It and the balance of two battalions on their way back into the salient were captured.[3]

While Barlow's men crowded into the eastern tip of the salient, Birney's troops had more difficulty securing the west side of the bulge. Monaghan's men retreated soon after Witcher fell back, but Walker's Stonewall Brigade held for a while. From behind traverses the Virginians fired at Federals who had penetrated the line where Monaghan used to be. When hit in front, the Virginians were forced to fall back, too.

But the Confederate retreat ended here. The brigades around Doles's Salient held firm and even launched local counterattacks to make sure the break did not widen. Elements of Harry T. Hays's old Louisiana brigade, to Walker's left; Junius Daniel's North Carolina brigade, which held Doles's salient; and Clement A. Evans's Georgia brigade, which was positioned in the secondary line to Daniel's rear, were responsible for this important stand. Apparently this secondary line of trench had been extended some distance to the right since May 10, but the left wing was still held by three of Evans's regiments.

Unaffected by the break, Cullen A. Battle's Alabama brigade pulled out of line on Ewell's far left as Brig. Gen. Joseph B. Kershaw's division of the First Corps extended to its right to fill the space left vacant. Then Battle moved his men behind the Rebel line to hit the Federals. At the same time, Robert E. Rodes also pulled Stephen D. Ramseur's North Carolina brigade out of line and threw it at the enemy. The Tar Heels passed the McCoull House and headed for a mass of packed Yankees between the right wing of the secondary line, vacant of Rebel troops, and the captured first line. This was the first of many bloody counterattacks on May 12. After a bullet hit Ramseur in the arm and forced him out of action, he was replaced by Col. Bryan Grimes. The Tar Heels crossed a section of the secondary line behind Doles's Salient and drove many Federals out of the area between the lines. Most took shelter just outside the forward parapet. Grimes now occupied a small space only yards from the enemy, separated from them by the width of the earthwork in front and by a series of traverses on the right. The proximity of the opposing sides was vividly demonstrated when a stout Yankee captured the adjutant of the 30th North Carolina by pulling him across the parapet by the hair. The 14th North Carolina began to fight its way to the right, traverse by traverse, to create more breathing space for Grimes's tightly packed men. Battle added the weight of his brigade when he advanced to this point on the seething battlefield, but it was a slow, tedious process.[4]

By the time Ewell's left prevented the Federals from tearing the hole in the salient's outer fabric even more, Hancock's Second Corps held about a mile of Confederate trench line. The top end, half of the west side, and all of the east side were in Union hands. Edward Johnson, George Steuart, and roughly 3,000 men were taken prisoner, while about twenty-four guns fell into Union hands. It was a battlefield disaster almost unprecedented in the history of Robert E. Lee's army. Only Pickett's Charge at Gettysburg, the capture of Ewell's forts at Rappahannock Station, the battle of Five Forks, and the battle of Sailor's Creek on the road to Appomattox compared to it.[5]

But this immense Union victory began to unravel quickly as confusion reigned just inside the captured Confederate works. Passing through the obstructions, crossing the parapet, and corralling prisoners had broken up all organization. To make matters worse, the Yankees poked about in search of flags and other trophies. Barlow later complained that Gibbon's division doubled the confusion when it entered the works and mingled with his men. A similar situation prevailed among Birney's troops when at least one of Mott's brigades, Col. Robert McAllister's, entered the captured works. Units "were inextricably mixed up in a howling and enthusiastic mob," recalled Capt. Edward C. Jackson.[6]

Despite this condition, chunks of Hancock's corps pushed forward to penetrate the salient. George D. Bowen of Gibbon's division found the going rough, as he had to clamber over brush and tree limbs that the Rebels had cut to make the revetment for their parapet. This was piled up just behind the line. The Federals got as far as the long reserve line that stretched across the breadth of the bulge halfway between the McCoull House and the Harrison House, held by elements of John B. Gordon's division. A few rounds from Gordon's troops easily convinced the scattered groups of Federals to retire. There was no organized effort to attack this line; the best that unit commanders could do was to regroup their men on the outside of the captured line of works. The presence of fresh Rebel troops within striking distance compelled Hancock's subordinates to seek shelter, and the stout parapet was the only kind available. The Federals therefore gave up any hope of further progress.[7]

According to some accounts, it was not easy to re-form the men outside the works. Already a patter of bullets was directed at them as Grimes and Battle fought their way slowly up the west side of the salient and Gordon began to direct a series of counterattacks across the interior of the bulge. Robert S. Robertson, an aide to brigade leader Nelson Miles, recalled that "it was only by coaxing, cursing, and threatening them that we could form a line of battle. It was only by the utmost exertions of the officers that the position was saved." In places, the Federals were packed five deep outside the parapet.[8]

Whatever Union troops remained inside the line of works were forced out by the counterstrikes that the Confederates now launched. Gordon sent Robert G. Johnston's North Carolina brigade from his reserve line toward Steuart's former position, but it was bloodily repulsed. Next, Gordon directed part of Evans's Georgia brigade, all of Col. John F. Hoffman's Virginia brigade, and what was left of Johnston's Tar Heels to drive again toward the northeast. This force received some enfilade fire from Col. Simon G. Griffin's brigade of Burnside's Ninth Corps, which went into action outside the right shoulder of the Mule Shoe Salient. Griffin was able to do this because he had just advanced and captured a segment of the Confederate line held by the 18th North Carolina and the 28th North Carolina of Brig. Gen. James H. Lane's brigade. This might have developed into a promising success for the Federals, but Cadmus Wilcox reacted quickly to engage the Ninth Corps troops. He sent in Brig. Gen. Edward L. Thomas's Georgia brigade and Brig. Gen. Alfred M. Scales's North Carolina brigade to help. The two units filled the gap between Lane and the right flank of Gordon's Reserve Line, and supported Lane's Tar Heels by driving Griffin out of the captured segment of the Third Corps trench. In this early stage of Burnside's fight, some of Brig. Gen. Robert B. Potter's units apparently used corpses to help fill the parapet of their newly constructed work, close in to the Rebel line.[9]

The combined weight of Evans, Hoffman, and Johnston could do no more than force the scattered Federals inside the salient to take shelter outside the works. The Confederates took position inside the trenches and bays, barely holding on while separated from the mass of Federals only by the width of the parapet. Evans was stretched out on the right, covering the southern half of the east side nearly to the right end of Gordon's Reserve Line. Hoffman extended to Evans's left, but well short of the East Angle.

Lee, desperate to shore up this embattled part of his army, pulled more units from other parts of the field. Brig. Gen. William T. Wofford's Georgia brigade of Kershaw's division came from the First Corps to bolster Daniel and Battle near Doles's Salient. William Mahone dispatched Abner Perrin's Alabama and Brig. Gen. Nathaniel H. Harris's Mississippi brigades from west of the Po River, Lee's extreme left. After a hard march, Perrin advanced to Grimes's right, retook a fifty-yard segment of the secondary line that Grimes's Tar Heels had crossed earlier, and advanced to the first line. While doing this, Perrin was hit and died instantly. Harris brought his men up behind Perrin's brigade and extended Confederate control of the inside of the salient's west face a little more to the right. There was considerable intermingling of all three brigades—Grimes's, Perrin's, and Harris's—but the Mississippi brigade managed to reach near the West Angle with its right flank. Harris's ability to extend right was facilitated by a unique construction of the trench line. Whoever had built one of the traverses had made a small tunnel under it so men could crawl from one bay to another. Even so, a considerable gap remained between Harris and Hoffman, one that included a stretch of trench on both sides of the East Angle.[10]

Samuel McGowan's South Carolina brigade came up from Wilcox's division to help cover that gap. McGowan hurriedly marched from near the courthouse and went into the salient soon after Harris. His Carolinians overlapped Harris's right and extended the line farther toward the East Angle, at least as far as the famous oak tree that would be cut down by small arms fire a few hours later. McGowan's left lay approximately at the West Angle, while his extreme right snuggled behind the shelter of a traverse. Only 200 yards of undefended trench lay between it and Hoffman's Virginia brigade.[11]

Remnants of Confederate works at East Angle. Looking northwest toward the West Angle, with the 15th New Jersey monument in the distance. (Earl J. Hess)

It was now about 10:00 A.M., and the Confederates had committed all of their available manpower to defend the salient. They could have covered the entire length of the line if they had not bunched up several brigades along the west side. Here their troops formed a thick line in the trenches and bays, while the line was dangerously thin on the east side. The 200-yard gap at the tip need not have worried Rebel commanders too much, for the Yankees had no will to exploit it.

By late morning Lee decided to hold the outer line of the salient until other troops could construct a new line at its base. Whatever men were available—mostly the remnants of Johnson's division—started to dig what often is called "Lee's Last Line." The commander counted on the veterans packed inside the salient to hold off the mass of Federals for as long as it took to make this line secure.[12]

The parapet along the bulge of the salient became a line of demarcation, a strange kind of no-man's-land that separated two opponents for nearly twenty-four hours of horrible fighting. The parapet enabled both sides to remain in static positions literally within a few feet of each other. It was a barrier crossed at the risk of death. No concerted attacks were launched across it for the rest of the battle, although individuals exposed themselves by standing or reaching across it for various purposes. Across this mound of earth and logs sailed uncounted tons of bullets and even some rounds of artillery ammunition. The parapet separated life from death.

On the outside of this mound, the Sixth Corps was called on just after 6:00 A.M. to assist Hancock. Horatio Wright had Thomas Neill's division at the Brown House and James Ricketts's and David Russell's divisions to the northwest at the Alsop House. Neill went forward to the West Angle, where Col. Oliver Edwards's Massachusetts and Rhode Island brigade lodged to the right of the Second Corps, his left at the angle. Brig. Gen. Frank Wheaton's brigade, to Edwards's right, was repulsed by Confederate fire and fell back a few yards to take cover in a swale. Another of Neill's brigades, led by Col. Daniel D. Bidwell, assembled to the rear and right of Edwards.

Neill's last unit, Col. Lewis A. Grant's Vermont brigade, went to the left to help Barlow, but the Second Corps division commander did not appreciate the effort. Barlow watched in dismay as the Sixth Corps troops double-quicked to his already disorganized command and mixed with them, increasing the confusion while providing no solution for the stalemate. He rode back to Hancock's command post at the Landrum House and testily told the corps commander, "For God's sake, Hancock, do not send any more troops in here." Barlow suggested that reinforcements should instead sweep down the Confederate line.[13]

Hancock got the message. He sent orders for Grant to pull out and further eased overcrowding by withdrawing Brooke's brigade of Barlow's division. These units were therefore available when Neill called for help at 8:00 A.M. Brooke was dispatched all the way to Wheaton's right, making a circuit around the salient, and at least part of Grant's command trailed after him. Later in the morning, Hancock further eased the crowded condition of Barlow's division by extracting Miles's brigade to re-form in the rear.[14]

Russell's division went in to shore up the right wing of Birney's division. When McGowan's South Carolina brigade advanced to the Confederate side of the parapet, McAllister's brigade had fallen back from the Union side of the work, creating a gap. Russell went in with more than enough men to cover this hole. Emory Upton moved his brigade to a swale 100 yards from the West Angle, from which he was able to fire at the gap. He also sent several regiments forward to the line but, seeing the punishment they received, ordered them back to the swale. Brig. Gen. Henry L. Eustis's brigade deployed on Upton's right in the open, its left close to the works. Col. Henry W. Brown's brigade advanced to Eustis's right, be-

Remnants of Confederate works at West Angle. Monument to the 15th New Jersey, Brown's brigade, Sixth Corps. (Earl J. Hess)

tween the rest of Russell's division and Doles's Salient. Brown's men got close to the Rebel line but lost heavily and retired.[15]

Ricketts's division also advanced to near the West Angle but was held in reserve. Also, Col. J. Howard Kitching's brigade of heavy artillerymen arrived from Warren's Fifth Corps to be held in reserve. By 10:30 A.M., both the Second and Sixth Corps had gone in and become stalled. There would be more minor shifting of units to come, but the major troop deployments remained stable for the rest of this long, costly day.[16]

The troops on both sides of the parapet were densely packed from the West Angle down to Doles's Salient. Eight Union brigades and eight Confederate brigades were arrayed along a line that was less than a quarter of a mile long. Grant and Meade were probably only dimly aware that the tactical stalemate along the outer perimeter of the Mule Shoe Salient was essentially permanent. By mid-afternoon, Grant had pressured Burnside into renewing his attack on the eastern base of the bulge, sending in Orlando B. Willcox's and Thomas L. Crittenden's divisions. They aimed at Heth's Salient, held by three of Henry Heth's brigades. It so happened that Lee had just ordered an attack of his own here, sending Lane's North Carolina brigade and Col. David A. Weisiger's Virginia brigade from their positions south of Heth's Salient to strike Willcox's left flank. These two Rebel units surprised John Hartranft's brigade as it advanced and forced it to retreat. Willcox's other brigade made a limited lodgment inside Heth's Salient but had to give it up because Crittenden failed to offer support. One of Crittenden's brigades got close to the Confederate works but was repulsed.

On the other end of the line, Grant and Meade pressured Warren to help. The Fifth Corps commander hesitated, arguing that "it does not take many men from the enemy to hold the intrenchments in my front." After repeated directives, Warren sent three divisions against Charles Field at Laurel Hill. This was no more successful than any of the other Fifth Corps attacks on this strong position. The 6th Wisconsin encountered an "abatis of sharpened stakes," stopped to fire a while, and then retired. Grant then urged Warren to send men to Wright so the Sixth Corps commander could organize an attempt to penetrate the outer line of the salient. He sent Brig. Gen. Lysander Cutler's division and two brigades of Charles Griffin's division. The difficulties inherent in such a push led Wright to delay so long that he never made the attempt at all. Wright adjusted his troop deployment, pulling Upton, Bidwell, and Col. Lewis Grant from their positions close to the parapet, but he kept Edwards in place. In fact, Edwards's exhausted men, who had been under fire longer than any other Sixth Corps troops, had to stretch out to cover the space vacated by the other units. Lee kept his concentration of manpower along the west side of the salient in place, although fire lessened considerably at dusk.[17]

TRENCH FIGHTING AT THE SALIENT

The battle of May 12 was the worst example of static trench fighting in the Civil War. Both sides were locked in a grueling contest, packed tightly in a small area, from about 7:00 A.M. on May 12 to 3:00 A.M. on May 13, when the fighting ground to a halt. It rained off and on all day and night, saturating the battlefield with a mixture of water and blood. The trenches were filled and the ground became slippery. In some places, especially early in the morning, fog limited visibility. The parapet loomed between the armies, protecting them but also standing in their way. It compelled both sides to stay put within lethal range of the enemy for so many hours that the battle became a gruesome nightmare. The parapet was both a blessing and a curse.

The mud was already a problem when Harris's and McGowan's brigades drove into the salient and took position inside the outer line. So many

Confederate works, possibly at Spindle Field, Spotsylvania. The number 112 is located on top of the parapet; the defender stood on the left, with a row of stakes and brush to the right of the parapet. The photographer's assistant can be seen in the mid-ground. (Massachusetts Commandery, Military Order of the Loyal Legion and the U.S. Army Military History Institute)

bodies littered the trench and bays that the Rebels had to drag them out during lulls in the firing. They also gathered abandoned muskets and kept them loaded, ready for use. Pvt. David Holt of the 16th Mississippi had seven muskets by his side. The steady drizzle not only soaked the ground and the wooden revetment, it also stained all of the accumulated water.

The men's clothes were red with blood and their faces were blackened with powder smoke.[18]

McGowan's men found the bloody mud knee-deep in places. They received fire not only from the front but also from the right and had to expose themselves a little to fire over the top of the traverses. The trenches as well as the pits that were dug to get more dirt for the parapet became pools of water, "so saturated with powder as to be nearly black as ink in places," recalled Berry Benson. An unidentified man in the 1st South Carolina vividly reported the disgusting mess in a letter to a Charleston newspaper. "I was splashed over with brains and blood," he wrote. "In stooping down squatting to load, the mud, blood and brains mingled, would reach up to my waist, and my head and face were covered or spotted with the horrid paint."[19]

The parapet locked both sides in a firefight that lasted for nearly twenty-four hours at close range. "We were held in a vise," as John Haley of the 17th Maine later put it. "We certainly couldn't advance, to retire was almost as difficult." Even though powder smoke mixed with the drizzle to form "a misty atmosphere" that hid objects only a few yards away, both sides unleashed a heavy volume of fire. Edwards's brigade held its position outside the works from just after 6:00 A.M. on May 12 until the fight ended about 3:00 A.M. on May 13. During these twenty-one hours, each member fired about 500 rounds. On average, that meant each man fired every two and a half minutes. Edwards's men fired even when the smoky mist or darkness hid the Confederates. The rifle musket tended to foul after about twenty-five rounds and had to be cleaned. Members of the brigade sent their weapons to the rear for cleaning and used muskets borrowed from other units until they were returned.[20]

Upton's brigade was 100 yards from the Rebel works for eleven hours, during which time each man fired about 350 rounds. That came to one shot every 1.9 minutes. Their lips were caked with powder, and their shoulders bore a layer of mud from holding the butts of their weapons. When the barrels became fouled with powder residue, Upton's men rammed the new charge as far down as possible and fired anyway. This worked, surprisingly, and allowed them not to bother about cleaning their weapons.[21]

A few combatants tried to cross the parapet. When the 49th New York of Upton's brigade went forward to the works, Maj. William Ellis attempted to lead it over the parapet. He was shot "through the arm and body with a ramrod" that some Rebel had forgotten to take out of his musket. But few men made serious attempts to go over the works. Mostly, troops hugging

Section of Mule Shoe Salient near West Angle, Spotsylvania. The photographer is standing atop the parapet, while the two men are standing in what was either a bay divided by traverses or an artillery emplacement. Note the heavy log revetment and the height of the parapet and traverse. (Massachusetts Commandery, Military Order of the Loyal Legion and the U.S. Army Military History Institute)

either side of the mound just tried to find ways to deliver fire across it or to defend themselves against enemy fire. Some soldiers knocked aside the barrels of their enemy's guns in order to jump atop the parapet and shoot at a packed mass only feet away. If one was quick at this, he could survive. A lieutenant of G. Norton Galloway's regiment exposed himself thusly and fired twice with impunity, using muskets handed to him by his subordinates. Just before he pulled the trigger a third time, he was hit, "his cap flew up in the air, and his body pitched headlong among the enemy."[22]

The vast majority of men on both sides of the parapet refused to expose themselves. They normally held their muskets over the top and pulled the trigger with their thumb. Many soldiers in McGowan's brigade grabbed the muzzles of Yankee muskets and held them up until the owner fired into the air, saving themselves and countless others. Most unit commanders found it was more efficient for half of their men to stay close to the work and fire while the rest reloaded and passed guns. If the muskets became too fouled, a bayonet turned them into a different kind of weapon. Thrusting over the top of the parapet or through crevices and holes in the revetment probably accounted for few casualties, but the attempt demonstrated the fierce emotions stirred up by this killing marathon at close quarters.[23]

Oliver Edwards, whose brigade probably was involved in the longest, most intense period of close-range firing at the Mule Shoe Salient, attempted to organize an effort to penetrate the Rebel position. He began to create detachments of fifty men each, led by an officer, to cross the parapet and secure a specified number of traverses. Mason Whiting Tyler was told to take charge of the first detachment. He gathered whatever intelligence he could and worked out a detailed plan with Edwards, but then corps commander Wright canceled the project before he started. Tyler was greatly relieved. "If we had made the attempt," he later wrote, "there is every probability that the whole detachment would have been sacrificed."[24]

As the battle continued, there was a notable slacking of aggressiveness on the part of the Confederates as well. Most of McGowan's men exposed themselves less and just huddled behind shelter, often sitting on corpses when there was no opportunity to remove bodies or the wounded.[25]

The prodigious volume of fire made it imperative that fresh cartridges reach every man. Mules hauled up supplies, 3,000 rounds on each animal, for the Sixth Corps units. They were led as close as possible, then men were detailed to carry the ammunition in. The Confederates strung out a line of soldiers in a hollow that led to the works and passed cartridge packets forward. They piled them in shelter tent halves and passed the bundle from man to man, or slung bundles on fence rails so that two men could move them. Inside the works, the cartridges were passed laterally along the battle line. David Holt improvised a method to get them across the traverses. He tied several packets together and used a ramrod to fling the cluster across.[26]

Surprisingly, there were attempts to employ artillery in this crowded infantry battle. A regular unit in the Second Corps, Lt. James Gilliss's Battery C, 5th U.S. Artillery, rolled up to the outer edge of the parapet. His men advanced the guns by hand over the dead and wounded. One piece fired nine rounds of canister and another fired fourteen, but the cost was high. Gilliss lost all but two gunners at these two cannon. Members of the 5th Wisconsin, Lewis Grant's Vermont brigade, and the 95th Pennsylvania volunteered to keep them firing before the futility of the effort became overwhelmingly apparent. Although at a range of only fifty-five yards, with the stout parapet in the way, the damage Gilliss did to McGowan's brigade was minimal. The two guns remained in place after the infantrymen lost interest in them, and the carriages were so nicked by musket fire as to be almost useless. The lid of one limber chest had twenty-seven bullet holes in it, while a sponge bucket was perforated with thirty-nine holes.[27]

Another attempt to provide artillery support was made by Company F, 15th New York Heavy Artillery, which set up eight Coehorn mortars to fire at the West Angle. These mortars had been designed by Dutch engineer Baron Menho van Coehoorn in the 1670s for use in sieges as antipersonnel weapons. Rated as 24-pounders, they were carried into position by four men and had a range of from 25 yards to 1,200 yards. The tube was fixed at a forty-five-degree angle, so differing ranges were achieved by employing greater or lesser amounts of powder. The New York Heavy Artillerymen could not accomplish much; most shells landed behind the Rebels or, when the range was adjusted, on the Federals. Sometime later, the Coehorn mortar proved to be an effective weapon at Cold Harbor and Petersburg. But gunners needed time to properly site it, and no mortar fire was ever so precise as to avoid injuring friendly troops who were close to the target.[28]

Few Civil War battles so severely tested the nerves and stamina of the troops as this one, and many men tried to surrender as a way to get out of the cauldron. Now and then shelter tent halves were raised to induce a cease-fire. When Union fire slackened, the willing Confederates jumped atop the parapet and gave up. G. Norton Galloway witnessed what happened to one group of about thirty Rebels who did this. They were startled by their first clear view of the massed Federals on the other side of the mound and hesitated for a second on top of the parapet. This gave enough time for other Confederates to fire, shooting most of them down. The idea that Lee's men killed their own comrades rather than allow them to surrender was not just a bit of postwar Yankee propaganda. Berry Benson of McGowan's brigade recalled what happened when some Confederates raised a white flag above the parapet. "'Shoot them fellows! Shoot them fellows!'" he heard a number of their comrades shout. A sputtering of rifle fire followed, and the flags instantly fell down.[29]

Opposite Evans's brigade, on the east side of the salient, the 26th

Michigan of Miles's brigade, Barlow's division, fired at the enemy for half an hour before a few Confederates began "waving handkerchiefs on their rammers" to signal a desire to give up. When the Michigan men stopped firing, every Rebel along an eighty-yard stretch of the parapet "rose up and started to come in." It must have been a thrilling sight to the Yankees, but then fresh Confederate troops arrived on the scene and all but twenty of those who attempted to give up took heart and jumped back into their own trench. The 26th Michigan fought the fresh troops another half hour before retiring.[30]

Sometimes, in the noise and confusion, it was difficult to tell who was trying to give up. A lull developed in the firing toward evening, and McGowan's men were surprised to see a Yankee officer jump atop the parapet. He told the Rebels that an order to surrender had been issued to them by a Mississippi colonel, and then he paced boldly back and forth in plain view while they tried to make sense of this man. Col. T. Frank Clyburn of the 12th South Carolina did not believe him. "Shoot, men, shoot!" he yelled, but Lt. Cadwallader Jones believed that the Yankees were trying to surrender and cautioned his men not to fire. The Federals even raised the butts of their muskets so the Confederates could see them over the parapet, to show that they had no intention to fire on them. This undoubtedly caused more confusion, as the inverted musket was a common signal of a willingness to surrender. This curious episode, which lasted only a minute or two, ended when someone fired a shot and everyone else joined in.[31]

Most of the evidence, both Union and Confederate, on attempts to surrender at the Mule Shoe Salient focus on Rebel efforts to give up under fire. But there were at least a few Federal attempts as well. Perhaps the confined environment inside the salient pressured more Rebels to try to surrender. Federal units had greater opportunities to pull out of the fight, while Lee's brigades were stuck there, held in place by the overriding need to support the line at all costs until a new position was entrenched at the base.[32]

With such an incredible volume of fire being delivered in a comparatively small space for so long, it is not surprising that the wood on the earthworks would be shredded. Awed observers noted that "the head logs of the breastworks were cut and torn until they resembled hickory brooms." This was a common comparison, for the many bullets broke apart the wood fibers into millions of small splinters.[33]

The most famous illustration of this effect was the cutting down of two trees, both oaks, that were severed by the rain of bullets. One of them was

East Angle, Spotsylvania. Most of the parapet remains, but the revetment appears to have been taken away. The man with a pole over his shoulder is standing at the exact angle, and the logs that constituted the parapet can be seen partially exposed between the other two men. (Massachusetts Commandery, Military Order of the Loyal Legion and the U.S. Army Military History Institute)

twenty-two inches in diameter and fell diagonally across the work after midnight, wounding a number of McGowan's men. Most of this tree cutting was done by the Sixth Corps, with a lot of help from the Second Corps.[34]

The fighting along the outer line of the salient lasted long enough for

Lee's men to erect a new work at the base. It was not easy, for the woods were thick and few men were involved. John O. Casler of the Stonewall Brigade vividly remembered working on the line after nightfall. Some men chopped down trees, which fell unpredictably in all directions, while others trimmed and carried the trunks to the line. Still other men used shovels, tin cups, and bayonets to pile dirt on them. The night was "so dark we could not see each other, and we so sleepy we could hardly stand up," Casler recalled. He used a pick, which got stuck in the numerous tree roots almost every time he plunged it into the ground. He found this "very aggravating." The men also were harassed by bullets that came sailing in from the battle line farther north.[35]

Lee's Last Line was ready by 3:00 A.M. The Confederate units quietly pulled out of their bloody trenches and moved south to man it. Berry Benson of McGowan's brigade had fallen asleep under fire before the withdrawal, but someone woke him in time to fall back with the rest. The firing sputtered out soon after. Much of the battlefield had fallen silent long before 3:00 A.M., but a handful of units, including Edwards's long-suffering brigade and some of Cutler's Fifth Corps regiments to its right, continued firing to the bitter end. The Confederates conducted the withdrawal so well that the Federals did not know the salient was vacant until dawn.[36]

At the end of this intense fighting, the Federal high command struggled to consolidate positions and plan for the next move. Meade told his corps leaders to strengthen their current lines in case the enemy counterattacked. "The trenches should be rendered as strong as possible," Meade informed Hancock, thinking not only of defense but also of sparing troops for a possible strike of his own. In carrying out these instructions, Hancock issued a circular requiring his division commanders "to see that the intrenching tools are properly cared for." Meade wanted Warren to extend his corps so as to block roads leading to the Union rear, making his fortified line as short and strong as possible. Potter's division of Burnside's Ninth Corps continued to strengthen its advanced position east of the salient. Members of the 7th Rhode Island used "bayonets, cups, wooden shovels, and a few intrenching tools" to throw together "a rough parapet of rails, logs, and earth."[37]

"This has been a most awful day," moaned John Haley of the 17th Maine in his journal, "and if there has been any benefit commensurate with the loss of life and limbs, I cannot see it." The fault did not lie with the men. "We did all that any body of troops could do or would do under like conditions. We held our own, but to do this amounted to nothing."[38]

 **Spotsylvania, May 13-20**

The Mule Shoe Salient presented a scene of horror to the exhausted Federals who surveyed its ground on the morning of May 13. "Horses and men [were] chopped into hash by the bullets," remembered Mason Whiting Tyler, "and appearing more like piles of jelly than the distinguishable forms of human life." Water and blood soaked the ground as red pools appeared in every depression. The trenches were filled with corpses, piled five or six deep by some estimates. Col. William H. Penrose of the 15th New Jersey counted 150 dead covering an area between two traverses that measured only twelve feet by fifteen feet. Wounded men still lay beneath corpses, distinguishable from the dead only when they writhed in pain. One injured Rebel was "completely trodded in the mud so as to look like part of it and yet he was breathing and gasping."[1]

The dead seemed mostly to have been shot in the head, and a great many guns, accoutrements, and personal belongings littered the field. "It was the most horrible sight I had ever witnessed," confessed G. Norton Galloway of Emory Upton's brigade. Many rifle muskets were still sticking through the fire slits, left there as the owner fell, and the tops of the parapet and traverses were lined with packages of cartridges. The Rebels had laid them out for quick reloading, but now they were completely soaked and useless. When Galloway's comrades began to bury the numerous dead, they pulled down the parapets and traverses on top of them.[2]

The Yankees began to call this place "the slaughter pen," and efforts to clean it up were haphazard. Many corpses lay unburied for days. The Confederates lost about 8,000 men in their effort to retain the Mule Shoe Salient, while the Federals sustained 9,000 casualties taking it.[3]

In some ways, it had been a useless fight on both sides, characterized by many mistakes. Grant gained nothing from it in terms of breaking Lee's position. He reduced the combat readiness of Ewell's Second Corps but at a huge cost in Union casualties. Massing 20,000 men in one group to smash into the tip of the Mule Shoe was a recipe for confusion and disorder, and piling up the Sixth Corps along a short segment of the western side of the salient was another poor use of good troops. These men had essentially no chance of crossing the parapet. Grant might have done better to send in a smaller attack force, say 10,000 men, and aimed to penetrate both sides of the salient near its base rather than to bludgeon the tip of it. The Federals should have done a better job of coordinating this initial attack with Burnside's and Wright's supporting movements.

The Confederates also were mistaken in their belief that the salient enclosed militarily valuable land. Subsequent events proved that the slight ridge was not used by the Federals to mount an effective artillery bombardment of the Rebel position, and Lee's line at the base of the salient held with no trouble for the rest of the fighting at Spotsylvania. If Lee had ordered the salient evacuated on the night of May 9, he could have avoided the 1,300 casualties involved in the repulse of Upton the next day and the 8,000 men lost while keeping Hancock, Wright, and Burnside at bay on May 12.

Historians have explained the initial Second Corps success in capturing the tip of the salient by highlighting the fact that many Confederates could not use their rifle muskets due to the dampness. Robert K. Krick believes that this was as important as the absence of artillery in the salient, while Gordon C. Rhea thinks even the outer line of the bulge would not have been taken if all rifle muskets had been operable that morning. Krick also notes that the works defending the salient were "the strongest yet seen in a field engagement on the continent."[4]

Given the immense force that Hancock had assembled and the example of Upton's success on May 10, it was probably inevitable that the Federals would take the outer line on the morning of May 12 regardless of whether all of the small arms had been working. Both Upton's and Hancock's initial assaults were successful because both commanders massed men and rushed them quickly onto the Rebel works. J. H. Hobart Ward's small attack at Laurel Hill on May 10 worked for the same reason, although neither Upton nor Ward had the advantage of facing Rebels with wet priming mechanisms. One must remember that William Witcher's Virginia brigade, which held the tip of the salient, had a history of poor battlefield performance stretching back to Chancellorsville. It probably would have folded just as quickly as it did even if all of its muskets had been in working order.

The most that can be said is that, with full Southern rifle capability, many more Federals would have been shot in the initial rush. This would have impaired the uniformity of Hancock's initial success. Some parts of the Confederate line might have held longer than others, but the result probably would have been the same.

The absence of artillery in the salient was a great disadvantage for the Confederates. Edward Johnson asserted that he could have held the position with proper artillery support. Edward Porter Alexander believed that the attack on May 12 should have been a wonderful showcase for Lee's long arm. Ewell's guns could have saved the salient, he thought, by tearing apart Hancock's massed formations at short range. This assumes, of course, that the gunners would have had enough time to load, aim, and fire before being overwhelmed by the massive attack.[5]

Despite the immense loss of life on May 12, the tactical situation at Spotsylvania remained the same. Grant shook off the failure to break Lee's line and planned more efforts. He wanted to shift the Fifth Corps and Sixth Corps from the right to the left, Warren to reinforce Burnside along Fredericksburg Road and Wright to extend the Federal line and outflank Lee's Third Corps, now commanded by Jubal Early. Grant hoped that the attack would take place at 4:00 A.M. on May 14.

But the roads were hopelessly muddy from all the rain that fell on May 11 and 12, and, as usual, Grant did not allow enough time for commanders and their staffs to prepare for such a complicated movement. Delays and continued bad weather forced him to postpone the attack. Meanwhile, Hancock constructed a new line of works stretching from the tip of the captured salient toward the Brown House, with a refused right flank, now that the other two corps had evacuated their positions. He also asked army headquarters for an "intelligent engineer officer, who could take proper advantage of the accidents of the ground and work in reference to the enemy's present line," to lay out a trench "cutting off the Salient which we took." Hancock was particular about this latter work, given that it would directly face Lee's Last Line and secure ground won at such dear cost. James Chatham Duane sent Nathaniel Michler to do this and to examine the Sixth Corps works before it left for Grant's mission to the Confederate right. When David Birney's division took up the new line from the tip of the salient to the Brown House, the men began to cut a military road running through the woods just to its rear and to slash the timber for at least eighty feet in front.[6]

By the afternoon of May 14, elements of the Fifth and Sixth Corps began to slowly feel their way into neutral territory beyond Burnside's left flank. Warren's men dug in south of Burnside's corps and north of Fredericksburg Road. It was still raining and the men called their trenches "'water works.'" A brigade from each corps took Myers Hill, halfway between Fredericksburg Road and Massaponax Church Road to the south. Upton's 800 men dug in to defend it, while the Fifth Corps brigade returned to Warren. They erected hasty works — fence rails with dirt piled on top — before Lee sent a counterattack to retake the hill. Early dispatched Brig. Gen. A. R. Wright's Georgia brigade, under Col. Matthew R. Hall, and Nathaniel Harris's Mississippi brigade. They outflanked Upton's position on both sides when they went in at 4:00 P.M. and easily forced the Sixth Corps troops to fall back across the Ni River. Lee also pulled Charles Field's division from Laurel Hill, now that Warren was no longer fronting it, and used his veterans to extend the Confederate line from Fredericksburg Road to cover Massaponax Church Road by dusk. Just before that, Warren and Horatio Wright cooperated to regain possession of Myers Hill. A few minutes before dark, a division from each corps advanced and forced the Confederates to retreat. The Federals worked hard to fortify the eminence that night.[7]

Grant continued efforts to outflank Lee's right on May 15. He instructed Hancock to pull Francis Barlow and John Gibbon out of line and rest near Harris Farm, well to the rear of the shifting Union line. From there, he hoped to move them south to help Wright find and turn Lee's flank. Confederate cavalry movements seemed to portend some offensive, so Barlow and Gibbon remained near the Harris Farm for the rest of the day. Birney remained between the salient and the Brown House to guard the Union right. He employed pioneers to shorten and strengthen the line between the Mule Shoe Salient and Burnside's right flank. Then Birney began to dig a new line from the Landrum House northeast to the Ni River to protect Meade's right flank. Grant hoped to move Birney to the left as well; he instructed Burnside to dig a new line from his right flank back to the Ni River to serve as the army's refused right flank after Birney had gone. Ninth Corps troops began to do so on May 15, also adding traverses to their main line facing west to protect against Confederate artillery fire delivered from the Landrum House after Birney evacuated that area. But Burnside warned that Birney would have to hold the newly made refused line of the Ninth Corps all the way to the river, because he did not have enough men to do it himself. Lee spent the day completing the shift of Richard Anderson's First Corps from his left to his right, retaining only Joseph Kershaw's division to guard Ewell's left.[8]

Union engineers remained busy during this period of maneuver. On the morning of May 14, Duane and Michler helped Warren locate the Confederate line. The pair caught glimpses of the Rebel works from some of the higher points of land north of Fredericksburg Road. The army's other engineer officers were busy on daily scouts along the lengthening Rebel line. Persistent problems over entrenching tools arose, prompting Second Corps headquarters to issue a circular urging commanders to safeguard whatever they had available. Many tools had been loaned to division leaders but had not been returned to the army depot, "and many, it is known, have fallen into the hands of the enemy, who is in want of nothing so much as entrenching tools."[9]

Perhaps the shortage of spades helps to account for the reason that corpses lay unburied for such a long time inside the captured salient. John C. Gorman, a Rebel in Stephen Ramseur's brigade, complained that the dead lay for five days following the gory battle of May 12. The corpses could be seen "filled with worms and poluting [sic] the atmosphere with their foul stench." Another reason might have been the difficulty of disposing of the bodies. They had become so decayed that "it is impossible to raise them," reported Surg. Daniel M. Holt of the 121st New York. "A hole has to be dug side of them and they rolled into it for burial. They were a complete jelly!"[10]

On the Confederate side of the line east of Spotsylvania Court House, the men also had difficulty coping with the constant rain and muddy trenches. Following its grueling experience inside the salient, Samuel McGowan's brigade took up a position and disposed of its remaining manpower as economically as possible. McGowan established a skirmish line 300 yards in front of his works, placing one out of eight men in the brigade in a line of rifle pits. The holes were ten paces apart and big enough for four men. One or two of the skirmishers in each hole were allowed to sleep.[11]

As the weather finally cleared on May 17, Grant renewed his plans to operate along Massaponax Church Road with the Second and Sixth Corps. But Wright, who was primarily responsible for supervising these operations before Hancock's arrival, sent two regiments out to test the Confederate defenses and found the intervening ground so covered with brush, and the works so strong, that he recommended against further operations. The Sixth Corps commander convinced Grant to plan another strike at Lee's left, assuming that it would have been weakened by now. Grant impulsively agreed, and plans were set to hit Lee's Last Line at the base of the Mule Shoe Salient. The Sixth Corps began to shift during the night, making a long march to reach the far right, while the Second Corps moved a much shorter distance from Harris Farm.

Ewell's men had been working for five days to perfect Lee's Last Line. Headlogs adorned the parapet, twenty-nine guns bolstered its defenses, and a heavy slashing lined the front. Despite the presence of Birney's division nearby, no significant efforts to reconnoiter this line had been undertaken, and it boggles the mind that anyone could think it was worth risking two corps in what almost was a reconnaissance in force to see if there were any Rebels holding it. Nevertheless, the Second Corps deployed outside the tip of the old salient with Gibbon on the right in two lines and Barlow to his left, also in two lines. Gibbon's right flank was near the West Angle, and Barlow's left flank was near the East Angle. A division of heavy artillerymen under Brig. Gen. Robert O. Tyler, newly added to the Second Corps, occupied a reserve position in a trench that the Confederates had dug from the Apex of the Mule Shoe Salient (just to the right of the East Angle) toward the Landrum House. Birney took position behind Tyler as another reserve force. As on May 12, Hancock assigned a role to engineer troops in the attack. He ordered them to "follow the command with the pioneer tools."[12]

The Sixth Corps deployed that night to Hancock's right. Thomas Neill's division connected with Gibbon but deployed in a column of brigades. James Ricketts's division extended the corps line to the right, and then David Russell formed the right flank. Grant wanted Burnside to support this effort by attacking near the point where Lee's Last Line joined the eastward-facing line held by Early's troops. Burnside chose only two brigades—one from Robert Potter and one from Crittenden—to make this assault.[13]

MAY 18–19

The Union assault began at 4:00 A.M. on May 18 with the opening of ninety-eight guns, half from the Fifth Corps and the rest from the Ninth Corps. Burnside sent Simon Griffin's brigade under cover of fog toward Edward Thomas's Georgia brigade, to the right of Ewell's corps and to the left of Henry Heth's salient. The Federals were stalled by heavy artillery and small arms fire, and by a contingent of Rebel infantry that came forward to fire into their flank. Brig. Gen. James H. Ledlie's brigade, led by Col. Stephen M. Weld Jr., advanced to Griffin's left and received enfilade fire from Brig. Gen. Joseph R. Davis's Mississippi brigade in Heth's

Salient. When the Confederates to Weld's front also opened fire and the Yankees encountered a heavy abatis, Weld's men gave up and retired.[14]

Hancock and Wright waited for Ricketts's division to get into place, but it was so delayed that they started at 4:35 A.M. without him. Three divisions went in — Barlow's, Gibbon's, and Neill's. They crossed the outer line of the salient, stepped over the yet unburied corpses inside the bulge, and immediately received a hail of Confederate artillery fire. The Union guns positioned on the Landrum Farm could not see the Rebel position and their covering fire was ineffectual.

The Union attack broke apart. Two of Gibbon's brigades took shelter in front of Gordon's Reserve Line, which stretched across the width of the salient between the McCoull House and the Harrison House, reversing the works for better protection. Another of Gibbon's brigades simply retreated, while the last one advanced diagonally southwest of Gordon's Reserve Line into a ravine in front of Ewell's left wing. This terrain feature was deep enough to offer significant cover from the artillery and small arms fire. Most of Barlow's division also stopped at Gordon's Reserve Line, although John Brooke's brigade advanced until it encountered a marsh fronting the Rebel position. Second Corps accounts of the attack emphasize the heavy abatis, 100 yards deep, that protected Lee's Last Line. Barlow called it "the most dense abatis he has ever seen," as Hancock reported to army headquarters. Neill's division fared little better. His formation, which straddled the western line of the salient, encountered "many natural and artificial obstacles in the vicinity of the enemy's old line of pits." The short secondary line behind Doles's Salient, with its traverses and abatis, in addition to severe artillery fire, broke up the formation of Frank Wheaton's brigade so that it could not continue the advance. Part of Neill's division stopped in line with Gibbon's men who were holding Gordon's Reserve Line, and the rest advanced into the ravine where they also stopped. Grant ordered a halt to further operations at 8:45 A.M., and the troops fell back to the outside of the Mule Shoe Salient's tip.[15]

Hasty preparation for an attack on a position whose great strength was unknown to anyone on the Union side doomed the assault. The Federals had time to survey the heavy slashing from their positions at Gordon's Reserve Line and in the ravine. A maze of trees had been cut down with their tops pointed in all directions. It should properly be called a "heavy slashing" rather than an abatis, but by whatever name this obstruction was thick enough to hang up the infantry attack. While they took shelter behind Gordon's Reserve Line, Hancock's men found themselves surrounded by rotting corpses from the May 12 attack. They "presented a hideous sight. Such a stench came up from the field as to make many of the officers and men deathly sick." Robert S. Robertson, a staff officer in Nelson Miles's brigade, noticed that many bodies still lay close to Lee's Last Line. The Federals during the past few days had not been able to bury them "on account of the danger from sharp shooters." To this was added 1,500 more Union casualties on May 18. The Confederates lost so few men that there was no attempt to tabulate Ewell's casualties.[16]

The attack on May 18 was a pitiful effort compared to the titanic struggle of May 12. The brigade and regimental commanders limited Union losses by taking shelter behind Gordon's Reserve Line and in the ravine when it became obvious that they could not penetrate the obstructions. Meade, who was leery of Grant's headlong assaults against fortified positions, smugly informed his wife that much had been expected of the May 18 attack. But "we found the enemy so strongly entrenched that even Grant thought it useless to knock our heads against a brick wall."[17]

Grant decided late on the morning of May 18 to abandon operations along the Spotsylvania line and make a wide flanking movement to the south. He wanted to dispatch the Second Corps to Milford Station as the first stage of his planned effort to step around Lee. Hancock pulled his men away from the Mule Shoe Salient and bivouacked to the rear at Anderson's Mill, where they rested in preparation for the move to Milford Station. Wright took his corps all the way to the Union left again in order to hold the area around Myers Hill. On May 20, Companies E and L of the 50th New York Engineers constructed a redoubt on Myers Hill. They placed it where the burned house had stood, cutting down fruit trees to make a clear field of fire. Infantry details dug connecting trenches on both sides of the fort. Meanwhile, Burnside pulled his Ninth Corps out of line to extend the Federal position south of Wright, beyond Massaponax Church Road, as Warren stretched his Fifth Corps troops to cover the space vacated.[18]

These dispositions were made to prepare for a shift of operations to the south, not for further offensive operations at Spotsylvania. Grant forgot a key element of defense in these new positions. He had overlooked the fact that there now were no Union troops between Ewell's corps and Fredericksburg Road. When this was discovered, J. Howard Kitching's brigade of heavy artillerymen established a picket line screening the road. Kitching could call on Tyler's heavy artillerymen, stationed at the Anderson Farm two miles away, if he needed help.

Curious to discover what was transpiring on the Union right, Lee sent Ewell's entire corps on a massive reconnaissance in force on May 19. This set up the last round of fighting at Spotsylvania, the only open field engagement of this phase of the Overland campaign. It also resulted in the first battle experience for the heavy artillerymen in Meade's army.

Ewell set out at 2:00 P.M., heading northwest then northeast in a wide arc toward the Union right flank. Kershaw's division, the extreme left unit of Lee's army, shifted to the right to hold Ewell's works while he was gone. The Second Corps advanced without artillery support, except for one battalion that tagged along behind the corps. Ewell struck Kitching's picket line with Ramseur's brigade, but the Federals held the veteran Tar Heels at bay until Tyler's reinforcements arrived on the scene. By then, Ewell had deployed his corps too, and a pitched battle developed across the open fields of the Harris, Alsop, and Peyton farms. The firing was fierce but the green Unionists held their own. Crawford's division of the Fifth Corps and Birney's division of the Second Corps came up to help, but they were not engaged. The battle resulted in a tactical draw, and Ewell disengaged at 10:00 P.M. to return to Lee's Last Line.

Lee had made a mistake in ordering Ewell forward. If gathering information was his sole objective, that could have been better attempted by a smaller force. But he obviously wanted to gather information and be ready to strike immediately with a large force, relying on Ewell's judgment to decide whether to press forward. Yet, in dispatching close to a third of his army, he risked seeing it cut off from support if the Union right was firmly held and Grant could respond quickly enough to counterattack. Also, Ewell's sally was a faint way of fulfilling Lee's stated desire to take the offensive against the enemy that had battered his army since May 5. Ironically, it gave Grant one of his pet desires: to see the Confederates come out of their trenches and challenge the Army of the Potomac in open battle. But the Federals could not take advantage of this golden opportunity to crush a Rebel corps. What took place on May 19 was a bundle of mistakes, half-fulfilled desires, and missed opportunities. Ewell lost 900 men while the Federals suffered 1,500 casualties.[19]

DEVELOPMENT OF TRENCH WARFARE

"The great feature of this campaign is the extraordinary use made of earthworks," reported Col. Theodore Lyman of Meade's staff on May 18. "It is a rule that, when the Rebels halt, the first day gives them a good rifle-pit; the second, a regular infantry parapet with artillery in position;

and the third a parapet with an abattis in front and entrenched batteries behind. Sometimes they put this three days' work into the first twenty-four hours."[20]

The Confederates also marveled at their own ability to entrench. "We finally built strong works for our protection," remarked William C. Jordan of the 15th Alabama in Anderson's First Corps. He was contrasting the light works at the Wilderness with the immensely strong fortifications at Spotsylvania. Jordan would have agreed with J. F. J. Caldwell of McGowan's brigade that the "system of fighting behind fortifications was now established, for it had become as necessary to us as it would formerly have been injurious." The Rebels adjusted very well to fighting from behind fieldworks. Jordan noted that his fellow Alabamians learned to secure their ramrods under the headlog in such a way that they stuck straight out. This way, they could reload more quickly by shoving the barrel forward onto the metal rod, "jerk the gun back, put on a cap and fire."[21]

The length of time spent on this fortified line—thirteen days for many units—came close to fostering some aspects of a siege. For the first time, with the possible exception of the Yorktown campaign, one sees the digging of bombproofs in the Army of Northern Virginia. Lt. Col. William T. Poague recalled that his surgeon had a large bombproof dug 100 yards behind the Third Corps Line and never left it. The heavy rains finally flooded the shelter, but the doctor remained inside, clinging to the log roof and saying, "'It was getting somewhat damp, but better to endure it than expose oneself needlessly."[22]

The Rebel line at Spotsylvania was astonishing. Six miles in length, it presaged the kind of fortification that crossed the line between a temporary fieldwork and a semipermanent earthen line, such as would be built to defend Petersburg only one month in the future. It was the most sophisticated field fortification dug by the Army of Northern Virginia to date, and it instilled great confidence in the men. "[W]e have got a splendid line of breastworks and we can whip any Army the Yankees can bring against us if the Lord is willing," crowed Pvt. Joseph F. Shaner of the Rockbridge Artillery.[23]

The Federals were not backward in digging their own works. The diary of Jacob Lyons indicates that the 71st New York, in Gershom Mott's division of the Second Corps, worked almost constantly on field fortifications during the Spotsylvania campaign. The regiment dug in as soon as it reached the battlefield at 6:00 P.M. on May 8 and continued building works during the next two days. The New Yorkers constructed earthworks on May 14 and concentrated on making traverses on May 17.[24]

Pvt. Arthur T. Chapin of Battery D, 4th Maine Artillery, which was part of the Sixth Corps, noted that the preparation of an entrenched position for his guns was a joint effort. Infantrymen did most of the work as forty men of the battery moved logs to the site. After occupying the emplacement, Chapin and his comrades went to work "digging holes to Lower the Limber chests into."[25]

The fortifications evoked feelings of confidence among the Federals as well. "We have finished our earthworks and now feel secure," noted Elisha Hunt Rhodes of the 2nd Rhode Island in the Sixth Corps. "Our works are strong and built of large trees covered with earth. Let the Rebels try to take them if they want to."[26]

But that was the rub. The Confederates would never make an attempt to take Union earthworks during the Spotsylvania phase of the Overland campaign, nor for the succeeding phases of this bloody drive south. This marks another turn toward the practice of trench warfare. The Confederates eagerly took the offensive at the Wilderness. Brigades of Ewell's Second Corps left the safety of their works to launch local counterattacks, and Gordon's assault on the evening of May 6 was a full-scale attempt to crush Meade's right flank. The First and Third Corps fought the whole battle with very few and light breastworks. Lee mounted a large attack on Hancock's fortified line along Brock Road on the evening of May 6.

Yet at Spotsylvania there were local counterattacks only on the Confederate right against Burnside's small-scale assaults. Lee ventured forth on a large strike on May 19 in an operation that was something of a cross between a reconnaissance in force and a determined grand tactical offensive, but it was an open field fight. Mostly, Lee's men took shelter behind their strong works and punished the many Union assaults that Grant and Meade threw at them. The Confederates used heavy fieldworks as a weapon to deteriorate the Union army's power.

Those many Union attacks often were characterized by inadequate planning and a lack of coordination, especially by a failure to coordinate supporting troops. The latter point probably was the most important in understanding why they generally failed. Grant had a tendency to set a timetable that did not allow subordinates ample opportunity to prepare. Sometimes, most notably with the breakdown of Mott's supporting role in the May 10 attack, key elements of planning fell between the cracks. Grant adopted a new twist on the pattern for May 12, massing an unusually large number of men to smash the tip of the Mule Shoe Salient. But this innovation was wrongheaded, as it merely increased the difficulties of control and maneuver by creating one of the worst traffic jams on any Civil War battlefield.[27]

Given that Grant was determined to press the campaign aggressively, the problem of how best to attack and crack open a line protected by strong earthworks became the Army of the Potomac's prime tactical problem for the remainder of the war. It was a very difficult problem to solve, and Meade's army would never come up with a clear-cut answer until near the end of the conflict, when Lee's weakened strength made it possible for the Sixth Corps to achieve a dramatic cleavage of A. P. Hill's Third Corps line at Petersburg on April 2, 1865. Until then, the Army of the Potomac lost thousands of valuable lives in futile attempts to find a way through Lee's trenches.

There is no doubt that the sophisticated earthworks were an important explanation for this lack of success, but they were by no means the only explanation. Earthworks could be penetrated. Ward did so on May 10 at Laurel Hill, Upton did so on May 10 on the west side of the Mule Shoe Salient, and Hancock did so on a massive scale two days later at the tip of the salient. The problem always lay in the lack of a good plan to throw in supporting troops at the right time and place to exploit the initial success.

Upton's attack is a good case study of this dilemma. That operation solved half the problem—the initial penetration of the defending line. This was best accomplished with a compact formation of men that was a cross between a single line of battle and a deep column. The key was to move fast over the killing ground with energy and determination and get into the fortified line quickly.

The second half of the problem was to find a way to coordinate a second wave, for exploitation was best done by fresh troops. They had a short window of opportunity after the initial break was made, for defending commanders would inevitably rush up reserves. The tendency in the Civil War was for the attacker to wait until there was a clear sign of initial success before sending in supports, but by then it often was too late. The supports needed time to traverse the no-man's-land between the lines and to negotiate the physical barrier of the parapet to get into a place where their strength could be felt. Ideally, the second wave should be able to get into the breach and widen it within ten or fifteen minutes after the first wave opened it. To do so required that they advance no more than a couple of hundred yards behind the first wave. The danger here was that if the first wave failed to make the initial penetration, the second wave would be disrupted by its retreat or run into a hail of fire from the defending force. This was why commanders normally preferred to wait until they knew there was an initial success before ordering in supports so as not to waste valuable manpower.

The physical problem of crossing the parapet using linear tactics was significant because moving a line across a parapet always broke it up. This forced units to spend time re-forming on the opposite side. Fighting within fortifications was impossible in linear formations. There was no training for trench fighting in the drill manuals; Civil War soldiers did it instinctually or they failed to do it at all.

Grant at least sensed the possibility of learning from Upton's failed attack on May 10, but he learned the wrong lesson. Instead of finding a more effective way to coordinate supports, he piled up so many men in the first wave that it would have its support within its own ranks. This was a recipe for chaos. Crossing the parapet broke apart all organization among 20,000 men as easily as it did for 5,000. Once the Rebels counterattacked and drove this disorganized mass back to shelter on the other side of the earthwork, there was little possibility of any further Union success. Yet Grant and Meade piled more troops—the entire Sixth Corps—into this mess, increasing the casualty list instead of maximizing the chance of victory. In hindsight, Grant would have been better advised to use far fewer men in the first wave while sending the rest of Hancock's corps to simultaneously attack the east side rather than trusting the unreliable Burnside in that sector. The stronger west side should have been ignored.

Why were lessons poorly learned, if learned at all? Admittedly, there were no institutional mechanisms in Civil War field armies to evaluate past performance and make recommendations for future adjustments. Such things were entirely up to the initiative of individual commanders, who usually were too busy running their commands to pay much attention. Grant was doggedly focused on the future, not the past, and determined to succeed in the end at any cost. The ease with which he accepted bloody failures and pushed on with undiminished enthusiasm was a key element in eventual Union success. Marching away from blood-soaked fields, Grant pushed the campaign forward without pause.

Grant lost 33,000 men at the Wilderness and during the worst phase of the Spotsylvania fighting, from May 5 to 12. This represented 28 percent of his available force. The Second Corps was worst hit, its strength deteriorated 40 percent during that period. During the same period the Confederates lost 23,000 men, or one-third of their number. The Second Corps suffered the most, with its troops reduced from 17,000 to 6,000. Johnson's division, which started the Overland campaign with 6,000 men, had only 1,500 left by the morning of May 13. After the armies finally moved on from Spotsylvania, Confederate ordnance officers collected over sixty tons of spent bullets from the battlefield and recast them into more projectiles.[28]

On May 10, with the help of two other doctors, Surg. Daniel M. Holt of the 121st New York took care of 350 wounded men from Upton's attack. Bullets fell onto the hospital site for an hour; one wounded man was hit even as Holt dressed his injury, and he later died. The last casualty was not sent to the rear until 5:00 A.M. on May 11, offering Holt and his colleagues a welcome opportunity to sleep. "I hardly know *what* to think of this wholesale slaughter in storming breastworks so well manned and stubbornly defended," he wrote. "*I don't believe it pays.*"[29]

Union soldiers widely recognized that Grant had inaugurated a new tone in Virginia operations. "This campaign beats all the rest in desperation and determination," wrote brigade leader Robert McAllister to his family. With it came increased demands on the physical and emotional stamina of the common soldier. In some ways Spotsylvania was the epitome of the whole campaign. Exhausted as they were by the Wilderness fighting, the men still had enough strength for another major battle soon after, and the intensity of combat on May 12 demonstrated how ready they were to engage the enemy.[30]

Yet that day marked the start of a decline in the combat effectiveness of Hancock's Second Corps, a fact admitted by its veterans. "We think the turning point in the fighting power of the Second Corps was at Spottsylvania," wrote John S. Jones of the 4th Ohio. "Its loss of officers and men at that battle rendered it physically and morally impossible for this corps to make another such fight without recuperation and reorganization." New York artilleryman Frank Wilkeson heard the first criticism of Grant from a man of the Second Corps on the night of May 12. Historian Carol Reardon believes that the whole Spotsylvania experience began to darken the optimism of men in the Army of the Potomac. She notes a range of factors, including sleep deprivation, poor logistical support, the difficulty of keeping clean in the muddy trenches, constant combat, and inefficient officers. A similar deterioration of morale was not evident in Lee's army, however, despite its high casualty rate.[31]

When Grant began the movement away from the Wilderness on May 8, he confidently informed Maj. Gen. Henry W. Halleck that his "efforts will be to form a junction with Genl Butler as early as possible and be prepared to beat any enemy interposing." Roadblocks appeared and battle was joined. By May 10, Grant vowed, "I shall take no backward step. . . . We can maintain ourselves at least and in the end beat Lee's Army I believe." The next day, he wrote his most famous pronouncement on the Spotsylvania phase of the Overland campaign when informing both Halleck and Secretary of War Edwin M. Stanton that "I propose to fight it out on this line if it takes all summer." Grant even convinced himself that the Confederate refusal to launch attacks from their well-fortified line indicated that Lee's men were losing their morale. They were "very shaky and are only kept up to the mark by the greatest exertion on the part of their officers." Two days later, the slaughter of May 12 apparently had made an impression on the man from Illinois. He wrote his wife Julia: "The world has never seen so bloody or so protracted a battle as the one being fought." He thought that Lee's men were digging in deeper and fighting harder because they realized that "their situation is desperate beyond anything heretofore known. To loose [sic] this battle they loose [sic] their cause." Grant believed that the Rebels "were really whipped" on May 12 and apologized to Halleck four days later for not throwing in another major attack. He assured the army chief of staff that only the heavy rains of the past five days had delayed the resumption of heavy fighting. Grant remained "very well and full of hope," as he had earlier informed Julia.[32]

Grant's impression of Confederate morale was skewed by his hopes of success. Despite the near catastrophe of May 12, the morale of the Army of Northern Virginia was generally high and Lee expressed worry only about the long-range implications of Grant's continuous campaigning. In a message to President Jefferson Davis on May 9, Lee stressed the defensive nature of his operations, promising to continue blocking Grant's short movements and avoiding a major battle whenever possible. Nine days later, after the disturbing threat posed by Upton's partial success on May 10, the terrible fighting of May 12, and the feeble Union thrust of May 18, Lee adopted a more aggressive tone. He felt frustrated at not being able to strike at Grant, for the Federals were too well fortified. He had no intention of wasting valuable manpower, but the Rebel commander promised to "continue to strike him whenever opportunity presents itself." Lee actually put that desire into limited practice the next day with Ewell's reconnaissance in force toward the Harris Farm. But there were few opportunities to launch serious offensives against a commander who was naturally unflappable and constantly on the move.[33]

Lee's men felt a certain sense of amazement at the repeated Federal attacks and at the moral fiber of a man who wasted so many lives. They did not know whether to condemn Grant or admire him. "Half such a whipping would have sent McClellan, Hooker, Burnside or Meade crossing to the other side of the Rappahannock," mused Capt. Thomas J. Linebarger of the 28th North Carolina. "It seems that Grant is determined to sacrifice his army or destroy Lee's." A few more attacks, Linebarger wrote on May 15, and "he will have expended his strength."[34]

6

Bermuda Hundred

Benjamin Butler's part of Grant's overall program had already run its course before the Spotsylvania phase of the Overland campaign came to an end. He was presented with numerous opportunities to wreak havoc far to Lee's rear, seriously threaten or even capture his choice of Richmond or Petersburg, and possibly bring the war to an early end. But several tentative moves were either aborted or turned back in small-scale fighting. Butler's most serious advance toward the capital was repulsed by a much smaller Confederate force, even though he had managed to occupy a portion of the defenses that stood in his way.

A recent historian has characterized the Army of the James an army of amateurs, and that is at least partly right. The regiments composing this field force of 34,000 men had been in service for a long time, since the first year of the war in many cases, but they had little combat experience. Mostly they had performed occupation duty along the Atlantic coast. The troops knew how to march, bivouac in the field, and do a variety of tasks normally done by soldiers, but they were not the tough fighters that Meade had under his command. The Tenth Corps had conducted the operations on Morris Island the previous summer, consisting of two sharp attacks on Battery Wagner followed by an efficient siege that reduced the fort. In contrast, the units of the Eighteenth Corps had almost no experience in battle.

Yet the men were of good quality, and they could quickly learn how to handle themselves under fire just as they had learned how to do all the other tasks normally assigned to soldiers. The most serious weakness in the Army of the James lay in its high command. Butler was a consummate political general. He had no military training or experience before the war yet received the first major general's commission offered to a volunteer, dating from April 16, 1861. The impressive seniority this appointment gave him failed to make a general out of Butler. Although in overall command when the battle of Big Bethel took place in June 1861, he did not lead troops in the field. Likewise, Butler commanded the small number of men who occupied the Outer Banks of North Carolina in August after the navy reduced the Confederate forts. Butler was always on occupation duty, most notably in New Orleans in 1862. He was among the least deserving of available candidates for command of the Army of the James. His political connections, his ability to network, cajole, and play the fawning subordinate to Grant both got him the job and enabled him to keep it despite his many failures.[1]

Unfortunately, Butler's two corps commanders, both of them professional engineers, had faults of their own. Maj. Gen. Quincy A. Gillmore had graduated at the head of his West Point class in 1849 and had served in the U.S. Army Corps of Engineers before the war. He was the chief engineer for the expedition that captured Port Royal in November 1861 and was primarily responsible for the reduction of Fort Pulaski the following April. Promoted brigadier general that month, Gillmore briefly commanded a division of infantry in Kentucky but saw no combat. He was given command of the Department of the South and launched the highly successful effort to seize Morris Island and capture Battery Wagner by skillful siege approaches in September 1863. He also reduced Fort Sumter to a pile of rubble by employing heavy-rifled artillery. Gillmore was promoted to major general in recognition of his achievements. Most of the troops in his department were gathered to constitute the Tenth Corps, and Gillmore led it to Butler's army early in 1864. He adopted "a square bastioned fort, very like a star in effect," as the corps badge. Although one of the premier engineers of either army during the war, Gillmore was out of his element as a field commander. The largest infantry attack he ever planned involved only three brigades, yet he found himself leading an entire corps.[2]

His colleague, Maj. Gen. William F. Smith, had also served in the Corps of Engineers after graduating fourth in the West Point class of 1845. Smith served on Brig. Gen. Irvin McDowell's staff at First Bull Run and was promoted brigadier general in August 1861. He led a division of the Sixth Corps in the Peninsula and Maryland campaigns and the corps at Fredericksburg. When he was offered promotion to major general, the U.S. Senate refused to confirm the appointment because he signed a letter highly critical of Burnside's performance as commander of the Army of the Potomac. Smith lost his Sixth Corps command as well. He became chief engineer of the Department of the Cumberland and did so well in the Chattanooga campaign that a number of superior officers, including Grant, praised him in their reports. He was promoted to major general in March 1864 and given command of the Eighteenth Corps when it was organized for duty with Butler's army. Smith was a good engineer, and he could have been an effective corps commander if placed under a decisive and competent army leader. But his tendency to bicker, complain, and connive was given full range of motion under Butler's tutelage, and the army commander himself would become the chief target of Smith's ire.[3]

The Army of the James had a lot of potential. In the right hands, it could have quickly evolved into a field force as effective as any Union army in the war. But its division and brigade leaders were no more experienced than Butler, Gillmore, or Smith.

The strategic outlines of the army's first campaign were initially suggested by Maj. Gen. Samuel P. Heintzelman in March 1864. He proposed that Butler's force land at Bermuda Hundred, a peninsula formed by the junction of the Potomac and Appomattox rivers. Here it could use nearby City Point as a logistical base. The army would be only fourteen miles south of Richmond and about the same distance north of Petersburg. The capital was garrisoned by a few thousand Confederates, and Petersburg and points south were lightly held by a few thousand more. Reinforcements would not likely be forthcoming from Lee once Grant initiated his Overland drive, and the nearest available help was under the command of Gen. G. T. Beauregard around Charleston. If Butler moved decisively, he could enter either city with enough strength to hold it.

Grant adopted Heintzelman's proposed line of advance and gave general guidelines for Butler to follow. If Butler had possessed sufficient initiative and experience, he could have taken these guidelines, revised them as needed, and charted his own course in the campaign. But the political general intended to proceed with a caution that increased with each passing day. Grant left it to him to decide, based on developing circumstances, whether Richmond or Petersburg should be his target. Instead, Butler focused on securing his bases at City Point and on the tip of the Bermuda Hundred Peninsula. He then planned to cut the railroad between Richmond and Petersburg before advancing on Richmond. Butler acted as if there was no need to hurry in any of these movements.[4]

Smith later criticized the entire approach. He argued, with some validity, that Butler should have landed all of his troops on the south side of the James and concentrated on Petersburg. Bermuda Hundred offered the Army of the James the opportunity to cut the railroad that ran between the two cities, but the actual approaches to both were difficult. The Confederates had strong earthworks stretching west from Fort Darling at Drewry's Bluff, covering the approach to Richmond from the south, while Swift Creek and the Appomattox River barred access to Petersburg. "Practically, the position taken up was between two fortresses with wet ditches," Smith commented after the war. Yet, even with these obstacles, good generals could have made the campaign a success. In fact, its outcome would be decided by the incompetence and fumbling of the Federal commanders.[5]

Butler set out on May 5, the first day of fighting at the Wilderness, from bases at Yorktown and Fortress Monroe. A division of black troops assigned to Smith's Eighteenth Corps occupied City Point, and other units secured the landing at Bermuda Hundred that evening. Butler listened to Gillmore and Smith, who advised securing both bases before advancing on Richmond. He ordered works constructed at Point of Rocks, on the north side of the Appomattox, and at other points to provide some security for the landing at Bermuda Hundred.

A brigade of the Eighteenth Corps set out on May 6 to reconnoiter toward the Richmond-Petersburg Railroad. It engaged in a small, open field fight near Port Walthall Junction and then returned to the landing. Another strike toward the railroad resulted in the second battle of Port Walthall Junction on May 7. A much larger Confederate force took position behind the railroad embankment, but the Federal commanders, who outnumbered it three to one, failed to press home their attacks. All they accomplished was the tearing up of 100 feet of track. The bulk of Butler's army spent May 6–8 digging in at the landing. The Eighteenth Corps on the left had a "naturally very strong" position, thought Gillmore, but his own Tenth Corps occupied ground on the right that could easily be approached by the Confederates. Gillmore planned a line of works from the James River to a ravine that lay in front of Smith's command to strengthen his position. News of the fighting at the Wilderness caused Butler to worry that Grant might not be able to reach his area anytime soon. He now was content to postpone a serious move on the Rebel capital while further securing his position.[6]

The two small fights at Port Walthall Junction alerted the Confederates to Butler's presence. Maj. Gen. George E. Pickett established a position on the south side of Swift Creek north of Petersburg. Col. David B. Harris, Beauregard's chief engineer, laid out works for Pickett to cover the Richmond-Petersburg Turnpike bridge. The line was long enough to

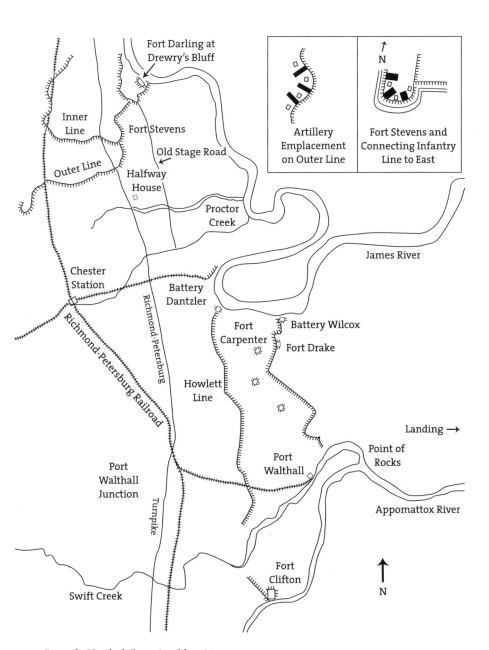

Inner Line

Fort Darling at Drewry's Bluff

Fort Stevens

Old Stage Road

Outer Line

Halfway House

Proctor Creek

Artillery Emplacement on Outer Line

Fort Stevens and Connecting Infantry Line to East

N

James River

Chester Station

Battery Dantzler

Fort Carpenter

Battery Wilcox

Fort Drake

Richmond-Petersburg Railroad

Richmond-Petersburg

Howlett Line

Landing →

Point of Rocks

Port Walthall

Port Walthall Junction

Appomattox River

Turnpike

Swift Creek

Fort Clifton

N

Bermuda Hundred Campaign, May 1864

hold 5,000 men and extended to the left to cover Brander's Bridge and to the right toward Fort Clifton. The Confederates dug this line on May 8 and 9, just in time to meet Butler's first major move out of his landing area on Bermuda Hundred. The irresolute general brought most of his army toward the railroad on May 9, leaving only three brigades and 500 additional men under Col. Harris M. Plaisted at the landing. Butler later claimed that his only goal was to snip the railroad in two, not to attack either city. The Federals easily gained the track and tore up short sections of it near Port Walthall Junction and Chester Station. Then they headed south to Swift Creek, where Butler repulsed a small band of two and a half regiments sent out to conduct a reconnaissance in force on May 9.

Butler seemed ready to attack across Swift Creek on May 10, but his corps commanders preferred to outflank Pickett's right. Butler readily acceded to this suggestion, then his nerves got the better of him. Further news from Grant seemed to indicate that the Army of the Potomac might be making faster progress toward Richmond than earlier expected, and Butler thought he should break off at Swift Creek and head for the capital to meet it. Then he got word that some Tenth Corps units left at Chester Station were being attacked by garrison troops from Richmond. Two Confederate brigades advanced from the works at Drewry's Bluff and engaged them in an open field fight east of the station on May 10. The Federals acquitted themselves well, even though outnumbered, and held off the Rebel units until Butler could send more help. This small battle and the host of uncertainties that accompany every campaign were too much for Butler. He decided to retreat to the landing, where Plaisted had spread his small force along the three-mile line and set it to work. The Federals further strengthened the Tenth Corps works by slashing timber in front. Plaisted had to arrest engineer Capt. John Walker for refusing to take orders from anyone except higher-ranking engineer officers and complaining at having to work on gun embrasures and platforms.[7]

Butler was ready to make his most serious effort on May 12 with the Eighteenth Corps and one division of the Tenth Corps. The rest of Gillmore's command was positioned facing south to protect his rear as he moved up the railroad toward Richmond. The slow-moving columns made it to Chester Station that evening and bivouacked. The next day, they moved on to find that the Confederates had abandoned their advanced position along Proctor's Creek. The Federals reached the Drewry's Bluff Line by mid-afternoon of May 13 and found it to be formidable. Smith personally reconnoitered the line. "Strong profiles, with an outside ditch extending for over a mile, were in sight," he later remembered. "Numerous embrasures were filled with artillery, and the ground had been cleared for a space of from 300 to 700 yards, which was entirely swept by the artillery in the works."[8]

Strong as it seemed, Smith was looking only at the Outer Line, a long extension of the Inner Line, which stretched from Fort Darling at Drewry's Bluff. This Inner Line curved north too soon to cover all of the approaches to Richmond, necessitating the construction of the Outer Line to sweep much farther westward. Fort Stevens was the anchor of these two lines, situated where they joined each other. Some Confederates did not share Smith's analysis of the Outer Line. Brig. Gen. Seth M. Barton, who had seen the works on May 7, called the line "very insecure." It was "too long, and far from support; is broken, and the timber is too close. There are roads which enable the enemy to turn it without great caution." Barton recommended that only the Inner Line be held. A week later, on May 13, the Confederates were still trying to occupy the Outer Line with too few men—only four and a half brigades under Brig. Gen. Robert F. Hoke.[9]

Gillmore's corps came up from the south and wheeled into place to the left of Smith's corps. Brig. Gen. Alfred H. Terry's division marched along the roads Barton had complained about to flank the Outer Line, approaching its anchor on Wooldridge's Hill a half mile west of the Richmond-Petersburg Railroad. The Rebel works on the hill were unenclosed, a serious drawback for the defenders. When the 3rd New Hampshire approached, Hoke's men jumped across the parapet quickly enough to repulse it by firing to the rear. The approach of another column to the Confederate front compelled Hoke to retire down the Outer Line. Terry occupied at least one mile of the works before dark.[10]

Early on the morning of May 14, Butler's army cautiously advanced to find the entire Outer Line empty. Hoke still held Fort Stevens, located on a hill just east of the Richmond-Petersburg Turnpike, as well as the Inner Line. Smith called Fort Stevens "a bastion salient on an eminence, completely commanding our position," but Butler more quaintly referred to the Confederate works as "square redoubts." Gillmore pushed along two and a half miles of the empty Outer Line to connect with Smith. After occupying one line and seeing the other, Gillmore thought that both Confederate works were equally well made, "judiciously located, of great strength, naturally and artificially; have deep ditches on their exterior at all available points." Terry reconnoitered the Inner Line and found it daunt-ing in appearance, fronted by at least some abatis.[11]

"I do not want you to assault the works in front," Butler admonished Gillmore at mid-afternoon of May 14. The Federals settled in along the Outer Line and began to skirmish with Hoke's command as all thoughts turned to defense. Butler's men began to dig in, converting the Rebel work into one that would offer better protection. Gillmore ordered his Second Division commander to "throw up a temporary breast-work in front of your lines to protect your command in case of an attack." Brig. Gen. Hiram Burnham's brigade of the Eighteenth Corps cut "a slight ban-quette" into the exterior slope of the Outer Line "on which a thin line could stand, protected by the original parapet." Other Eighteenth Corps units simply made "a rude breast-work of logs." The Federals used proper tools wherever available but put tin cups and bayonets into play as well. Part of the Eighteenth Corps line ran through some woods, so the men put headlogs on top of the parapet.[12]

On the night of May 14, at Butler's urging, Smith reported that the only place he might be able to attack was between two large works on the Inner Line opposite his corps. Butler experienced a spurt of enthusiasm for the idea, which Smith did not share. Yet he realized that the army commander was keen on an attack, so he insisted that engineer Lt. Peter Michie help him plan the move. Smith's lack of confidence in the offensive led to its cancellation. Gillmore fed the feelings of doubt at both Eighteenth Corps and army headquarters by relaying information, gathered from an inter-view with someone who had helped construct the Inner Line, that the strongest part of it lay in front of Butler's position.[13]

Rather than advancing, Butler's men further strengthened their defen-sive works. Smith was responsible for the fact that some units constructed a wire entanglement along parts of the line. He ordered two division leaders, Brig. Gen. William T. H. Brooks and Brig. Gen. Godfrey Weitzel, to collect telegraph wire and string it around stumps along their front. The wire was taken from poles planted along the turnpike. When it was reported that there was not enough wire to go along the whole line, Smith decided to place it where the Federal position was closest to the Rebels. The wire was strung about a foot from the ground in areas where there was substantial underbrush to hide it. This apparently was only the second time in the war that such an obstruction was placed on a battlefield; the previous instance occurred during the Knoxville campaign in November 1863.[14]

Smith had ordered Brig. Gen. Charles A. Heckman, whose brigade belonged to Weitzel's division, to string wire. But for some reason he never received the order. Heckman built new works but then two regiments came up to reinforce him, as his command held the extreme Union right. In extending the line, Heckman failed to position or fortify his additional units properly. His extreme right now barely covered Old Stage Road. Heckman's troops were tired from their previous digging and it was late in the evening, so they did a poor job of reinforcing the extreme right with fieldworks. The 9th New Jersey, on the end of the line, apparently had no works at all even though it straddled the road.[15]

On other parts of the Union line, various units made small adjustments to their defensive preparations. They moved picket lines to more favorable ground and dug rifle pits to protect them as Butler ordered Gillmore to bring forward troops of the 1st New York Engineers to make fascines. Lt. Col. Winslow P. Spofford advanced his 11th Maine forward to an outpost and worked his men by reliefs all night of May 15. They made a kind of fort consisting of three infantry parapets enclosing a house and several acres of land, with the fourth side of the square more or less protected by a section of the Outer Line.[16]

Butler's extreme right was vulnerable because of the inexperience of his brigade and division commanders, but the rest of the Union position was strong. The weakness, however, in the Army of the James was the complete lack of any plans for offensive action. Butler seems to have been content to wait in his partially captured, partially refortified Confederate fieldworks for something to happen. He had many more troops than the defending Rebels and all of the advantages in terms of strategic momentum. Few other campaigns of the Civil War demonstrated more appalling waste of tactical and strategic opportunities.

The Confederate commander, on the other hand, refused to waste any opportunities. Beauregard rushed up from his department headquarters at Weldon, North Carolina, riding around Butler's left flank, and reached Drewry's Bluff early on the morning of May 14. He consulted his chief engineer and Col. Walter H. Stevens, who was chief of construction in Lee's Department of Northern Virginia. They filled him in on the state of affairs as Stevens produced a good topographical map of the area. Hearing the latest news from Lee as well, Beauregard concocted a plan to win the war in one stroke. He wanted Lee to break off contact with Grant and pull back to establish a defensive position along the Chickahominy River. This would enable him to send 10,000 men to Beauregard, who would then attack and crush Butler. There would still be time to shift most of these men back to Lee so the two Confederate commanders could strike Grant's left flank and crush him too.

This was typical of Beauregard's grandiose schemes, and the general rushed Stevens off to Richmond to propose it to the authorities. Stevens could not see Jefferson Davis, but Gen. Braxton Bragg, who was acting as the army's chief of staff, liked the proposal and went to Drewry's Bluff to talk to Beauregard. Bragg then took the idea to Davis in Richmond, who wisely killed it. From every perspective, it was an unworkable plan. Davis noted that it would destroy public morale to have Lee deliberately retreat from Grant's army. He could well have pointed out that Grant was not the kind of general to meekly wait for several days along the Chickahominy for the Confederates to attack him. Bragg got the message. Days later, he explained to Beauregard why the plan would not have worked.[17]

Beauregard was right in only one way—that the Confederates could not afford to act on the defensive when faced with such a large enemy force. He planned an attack to take place early on May 16. While all of his available manpower would advance from the Inner Line to drive the Yankees south, he also arranged for Maj. Gen. William H. C. Whiting to advance northward from Petersburg to cut Butler off from his base at Bermuda Hundred. Although outnumbered, Beauregard's army was formidable. Maj. Gen. Robert Ransom held the left with four brigades and was to advance along Old Stage Road to turn Butler's right flank. Hoke was to advance in the center and left with four brigades, while two remaining brigades would constitute a general reserve. Beauregard planned to throw 17,500 men into action. Whiting had an additional force of four brigades that would take position at Port Walthall Junction and wait for the sound of Beauregard's fight.[18]

Beauregard's decision to attack was motivated not only by his desire to seize the initiative, but also by the untenable nature of his defensive position. The Drewry's Bluff Line was not well suited to withstand a siege. It had been built in 1862, when the Confederate capital was threatened by the Army of the Potomac. The base of this defensive system was Fort Darling, a large bastioned work protecting the river batteries that defended Richmond. Named for landowner Capt. Augustus H. Drewry, the bluffs were ninety feet above the James River and about eight miles downstream from the capital. Started on March 17, 1862, Fort Darling had three large guns by the time a Federal squadron of two ironclads and three gunboats attacked on May 15. The Confederates also had emplaced six heavy guns in positions outside the fort. The fire of these nine cannon decisively turned back the only naval attempt to reach Richmond during the war.[19]

A great deal of construction took place after that Confederate victory. Fort Darling was reinforced with emplacements for field artillery on its land side, and a line of works was built in a wide circle to enclose the fort. Then the Confederates built the Inner Line stretching from the Fort Darling complex to the southwest. From Fort Stevens, the Inner Line headed due west to the railroad, then it made a right-angle turn to the north and crisscrossed the railroad to conform to the high ground, ending two miles north of the right angle. All told, the Inner Line stretched for five miles. An extremely well-preserved segment of it shows that the line was constructed in a manner similar to most other semipermanent works in the early part of the war. There are no traverses and no trench, but the ditch is deep and the parapet is large and well formed. The artillery emplacements have a reinforced parapet that even today is about six feet tall, fifteen feet wide at the base, and three feet wide at the top. The ditch in front of the artillery emplacement is six feet wide, and the artillery platforms have deep embrasures.[20]

Fort Stevens should more properly be called a battery, for it was built as an artillery emplacement open to the rear. It has big parapets with wide and deep ditches, but there are no trenches inside the parapet. Not even the connecting infantry line to the east has remnants of a trench. Inside the fort, three ground-level platforms for heavy guns are separated by two ramps that have platforms for field guns on their tops. These features, in effect, serve the double purpose of traverse and ramp. There is also a more traditional traverse to the rear, nearly enclosing the work.[21]

Not much of the Outer Line is left to demonstrate its design, but undoubtedly it was built after the Inner Line was finished. The Outer Line stretches from Fort Stevens south for a short distance, then southwest to cross the turnpike. Here it heads due west before resuming its southwestern course at the railroad. If this line had continued westward it might have served as the basis for a long-term defense of the approaches to Richmond, but there was no imminent danger in this quarter when the Drewry's Bluff Line was built. The Outer Line therefore ends rather abruptly with a retrenchment after stretching across the countryside for four miles. Butler's army was large enough to outflank this line on the evening of May 13. After they abandoned the Outer Line, the Confederates had no hope of blocking a vigorous Union advance toward Richmond except with offensive action because the Inner Line faced west rather than south in this area. What is left of the Outer Line indicates that the work had no traverses except in the artillery emplacements, one of which has room for three or four field guns inside a slight bulge in the parapet. There are sizable traverses dividing the gun platforms.[22]

Attacking on May 16 was not only the right choice for Beauregard, it was his only feasible course of action. Fortunately for the Confederates, outnumbered two to one, their counterparts had no idea that they were to be the targets of offensive action.

MAY 16

The Confederate attack began at 4:45 A.M., aided by a heavy fog that settled over the eastern half of the battlefield. As Ransom's division approached Butler's right, his front line, consisting of Brig. Gen. Archibald Gracie's Alabama brigade on the left and Lt. Col. William G. Lewis's North Carolina brigade on the right, managed to get close to the Union position before it was detected. Heavy fire forced both brigades to stop, but not before Lewis had veered far enough west to get his rightmost units entangled in the wire fronting Burnham. When Gracie's leftmost units discovered that they had an opportunity to outflank Heckman, the advance continued. At first, Heckman's 9th New Jersey refused three companies and held its own, forcing Gracie's Alabamans to take cover by lying on the ground short of their objective. When Gracie called for help, Col. William R. Terry's Virginia brigade came up from the second line and extended to the left far enough to overlap the Jerseymen. Butler's extreme right flank collapsed, the 9th fled in disorder, and Heckman was taken prisoner.[23]

Hoke started his advance in the Confederate center at 6:00 A.M. to give Ransom time to mangle the Union right. But Hoke's brigades fared worse than Ransom's, for their attack was not a surprise and they ran into the wire entanglement. Brig. Gen. Johnson Hagood's South Carolina brigade advanced east of the turnpike while Brig. Gen. Bushrod R. Johnson's Tennessee brigade attacked west of it. At first, heavy fire forced Hagood's men to seek shelter behind the part of the Outer Line that extended southward from Fort Stevens; although facing east instead of south, it offered some degree of protection. Then Hoke ordered Hagood to try again, wheeling to the west on the assumption that Ransom's flanking movement was successful. Hagood's regiments ran into the wire entanglement and received severe flank fire as they wheeled right. When the men of the 7th South Carolina Battalion came on the wire, they were thrown down "in a mass to the ground" and suffered heavy casualties while struggling to re-form. A company of another regiment in Hagood's brigade lost twenty-two of its thirty-six men in the same manner. Hagood's command spent twenty minutes in the wire, hoping for support from Ransom, but it never came. Finally, the men retired to the Inner Line.[24]

Johnson's brigade also advanced only to become entangled in the wire. Here, at a distance of thirty yards from the Union line, the Tennesseans were devastated by rifle fire. The men "were dazed" by the unexpected obstruction and stunned by the heavy losses they suffered while stuck in the maze of wires. The confusion was worse in some units than in others. Capt. J. H. Curtis of the 25th Tennessee was among the first to stumble on the wire and fall down, but he managed to get up in time to yell a warning to his men. Nevertheless, most of Johnson's brigade stalled in the entanglement. The consolidated 25th and 44th Tennessee took shelter behind a retrenchment that angled away behind the Outer Line, only a few yards from the Yankees, but it could go no farther. Johnson's only success was that a portion of his leftmost regiment managed to make a tiny lodgment in the Union line after the 8th Connecticut of Burnham's brigade retired because the Federals were afraid that Hagood's wheeling movement would outflank its position, but the Confederates were unable to exploit this minor advantage. At least one Rebel officer discounted the effect of the wire entanglement on his unit. Col. R. H. Keeble of the consolidated 17th and 23rd Tennessee referred to it as a "trick (emphatically a Yankee one)" that was "soon discovered and surmounted." But the weight of evidence supports Weitzel's contention that the attackers were "piled in heaps over the telegraph wire" and the entanglement was "of immense service."[25]

As a result, Hoke's advance ran out of steam after Ransom's initial success on the left stalled. The collapse of the 9th New Jersey spread to three other regiments in Heckman's command, but the rest of the brigade shored itself up. The remainder of Weitzel's division solidly held its own east of the turnpike, and Burnham's brigade (except the 8th Connecticut) was in position west of the roadway.

Then the turning point of the battle occurred as William F. Smith lost his nerve. Shaken by reports of Confederate cavalry probes around his right flank, he ordered a retreat at 7:45 A.M. Even though Smith was unaware of the true state of affairs along his front, there was no excuse for doing this. As the fog lifted, it became obvious that there were no imminent attacks, only a pile of dead and wounded entangled in the wire.

Brooks's division west of the turnpike was reluctant to fall back. His subordinates sent out detachments to gather some prisoners, then the division slowly retired, soon followed by the rest of the corps. The Confederates did not immediately pursue; they were disorganized and not fully aware of what was happening.[26]

Confusion reigned at Tenth Corps headquarters even though Gillmore contended with little more than skirmishing and a few halfhearted Confederate probes. Poorly worded orders from Butler and a need to shift regiments to the right to maintain connection with the Eighteenth Corps kept Gillmore in a fuddle. In a sense, Smith's withdrawal cleared up the confusion and Gillmore ordered his corps to fall back too. Both corps retired to the Half Way House, a hostel located on the turnpike just north of Proctor's Creek, where Butler ordered them to retire all the way to the entrenchments at the neck of Bermuda Hundred. They handled the retreat well, and the Confederates did not pursue closely. This was partly because Beauregard did not want to push the enemy too fast, hoping that Whiting might be able to get in their front, but it was a wasted hope. Whiting lost his nerve that day, bluffed by a small group of Tenth Corps men into believing that he was opposed by a large Federal force. Whiting dallied, fretted, and then ordered a retreat to Swift Creek.[27]

The biggest battle of the Bermuda Hundred campaign resulted in 3,000 Federal casualties and an equal number of Confederate losses. Butler reached the landing by 10:00 P.M., having seen his bright hopes completely dashed. He tried to put the best gloss on his failure by reporting that he retired to secure the landing as a base of operations for Grant. Butler even claimed that he had never had any plan to capture Richmond, merely to allow his cavalry division to make a raid to the west of the capital.[28]

Beauregard came up to Butler's position across the base of the peninsula by the afternoon of May 17 and began to skirmish and dig in. The Confederates started with a large fort at Dr. Howlett's House on the south bank of the James River. The 1st Virginia of Terry's brigade worked on the fort under the fire of Union gunboats all day of May 18. The Virginians had some protection as soon as they threw up a bit of parapet, but the shelling tried their nerves as well as took lives. One projectile exploded so deep in the ground that it partially covered a group of men who were working in the bottom of a trench. Already exhausted, they had difficulty digging themselves out. The regiment lost two men killed and several wounded that day. "Darkness came and we left that awful pit looking like a set of miners returning from the bowels of the earth," recalled Charles T. Loehr.[29]

The work initially was called Fort Howlett, but the name was changed to Battery Dantzler to honor Col. Olin M. Dantzler of the 22nd South Carolina, killed in a skirmish on June 2. Battery Dantzler became the northern anchor of a strong line of field fortifications known as the Howlett Line. Away from the James River, it traversed ground that in many places was "a wild, thickly wooded country with few clearings, and in many places broken up in short but steep hills." Fort Clifton, built sometime before on the north bank of the Appomattox River, became the southern anchor of the Howlett Line. Like Fort Stevens, Fort Clifton should be called a battery. It is an unenclosed position for four or five heavy guns with big parapets and traverses but no positions for infantry.[30]

The Confederates continued working on the Howlett Line as Beauregard ordered limited attacks designed to shorten it and allow him to spare troops for Lee. Some of his units advanced three-quarters of a mile and captured Union pickets on the Tenth Corps sector on May 20. Federal counterattacks failed to drive them back. The Confederates lost 800 men and the Federals suffered 702 casualties in this short fight, but a portion of the Howlett Line was dug closer to the enemy. Beauregard planned to further strengthen the line so that only 10,000 troops could hold Butler's army at the tip of the Bermuda Hundred peninsula. As part of this plan, Hagood took his men into position on the southern portion of the line on the afternoon of May 22. He found that the main Federal position was 800 yards away. His picket line was only 50 yards in front of his own works, and the Yankee pickets were 250 yards in front of his skirmishers. Hagood decided that this was too close for the comfort of his troops. That night, he pushed forward a reinforced skirmish line and drove back the Federal pickets. Then his South Carolinians dug in, two men to a skirmish pit. This action made it safer for his men to move around in the main line.[31]

Although an accomplished engineer, Beauregard was too busy with departmental duties to oversee the construction of the Howlett Line. He appointed Maj. Gen. Daniel H. Hill as superintendent of the works. Hill had held a prominent division command early in the war in Virginia but had fallen out of favor due mostly to his irascible nature. He had been acting as a volunteer aid for Beauregard and adviser for Whiting before this assignment. On May 24, Hill issued a circular that spelled out a number of details regarding duty in the trenches. Sentinels were never to lie or sit down, and they were to walk on top of the parapet wherever that was safe. The trench had to be eight feet wide and free of obstacles. Hill ordered traverses cut through if they blocked the trench. He wanted obstructions placed before the line at least fifty yards from the parapet. Bombproofs were "objectionable" to Hill but, if built, should have roofs with at least ten feet of earth. Hill had no objection to the construction of shelters to protect the men from the sun, but they had to be taken down if an attack was on the way. He arranged for a general officer of the day, with two more subordinate officers of the day for each wing. These men were responsible for posting the pickets and inspecting the works. Hill divided the troops into two reliefs, one to come to the aid of the skirmishers if attacked, and the other to be called up if the skirmish line was pushed back to the main line. Finally, Hill called on brigade commanders to make sure their connections to the units on either side were secure.[32]

The Confederates worked for many days to improve the Howlett Line according to Hill's guidelines. Two days after his circular appeared, the pioneer companies of Hagood's and Brig. Gen. Thomas L. Clingman's brigades were busy widening trenches and clearing out all the obstacles in them, although Clingman's troops had only "a limited supply of tools." On other parts of the line, details of up to 500 men were assigned larger tasks. Brig. Gen. Stephen Elliott's South Carolina brigade held a naturally strong part of the position, and therefore its works were "much lighter than on any other portion of the line, and more thinly manned." The Howlett Line stretched for three miles from river to river and was on average about two-thirds of a mile from the Union position. After several days of occupation, Beauregard's pickets seemed to become too friendly with the Union pickets. This prompted the department commander to issue orders forbidding all communication between them, including the exchange of newspapers, and urging all Rebel pickets to fire on the Yankees at every opportunity.[33]

On the evening of May 17, the Federals began to dig in opposite the Confederate position. Smith pushed out large work details to slash trees in front of the Eighteenth Corps as Gillmore instructed fatigue parties to "work on the intrenchments tonight along my whole front." Superintended by Lt. Col. Edward W. Serrell of the 1st New York Engineers, Tenth Corps troops also began slashing timber for at least 750 yards in front of their works on May 18. Skirmishers had to hold the Rebels back while their comrades cut trees to the rear. On Brig. Gen. Adelbert Ames's

Third Division front, the pickets sheltered behind rifle pits made of rails covered with earth. Ames also recommended that abatis be placed in front of his battery positions. Tenth Corps troops soon became accustomed to life in the trenches. Cooks prepared food at the rear and brought it forward to the entrenchments. When a Confederate battery began to enfilade the position of the 39th Illinois, the men grabbed shovels "and went to work with a good will throwing up trav[er]ses." They could hear the Rebels—300 yards away—digging, chopping, singing, and whistling through the early part of the night.[34]

Before long, an officer on Beauregard's staff came to the conclusion that the Confederates would be slaughtered if they attempted to storm the Union works. Yet the Tenth Corps apparently was less well prepared than the Eighteenth Corps. Gillmore's men had fewer tools and apparently coordinated their work less efficiently. Serrell complained that there were "various changes made in the line, places exposed, details put on and taken off by various officers." He advised headquarters that lines of authority be established to clear up the confusion.[35]

Part of the trouble was that Butler's chief engineer, Capt. Francis U. Farquhar, was too ill to oversee the construction of this line. Butler named one of his division commanders, Godfrey Weitzel, as his acting chief engineer and sent him to inspect the works. Weitzel was a protégé of Butler's. Born of German immigrant parents in Ohio, he graduated second in his West Point class of 1855 and served in the Corps of Engineers. Like many engineer officers, he taught briefly at West Point before the outbreak of war. Weitzel was Butler's chief engineer when the latter commanded occupation troops at New Orleans, and Butler later made him his second in command and mayor of the city. Weitzel was promoted to brigadier general in August 1862. He competently led a division during the Port Hudson campaign before rejoining Butler in time to take a division in Smith's corps. Butler assigned engineer Lt. Peter S. Michie as Weitzel's assistant.[36]

Weitzel inspected the line and wrote detailed instructions to Gillmore on May 20. He found numerous faults with the lines held by two of his divisions and recommended that Ames construct a new redan and a new redoubt. The meager abatis in front of the line was studded with fence rails that served no purpose as an obstruction. Weitzel wanted Ames's men to remove the rails and strengthen the abatis properly. He also instructed Ames to strengthen his traverses and parapet, cut embrasures for the artillery, and chop down trees near the works. Because a portion of Ames's line had been built on low terrain, Weitzel advised retrenching to higher ground to the rear and leveling the ineffective work. Terry's division line had fewer deficiencies. Altogether, Gillmore must have been embarrassed by Weitzel's long list of recommendations, which the new chief engineer had carefully numbered in order of priority.[37]

Butler pushed Gillmore to correct these weaknesses immediately, urging him to place his Third Division in reserve behind Ames in case the Confederates attacked at dawn on May 21. Gillmore complied, sending 600 men to work that night and making sure the reserve division was in place. This immediate crisis passed with no Rebel attack, but work on the line continued. Weitzel pushed for more abatis, for cutting more trees, for more traverses, and for the construction of new redoubts and banquettes wherever needed. Maj. Frederick E. Graef of the 1st New York Engineers supervised the stringing of "one line of wire entanglement" between Battery No. 1 and Battery No. 6 on the night of May 27. To accomplish all that Weitzel wanted demanded a great deal of Butler's troops. Regular work details were busy every day and night, and an additional draft of 200 men and 25 engineer soldiers was levied on Gillmore. The Tenth Corps commander had enough tools only for one out of three men on this detail. The men were getting tired; reportedly they "drop down in their tracks, and cannot work any more," wrote Serrell. Smith gave Eighteenth Corps fatigue details a day off and allowed whiskey, quinine, or coffee to be issued to the infantrymen ordered to stand to in their trenches at 3:30 A.M.[38]

Butler named Col. Henry L. Abbot of the 1st Connecticut Heavy Artillery chief of the artillery defenses along the line. Ames believed that the segment between Batteries No. 1 and 6 was the most likely point for a Confederate attack. At least 4,000 troops should man this segment at all times, he recommended, and they should be instructed to remain close to the parapet in case a sudden burst of Rebel artillery fire descended on the works. Abbot also urged the construction of a second line behind Batteries No. 4 and 5. Weitzel wanted to cover the embrasures of artillery emplacements with mantlets—shields made of wood, iron, or rope that could be raised when firing or that had a hole fitted for the artillery tube. Chief Engineer Richard Delafield initiated a search for at least eighteen mantlets used at Yorktown in McClellan's Peninsula campaign two years earlier, and laid plans to make new ones if the old ones could not be found. Meade's artillery chief, Henry J. Hunt, also advised using the Yorktown mantlets but was not certain if rope or iron would make a better cover.

He thought the iron mantlets might splinter if directly hit by an artillery projectile.[39]

Adjustments in the Union line continued for many months to come as the Federals turned the Bermuda Hundred peninsula into a fortified camp. The 1st New York Engineers built Battery Wilcox east of Confederate Battery Dantzler and placed a 10-inch mortar in it. The engineers also constructed Fort Drake on the main Union line, naming it for the 112th New York's Col. Jeremiah C. Drake, who was killed later in the campaign. Fort Carpenter, named for Lt. Col. E. P. Carpenter of the same regiment, was one of three advanced works forward of the main line. It could hold 100 men and four guns. Six batteries, numbered from right to left, studded the main line. They were enclosed works with stockades, palisades, and abatis, and the picket line was fully fortified. The Federal line was constructed with defense in depth—not as part of a master plan, but through circumstance and improvisation to deal with trouble spots. It was "unusually strong," in the words of Chief Engineer Delafield, and stretched for 6,058 yards from a point about one mile downstream from the Howlett House to the Appomattox River. "Great is our confidence in our ability to hold our position," asserted a Tenth Corps infantryman.[40]

As soon as both sides dug in, their respective authorities began to siphon off troops from Bermuda Hundred. At first Ransom and Hoke were taken from Beauregard and sent to Lee's aid, but then more and more Rebels were given orders to march northward. Within a few days, Beauregard was left with only 5,400 men and some militia troops. He had to hold the Howlett Line and protect Petersburg and, to a degree, Richmond, with this small force. Fully one-third of his men served on the picket line at all times.[41]

Grant also eagerly awaited reinforcements from Bermuda Hundred. He sent Brig. Gen. Montgomery C. Meigs and Brig. Gen. John G. Barnard to study the situation and make recommendations. The two generals believed that Butler's line could be held by 10,000 men and the rest should be shipped northward, so Grant ordered Smith's Eighteenth Corps to join Meade. Smith took two of his divisions and a few Tenth Corps regiments to make a reinforcement of about 15,000 men. These troops would play a heavy role in the fighting at Cold Harbor. Butler continued to hold City Point as well as the peninsula with the rest of the Army of the James.[42]

The troops left behind at Bermuda Hundred continued to work on the Union defenses, completing the shorter line between Batteries No. 3 and 6 that Abbot had earlier recommended. Gillmore worked to finish the three advanced redoubts in front of Batteries No. 1, 3, and 6. He erected "barriers at the entrances" and issued instructions that the redoubts should be stocked with three days' rations and that the garrisons dig wells. Gillmore wanted the advanced redoubts "to be held at all hazards" as forward points of resistance to break up Rebel attacks. He recommended that another one be built atop a piece of high ground on John W. Turner's division front. Weitzel approved but suggested the redoubt remain open to the rear so the enemy could not take and hold it without subjecting themselves to Union fire.[43]

Butler ordered six coils of telegraph wire for stringing before the works, but engineer officers again began to complain that work details were poorly handled. Detailed infantrymen arrived "late and short-handed," and not always with very explicit orders. Weitzel dealt with a shortage of sandbags by requiring Gillmore to inspect his camps and confiscate any that were "illegally used by soldiers." Many men protected their tents in the rear of the works by erecting "heavy banks of earth" around them.[44]

After two weeks of desultory action, the Bermuda Hundred campaign came to an end. While the Confederates relied on fieldworks at Swift Creek and Drewry's Bluff, they were quite ready to strike out into the open field to protect the railroad (as in the two Port Walthall Junction fights) or to take advantage of a small, isolated Union force (as at Chester Station). Beauregard's decision to attack on May 16 was inspired to a degree by the fact that the Drewry's Bluff Line was inadequately positioned to hold back a large force like Butler's.

The Federals began the campaign with tentative moves that resulted in open field fights, then partially occupied a major Confederate fieldwork. Repulsed on May 16, and pressed by the immediate presence of Beauregard's troops, they dug in extensively for the first time in the campaign. Union and Confederate soldiers held the lines at Bermuda Hundred longer than any other fieldworks of the war—from May 17, 1864, until April 3, 1865, a month longer than the works at Petersburg.

Grant popularized a common phrase, which ran current in the weeks following May 16, to the effect that Butler had been bottled up by the construction of the Howlett Line. It influenced conceptions of the Bermuda Hundred campaign that are still widely held today. To a degree, that conception was accurate. The Howlett Line certainly did prevent the Federals from ever sallying forth from the peninsula to threaten either Richmond or Petersburg. But Butler was by no means bottled up, for he had complete freedom of movement out of the peninsula by boat. The transfer of half of his available manpower within two weeks of the construction of this line amply demonstrates that point. This freedom of movement allowed Grant the opportunity to continue to use the Army of the James to support his offensive operations against Lee.[45]

7 North Anna

Butler's defeated army was fortifying at Bermuda Hundred when Grant broke away from the battlefield at Spotsylvania and continued moving to Lee's right. The failed attack on May 18 finally spurred him to seek a more advantageous position elsewhere. He began a large flanking movement to gain the North Anna River, and to lure Lee out into the open so the Army of the Potomac could strike him. The Second Corps was to move first, far enough from the rest of the army to tempt Lee but close enough so support could reach it. Hancock would move via Guinea Station and Bowling Green to Milford Station on the Richmond, Fredericksburg, and Potomac Railroad. If Lee took the bait, other units would proceed south down Telegraph Road and hit his left flank. Even if the Confederates did not expose themselves, Grant could alter the plan and have Hancock lead the way south.

Grant's move was delayed because of Ewell's reconnaissance in force to Harris Farm on May 19. The Federals waited the next day to make certain no other forays were planned, then Grant set dusk of May 20 as the starting time for Hancock's advance. Lee assumed that the Federals would try once again to move around his right, but he guessed that it would be along Telegraph Road. Ewell prepared to march toward Mud Tavern on that thoroughfare to block them; if he failed, Lee could fall back to the North Anna River. The 1st Confederate Engineers and some cavalrymen dug a line of works along the Po River at Stanard's Mill, just north of Mud Tavern, for Ewell. Meanwhile, Lee used some of the new units being shifted from G. T. Beauregard to safeguard his logistical support. William R. Terry's Virginia brigade of George Pickett's division arrived at Milford Station, the closest rail station to Spotsylvania, on the night of May 20.[1]

The two armies began their departure at nearly the same time. Hancock started with 20,000 men at 10:00 P.M. on May 20 and reached Guinea Station by dawn. Lee set Ewell in motion at 4:00 A.M. on May 21. Ewell easily reached the works near Stanard's Mill by mid-morning as Grant changed his strategy. He set the Fifth Corps in motion behind Hancock and urged the two corps leaders to head for the North Anna River, rather than offer battle near Mud Tavern or Milford Station. But there was a considerable time lag in executing this change of plans, for Hancock was miles away from army headquarters and Warren needed time to pull his corps out of line. Meade also had to readjust the defensive positions around Spotsylvania on May 21. After Warren disengaged, the Sixth Corps refused its right but continued to hold Myers Hill. Grant and Meade sent engineer officers and a tracing of an appropriate map to help Wright. The Sixth Corps now constituted Meade's right wing east of Spotsylvania and Burnside held the left, adjusting his line a bit to conform to Wright's new position. Army headquarters warned both corps commanders to be ready to evacuate their positions that night.

Lee pieced together Grant's move from various reports and began to shift his forward base from Milford Station to Hanover Junction, only twenty-five miles north of Richmond. He began this movement by ordering Ewell to give up his works at Stanard's Mill and move south on Telegraph Road. This took Chief Engineer Martin L. Smith by surprise. Smith was busy laying out another line along the Po River and had just started to position some of Ewell's troops along it to begin digging when the order to head for the North Anna River arrived. Ewell started his corps on the evening of May 21.[2]

Hancock reached Milford Station late on May 21, after his cavalry advance skirmished with Terry's 500 Virginians. Second Corps infantry easily pushed the Rebels out of their works on the north side of the Mattaponi River and crossed the small stream. As Terry fell back, another Virginia brigade and a division of cavalry joined him, all of which were posted on various roads running west. The Federals were content to stay near Milford Station. They dug a strong line of works along the irregular bluff of the river valley, which was about 100 feet high and one mile west of the Mattaponi. Fronted by abatis, the line was long enough for three divisions. One of Hancock's staff officers later called it "a marvel for the skill and industry it displayed," while a Second Corps surgeon was "surprised to see the formidable breastworks all along our lines." Later, when Burnside saw the trenches, he "could scarcely believe that these had not required days for their construction."[3]

That evening, Grant suffered an unusual bout of anxiety. He had no idea where Hancock was and began to worry that he could not support him if Lee chose to strike. Grant issued orders to assume a defensive position. The Fifth Corps was to deploy between Mud Tavern and Guinea Station, the Ninth Corps to evacuate its position east of Spotsylvania and move down the Telegraph Road to Mud Tavern, and the Sixth Corps to disengage and follow the Ninth. Grant had no way of knowing that attacking was far from Lee's mind. In fact, Lee's hastily drawn-up defensive arrangement offered the Federals a wonderful opportunity to strike the Confederate army as it moved south. Lee ordered all of his men to give up their muddy trenches around Spotsylvania and head for the North Anna River that evening. All night the gray regiments marched, Richard Anderson's First Corps following Ewell along Telegraph Road and A. P. Hill's Third Corps, which accompanied the army's trains, using a road farther west via Chilesburg. Burnside was unable to approach this moving column, for screening Rebel cavalry and the 1st Confederate Engineers blocked his crossing of the Po River at Stanard's Mill. The engineers did creditable duty on the skirmish line and helped to keep Burnside from realizing how weakly the Confederates held their earthworks. The Ninth Corps doubled back up the road and headed east to follow the route of the Second and Fifth Corps, but Warren's right flank was only one mile east of Mud Tavern. If Grant had known the situation, he could have ordered the Fifth Corps to move west and slice into the gray column.[4]

Fortunately for Lee, confusion and disorientation kept the Federals inert. At dawn on May 22, Grant regained his usual confidence when he realized that Lee was well on his way to the North Anna River. At this point the Federals were faced with two alternatives. They could continue south and east from Hancock's position at Milford Station and make a wide flank movement to cross the Pamunkey River, avoiding the North Anna altogether. This alternative was favored by Meade, who usually preferred to maneuver rather than fight to gain his objective. But Grant liked the second choice—a shorter movement south along Telegraph Road. This would keep the Army of the Potomac much closer to Lee. Grant reasoned that the Confederates were just as likely to have time to dig strong works guarding the crossing of the Pamunkey as they were to defend the crossing of the North Anna. He preferred to keep up the pressure as consistently as possible along the shortest route to his objective. As a result, the Army of the Potomac moved a short distance south on May 22, then rested. While Hancock stayed at Milford Station, the other three corps positioned themselves south and east of Mud Tavern.[5]

The lead element of Ewell's corps reached the North Anna River early on the morning of May 22, while Lee's headquarters arrived at mid-afternoon. Chief engineer Smith began to scout the terrain in preparation for the order to dig in, but Lee hesitated. He had a feeling that Grant would try to take the longer of the two options open to the Federals, to move toward the Pamunkey River, and he wanted to rest his men a few hours and keep them ready to move east if needed. He also worried that his long march south might alarm the authorities in Richmond. "I should have preferred contesting the enemy's approach inch by inch," he assured President Davis, "but my solicitude for Richmond caused me to abandon that plan."[6]

While Smith scouted, Lee asked Ewell's topographer, Jedediah Hotchkiss, to recommend a site for the army to fortify. Hotchkiss did not like the south bank of the North Anna because it was irregular and many places along the north bank dominated the landscape south of the stream. He recommended the line of the Virginia Central Railroad, which ran along the high ground dividing the watersheds of the North Anna River and the Little River to the south. Lee liked the idea. The railroad offered a very straight line; Lee told Hotchkiss that there should be no more salients like the one at Spotsylvania.[7]

MAY 23

The Federals started their move to the North Anna River at dawn on May 23. Hancock marched south along Telegraph Road, expecting to cross the river at Chesterfield Bridge. Warren aimed to cross farther upstream at Jericho Mills. Burnside tried to find a suitable crossing between the two, while Wright's column trailed behind Warren's. Lee had not fortified any of the crossings because he had no intention of holding the Federals north of the river. As Hotchkiss had already informed him, the ground was unsuitable for a defensive line on either bank. But Lee allowed a small South Carolina brigade under Col. John Henagan to hold an earthwork that had been built on the north side in 1863 to cover Chesterfield Bridge. Apparently he wanted to maintain a toehold on the north bank in case Grant headed for the Pamunkey River instead of straight down Telegraph Road. Now called Henagan's Redoubt, it was located on a bluff about fifteen feet high, facing north, and was unenclosed. The 2nd South Carolina manned the work while the 7th South Carolina filled a connecting infantry trench to the west. The 3rd South Carolina occupied a similar trench to the east, on the other side of Telegraph Road. The tiny 3rd South Carolina Battalion tried to fill the space between the road and the redoubt. This position was

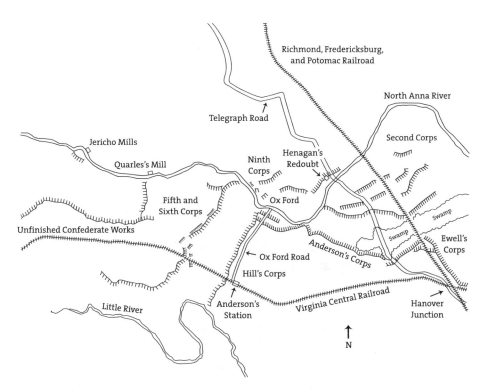

Union and Confederate Defenses at North Anna River, May 23–27, 1864

well suited to defend against cavalry raids, the main threat before Grant brought his army to the North Anna, but it was so poorly suited for defending against Hancock's Second Corps that the Carolinians should have been pulled out long before.[8]

Hancock deployed three divisions against this small force on the other side of a cleared space of ground that stretched 600 yards to the redoubt. There were several more Confederate brigades on the south side of the river, some dug in to cover the railroad bridge, and Rebel artillery soon engaged the Federals in a long-range duel.

At 6:00 P.M., two Federal brigades, numbering 3,000 men, advanced in three columns against both wings and the center of Henagan's position. The attackers took their time, taking advantage of every swale, gully, and ravine they could find to close in on the Rebel works. The 7th South Carolina on the left, recognizing the futility of its situation, fled before contact was made. The other units held on a bit longer but soon followed suit. They crowded while retreating across Chesterfield Bridge and the nearby railroad bridge. The latter was burned as soon as they crossed it,

Henagan's Redoubt, occupied by Federals, North Anna, May 25, 1864. The original Confederate fort was open to the rear; the Federals have closed it with a parapet and emplaced the gun on the far left of the view, overlooking the valley of the North Anna. Note the living arrangements inside the fort. (Library of Congress)

but Chesterfield Bridge remained intact. Henagan lost 155 men, while Hancock suffered about 300 casualties. The 7th New York Heavy Artillery occupied the redoubt, and Battery G, 1st New York Light Artillery, placed guns in it. The men added another parapet to the unenclosed rear of the work and reversed the connecting infantry trenches to face south.[9]

Warren had a much tougher time crossing upstream because of the steep bluffs and a poor road. He found Jericho Mills undefended, although Samuel McGowan's South Carolina brigade was positioned due south of the mills and a bit south of the Virginia Central Railroad. Warren pushed units across the narrow valley and ordered them to dig in on high ground, to form a fortified bridgehead to protect the rest of his corps and Wright's command as they crossed. As soon as he received word of these developments, A. P. Hill ordered Cadmus Wilcox's division to attack. By the time Wilcox struck, Warren had managed to get all of his men over the river, some walking across on a pontoon bridge and others wading the four-foot-deep stream. The line they assumed was one and a half miles long across the base of a salient of land that protruded northward, formed by the curving river. The crossing was at the northern curve of this bulge. Samuel Crawford's division was placed on the left, Charles Griffin's in the center, and Lysander Cutler's on the right. Both ends of the Union line touched the river, and most of the left and center was at least partially fortified. Cutler, however, was a bit late in taking position.

The Confederates attacked at 6:00 P.M., the same time that Hancock hit Henagan. James Lane's brigade was on the right, McGowan's in the center, and Brig. Gen. Edward L. Thomas's Georgia brigade on the left. Another unit, Alfred Scales's North Carolina brigade, followed Thomas in an effort to help him turn the Union right. Cutler was just beginning to arrive on the field when the Confederates came in. Thomas hit his lead unit, Col. William W. Robinson's Iron Brigade, as Scales rounded the Federal right flank. This forced Robinson to retire and began what might have turned into a collapse of Warren's right flank. This part of the battle of Jericho Mills was an open field fight, with the Federals unprepared to meet the Rebel advance.

Fortunately for the Fifth Corps, three of its batteries were in a good position to deliver fire on the Confederates once Robinson's retreating men were out of the way. In addition, three regiments of Joseph J. Bartlett's brigade counterattacked from a reserve position they had earlier assumed to the rear, after protecting that location with "a hastily constructed breastwork of rails." Col. J. William Hofmann's brigade of Cutler's division also made a determined stand, although caught in motion while moving up behind Robinson. The tables were turned pretty quickly. Thomas and Scales retired in disorder, but Warren chose not to follow up his advantage. McGowan advanced on the Union center, his sharpshooters skirmishing up to what Maj. William Dunlop called "a strong line of earthworks" that protected Griffin's front, but the Confederates made no headway against the rest of Warren's Line. The Fifth Corps lost 350 men while Wilcox suffered 730 casualties in this sharp fight. That night the Confederates began to dig a line that stretched west to east between the Virginia Central Railroad and Jericho Mills. On the right, it projected northward to join the river just west of Quarles's Mill. The Rebels never finished the fortification because on the same night orders arrived from Lee to dig in elsewhere.[10]

As night closed along the North Anna River, the Fifth Corps was firmly bedded south of the river and the Second Corps was preparing to cross it. Now faced with the need to fortify his position, Lee held a conference attended by Ewell, Anderson, and several engineers, artillery commanders, and staff officers. It was an unusual moment, for Lee seldom needed to consult his subordinates in this fashion. But he was suffering from exhaustion and a stomach ailment. The general even brought up the question of whether the army should hold here at all.

Everyone agreed that it was essential to protect Hanover Junction and the Virginia Central Railroad, the army's link with the Shenandoah Valley, but Hotchkiss's idea of forming the line along the tracks was no longer feasible. Warren could advance from his bridgehead and threaten the army's exposed left flank. Here is where Martin L. Smith played a key role in the North Anna phase of the Overland campaign. Lee had grown to rely on him ever since Smith had pointed out the usefulness of the unfinished railroad grade at the Wilderness. Smith had also laid out the line at the base of the Mule Shoe Salient. He was an indefatigable scout who understood terrain and fortifications equally well. Smith had scouted the land between the North Anna River and the Little River on May 22 and 23. This allowed him to realize that the Old Stage Road from Richmond passed by Anderson's Tavern and across the Virginia Central Railroad on its way to Ox Ford on the North Anna, where the south bank dominated the north side. This road, which had been rendered a backcountry track by the Telegraph Road, nevertheless ran along a ridge facing northwest, angled enough to offer a firm roadblock to any advance by Warren from Jericho Mills. The left of the line could be anchored on Little River and continued along a stretch of the North Anna River for about half a mile, then angled southeastward toward Hanover Junction. Swampy land lay northeast of the junction, and the engineers debated whether the line ought to run in front of or behind this morass. Listening to both sides, Lee decided to place the line behind the swamp. He wanted the right flank refused as well.

Thus was born the famous inverted V, a rather unusual configuration for a fieldwork as it actually created a giant chevron pointing toward the Union advance. Lee adopted it because it offered a peculiar set of advantages to the Confederates. The left wing would fully block Warren's and Wright's corps as they advanced the next day from their bridgehead. And, by connecting to the south bank of the river between Warren and Hancock, Lee could use the works to prevent Grant from forming a continuous line south of the North Anna River. As the Union right and left advanced, the center would be held up on the north side. The Army of the Potomac would be fragmented, with each part finding it difficult to support the other. The swampy land on the far right would serve as an effective obstacle. Most of all, the position protected Hanover Junction and gave Lee a welcome alternative to retreating.

Gordon Rhea has called this "the cleverest defensive formation" in the history of the Army of Northern Virginia. Lee was never better served by his engineers than he was in that nighttime conference. They offered him a perfect solution to a vexing problem. The engineers, especially Smith, turned what might have been a tenuous position into one of the most solid defensive stands the Army of Northern Virginia ever made.[11]

"I seem to have acquired the confidence of Genl Lee to the extent of his being willing to place his troops on the lines of my selection and stake the issue of a battle," Smith quietly bragged in a letter to his wife. "[M]ore than this is hardly to be expected." Smith set out with other engineers, including topographer Hotchkiss, to lay out the line that night and oversee the troops as they dug in. The soldiers worked hard all night. Hill held the left from Little River to Ox Ford, Anderson held the center, and Ewell's depleted corps continued the line toward the swamp.[12]

MAY 24

The Federals advanced carefully on the morning of May 24. Wright brought his Sixth Corps over the river at Jericho Mills as Warren advanced southward across the Virginia Central Railroad. Farther east, Hancock's Second Corps crossed at dawn and took up a position facing south, straddling both Telegraph Road and the Richmond, Fredericksburg, and Potomac Railroad.

Burnside had a most frustrating day in trying to find a way to cross the river and link the two Federal wings. The Confederate works, the apex of the inverted *V*, blocked his attempts to cross at Ox Ford. His subordinates found that a crossing was feasible upstream at Quarles's Mill. Then Hancock asked Burnside for help in an attempt to clear the Confederates from Ox Ford. The Second Corps commander had sent Nelson Miles's brigade toward that point to silence some Rebel artillery that annoyed him, but Miles found the newly dug Confederate line and could not get close to the ford. Burnside devised a plan to help Hancock and cross the river too. He would send Robert Potter's division to help Miles, crossing the North Anna at Chesterfield Bridge. Thomas L. Crittenden's division would cross

Federals occupying trench near Chesterfield Bridge, North Anna, May 25, 1864. Most likely, these are men of Willcox's division, Ninth Corps, overlooking the valley of the North Anna. This is one of the best photographs depicting how soldiers accommodated themselves for comfort while holding a trench. (Library of Congress)

at Quarles's Mill, while Orlando Willcox's division would hold on the north side opposite Ox Ford. Willcox would be the only tenuous link between Hancock and the rest of the army.

Warren also helped Burnside implement this plan. He sent Crawford's division down the south bank of the river to establish a bridgehead at Quarles's Mill. Confederate skirmishers had advanced from Hill's line to this area, and the two sides threw up crude works made of fence rails with a little dirt thrown on top. Crawford formed a semicircular line protecting the crossing and sent out two regiments to drive the stubborn Rebels away. Three attempts failed to push them back to the main line, but at least Crittenden was able to begin crossing the river.[13]

Crittenden sent out Brig. Gen. James H. Ledlie's brigade to drive the

Rebel skirmishers away. This was done easily, the skirmishers falling back to the main line as they were wont to do when confronted with superior force, but Ledlie completely lost control of himself and his command. Blatantly drunk, he ordered an assault on the works. Ledlie sent a messenger back to ask Crittenden for help, but the division leader cautioned him not to attack unless it was a sure thing—he did not yet have all his division across the stream. Without waiting for a reply, Ledlie pushed his brigade forward at 6:45 P.M. This unauthorized, unsupported, and unnecessary attack had no chance of success. A rainstorm suddenly came over the battlefield in the middle of it, and the men broke ranks in their hurried dash across the rough ground.

Ledlie aimed at the far right of Hill's line, near the apex of the inverted *V*. Holding here were Nathaniel Harris's Mississippi brigade and Col. John C. C. Sanders's Alabama brigade of Brig. Gen. William Mahone's division. They were pleasantly surprised to see this lone Yankee unit approach them in the rain. As soon as Ledlie's advance stalled well short of the strongly fortified line, Mahone ordered three regiments from Harris and Sanders to go forward and outflank the Yankees. Ledlie's disorganized command tried to make a stand, then retreated as fast as possible.[14]

If any good came out of this affair, it was to prove that the Confederate works were strongly held. Everyone else in the Army of the Potomac understood that by the end of the day. Potter crossed at Chesterfield Bridge and advanced in the direction of Ox Ford, but he ran up against Anderson's segment of the Rebel line and stopped. He dug in with his right resting on the riverbank and his left connecting with the Second Corps. All evening Hancock's men tried to push south to close in with Ewell's section of the line. The Confederates aggressively sent out units to spar with them, much of the fighting taking place on the Doswell Farm. It was a seesaw, open field battle for the most part, which resulted in minor Federal gains. Hancock got close enough to see that his way was blocked by fortifications and the swamp.

The events of May 24 gave the lie to a common assumption within the Union army that Lee had fallen back to the South Anna River and left only a rear guard manning the fortifications at Ox Ford. Grant had been eager to push on quickly and catch up with the retiring Confederates all day. He did not realize until late in the evening that a long and well-made line of works confronted his army. Lee held the advantage of position here, so Grant ordered Hancock to dig in. The Second Corps was vulnerable and needed protection. It was possible for Lee to hold Warren and Wright with Hill, and to use Anderson to prevent Willcox from crossing the river. That freed Ewell to launch a strike against Hancock. The result of such an action was unpredictable; with fortifications, Hancock's men probably could have saved themselves from disaster. But Lee never took the chance, even though he had earlier expressed a strong desire to attack Grant with such an advantage on his side. Lee was hit with a severe ailment, some sort of intestinal disorder, and was forced to stay in his tent all of May 24. He did not trust his corps commanders as he had once trusted Stonewall Jackson and felt that he needed to be personally in charge of any risky operation. Gordon Rhea has rightfully warned us not to exaggerate the impact of this lost opportunity for Lee to take the offensive. Even if the Union Second Corps had been mauled, the survivors most likely would have been able to retreat across the river. Grant had taken severe losses before and yet kept moving south. Any victory by Ewell on the morning of May 25 likely would have resulted in only a temporary advantage, and there was no certainty that Ewell would have been successful. He had not conducted the reconnaissance in force on May 19 with much skill.[15]

Grant was saved from having to fend off a Rebel thrust, but could he have continued the offensive? The answer is a decided no. His only options would have been to frontally attack the Rebel line or try to skirt its right, further dividing his army. Hancock's staff officer, Francis Walker, admired the line Smith had laid out for Lee. "[S]o great was the natural strength of the ground, so well were the intrenchments traversed, so tenacious was the Southern infantry, that it seemed impossible to produce any serious impression upon them." Walker concluded that to have "attacked the Army of Northern Virginia across intrenchments of the character found here, would have involved a useless bloody repulse."[16]

The Army of the Potomac dug fieldworks wherever individual units found themselves that evening. Warren and Wright formed a line facing southeast, confronting Hill across the breadth of land separating the North Anna from Little River. When the 139th Pennsylvania in Thomas Neill's division of the Sixth Corps was told to dig in, it found that all available tools were already being used to tear up the track of the Virginia Central Railroad. The men had to use fence rails and boards from a nearby barn to break up and move the dirt, yet they managed to fashion a good trench and parapet. Brigade leader Frank Wheaton showed it to Wright, who called it a "curiosity in its way . . . highly creditable to the men." The Army of Northern Virginia also spent May 24 working on its entrenchments. First Corps officers busied themselves "in examining and improv-

Federal engineers improving road at Jericho Mill, North Anna, May 24, 1864. This photograph depicts Maj. E. O. Beers's 2nd Battalion of the 50th New York Engineers widening a narrow road. (Library of Congress)

ing the line," and eliminated an angle close to Evander M. Law's Alabama brigade by straightening the trench line.[17]

While the Union infantrymen made themselves safe, the engineers worked all night to secure communications across the river. During the day, under artillery fire, Maj. Wesley Brainerd's 50th New York Engineers had built three bridges downstream from the railroad bridge behind Hancock's rear. Burnside then asked Brainerd to build a bridge for him near Quarles's Mill, and the willing major did so with two of his companies. They worked throughout the night, drenched by rain. While some engineers cut trees, others notched them and still others rolled them into place. They constructed cribs to serve as piers, filled with stones to stabilize them in the current that grew stronger as the rain continued to fill the narrow river. Six feet wide and ten feet long, the cribs were placed lengthwise to the current fourteen feet apart. Brainerd's men then laid a corduroy road atop the cribs, with a layer of heavy logs as the foundation, capped by a layer of lighter logs. They finished at dawn, just in time to return to the Second Corps and build yet another bridge.[18]

Engineer troops also enhanced the rear support of Meade's army by improving the fords. Timothy O'Sullivan took a picture of the 2nd Battalion, 50th New York Engineers, as it worked with shovels to improve the road leading up from Jericho Mills. It is one of only two known photographs of the war that show such a basic task being performed by engineer troops.[19]

MAY 25

Both Hancock and Warren further developed the Confederate line by advancing skirmishers on May 25, only to confirm what was already known—that it was far too strong for an attack. Grant spent the rest of the day trying to decide his next course of action. Meanwhile, the Federals continued to tear up the tracks of both railroads.[20]

Morale remained high in the Confederate army. "Our troops are remarkably lively and cheerful," reported Capt. Thomas J. Linebarger, "considering the extreme fatigue of the last three weeks." South Carolinian James S. Wingard had gotten only two nights of good sleep in the past twenty-one, but he noted that the losses in his regiment had lessened considerably since it had started to fight from behind earthworks. Many Rebels were disappointed that Grant did not waste his strength by attacking the inverted *V*, "for we know that we have to fight, and we want it over with," as Joab Goodson of the 44th Alabama put it. Lee, according to staff officer Charles S. Venable, was even more anxious for action. "We must strike them!" he exclaimed while lying on a cot in his headquarters tent. "We must never let them pass us again!" Actually, Lee had already sent engineer Martin to scout the ground along the South Anna River on May 25 to locate a fortified line in case he was forced to fall back. Martin reached the area too late that day to accomplish anything, but he spent May 26 and 27 riding about the countryside with a local civilian as guide. By the time he finished, the armies were starting to move away from the North Anna, to the east rather than south. Lee also came to think on May 26 that Grant might yet attempt an assault. Reports reached him that Union skirmishers were carefully advancing on Anderson's segment of the line by protecting themselves with fascines. He alerted Anderson to the possibility of an attack and ordered Ewell to be ready to send help if needed, but an attack never came.[21]

On the other side of the heavy parapet from Lee's men, the Federals enjoyed a suspension of Grant's relentless drive. The Army of the Potomac had lost more than 36,000 men since May 4, about 31 percent of its strength. Officer casualties were staggering. One of the four corps leaders was down; four of the thirteen division commanders and twenty-four of the army's forty-one brigade leaders were also casualties. Half of all commanders above the regimental level had been replaced by men new to their jobs. The Second Corps suffered the most because of its horrendous fight on May 12. It started the campaign with 28,333 men. Hancock had lost 11,734 of them by May 20, in addition to losing 35 percent of his officers. Replacements began to flow southward from Washington to help make up for the loss of manpower, but they were mostly inexperienced heavy artillerymen. By May 20, the Army of the Potomac had received 17,250 replacements, 1,800 of whom were draftees.[22]

The morale of Meade's men suffered correspondingly with each grueling day of the campaign. "How we feared that Grant would keep sending us to the slaughter," remembered Frank Wilkeson, an artilleryman in the Second Corps. Wilkeson noted that the skirmish firing along the North Anna was more vicious than at previous locations. It greatly tried the men's nerves. The Rebels often fired on them even as they tried to relieve themselves in the woods. Wilkeson heard the first complaints against Grant's tactics here at the North Anna. The willingness to give this new man from the west the benefit of the doubt had begun to evaporate; it was replaced by bitter resentment at the waste of manpower against impregnable earthworks. "How we longed to get away from North Anna," Wilkeson confessed, "where we had not the slightest chance of success." As a modern historian has noted, the North Anna phase of the Overland campaign saw the beginning of a trend among many units in the Army of the Potomac. They "would attack more cautiously without the elan of old."[23]

Grant seemed unaware of this change in the mood of the troops. He boasted that Meade's men "feel that they have gained morale over the enemy and attack with confidence. I may be mistaken but I feel that our success over Lees [sic] Army is already insured." The general-in-chief based this analysis on the fact that many Confederate prisoners seemed demoralized, and that Lee was making no move to meet him in the open field. "A battle with them outside of intrenchments, cannot be had," he admitted to Henry Halleck on May 26. Grant had always considered that achieving a morale superiority over his enemy was the key to victory, but he too optimistically gauged the mood of Lee and his army and ignored signs of deteriorating morale among Meade's troops.[24]

The stalemate near the North Anna River lasted two days. Meanwhile, if Lee would not come out of his works, nothing prevented a small force of Confederate cavalry from attacking a strongly fortified Union position some distance to the southeast. Butler had sent one of his subordinates, Brig. Gen. Edward A. Wild, to occupy Wilson's Wharf, on the north side of the James River some twenty miles downstream from Richmond. Here Wild improved Fort Pocahontas to guard the wharf with his brigade of black troops.

Maj. Gen. Fitzhugh Lee took three brigades of his cavalry division, totaling 2,500 men and one gun, to eliminate this Yankee outpost. He arrived near noon of May 24, as Grant was trying to chase Lee from the North Anna River. The post was held by 1,100 infantry, supported by a New York battery. Fort Pocahontas was a semicircular work with a good ditch and abatis in front. Although it was incomplete, a gunboat anchored in the river provided fire support. Wild refused to be intimidated, forcing Lee to attack. The cavalrymen advanced on foot, some penetrating the abatis and entering the deep ditch, but no one on the Rebel side noticed the incomplete section of the work. The attack was repulsed with 200 Confederate casualties. Wild lost only 46 men. Some black skirmishers were taken prisoner, a few were shot as Lee's defeated column retreated, and one was sent back to his former master in Richmond. Butler congratulated his subordinate on winning what a modern historian has called the "first major encounter" in which elements of Robert E. Lee's army met black troops in battle.[25]

LEAVING THE NORTH ANNA RIVER

Grant decided on May 25 to disengage and continue his attempts to move around Lee's right. He set in motion a plan to go southeast and cross the Pamunkey River, the route Meade had earlier favored. Staff officers prepared the necessary orders for the trains and the artillery to pull back across the North Anna after dark on May 26, to be followed by the infantry. Hancock ordered that any Federal earthworks south of the river that the Confederates could use to fire on the retiring column should be "impaired" before evacuation.[26]

Hancock wanted to save the pontoon bridges to his rear, so he worked out a plan with Wesley Brainerd for the engineers to construct a temporary bridge strong enough to carry the pickets, who would be the last to withdraw across the river. This would allow Brainerd's men to take up the pontoons as soon as the infantry crossed; the temporary bridge could be abandoned after the pickets used it. This was a good plan, but Brainerd was utterly exhausted and gave the assignment of building the bridge to one of his subordinates. By the time Brainerd rested and got around to inspecting the subordinate's work, he was appalled to find that the temporary bridge was too short and flimsy to withstand the strong current of the North Anna. When pushed into the stream, the span nearly broke loose. Brainerd was able to lash a rope around it just in time to keep it from sweeping down and crushing the pontoon bridges only 100 feet downstream.

Disaster averted, the Federal withdrawal went smoothly. The Sixth Corps crossed at Jericho Mills, while the Fifth and Ninth Corps used the ford at Quarles's Mill. Hancock's artillery crossed Brainerd's bridges first, then set up on high ground north of the river to cover the crossing area. The trains and then the infantry marched silently northward, after which the engineers went to work to save all the bridging material they could. The pickets retired to the sole remaining pontoon, for the temporary bridge was unusable, and the entire corps was across by 4:00 A.M. of May 27. Brainerd's men worked feverishly to take up the last pontoon bridge in only twenty-seven minutes. Confederate skirmishers immediately appeared on the south bank of the river but halted as soon as they saw the Second Corps guns frowning from the bluffs on the north side.[27]

Grant's drive to the North Anna River was the only confrontation of the Overland campaign that did not result in major fighting. The pugnacious general recognized the futility of assaulting the inverted V and for once refused to waste valuable manpower. Unlike the other battles, he decided to break off contact and maneuver rather than lock the army in a round of poorly planned and uncoordinated assaults. In the next phase of the campaign, however, Grant reverted to the pattern set at Spotsylvania, and the result was a dismal failure that took thousands of good troops out of action. Cold Harbor would come to symbolize the futility of Grant's tactical plan to break the trench warfare practiced by Lee's army.

Cold Harbor, May 27–June 2

The immediate objective of Grant's move away from the North Anna was to cross the Pamunkey River, but he would set subsequent goals on a daily basis depending on what the Confederates were up to. Grant asked Halleck to draw as many men as possible from the Army of the James and transport them by boat to White House Landing, a few miles up the Pamunkey from its junction with the York River. This landing, which had been used by the Army of the Potomac during McClellan's Peninsula campaign two years before, was transformed into Grant's new base.

Meade began to move on the night of May 26. A cavalry division secured Dabney Ferry near Hanovertown and Nelson's Bridge farther upstream, and the 50th New York Engineers constructed two pontoon bridges to take three of Meade's infantry corps across the Pamunkey on May 28. The cavalry moved ahead to fight a sharp battle west of Haw's Shop that day, well forward of the Union position. They found the Confederates imperfectly sheltered by "a temporary breast-work of rails" and drove them away. Philip Sheridan's men then constructed works of their own, consisting of "a few rails laid up, and dirt scooped out with hands and bits of sticks." A regular engineer who examined the Union entrenchments a few days later marveled that he could see "the prints of their hands where they had patted down the soil[,] being just enough to cover a person from rifle bullets." The Second, Fifth, and Sixth Corps, meanwhile, established a defensive line about a mile south of the Pamunkey. Meade sent James Chatham Duane and Nathaniel Michler to examine the terrain and help form the units on the best ground. The engineer and cartographer helped to create a continuous, strong position that some units managed to entrench before dark. Col. James A. Beaver of the 148th Pennsylvania in the Second Corps called it "an advantageous position a short distance from the River," supported by "strong earth works." Hancock instructed his subordinates to make arrangements for artillery and infantry to pass through the works wherever they crossed a road.[1]

Warren enjoyed helping his Fifth Corps construct earthworks near Dr. Brockenbrough's house on the evening of May 28. Charles S. Wainwright admired the result. The works "for once . . . were made with some knowledge," he concluded. Warren placed large openings at the reentering angles to allow for the movement of guns and men through the line. This was recommended in the fortifications manuals but not normally done in practice, and many men and officers gazed uncomprehendingly at them. Wainwright placed six batteries in this line and had time to assist Warren in laying out the entrenchments. "[Warren] liked the work and was consequently in good humour," Wainwright recalled, "so that I had a very pleasant time aiding him."[2]

While Warren made sure that Meade's left was protected, fortifying took place on the Union right as well. "Great is the shovel and spade," proclaimed Elisha Hunt Rhodes, an officer of the 2nd Rhode Island in Wright's corps. "Well I would as soon dig the Rebels out as to fight them," he concluded. Away from the impossible situation at the North Anna River, some buoyancy returned to the army. George D. Bowen of the 12th New Jersey was getting only four hours of sleep each night, but he did not mind the digging. "We are pretty well exhausted but cheerful," he recorded in his diary.[3]

By the morning of May 29, the Army of the Potomac had a continuous line of trench south of the Pamunkey River. The next stream, Totopotomoy Creek, was the dividing line between the contending armies. It flowed west to east and drained into the Pamunkey, which flowed southeastward to the York River. The Federals probed southward toward the creek on May 29, only to find Lee's army south of the stream. Ewell's Second Corps held the right near Pole Green Church, Anderson's First Corps was behind him, and Hill's Third Corps held the left. Hill's Line extended far enough to cross the Virginia Central Railroad north of Atlee's Station. A small division under Maj. Gen. John C. Breckinridge, recently arrived from the Shenandoah Valley, connected Hill and Anderson. Skirmishing took place as the Federals wheeled to the right, establishing a solid line from the Pamunkey to the Totopotomoy by noon of May 29. Meade was careful that his subordinates get their men "in position, intrenched, at the earliest possible moment," and prepared to make troops available for other movements if called upon.[4]

On the Union center, Francis Barlow's and David Birney's divisions advanced to the Shelton House just north of Totopotomoy Creek. They could see the Confederates digging in to the south, yet only Birney's division constructed fieldworks. Nelson A. Miles urged Barlow to fortify, "but he did not consider it necessary."[5]

A similar attitude was held by a few men on the other side of the creek. Some Confederate units constructed works but others did not. Martin L. Smith noted in his diary on May 29 that the troops were bivouacking "without [works], awaiting appearance of Enemy with a vision of attacking." Lee was trying to keep his options open in case the Federals presented a disjointed front while crossing the stream, but no such opening became apparent.[6]

In the absence of general orders to refrain from entrenching, many of Lee's men dug in on May 29. "Virginia will be one great network of them," wrote John F. Sale of the trenches. "I once thought the Yankees could beat us throwing them up." Sale found it "right amusing" to see his comrades dig with anything that came to hand. They made good use of bayonets to break up soft dirt and everything from old wooden shovels found in nearby barns to tin cups, plates, frying pans, tins from cartridge boxes, and even hands came into play. "Truly, 'Necessity is the mother of invention,'" Sale concluded.[7]

BETHESDA CHURCH, MAY 30

The Confederates struck only when Meade began to push south of Totopotomoy Creek. The Fifth Corps crossed the stream and began to advance west along Shady Grove Road to find the enemy. Lee was aware of this movement and planned to take advantage of the fact that Warren's command was the only Federal infantry south of Totopotomoy. Some units of the Confederate Second Corps, now led by Maj. Gen. Jubal Early because Ewell was in poor health, straddled the road to block Warren's advance. They fortified a position along the western edge of a ravine and forced Brig. Gen. Romeyn B. Ayres's brigade to dig in opposite. Warren was vulnerable to a Confederate strike from the south around his left flank. Sheridan was supposed to cover that flank but wandered off post and got involved in a fight with Confederate cavalry. Warren detached two of Samuel Crawford's brigades to Bethesda Church to cover the left flank, while the rest of the division supported Ayres in the westward-facing line.

Early planned to overwhelm the two Union brigades at Bethesda Church with Robert Rodes's and Stephen Ramseur's divisions, while units of Anderson's First Corps would attack Ayres along Shady Grove Road.

One of those Federal units at the church, Col. Martin D. Hardin's Pennsylvania brigade, had constructed light fieldworks as soon as it had arrived. The Confederates took Hardin by surprise, outflanked him, and easily drove his troops from their entrenchments. The other unit, J. Howard Kitching's brigade, moved up to help but was hit in transit in the open field and driven away. Warren was taken unaware but reacted effectively to save his flank, consolidating his corps in a strong defensive position along Shady Grove Road facing south. Everyone now hastily threw together breastworks and finished in time to devastate John Pegram's brigade when it attacked this position about 6:00 P.M., even though some Confederates managed to cross the Union breastwork. Anderson failed to support Early's attacks. He pushed George Pickett's division only up to the fortified post previously established by Early's men on the west side of the ravine along Shady Grove Road, but then he saw the strongly fortified Union position on the east side and decided not to attack. The Confederate offensive stopped Warren's tentative advance. Federal casualties amounted to 417 while Early lost 450 men. Both sides readjusted their positions on the evening of May 30. Early and Anderson firmed up their lines running north and south across Shady Grove Road and Old Church Road to the south. Burnside's Ninth Corps moved up to fill in the space between Warren and Totopotomoy Creek.[8]

North of the Totopotomoy, the Federal Second and Sixth Corps continued to skirmish and strengthen their position with entrenchments on May 30. Hancock visited the Shelton House and saw that Barlow had not fortified. Commenting that he should have done so the evening before, Hancock told him to dig in immediately. Many men in Miles's brigade had to work under fire in a wheat field, which was the best place to locate the trench. "They would cast up a shovel full of dirt and then lie down in the wheat until the bullets which the throwing up of the earth attracted had passed over, then resum[e] their labor," noted staff officer Robert S. Robertson. "This delayed the work of intrenching until a bank had been thus raised high enough to afford a partial protection to the working party when we progressed much more rapidly." Rather than logs, the men used cordwood from a large pile of firewood near the house to form the base of their parapet. The line was nearly done by dusk, but it had to be extended because the 2nd New York Heavy Artillery was added to Miles's brigade. The work did not cease until 2:00 A.M.[9]

On the evening of May 29, Hancock had ordered that artillery emplacements be dug close to his infantry line near the Shelton House, but a misunderstanding led responsible officers to place them 400 yards to the rear, where they "were useless." Col. John C. Tidball, Second Corps artillery chief, detailed men from various batteries and the heavy artillery units to dig them in open ground where originally planned, during daylight and under fire, on May 30. By the evening, Tidball had sixteen guns and six Coehorn mortars in place near the house.[10]

The next day, May 31, Nelson Miles sent out details to cut and place abatis in front of his brigade line. John Brooke's brigade also worked hard on its entrenchment, termed a "heavy work" by James Beaver. His men had few tools, which accounts for the fact that it took all night of May 31 to complete the fieldwork.[11]

On the Confederate side, Breckinridge's division entrenched opposite the Union Second Corps south of Totopotomoy Creek. Most of the men had no tools, so they improvised by splitting open canteens, "making scoops of them," and moving the sandy soil with their hands. Lee's men generally were happy with purely defensive measures. "Our policy now seems to be to receive the attacks of the enemy behind breastworks," noted Joab Goodson, an officer of the 44th Alabama in Charles Field's division. "All we ask is to get into position, and have an hour or two to fortify our line; then we are ready."[12]

MAY 31

With half of his army south of Totopotomoy Creek, Meade urged both Burnside and Warren to move forward on the morning of May 31. Burnside advanced three-quarters of a mile and captured Confederate skirmish posts protected by "a line of detached rifle-pits." He established his Ninth Corps battle line there. Anderson's Confederates were well fortified in his front, and "difficult" ground intervened. Anderson's left wing faced north but his right wing, near Pole Green Church, faced east to confront Burnside. Meade authorized the Ninth Corps to dig in rather than attack. Early also was well fortified. His left wing faced east but his right wing faced northeast, toward Bethesda Church. Warren pivoted his Fifth Corps so that part of it faced west while his left wing continued to face south. The latter served as a refused line guarding Meade's left flank. Cold Harbor, the next important crossroads, was two and a half miles to the south. Warren's men heard Early's troops chopping down trees on the other side of no-man's-land.[13]

There was no prospect of offensive action for the other half of Meade's army that still lay north of Totopotomoy Creek. Miles could also hear the

Rebels chopping trees and even see them digging along their skirmish line on the south bank of the creek, some 300 yards ahead of their main line. In places, the stream had a swampy bottomland 300 yards wide, with steep bluffs. On the Sixth Corps front, the Rebel line rested on "a high ridge, difficult of ascent, and in some places perpendicular," Wright reported. "The timber is slashed on the slope of the ridge, and immediately in front of the intrenchments (which are some distance back from the brow of the ridge) is an abatis." James Ricketts's division nevertheless pushed skirmishers across the swamp to hold a section of the Rebel skirmish line, but David Russell could not cross the morass. Hancock also managed to get his two wings across the stream, but his center division, Barlow's, was stuck on the north side. As a result, the Second Corps line was one-third longer than it had been in the morning, with just as few troops to man it. Hancock felt that his forward position was no good except for launching an attack, which he had no desire to do, and sought permission to retire that evening after he learned that Wright was to pull the Sixth Corps out of line and move to the army's left flank. Initially, Meade authorized a pullback and Hancock issued a circular to that effect, reminding his two division leaders to make sure no entrenching tools were left behind. Then late on the night of May 31, reluctant to give up any hard-won ground unless it was absolutely necessary, Meade instructed Hancock to cancel his planned withdrawal.[14]

Cold Harbor became the next objective in Grant's creeping movement toward Lee's flank. What locals called Old Cold Harbor, ten miles northeast of Richmond, was a crossroads halfway between Totopotomoy Creek and Chickahominy River where five roads intersected. One road came from the north, another connected Cold Harbor with White House Landing, two roads extended to the southeast and eventually crossed the Chickahominy, and the fifth road went west toward Richmond. One mile to the southwest was another, less important junction called New Cold Harbor.[15]

A brigade of Fitzhugh Lee's cavalry division and Thomas Clingman's North Carolina brigade of Robert Hoke's division held Old Cold Harbor. Three brigades of Sheridan's cavalry attacked them on May 31. The Rebel horsemen fought from behind "temporary . . . breast-works of . . . rails, logs, and earth" at Old Cold Harbor. Sheridan's troops drove them away and began to reverse the entrenchments for their own use. This little battle drew everyone's attention to the strategic junction. Robert E. Lee began to direct all of Hoke's arriving division there that evening and later transferred all of Anderson's First Corps. He did not intend to abandon any other part of his position, forcing his corps commanders to thin out their dispositions to hold the entire line from Totopotomoy Creek down to Cold Harbor. Anderson pulled his men away from Shady Grove Road at 4:00 P.M. Wright's Sixth Corps began moving from the extreme Union right toward the junction on the night of May 31. William F. Smith's Eighteenth Corps was due to reach the Army of the Potomac very soon; it could be used to fill in the gap between Wright's intended position at Old Cold Harbor and Warren's left wing north of Bethesda Church.[16]

JUNE 1

The Confederates had a shorter line of march toward the junction than Wright, who faced a long, hard trek across unfamiliar territory. He left his position on the right of Meade's army before midnight of May 31 and moved twelve miles in the hot, dusty night. It would be at least 9:00 A.M. on June 1 before the head of Wright's column reached the crossroads at Old Cold Harbor. The reinforcements from Butler were also directed to the crossroads. William F. Smith had embarked two divisions of his Eighteenth Corps and one division of the Tenth Corps at City Point at 2:00 A.M. on May 28. They steamed to White House Landing and began to unload at 11:00 A.M., May 30. Smith left the landing by 3:30 the next afternoon, but confusion about the route and destination delayed his march. The head of his column did not reach the vicinity of Cold Harbor until mid-afternoon of June 1.[17]

The Federal cavalry held the crossroads until the infantry arrived. They dug in on the night of May 31 but made only "slight" earthworks at the crossroads and northward up the road toward Beulah Church. The Confederates tried to retake Cold Harbor before Wright appeared. Hoke managed to bring the rest of his division to the area by early morning of June 1, and Joseph Kershaw's division, the van of Anderson's corps, neared Cold Harbor by dawn. Kershaw advanced to the crossroads right away, sending his lead brigade, which, unfortunately for the Confederates, was commanded by his least experienced brigade commander. Col. Lawrence M. Keitt's 20th South Carolina, only recently shifted to Lee from garrison duty around Charleston, had been attached to John Henagan's brigade, Kershaw's old unit. As senior officer, Keitt assumed command of the brigade even though he had little combat experience. He struck Alfred T. A. Torbert's troopers north of Cold Harbor early on the morning of June 1, advancing across open ground supported by Col. Goode Bryan's Georgia brigade. Keitt ran into a hail of gunfire, much of it from troopers armed with repeating rifles. He was mortally wounded and his brigade faltered. Kershaw's supporting troops could make no better headway, and Hoke's division failed to help.[18]

Following this fight, Kershaw dug in facing east, extending the Confederate line northward. Hoke connected with Kershaw at what Edward Porter Alexander called a "swampy thicket, along a small stream" that ran east to west. Actually, it was what modern historians call the Southern Ravine, because it is the southernmost of three ravines that drain west toward Gaines's Mill Pond. Preserved in the Cold Harbor Unit of the Richmond National Battlefield Park a quarter of a mile north of Cold Harbor Road, it is often called Bloody Run. There was a seventy-five-yard gap in the Confederate line because of this terrain feature, and it would be a sore spot for the defending Rebels. The second ravine, three-eighths of a mile north of Bloody Run, is today at the northern border of the park. Kershaw rested his left flank at the third ravine, half a mile north of the second. The terrain in this area is flat and covered with a thin growth of pine trees and occasional clearings. The Rebels were on a slight rise in the ground, the only advantage to be had in this countryside, which became the basis of Lee's new position in the Cold Harbor vicinity. His army aligned north and south of here for the next two weeks. It was a position taken up by circumstance, not planning. Confederate cavalry and Clingman's infantry brigade had initially settled here when they had been driven from Old Cold Harbor. Now Hoke and Kershaw also aligned on the position, to be followed by more units of Anderson's corps that filled up the line north of Kershaw and south of Early's Second Corps. For the time being, the Confederate line barely extended southward enough to cover the road leading westward from Old Cold Harbor. New Cold Harbor lay to Hoke's rear.[19]

Not only had the Rebels failed to retake the road junction, they would have to fight to maintain the new line they had just assumed. The Sixth and Eighteenth Corps trickled into the Cold Harbor area nearly all day on June 1, forming a line by 5:00 P.M. that stretched from positions southwest of Old Cold Harbor up to Beulah Church. A gap of two miles existed between their right and Warren's position, now advanced southward enough to encompass Bethesda Church. Smith found that he did not have enough men to close up with Warren, so he concentrated his strength near Wright to support the Sixth Corps attack. John H. Martindale's division, on Smith's far right, faced north to cover the Eighteenth Corps flank. In fact, both flanks of the Wright-Smith line were refused. South of the Sixth

Corps lay one and a half miles of open country, all the way to the Chicka-hominy River. The gap between Smith and Warren did not worry Grant, for he wanted Wright and Smith to attack immediately, throwing off any Confederate attempt to exploit the hole in Meade's line.

Grant and Meade had gambled that Smith and Wright could attack be-fore the Confederates had time to fortify, but that was a forlorn hope. Hoke and Kershaw had plenty of time to dig in—close to twenty-four hours in Hoke's case. That officer placed two brigades, James G. Martin's and Johnson Hagood's, south of Cold Harbor Road. Hagood's men an-chored the southern end of the Confederate line. They tossed down rails and used their hands, tin cups, plates, and a few available entrenching tools to raise a parapet over them. "The rapidity with which this was done was laughable," later recalled Hagood, "and would have been incredible to anyone who had not seen soldiers who knew the value of earthworks, how-ever slight, work under similar circumstances." Meanwhile, Field's and Pickett's divisions of Anderson's corps took position north of Kershaw.[20]

The scene was set for the first major attack of the Cold Harbor battle, involving 20,000 Federals in four divisions. Two more divisions—Martin-dale's to the north and Thomas Neill's to the south—were on the field but dedicated to protecting the Union flanks. The attacking units advanced across a front of one and a half miles against 10,000 men in Hoke's and Kershaw's divisions. South of Cold Harbor Road, the Federals advanced with little coordination. Some units managed to reach a spot only fifty yards from Hoke's line but could go no farther.[21]

North of Cold Harbor Road, Emory Upton's brigade encountered a slashing of pine trees extending at least seventy feet in front of the Rebel works. It was well made, the limbs were "interlocking with each other and barring all farther advance." Through the maze Upton's men found two paths several yards wide, enough for four men to march abreast. But Clingman's and Alfred Colquitt's brigades were already pouring fire onto those paths. Most of Upton's troops never made it through the slashing; only a handful of intrepid warriors managed to reach the Confederate parapet, where they were either shot or taken prisoner.[22]

Col. William S. Truex's brigade of Ricketts's division was the next unit to Upton's right. It pushed Rebel skirmishers out of a light work 150 yards in front of the main Confederate line, shielding the seventy-five-yard gap at Bloody Run. The extreme left wing of Col. Benjamin F. Smith's bri-gade, to the right of Truex, also captured a part of this fortified skirmish line. Then the two brigades pushed on. Truex had his right wing in Bloody

Run and his left wing in the open, while a good part of Smith's brigade was engulfed in the wooded ravine. The Federals became somewhat mixed up, but they retained enough cohesion to exploit the gap between Hoke and Kershaw. Clingman's leftmost regiment, the 8th North Carolina, refused its line to face north, but the Yankees managed to find and turn the unit anyway. The 8th North Carolina fragmented; while many men ran away, the rest stayed and were surrounded. This started a chain reaction down Clingman's line, with the 51st North Carolina reacting in the same way and the 31st North Carolina retreating as a whole to escape a similar fate as its sister regiments. Only Clingman's rightmost unit, the 61st North Carolina, remained in position.[23]

At almost the same time, a similar course of events took place on the north side of Bloody Run. Col. Jeremiah C. Drake's and Col. William B. Barton's brigades of Brig. Gen. Charles Devens's division in the Eighteenth Corps attacked Brig. Gen. William T. Wofford's Georgia brigade of Kershaw's division. They crossed 1,250 yards of open ground before penetrating slashings and entanglements. Under heavy pressure from the front, and probably threatened by the Federal effort to work around their right flank, Wofford's men gave way. Bryan's brigade, to his left, also fell back in the face of the Union advance. This widened the seventy-five-yard gap into a half-mile hole in the Confederate line; suddenly, the 10th Georgia, the leftmost regiment of Bryan's brigade, became the northern shoulder of this gap. North of Bryan's former position, the Confederates held firm. Three brigades of William Brooks's division captured sections of the Rebel picket line, which was poorly protected by "slight rifle-pits," but failed to push back Benjamin G. Humphreys's and Henagan's main lines. Martindale remained in position to guard Smith's right flank.[24]

Despite all of the delays, the Federal attack on June 1 nearly succeeded. But the Yankees failed to exploit the break they made at Bloody Run. Clingman organized a new, refused line based on the position of the 61st North Carolina, mostly made up of a handful of units sent by Colquitt. He directed this improvised line forward in a counterattack at dusk. Aided by the confusion and darkness, Clingman managed to retake most of his former position. On the north side of Bloody Run, Kershaw dispatched two units from Henagan's brigade that were able to drive what few Federals remained in the ravine out that evening.

The Confederates worked hard to shore up the line in this vulnerable sector on the night of June 1. Some Federal units dug in only fifty yards from Clingman's front, but his brigade was in no shape to reliably hold the line. Later that night, Col. Eppa Hunton's brigade of Pickett's division arrived to replace him. Clingman vacated 150 yards of trench to make way for the Virginians, but the Federals were alert. They advanced and occupied the position before Hunton arrived. This forced the 28th Virginia to counterattack and clear the trench before Hunton could take up his new post. The rest of Clingman's position was filled by Hagood's brigade. In addition to restoring the old line, Anderson insisted on positioning troops in a secondary line well to the rear, sweeping around the former gap in Bloody Run. Three brigades from Field's division—John Gregg's, Evander M. Law's, and George T. Anderson's—filed into place along the secondary line that night.[25]

In this promising but unsuccessful attack, Smith and Wright lost about 2,200 men while the Confederates suffered 1,800 casualties. No other action along the Cold Harbor line on June 1 offered a better chance of victory. The Second, Fifth, and Ninth Corps held a line five miles long north of the two-mile gap between Warren and Smith. Hill, Breckinridge, and Early opposed them. There was considerable skirmishing along this line during June 1. Barlow's division pushed across Totopotomoy Creek and drove the Rebel skirmishers, coming close enough to the Confederate main line to hear officers tell their men to "'lie down.'" The troops in Joshua T. Owen's brigade of John Gibbon's division constructed traverses to protect themselves from fierce Confederate skirmish fire, and elements of the Ninth Corps reported that their skirmish line was no more than thirty yards from the Rebel skirmishers. Only two significant, small-scale attacks took place. At 4:30 P.M., Gibbon advanced two brigades near Hundley's Corner to see if the Rebels were evacuating their position. Most of the Union troops went far enough to draw Confederate fire and stopped, but four companies of the inexperienced 36th Wisconsin continued to advance and suffered 140 casualties out of 240 engaged. Later that evening, about the time that Smith and Wright were achieving their greatest success along Bloody Run, Early launched an attack by John Gordon's division, supported by Rodes to his left, along Shady Grove Road. Because Burnside was well fortified, the Confederate thrust amounted to little more than a sharp firefight.[26]

The futility of attempting any more offensive operations along the Union right was apparent to all officers there. Hancock spoke for them when he informed army headquarters: "I do not believe that these assaults upon intrenched [positions] through thick woods, where we do not know the ground, are likely to be successful where the enemy hold their line in force."[27]

JUNE 2

Grant and Meade hoped to renew the assault from their left wing at dawn on June 2 with the Second Corps as reinforcement. "If we give [the Confederates] any time they will dig so as to prevent any advance on our part," Meade wrote. Orders went out for Hancock's men to leave their position on the Union right, but they did not set out until 11:00 P.M. The vanguard of the Second Corps reached Old Cold Harbor at 6:00 A.M. on June 2, and the rest dribbled in during the next several hours. Grant postponed the attack until 5:00 P.M. The Second Corps planned to take position south of Cold Harbor Road, while Wright shifted most Sixth Corps troops north of the road. Hancock established his line half a mile from the Confederates. As he deployed to Wright's left, he found that the Confederates had placed more troops in his front. Lee had shifted Breckinridge's division during the night of June 1, then moved Cadmus Wilcox and William Mahone of Hill's corps on June 2. This put Henry Heth's division on the far Confederate left with Early's Second Corps next to him. Because of "heat and want of energy among the men from moving during the night," Grant rescheduled the evening attack for 4:30 on the morning of June 3.[28]

Lee had authorized Early to attack if he saw an opportunity, and the aggressive corps commander did not hesitate when he saw the Federals pulling back in his front. This was part of an effort by Meade to consolidate his new position. Warren closed up to his left, hoping to fill the gap that existed between the Fifth and Eighteenth Corps, although his command was stretched to the breaking point to hold a four-mile sector of the battlefield. "It is only a single line assisted by intrenchments and swamps, and nearly without reserves," as Warren put it. Burnside moved left to maintain his connection with Warren. The Ninth Corps now found itself holding the army's right flank, and Meade advised Burnside to refuse his right back toward Totopotomoy Creek. Early sent Rodes and Gordon, and enlisted the cooperation of Heth, in his attack on the afternoon of June 2.[29]

It was touch and go for some elements of the Ninth Corps when the Confederates struck as they were moving to their new position. Most of the fighting took place in the open, but a part of Elisha G. Marshall's brigade managed to occupy some old Fifth Corps trenches, dug on May 30 south of Shady Grove Road, just minutes before the Confederates reached that point. This stabilized the fluid fighting on Rodes's sector. Gordon managed to capture a lot of Federal pickets along Warren's front, but Charles Griffin's division successfully retired to the May 30 battlefield near Bethesda Church and dug in. Gordon did not press him any further but constructed new works nearby.[30]

Heth's division advanced about two miles before making contact with the enemy. It advanced east and then curved southward, much of the time pelted by a fierce rainstorm that suddenly rushed across the area. Simon Griffin's brigade of Robert Potter's division turned around as Heth approached and hurried back to that line of trench dug by Warren on May 30 south of Shady Grove Road. From here, it stopped Heth's skirmishers with well-directed fire. The Confederates continued to move up to the road but could advance no farther. Then they grabbed fence rails and used them as the base of a parapet, digging in as night fell. Early's attack amounted to nothing more than a heavy reconnaissance in force, delineating the shifting lines by dusk and resulting in 1,000 losses for Burnside, 500 for Warren, and close to 600 for Early.[31]

Most Confederate activity on the afternoon and evening of June 2 centered on filling up the right wing, extending and strengthening the line south of Cold Harbor Road. Breckinridge's division arrived about 3:00 P.M. and took position south of Hoke's command. Col. George M. Edgar led his 26th Virginia Battalion of Col. George S. Patton's brigade into a salient formed by a small rise of ground, known locally as Watt's Hill. The area had been held by cavalry behind "very light breastworks." Heavy Union artillery fire and sharpshooting proved to Edgar that he needed better protection, so his men went to work with the few shovels and picks available. Capt. T. C. Morton of Edgar's battalion admired his men's efforts. They "were handy with dirt—being most of them farmers and laboring men," and soon erected stout fortifications.[32]

But even with good fieldworks Edgar's position was vulnerable because he was forced to form his battalion in a salient. The chevron-shaped formation had two faces, each about two hundred yards long. Breckinridge spread his men pretty thin; Edgar had only his own battalion and a company of the 22nd Virginia, about 450 men, plus a couple of field guns. He placed his right wing in the salient and his left connecting with it to the north. Each man stood three feet from his neighbor. Edgar became alarmed when, on examining the lay of the land more closely, he found a depression that created a dead space from forty to eighty yards deep directly in front of his men. Dispatch Station Road, an "old, deeply washed-out road, covered with stunty pines," ran north to south just on the east side of the depression.[33]

Edgar became "much depressed with a sense of impending catastrophe" when Patton informed him that there were no spare troops to reinforce his position at the salient. He then suggested that the line be moved back and straightened so as to demand fewer men, but Patton did not feel authorized to do this. The brigade commander sent the idea on to Breckinridge but never heard from the division leader. Patton could only encourage Edgar to make his works as strong as possible, and the Virginians dug nearly all night, much of the time in a drizzly rain. They rested for only a couple of hours before dawn.[34]

Two more divisions arrived on the evening of June 2 to continue the Confederate line southward. Wilcox deployed along Turkey Hill to Breckinridge's right, with his extreme right half a mile from the Chickahominy River. Mahone's division acted as a general reserve to the rear of Colquitt's and Martin's brigades of Hoke's division.[35]

A great deal of work took place along other parts of the line as covering units sought to seal up weak spots in the Confederate position. Hunton's Virginia brigade of Pickett's division straddled Bloody Run and continued the line northward. Gregg's brigade joined Hunton's left and took the line across Middle Ravine, while Bryan's and Wofford's brigades were positioned to the rear as a reserve. These units, from Hunton to Wofford, formed a line that curved well to the west of the main position. This horseshoe line had a five-foot-high parapet and a banquette.[36]

Law positioned his Alabama brigade on the north side of Middle Ravine to protect the angle where the main Confederate line began to head west to join this horseshoe line. The main line was angled here in such a way as to form a salient near a lone gun of Callaway's Battery, which had been positioned at the site on the evening of June 1. Law remembered the Mule Shoe Salient at Spotsylvania as he noted a low, swampy area directly behind the Confederate position. To shorten the line, flatten the salient, and take advantage of the swampy area as an obstruction, he suggested moving the line behind the low ground. Gregg's men leveled the fieldworks as best they could on the abandoned part of the position as Law's men and George T. Anderson's Georgia brigade worked on the new line. Law personally laid it out. Two of his staff officers carried stakes, and Law drove them into the ground with a hatchet. The men quickly constructed the trench and parapet as artillerymen placed guns at both ends. A skirmish line was left at the abandoned fieldworks. Col. Henry C. Cabell, commander of an artillery battalion in Richard Anderson's First Corps, directed the cutting of a road through the timber so guns and ammunition could be brought up to Law's new position. Robert Stiles, an officer of Cabell's battalion, oversaw the construction of three small bridges over the ravines that bisected this part of the battlefield. All of this work was done by the division pioneer corps. By early morning of June 3, this vulnerable sector of the Confederate line was made very strong.[37]

Other than Edgar's Salient on Breckinridge's front, there were no longer any weak spots along the Confederate position by dawn of June 3. The 20th South Carolina, which had been worsted by Union cavalry on the morning of June 1, heavily fortified its part of the line on the evening of June 2, while the skirmishers of Clement Evans's brigade in Gordon's division entrenched 100 yards in front of the main line. They dug "good rifle pits about twenty-five yards apart, with about five men placed in every pit."[38]

When finally firmed up, the Confederate line extended for six miles from Shady Grove Road near Totopotomoy Creek toward Chickahominy River. It firmly blocked Grant's most direct line of approach to Richmond. Heth and Rodes aligned along the road facing south, while the rest of Lee's divisions — Gordon's, Ramseur's, Field's, Pickett's, Kershaw's, Hoke's, Breckinridge's, and then Wilcox's — faced east. Only Mahone was in reserve, but he fortunately was placed near the weakest spot. As Gordon Rhea has pointed out, the Confederate position was taken up in stages by the force of circumstances rather than as part of a general plan. Yet it "masterfully exploited the terrain" and was "as strong as any [Lee] had held since the Wilderness."[39]

The Federals dug in on June 2 as well. Hancock's men found mostly light fieldworks when they filed into position south of Cold Harbor Road. Capt. J. Henry Sleeper's 10th Massachusetts Battery entered some works already dug by heavy artillerymen, and "they seemed quite tenable." But the gunners improved them all night, raising the parapet higher, building traverses between the gun positions, and digging holes so they could lower the limber chests for protection. They also placed brush to screen themselves as much as possible. This reinforced battery position saved many lives during the heavy artillery firing the next day.[40]

On Wright's front there was ample room for improvement of the existing fortifications. Company B of the U.S. Engineer Battalion dug trenches under Confederate skirmish fire, and some of Upton's troops erected headlogs on top of their parapet. They also improvised embrasures for sharpshooters by filling empty ammunition boxes with dirt and arranging them to suit their needs. A few of the more enterprising men of the 121st New York set up decoys to fool the Rebel skirmishers into firing, so that counterfire could be directed at their puffs of smoke. Another trick was for "someone in a tone of command" to shout orders for a charge. This brought a volley of balls from the main Confederate line that fell harmlessly in no-man's-land. More Sixth Corps artillery went into position. Capt. Greenleaf T. Stevens used the pioneer company of the 5th Maine to dig "rude, but . . . substantial" gun emplacements for his battery. The Federal gunners pushed two pieces 100 yards through the pine woods into this work, which lay only 275 yards from the Confederates, and then lowered four ammunition chests into holes for protection.[41]

The Federals had also taken up their position by force of circumstances, but it was a bit more compact than Lee's. The line stretched from the right of the Ninth Corps, which lay more than one mile northeast of Bethesda Church, to the left of the Second Corps, nearly two miles south of Cold Harbor. Potter, Orlando Willcox, and Thomas Crittenden faced north along Shady Grove Road, while Griffin, Lysander Cutler, and Crawford faced west. Early's attack on June 2 had disrupted the repositioning of the Fifth Corps so that a gap of three-fourths of a mile still existed between it and the Eighteenth Corps. William F. Smith placed Devens, Martindale, and Brooks from right to left; Wright placed Neill, Ricketts, and Russell in line; and Hancock put Gibbon on his right and Barlow on his left while holding Birney in reserve.[42]

Everyone realized that Grant's repeated moves to Lee's right had taken both armies onto historic ground. The southern portion of the battlefield had been the scene of severe fighting during the Peninsula campaign, when McClellan's Army of the Potomac had driven to the gates of Richmond. The battle of Gaines's Mill had been fought just to the rear of Lee's right wing as the Confederates took the offensive in the Seven Days campaign and drove McClellan away from the city. Now, on June 2, some of Mahone's men found physical evidence of that earlier engagement. While digging works in their reserve position, they uncovered skeletons of several men who had been killed two years before. "None knew whether they were the remains of friends or foes," commented John F. Sale of the 12th Virginia.[43]

Attack and Siege—
Cold Harbor, June 3–7

The usual delays forced the Federals to postpone their attack so that Grant ordered a general assault along the line, rather than just an advance on the left, to take place at dawn on June 3. It would be the first planned general assault since the Wilderness. The tremendous effort of May 12 at Spotsylvania also involved all corps of the Army of the Potomac, but that general involvement had evolved due to circumstances. No effort was made on June 3 to find a weak spot in the Confederate line; in fact, save for Edgar's Salient, there were no weak spots.

It is likely that Grant wanted to demonstrate the strength of the Army of the Potomac and challenge the morale of Lee's army. He continued to believe that the Army of Northern Virginia was losing its offensive spirit, that Lee was psychologically beaten and thus content to act on the defensive. Moreover, the Federals could not turn either of Lee's flanks, and they were only about nine miles from Richmond. If they could break through on June 3, Lee's army would be in trouble. As a recent historian has put it, the attack of June 3 "made eminent sense" from Grant's standpoint.[1]

JUNE 3

The assault began at 4:30 A.M. On the Union left, Hancock's Second Corps went forward to test the new Confederate line that stretched south from Cold Harbor Road. Francis Barlow was on the left, with John Brooke and Nelson Miles in his first line. John Gibbon was to the right, with Robert Tyler and Thomas Smyth in front. Gibbon's men made little headway. The swampy headwaters of Boatswain's Creek interfered with Tyler's advance, but the 155th New York closed to within fifty yards of the Confederate line and held there for half an hour. It then fell back 100 yards to a rise of ground and began to dig in, using bayonets and tin cups to pile dirt onto fence rails. Another regiment of Tyler's command, the 8th New York

Heavy Artillery, dug in only 80 yards from the Rebels after retiring from a position as close as 20 yards short of the defender's trench.

Smyth's brigade advanced to Tyler's left through a patch of thin woods and captured the Confederate pickets, who thought it was too dangerous to retire in the face of the Union advance. Then the Federals came to an open field with the Rebel line 200 yards away. They could see a second line behind it, and abatis lined the forward parapet. Smyth's men double-quicked across the open, taking many casualties, until the survivors could plainly see that it was a hopeless venture. Then the rank and file stopped about 60 to 100 yards from the enemy. While some took "such shelter as presented itself" and soon began to construct "a rude breast-work," others retired. "There was no break, no rout," reported George D. Bowen of the 12th New Jersey. "They realizing that they had done all they could, just retired keeping good order." Smyth's Federals retreated to the edge of the woods and re-formed in a slight depression. Bowen remembered that the order to try again soon filtered down. "This the men positively refused to attempt notwithstanding all our efforts to drive them forward. Our men have so much experience that they understand what they can and cannot do just as well as our commanding officers." Instead, Smyth's brigade began to dig in at the edge of the woods, using tin plates and cups. Although under small arms and artillery fire, they soon had a good trench. Some of the more advanced units, like the 10th New York Battalion, were 150 yards from the Rebels.[2]

Gibbon's supporting brigades moved up to the rear of Tyler and Smyth but could not close with the Confederates. Most of Col. H. Boyd Mc-Keen's veteran regiments stopped behind Tyler, but the newer 36th Wisconsin advanced to a point seventy-five yards from Alfred Colquitt's Georgia brigade before stopping and asking for tools to be brought forward so the men could entrench. Joshua T. Owen's Philadelphia brigade moved ahead to Smyth's left and lodged about 100 yards from the north face of Edgar's Salient. Gibbon's losses were substantial. The 8th New York Heavy Artillery suffered 505 casualties, including its Col. Peter A. Porter, accounting for more than half of Tyler's brigade losses. Tyler himself was wounded in the attack.[3]

Barlow achieved limited success against John Breckinridge's under-manned division. Brooke's brigade connected with Gibbon to the right and fronted Edgar's Salient. The 7th New York Heavy Artillery emerged from some timber before its men saw the bulge in the Confederate line. Sensing a weak spot, they began to double-quick, receiving only light fire

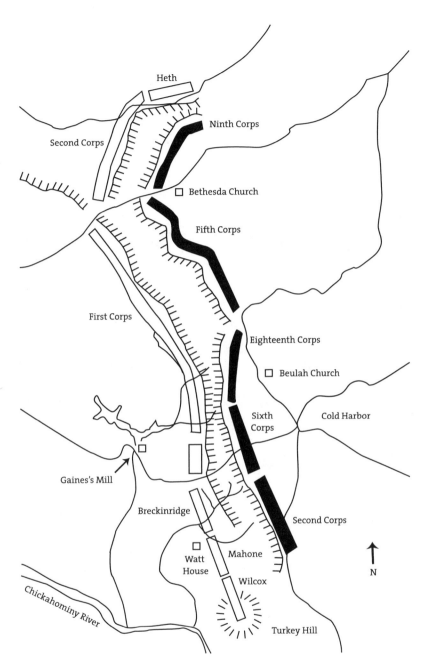

Heth

Second Corps

Ninth Corps

Bethesda Church

Fifth Corps

First Corps

Eighteenth Corps

Beulah Church

Sixth
Corps

Cold Harbor

Gaines's Mill

Breckinridge

Second Corps

N

Watt
House

Mahone

Chickahominy River

Wilcox

Turkey Hill

Cold Harbor, June 3, 1864

along the way. They were helped by the low ground fronting the salient along Dispatch Station Road. George Edgar saw the Federals approach and roused his men to open fire when the enemy were within "easy range." The left battalion of the New York regiment was stopped by effective fire south of the salient, but the center and right battalions paused at the base of the slope. One of their number, Corp. Terrence Begly, shot the color bearer of the 26th Virginia Battalion, which inspired his comrades to trot grimly up the low hill.[4]

The New Yorkers were slowed by a line of sharpened palisades placed in front of the parapet, but the men helped each other across and then climbed the parapet to meet Edgar's men. Hand-to-hand fighting failed to stop them. Edgar later reported that his small battalion was "completely overpowered by superior numbers and brute-force." He lost virtually all the troops holding the salient, an estimated 219 out of 250 soldiers. The left wing of Edgar's battalion, about 200 or 250 men, held firm to the north of the salient.[5]

The 7th New York Heavy Artillery duplicated the Second Corps success on May 12 on a far smaller scale, and the same problem hampered its ability to exploit that victory. Running across no-man's-land, trotting up the slope, and engulfing Edgar's troops had taken the steam and the cohesion out of the regiment. "We had lost all semblance of organization," later reported Pvt. Augustus DuBois of Company F. The two battalions had degenerated into "a veritable mob," milling about inside the captured works.[6]

But a regiment of Miles's brigade on the left of Barlow's division came forward to help the New Yorkers. While most of Miles's units took shelter in the foot-deep depression of Dispatch Station Road, the 5th New Hampshire continued forward. Its colonel could see the hand-to-hand struggle atop the hill at Edgar's Salient and wheeled his regiment to the right to offer assistance. The New Hampshiremen advanced diagonally across the Confederate front for 400 yards and climbed up the southern face of the salient. They managed to struggle through the clusters of disorganized New Yorkers and captured Confederates, and continued to advance toward the Rebel rear. Fortunately for Lee, elements of William Mahone's reserve division were right in the way. Brig. Gen. Joseph Finegan's Florida brigade and the 2nd Maryland counterattacked when the New Hampshire regiment was only eighty yards away. They not only stopped the Union advance but also pushed the Federals into the salient, where the Yankees failed to organize a defensive position. Almost quicker than anyone realized it, the small part of Lee's line that fell to the Union attack was cleared of its captors.[7]

The rest of the brigade failed to help the 7th New York Heavy Artillery. Brooke tried to rush up his second wave but was wounded by canister fire. Col. James A. Beaver of the 148th Pennsylvania replaced him and managed to get the troops to the base of the slope. They took position anywhere from thirty to seventy-five yards from the Confederate works and started to dig in about the time that the New Yorkers and New Hampshiremen retreated from Edgar's Salient. Beaver was able to establish a position for the refugees to fall back to. In Beaver's words, his men "got a little earth thrown up which now grew into a rifle pit." One of Hancock's staff officers dramatically described Beaver's men entrenching "themselves by throwing up the sand with their bayonets, hands, & c., under a scathing fire of musketry." Barlow did not send in Clinton D. MacDougall's brigade since it seemed that the opportunity to exploit the advantage had passed, and Richard Byrnes's brigade could accomplish no more than Miles's command had already done.[8]

The action at Edgar's Salient was the only small success achieved by the Federals on June 3. It lasted no more than twenty minutes and led to the loss of 422 out of 1,500 members of the 7th New York Heavy Artillery and 202 men of the 5th New Hampshire. The Confederates lost 312 men.[9]

By 8:30 A.M., Hancock reported that any chance of success had long since passed, but he "volunteered . . . that we would cling to the advanced positions gained, so that, if any successes were gained by other corps on our right, we would feel ready to try it again." Francis Barlow had more faith in a renewal of the attack, arguing that Coehorn mortars could be readily brought forward to shell Edgar's Salient as a prelude to another push by Beaver's men. Hancock did not have much confidence in the prospects but allowed Barlow to plant the mortars only forty yards from the salient and open fire. John Tidball also brought forward several batteries within 200 yards of the Confederates to support both Barlow and Gibbon, but the infantry never attempted another attack.[10]

Wright's Sixth Corps also began to advance at 4:30 A.M. to the north of Hancock's position. David Russell's division straddled Cold Harbor Road but failed to attack at all. To the north, James Ricketts's division advanced disjointedly, with William Truex's brigade moving along Bloody Run. The Rebels held this sector much more firmly on June 3 than they did on the evening of June 1, and the Federals failed to break through. The Union troops dug in relatively close, however, when their advance lost momentum. Ricketts's other brigade, commanded by Col. Benjamin F. Smith, was held in reserve for two hours and then took position in line with Thomas Neill's division. Smith's men received so much Confederate fire that they found it "necessary to protect ourselves in some way," as Lt. Col. Otho H. Binkley of the 110th Ohio put it. They "commenced making excavations, by digging with their bayonets and scooping up the earth with their tin cups and plates." A few shovels arrived, and the Federals "went vigorously to work—the enemy continuing their fire, occasionally killing or wounding one. In a short time they had a line of logs and earth thrown up sufficient for them to lie behind and return the enemy's fire with comparative safety." To Ricketts's right, Neill's division deployed in a column of brigades rather than a line, but this tactical formation failed to offer Neill any advantage. Frank Wheaton's brigade, which led the column, took the skirmish line fronting John Gregg's and Anderson's brigades, but stopped about seventy-five yards short of the main line. Wheaton's men fell back to the Rebel skirmish trench and worked hard to reverse it for their own protection. The Sixth Corps artillery also moved forward to offer better support. All available men belonging to Battery A, 1st New Jersey Light Artillery, were detailed to "throw up works, and the ground being very loose and sandy, the men were soon well protected."[11]

William F. Smith's Eighteenth Corps faced the Middle Ravine and its strengthened defenses. Not knowing how strong they had become, the Federals deployed Martindale's division in column so that it mostly entered the ravine itself, but part of it lapped onto the higher ground north of the watercourse. Brooks's division also deployed in column, for the most part, to Martindale's left, although it failed to offer much support to Martindale. Brooks's lead brigade, led by Brig. Gen. Gilman Marston, captured Confederate skirmish pits but halted partway to the Confederate line when pelted by fire from Anderson's brigade south of the Middle Ravine, as well as by oblique fire coming from Evander Law's brigade north of the ravine.

Stannard's brigade of Martindale's division made the main effort to strike through the Middle Ravine area. It angled across the ravine, south to north, advancing directly into the fire of Law's command only a few minutes after Marston halted. Stannard easily took the Confederate picket line, located at the abandoned and partially demolished main Rebel position; then the 25th and 27th Massachusetts continued across the low ground toward Law's new position. The Alabamians opened fire at a range of seventy-five yards and devastated the Massachusetts units. Law's rear rank loaded muskets for the men in the front rank, increasing the rate of fire. One soldier, Pvt. James Daniel of the 47th Alabama, reportedly fired sixty rounds. Law walked along the line, fearing that his men would run out of ammunition. The Alabamians were "in fine spirits, laughing and talking as they fired." Law found the slaughter among the Federals, who were "a mass of writhing humanity," worse than at any previous battle he had seen. "It was not war; it was murder," he concluded. The 25th Massachusetts lost two out of three men in the ranks that morning, and the 23rd Massachusetts suffered when it entered Law's trap to offer support. The three units were forced to fall back to the Confederate picket line and take whatever shelter they could find behind it.[12]

The rest of Brooks's division did little that day. Henry's brigade advanced until it found some abandoned Confederate skirmish pits and laid claim to them. Hiram Burnham's brigade did not attack at all but remained as an unused reserve. Nevertheless his men dug in, using bodies left over from the June 1 fighting in this area as the base of a parapet.[13]

Meade gave Warren only general directions about what to do on the morning of June 3, encouraging him to cooperate with Burnside and to exploit any success by turning south to roll up the Rebel line. Yet the Fifth Corps did little other than skirmish, while the Ninth Corps made limited efforts. Curtin's brigade of Robert Potter's division advanced on John Cooke's North Carolina brigade along Shady Grove Road and took its skirmish line, but Curtin was stopped fifty yards short of the main Confederate position. The Federals piled up logs from a nearby patch of woods and put dirt on them during lulls in the firing. Potter's division pioneers lent a hand by chopping down more trees in the woods, which were manhandled forward to strengthen the parapet as soon as it was high enough to allow some freedom of movement to the rear. On Curtin's left, John Hartranft's brigade of Orlando Willcox's division captured the Confederate skirmish line but stopped anywhere from 75 to 300 yards from the main position.[14]

When Burnside requested the opinion of his division commanders on whether a renewal of the attack was feasible, Willcox consulted engineer James St. Clair Morton and his two brigade leaders. He concluded that it might work if he could get enough artillery into position to counter the Rebel guns. Willcox instructed Capt. Albert B. Twitchell to put four pieces about 350 yards from the Rebel main line and to use infantry details to dig works for them. Gunners and infantrymen alike labored under fire; they "were shot down every moment," according to Willcox. After two hours of this harrowing work, Twitchell opened fire about 10:00 A.M. with two guns he had managed to build some protection for, but the other works took longer to make ready.[15]

Throughout the morning, Meade issued calls to his corps commanders for renewed attacks. These calls filtered down the chain of command to be ignored by some subordinates, or they elicited an inquiry by corps commanders to division and brigade leaders as to whether there was any way to execute them without wrecking their units. In some cases, lower-level commanders obeyed the calls, in a manner of speaking, by intensifying their fire from the improvised fieldworks under construction. William F. Smith later contended that Cyrus Comstock came from Grant's headquarters to inspect the state of affairs. Smith sent his engineer, Captain Farquhar, to accompany him. Farquhar later assured Smith that Comstock understood the futility of further action, and Smith felt justified in not responding to Meade's urgings.[16]

Meade also sent engineer Nathaniel Michler to inspect the forward positions of the army soon after the attacks stalled. Farquhar accompanied Michler when he reached the Eighteenth Corps. The inspection, much of it conducted on his hands and knees, convinced Michler that it was foolish to continue attacking, and he reported this to Meade.[17]

Grant put an end to further attacks in a message to Meade, issued at 12:30 P.M. "Hold our most advanced positions and strengthen them," he instructed the army leader. This was not only a humane order but also necessary given the state of affairs. But then Grant went on to initiate a new phase of the Overland campaign: "Reconnoissances [*sic*] should be made in front of every Corps and advances made to advantageous positions by regular approaches." At no previous point in the brutal march from the Rapidan had Grant contemplated the use of siege approaches to reduce Lee's strongly fortified positions. Most likely, Comstock's report on the short space that now separated the two armies led Grant to envision this type of approach. The man who had commanded the Army of the Tennessee during the war's classic siege at Vicksburg now urged the Army of the Potomac to do likewise at Cold Harbor.[18]

Meade issued orders at 1:30 P.M. suspending further attacks. He also ordered his subordinates to dig in at their advanced positions and make preparations for "moving against the enemy's works by regular approaches." This order arrived barely in time to stop the only Federal attack in preparation, that by Willcox's division of the Ninth Corps. Burnside had instructed Willcox to go in at 2:00 P.M., but he was delayed by the need to shift Hartranft's brigade farther to the right so it could start from the most advanced position. Hartranft was finally ready to go an hour later, but Meade's order arrived in time to cancel the advance.[19]

The famous attack of June 3 at Cold Harbor was mostly carried by a few units in the Second, Sixth, and Eighteenth Corps. Only seven of twelve brigades in Hancock's command, one of ten Sixth Corps brigades, and three of seven in Smith's Eighteenth Corps conducted serious attacks. Federal losses have been exaggerated by many observers and historians over the years, but the most recent estimate of Union casualties places them at 3,500 in about one hour of fighting. This amounted to 27.3 percent of total Union casualties during the Cold Harbor phase of the Overland campaign. The Confederates lost about 700 men in repulsing the attack.[20]

The morale of the Army of the Potomac suffered, although most men were still willing to do their duty. They began to assume more responsibility for deciding whether that duty included wasting their lives. Engineer Wesley Brainerd witnessed the fight from the relative safety of Hancock's headquarters, yet the "horrors of that bloody assault have made such an impression on my mind that I can never forget it." He saw the confidence of the Second Corps shaken by the failed attack. "There was no demoralization visible but a settled commotion which showed itself plainly in the faces of every Officer and every man."[21]

There is evidence of a refusal to fight among Second Corps troops. George D. Bowen contended in his diary that Smyth's brigade rejected an order to make a second advance. This was never officially reported and thus passed without making a ripple in army affairs. Henry Richard Swan, who survived the bloody attack in the ranks of the 8th New York Heavy Artillery, argued in a letter written on June 4 that many veterans who served in Tyler's brigade "refused to charge & one Regt was driven out of our intrenchments by the Provost Gd. at the point of the Bayonnett." Swan's evidence is less convincing than Bowen's, for he did not personally witness the incident.[22]

The morale of Hancock's command suffered more than that of any other corps in Meade's army. The deterioration started with the attack on the Mule Shoe Salient on May 12 and continued with each grueling attack thereafter. Hancock's men "were badly worn out and sadly in need of rest," noted John S. Jones of the 4th Ohio in Smyth's brigade. They felt that they were being asked to do too much. A month of extraordinary work in the field had "its legal effect," as Maj. William Houghton of the 14th Indiana, another regiment in Smyth's brigade, put it. "The men look pale & careworn," he wrote home, "their systems are exhausted, they are weak, and men die from scratches because they have not physical resistance to recover from a slight prostration."[23]

The rest of the army suffered as well, but to a lesser degree. Andrew Glaser, a soldier in the 14th U.S. Infantry of Griffin's division, Fifth Corps, frankly told his brother that "the men are played out, and half of our army is without shoes." He claimed that his regiment started the campaign with 528 men and now had only 135 left.[24]

Meade had a feeling of smug satisfaction on one issue: that his own history of hesitating to attack strong Confederate positions was vindicated. He had received a great deal of public criticism for not assaulting Lee's strongly defended line at Williamsport in July 1863, during the Confederate retreat from Gettysburg, and at Mine Run the following November. After a month of Grant-like warfare in Virginia, Meade concluded that anyone who dared attack a well-fortified position was asking for failure. He had chafed under the peculiar command arrangement that placed the general-in-chief near his headquarters and now derived a certain morbid satisfaction from the results of the campaign. "Grant has had his eyes opened, and is willing to admit now that Virginia and Lee's army is not Tennessee and Bragg's army." Meade accurately summed up the army's accomplishments: "Up to this time our success has consisted only in compelling the enemy to draw in towards Richmond; our failure has been that we have not been able to overcome, destroy or bag his army."[25]

The attack of June 3 was no more horrendous than any other during the Overland campaign; it had no fewer chances of success or failure than the others. Indeed, the attack of May 12 was a far worse experience that achieved little more for the Union cause (other than the significant capture of several thousand Confederates). The attack of June 3 was unusual in that it was a general attack with no special instructions for the assaulting troops, no single point identified as a target, no plan to coordinate the movements of supporting troops. As a result, according to John C. Ropes, the assault was rather like a gigantic reconnaissance in force.[26]

But the action on June 3 was remarkable in another way. "A singular thing about the whole attack," mused Col. Theodore Lyman, "and one that demonstrated the staunchness of the troops, was, that our men, when the fire was too hot for them to advance and the works too strong, did not retreat as soldiers often do, but lay down where some small ridge offered a little cover, and there staid." On no previous field did the Army of the Potomac do this in such large numbers. By evening of June 3 much of the army's line was only forty yards from the enemy, and it was already so well entrenched as to be impregnable. Lyman marveled at how the opponents could go to sleep that night with no-man's-land "ploughed by cannon-shot and clotted with the dead bodies that neither side dared to bury!" After four weeks of continuous marching, digging, and fighting, the two armies lay down "with their heads almost on each other's throats!"[27]

Ironically, Meade issued a circular to his corps commanders at 6:30 P.M. asking them to report on the exact condition and position of their commands, and recommend what should be done the next day. He apparently still held open the possibility of attacking, if feasible. The response was strong from Horatio Wright, who reported within fifteen minutes that much of his Sixth Corps was already well protected by new earthworks and the rest would wait until dark offered an opportunity to dig in. "It is so difficult getting along our front line before it is fully intrenched that anything like a correct reconnaissance cannot be made, and I cannot, therefore, say with any certainty what it is practicable to do to-morrow." Yet Wright doubted that he could attack at all.[28]

Similar views came from the Second Corps, although Barlow was enthusiastic about planting a dozen cannon close enough to Edgar's Salient to drive the Confederates out of it. Gibbon strongly recommended regular approaches rather than further attacks, but he also noted that even if he could pry the Rebels from one line, they had more to fall back to. Reducing all of them would "be a work of time." Meade nevertheless reported to Grant that tonight "we will begin all along the lines, digging up to the enemy's works."[29]

Meade was too optimistic, for his army spent the night of June 3 consolidating its forward position. Hancock's artillerymen continued to dig gun emplacements, adding embrasures the next night. Some of his infantrymen braved Confederate fire to complete their entrenchments, and two brigades of Gibbon's division constructed covered ways to the rear. An adjustment of the forward line in Neill's division of the Sixth Corps allowed Wheaton's brigade 200 additional yards of space, which "was but imperfectly intrenched" during the night by the 62nd New York.[30]

Eighteenth Corps troops also worked hard all day and night. "[W]e just began to protect ourselves," remembered Daniel W. Sawtelle of the 8th Maine in Col. Griffin A. Stedman's brigade of Martindale's division. He and his comrades used their knapsacks as shields until they could scrape up enough dirt to form a rude parapet. When the loose topsoil was gone, they broke up the harder layers below it with knives and bayonets. Tin plates and cups served as scoops to form it into an ever-rising parapet. "It is wonderful what a pile of dirt a regiment will throw up when once they start at it," commented Sawtelle. By noon of that day, the 8th Maine had a work that was shoulder high. This allowed the men to stoop while going to the rear to build fires and boil coffee. At dusk, the Maine troops received a supply of spades and intensified their efforts. The regiment went to the right and formed a line of battle in the dark on open ground. The men in the first rank dug quietly while those in the second rank were ready to cover them if firing broke out. They also relieved their comrades in the front rank when they became tired. In this way, the 8th Maine constructed a strong work with loopholes by dawn of June 4.[31]

Following its traumatic attack against Law's brigade, the 25th Massachusetts sought what cover "the nature of the ground" could offer until dusk on the evening of June 3. Then the men constructed works using "their hands and tin cups." In contrast, the 21st Connecticut dug in all night "with only occasional interruptions from the enemy's pickets, who were but a few yards from our own."[32]

The U.S. Engineer Battalion divided its units among the corps most in need of extra hands. Companies A and B worked on the Sixth Corps front constructing a battery and strengthening infantry parapets only 100 yards from the Confederates. Company D dug a new skirmish line on the Eighteenth Corps sector well forward of the existing skirmishers on the night of June 3. Led by Farquhar and Sgt. P. H. Flood, the company deployed with each man six feet from the other and quietly dug in all night, finishing by dawn.[33]

Some Confederates also worked on their fortifications on June 3, often using only their hands and bayonets. Lee had heard rumors that the works on Breckinridge's front were "too high" and wanted the division commander to lower them or construct a banquette for the men to gain enough elevation to fire over it. Lee's artillery chief also experimented with using 24-pounder guns as mortars to annoy Federal working parties.[34]

Mostly, however, the Rebels sniped and slept during this memorable day. Surprised that so few wounded came to his field hospital, LeGrand J. Wilson, surgeon of the 42nd Mississippi in Heth's division, wandered up to the front line and found two-thirds of his regiment asleep. The men were "lying in every conceivable position, propped up or leaning against the breastworks, or lying in the ditch, with a cartridge box or blanket for a pillow." The rest were constantly taking shots at the Federals. Whether awake or asleep, Wilson saw that everyone was "clasping his Enfield rifle." The Alabamians in Law's brigade needed a secure source of water, so they dug a zigzag communication trench from the center of their line toward a spring a few yards to the rear.[35]

Finegan's Florida brigade was the only Confederate unit that conducted small-scale attacks on June 3. It firmly held the salient but was subjected to harassing skirmish fire from three sides at close range. The Floridians kept their heads down and passed orders along the perimeter of the salient in a cap box. Finegan ordered the Yankees driven back to a more comfortable range, so Lt. Col. John M. Martin and Maj. Pickens B. Bird led a skirmish line out beyond the parapet at about 10:00 A.M. Bird and many of his men were shot before the survivors jumped back across the parapet to the relative safety of the salient. Three soldiers braved the Yankee fire in an effort to retrieve Bird, but all were shot. Sgt. P. N. Bryan of the 6th Florida saved one of these men by dragging him back behind the parapet and laying him gently in the shelter of a traverse. That evening, Finegan unwisely ordered a second attempt to push the Federals back. Capt. Charles Seton Fleming of the 2nd Florida led this effort at 8:30 P.M., but he was quickly killed and most of his men were lost. A supportive advance by Martin's brigade against Smyth and Owen at the same time, which was preceded by thirty minutes of Confederate artillery fire, resulted in 100 Rebel losses and nothing to show for the sacrifice. Only the onset of darkness offered Finegan's men some relief from the relentless sharp shooting, and Smyth kept half of his men awake and ready to repel another attack all night.[36]

"We have had an order read to us that we are to assume the defensive instead of the offensive," commented William B. Greene to his mother. This member of the 2nd U.S. Sharpshooters heard plenty of rumors that Meade's men were "to use the shovel & pick ax now for a while." Greene was right. The attack of June 3 was by no means the end of the Cold Harbor confrontation, nor was it the end of the Overland campaign. Two important things happened that day. A large part of the Army of the Potomac and of Smith's Eighteenth Corps began to engage in a determined effort to refortify their positions much closer to the Confederates. This occurred nearly all along the line and constituted a major work project in itself. The second thing that happened on June 3 was that the Army of the Potomac began conducting siege approaches on a significant scale. Its only previous experience at this was a limited effort at Yorktown in April 1862. This was a high-level directive, originating with Grant and endorsed by army headquarters. But when the directive filtered down through corps, division, and brigade levels, it was taken seriously by only a few subordinates, and Grant himself ordered work on the approaches stopped four days later. The last phase of the Overland campaign (and of the Cold Harbor period of that campaign) lasted from June 7 to 13, during which the men lived and fought in the strong trench systems they had constructed while Grant planned to shift the theater of operations south of the James River and make Petersburg his target. The most intense period of fortification use during the whole of the Overland campaign occurred from June 3 to 13.[37]

SIEGE APPROACHES, JUNE 4–7

The immediate effect of Grant's directive to begin siege approaches was not felt on June 3 or 4, mostly because the troops were too busy refortifying their new, close-in positions to the Confederate line. Beaver's brigade worked hard to strengthen its fortifications and install artillery on the night of June 4. In Smyth's brigade, the 12th New Jersey had been able to construct light fieldworks by the evening of June 3 but "went to work like beavers" after dusk. By dawn of June 4, they had a parapet ten feet thick topped with headlogs, located about 200 yards from the Confederate line. George D. Bowen used a detail of twenty men to fortify a skirmish line for the 12th New Jersey. It was only twelve yards in front of the division's newly made trench, but Bowen's detail received fire as it worked throughout the night of June 4. He put the men five paces apart and ordered each one to dig a shelter pit, with the dirt thrown up all around. Bowen ignored the danger and remained on top of the ground to encourage the men. When they finished their pits, he told them to dig toward each other and create a parapet. Before long, they had a continuous trench. Other troops dug communication trenches in a zigzag pattern to connect the skirmish line with the main line. They also fashioned triangular loopholes of boards taken from cracker and ammunition boxes and placed them in the forward parapet of the skirmish line.[38]

In the Sixth Corps sector, Neill's division built traverses along the Confederate skirmish trench it had captured in the attack of June 3. Neill's men established their skirmish line forty yards in front of this position on the night of June 4. Ricketts strengthened the works on his division skirmish line, but Russell did little more than construct gun emplacements on June 4.[39]

Members of the U.S. Engineer Battalion continued work in the Eighteenth Corps sector on the night of June 4, laying out a line across an open space under skirmish fire so that infantry details could dig the trench before dawn. The regulars stockaded a redoubt and installed abatis during the next couple of days. Stedman's brigade, which included the 8th Maine, constructed a new trench that both shortened its line and placed the men 100 yards closer to the enemy. Among Burnside's troops, orders went out to dig covered ways behind each brigade for up to thirty yards behind the line. This was to allow for covered passage to and from the trenches, but the orders also specified that brigade commanders were to make sure the men did not lie in or obstruct the covered ways.[40]

With the lines so close to each other, Hancock's men received the brunt of heavy Confederate artillery fire that commenced at 10:30 on the morning of June 4. It slacked off later that day, and troops from the 4th New York Heavy Artillery who were manning Coehorn mortars returned fire. Capt. James H. Wood could even see two headless bodies thrown ten feet into the air as a result of some direct hits. Rebel artillery fire increased when Confederate infantrymen delivered heavy musketry at Smyth's brigade at 8:40 that evening. Grant suggested that the Federals retaliate with their own artillery fire at midnight to wake up and annoy the enemy. Although Meade did not want to do this, noting that it would result in an exchange that would wake everyone up, he authorized his corps commanders to do so if they thought it would not interfere with the construction of siege approaches. Hancock and Wright were unenthusiastic about the idea but vowed to open their artillery if compelled to do so. In the end, neither did, using the excuse that Meade offered them regarding the interference with siege approaches.[41]

Both armies significantly adjusted their lines on June 4. Jubal Early's Second Corps units fell back from Shady Grove Road to the line they had occupied before the June 2 attack. This placed them facing northeast rather than south and southeast, and eliminated the forward curving end of the Confederate line. Henry Heth's division marched to the far right to rejoin A. P. Hill's Third Corps. It left the trenches at 3:00 A.M. of June 4 and rested that day and the next before taking its new position on the right.[42]

On the other side of the field, Meade responded to Early's withdrawal by starting to contract the Fifth and Ninth Corps line so they could close up on Smith and fill the gap that had existed for several days between the Eighteenth Corps and Warren's command. David Birney's division of the Second Corps had moved into this area on June 3 and had begun to entrench, but it could not cover the gap entirely. The intention was to rest Burnside's right flank at Bethesda Church, but Meade changed his mind before this could be done. To relieve Hancock's hard-pressed troops on the far left, he wanted the Ninth Corps to fill the hole alone while sending Birney and Warren off to that sector. Whereas Potter and Willcox moved during the daylight hours of June 4, Crittenden did not complete the Ninth Corps shift until after dark. Burnside had no opportunity to set up his artillery, even if he had wanted to open it at midnight to annoy the Confederates. He could not even begin to fortify his new position because the night was too dark for engineer Morton to survey the ground. Birney was on his way back to Hancock, but until Burnside was well situated, Warren postponed his move.[43]

On June 5, Burnside received orders to relieve a brigade of the Eighteenth Corps as well, thus extending his corps line to a total of three and a half miles, with the right resting near Bosher's House. Willcox, who connected with the Eighteenth Corps, began building an earthwork called Fort Fletcher in front of and to the right of Smith's old right flank, now held by one of his own brigades. Morton supervised the construction. By mid-morning of June 5, army headquarters wanted Burnside to adjust his line again. He was still to maintain firm connection with Smith on the left, but the rest of his corps line was to angle toward the northeast instead of the north, along the main stream of Matadequin Creek, past Allen's Mill, and to the fork of Old Church Road and Cold Harbor Road, where Burnside's black division was positioned. Burnside and Morton "carefully" looked at this ground for several hours and did not like it. Although the new line would be only slightly longer than the one he already held, there were few natural obstacles in front and numerous swamps and ponds to the rear. Like the position he had already assumed, this new one ran through dense woods for much of the distance, requiring much cutting of timber. Burnside also pointed out that Fort Fletcher, while a strong earthwork, was well forward of his main line and thus vulnerable. He would have to post a full brigade to hold the fort and its connecting trenches, leaving too few men to man the rest of the proposed line. By the end of June 5, Meade allowed him to stay put but directed him to refuse the far right of Potter's division a little near Bosher's. On the night of June 5, Warren began to pull out his Fifth Corps troops from the line they had held for nearly a week. They moved to the army's left to picket the north bank of the Chickahominy River and guard its crossings.[44]

Ninth Corps efforts to secure the army's right flank raised some snide comments among the staff at Warren's headquarters. "Burnside's men are great at throwing dirt," Col. Charles S. Wainwright commented in his diary, "all this army have got to be very expert diggers, being able to do a full days' work with no more than a tin plate and their bayonet; but the

Ninth Corps far surpasses all others that I have seen both in the height and number of their breastworks." Wainwright may have been referring to Fort Fletcher, which was noted among observers as an unusually large redoubt.[45]

Meade issued instructions for all corps commanders to begin siege approaches on the night of June 4. Hancock appointed Barlow and Gibbon to direct Second Corps work in this direction, while assigning engineer Lt. Ranald S. Mackenzie to advise them. Also, men of the U.S. Engineer Battalion were available "for the instruction of the troops in running the approaches." Word circulated through the army that the Second Corps would be the prime mover in this endeavor, as its line was closer than the other corps'. Surg. Jonah F. Dyer of the 19th Massachusetts, a regiment in Gibbon's division, reported that "the siege of Richmond will be a part of the program" from now on. Wright merely suggested to Ricketts that he fully fortify his skirmish line that night and move his main line to it, apparently with the intention of starting his approach from there. Warren did not seem at all inclined to participate. Having sent his engineer troops back to the rear for rations, he reported that he could advance his left wing "at a jump without regular approaches" if such a move could be supported with an advance by Burnside to his left. Nothing came of this suggestion.[46]

The bulk of the work on siege approaches fell to the Second Corps, with a little effort by the Sixth and Eighteenth Corps. The Fifth and Ninth Corps did almost nothing in this line. Even so, Meade distributed available engineer officers and troops evenly across the army. Company A of the U.S. Engineer Battalion went to Hancock, Company B to Wright, and Company C to Warren; Burnside and Smith shared Company D.[47]

Barlow pushed forward the approaches more energetically than any other division commander in the army. During the night of June 5, his men worked on two parallels, digging laterally to connect them. At the closest point, he was only thirty yards from the Confederate line. The rest of the parallel system angled away from the enemy to conform to the crest of the shallow rise of ground the Federals occupied. Barlow reported slow progress due to intense Confederate fire. He found that it prevented his men from digging any faster at night than was possible during the day.[48]

Barlow also initiated the construction of a mine, dug by a detachment of Company A, U.S. Engineer Battalion. Helped by the infantrymen of Beaver's brigade, the engineers dug an approach ramp to this mine on June 5. The next day they began digging the gallery from the closest point to the Rebel line. The length of the ramp and gallery combined totaled forty feet by the evening of June 7. This was the first time that the Army of the Potomac engaged in mine warfare, something it would do on a more important scale at Petersburg.[49]

The stormy night of June 6 impeded Barlow's efforts, although his men worked "as vigorously as possible." He pushed forward saps from the right and left wings of one parallel, aiming toward a point on the Confederate line that was opposite the center of the parallel. Lightning lit up the sky and revealed the working party, which gained only six yards on the left and four yards on the right because of the resulting Confederate fire. Moreover, only one man could dig at each sap at a time. The Confederates saw the sap roller, a mobile protective device to shield the sappers from enemy fire. At this close range their artillery so damaged the roller that it was nearly impossible to continue. Col. T. M. R. Talcott of the 1st Confederate Engineers prepared to dig a countermine to blow up the sap roller in case the Federals managed to devise a strategy to keep it moving forward.[50]

In addition to working on the approaches, Hancock's men continued to improve their works by connecting detached skirmish pits and digging communication trenches to more firmly connect the skirmishers with the main line. On some parts of the Second Corps line, Confederate skirmishers were pushed farther away to give more protection to the Federals who held secondary positions behind the Union main line, for their bullets were carrying some distance to the Federal rear. When the Rebels advanced their own skirmish line on the night of June 5, Col. Theodore G. Ellis of the 14th Connecticut assumed that it was a prelude to an attack. The Connecticut men opened fire and the Rebel main line responded. The two sides fired heavily for twenty minutes before both realized there was no need to do so. "Such mistakes as this cannot always be avoided when the enemy is in such close proximity," Ellis explained.[51]

Gibbon's division made little progress in its siege approaches. Owen, whose brigade constituted the left wing of the division, jumped men twenty feet ahead of the line during the night of June 5 but found the new position difficult to fortify. "He needs sand-bags or gabions very much," Gibbon informed corps headquarters. Owen hoped to "harass the enemy to his left and front" from this new line. Gibbon's other brigade leaders reported the ground to their front "very difficult to work in and not much can be done." Meade issued a circular urging his corps commanders to "continue pushing up their works to the enemy, especially during the night" and promising that "forage sacks and sand-bags" would be issued by his quartermaster as needed. Hancock relayed this imperative to his division commanders while offering "Grain bags" to them. In response, Owen jumped more men ahead on the night of June 6 and instructed them to dig in as best they could. He planned to connect both spots with a parallel and begin to form a continuous line twelve to fifteen yards ahead of the rest of the division. The other brigades made even smaller gains while advancing men across the difficult ground in their front. As Owen, Smyth, and Ramsey tried to work forward, Pierce's brigade concentrated on working backward. His men constructed reserve lines to the rear and corduroyed a swamp that bisected the brigade line. Both Gibbon and Barlow sent maps to corps headquarters to document their daily progress.[52]

Birney's division extended Hancock's line to the left on the evening of June 5, completing that move before dawn the next day. Therefore, Birney had not yet begun to construct siege approaches. On June 7, Hancock ordered him "to run zigzags and parallels until you attain a position from which the enemy's works can be readily assaulted, or batteries placed to enfilade their lines." He wanted Birney to aim at a point where the Confederate line angled toward the rear, assuring him that the engineers were making gabions useful for revetting earthworks and that his division could obtain "a small number of these . . . from day to day."[53]

The Sixth Corps invested less energy in its siege approaches than the Second. A detachment of regular engineers went forward on the left of Wright's line during the night of June 5 to establish an advanced position on ground once occupied by Confederate skirmishers. During the day and night of June 6, the engineers improved the fieldwork and connected it to the main line with a communication trench. Then they began to do the same on the center of Wright's line. No such activity took place on his right, and the two small advanced works on the left and center were never connected. Nevertheless, two Sixth Corps subordinates later reported that "gradual approaches were made toward the enemy's works by means of zig-zag lines."[54]

Smith's Eighteenth Corps also advanced men during the night of June 4 to a point near the center of the corps line where they dug in. Two nights later, they constructed a parallel from that point to the Northern Ravine and then dug a communication trench connecting the parallel to the main position. This had the effect of "throwing forward my troops in line and making the line of battle straight," as Smith put it.[55]

Burnside's effort to advance across no-man's-land was delayed by the need to reposition the Ninth Corps on the night of June 4, which turned out to be a much longer process than expected. After relieving Birney's division north of the Eighteenth Corps position, Burnside hoped to take possession of a rise of ground about 100 yards ahead that would enable him "to push our approaches with greater facility." Whether his men were able to take this rise is unclear, but Morton instructed division leader Willcox to "prosecute the works of approach along your line" on June 6. Willcox apparently was able to establish an "advanced parallel," perhaps on the rise of ground, but he never started any approaches.[56]

The Federals never fully implemented the traditional process of sapping forward that had been developed scientifically by French engineers in the seventeenth century. Only one sap roller was deployed, on the Second Corps front, to protect the digging of an approach trench across no-man's-land, and it made little headway. More commonly, the Federals advanced their positions by what the engineer manuals termed the "flying sap"—sending detachments out over the open ground at night to dig in at a designated point forward of the main line, then consolidating that position by digging a parallel to both sides of it and a communication trench to the rear.[57]

Brig. Gen. John G. Barnard offered Grant advice on how to proceed with the siege works. Barnard had spent much of the war engineering the massive defenses of Washington D.C., and Henry Halleck sent him to Grant in late May to be useful. Having served as McClellan's chief engineer during the Peninsula campaign, Barnard had accumulated considerable knowledge of the area along the James River. Grant obliged on June 5 by putting him on his staff and naming him chief engineer "of the armies in the Field." "It is quite probable that the present campaign may result in heavy siege work," Barnard lectured Grant the next day, "and your own experience at Vicksburg must have shown you the need of a sufficient number of engineer officers." Barnard recommended that each corps and, if possible, each division should have an engineer assigned to it. He also suggested that a siege train be accumulated at Fortress Monroe. As both suggestions had already been acted on, there was little need to respond to this sound advice. Grant instructed Barnard to send his reports directly to Meade beginning on June 9.[58]

In the middle of their limited progress on the siege approaches, Meade sent a message to his corps leaders asking if they thought an attack was possible on their front. The answer was resoundingly negative. Wright consulted his division leaders and determined that it was "impracticable." Even if he could take the first line, it was highly unlikely that he could penetrate the secondary lines as long as those rear positions were "defended with ordinary obstinacy." Barlow reported the same problem. He further noted that the Confederates were able to deliver a raking fire across no-man's-land on his front, due to the bulge in the Rebel line at Edgar's Salient. He had no place to form his assault column in safety, and, even if he did, the formation would be completely broken up by crossing his own works. Barlow believed that an attack launched on the evening of June 2, as originally planned, might have worked. But the Rebels had had four days to prepare, and it would be foolish to attempt an assault now. Gibbon concurred as well.[59]

Whereas Smith simply reported that attacking was impracticable, Hancock explained more fully and eloquently the basic problem affecting all units in the Union army by this stage of the campaign: "I am averse to an assault, simply because my men have been so constantly out at the front, lying in the trenches all the time for three days, and are so fatigued that I fear they have not the dash necessary to carry them through the obstacles of a second line. They have lost the officers who have been accustomed to lead them, and as the enemy have been working constantly since we came here, the obstacles are now materially greater than they were on the first day." Although the Federal entrenchments were strong enough to repel any counterattack, Hancock felt that the Confederate works were "better regulated and more secure than our own, they having had a better opportunity of constructing them."[60]

Whether or not the Rebel works were superior to those of the Yankees, the men of the Army of the Potomac were clearly aware of Grant's change in tactics. "This certainly had the appearance of a siege," thought Wesley Brainerd when told to put his troops to work making gabions. "We had now no idea but that we were to approach Richmond from this point." His battalion constructed 300 gabions, most of which were used on the Second Corps works. There was a general recognition, especially in Hancock's command, that "charging is played out now" and that success will have to be achieved "by undermining their works and sieging." Awareness of this tactic extended to the Sixth Corps, but it does not seem to have been general all along the line.[61]

The Confederates certainly were aware that they had become the target of Union siege approaches. "This is beginning to be something like Vicksburg," commented John F. Sale of the 12th Virginia. A few days later he defied Grant to dig his way across no-man's-land. "[H]e will find that a large army in the field is quite a different affair from the little garrison at Vicksburg, cut off from all communication and under an incompetent officer." Another soldier who was stationed on Lee's right did not fear the result. He knew the strength of the Confederate works and believed that the men could withstand anything the Federals brought against them.[62]

These Rebels had no need to hurl defiance at the Union sappers, for Grant decided not to push the siege approaches after all. On June 6, he announced his resolution to shift the Army of the Potomac to the south side of the James River and operate against Petersburg. William F. Smith received a hint of this decision on June 5, when Meade made some comments to Farquhar, leading Smith to drop all plans to continue approaches to the enemy line. Meade issued a circular on June 7 telling his corps leaders to "suspend pushing their works up to the enemy, limiting their operations to completing those necessary for their security that have been commenced."[63]

Siege work did not cease immediately. Efforts continued on June 7 before orders went out for the various companies of the U.S. Engineer Battalion to report to battalion headquarters, a sure sign that offensive digging had been canceled. The men of Company A continued plugging away in Barlow's mine on June 8, advancing it a few more yards, before they left. By June 9, it was obvious to any observer that the siege work had stopped. "[O]ffensive operations ceased," noted James A. Beaver, "indicating a change of base."[64]

Was Grant serious about conducting siege approaches at Cold Harbor? There is some reason to doubt it. "I do not think General Grant intended to begin a siege here," noted Surg. Jonah F. Dyer of the 19th Massachusetts, "for he did not bring anything to do it with." Grant could not, however, continue making short runs around Lee's right flank, as the Chickahominy River stood in the way. Crossing that river and operating south of it had not worked for McClellan in 1862 and would likely reestablish the Army of the Potomac in a similar position as it already held at Cold Harbor. The best option was to cross the James River and operate in the more open area against Petersburg. How early Grant was thinking of this alternative is difficult to know—perhaps as soon as May 26, when orders to dispatch bridging equipment to the theater of operations went out. It is certain that by June 6 he was committed to the move.[65]

Were the siege approaches at Cold Harbor feasible in a practical sense? The sapping operations that Barlow conducted certainly were not practicable. In contrast to Vicksburg and the siege of Battery Wagner, the defender was able to tear apart the sap roller fairly easily. The only explanation for this must lie in the height advantage the Confederates enjoyed opposite Barlow's division, which allowed their field artillery to dominate the low ground from which the Federals were trying to advance.

Barlow's mine was a different matter. There is no reason to doubt that it could have been completed. In fact, the Federals had the advantage here, for they started it from a covered, depressed area of ground and dug the gallery horizontally into the sloping terrain. After three days of work, the gallery was at least twenty feet long, most probably about thirty or forty feet long, by the time the regular engineers stopped digging it on the evening of June 8. They would have had to dig the gallery at least 100 yards long to place a powder chamber some twenty feet below the apex of Edgar's Salient. There is no evidence that the Confederates were aware of the mine, but most likely they would have detected signs of it as the engineers neared their target. This would have given the defenders some opportunity to take effective countermeasures. Moreover, blowing up Edgar's Salient might not have broken Lee's line anyway. The 7th New York Heavy Artillery took possession of the salient on June 3 and lost it again, in some ways as the Ninth Corps would seize another salient at Petersburg on July 30 only to lose it to spirited Confederate counterattacks. In short, while technically feasible, Barlow's mine likely would not have had a dramatic effect on the outcome of the Cold Harbor phase of the Overland campaign.

What occurred at Cold Harbor from June 3 to 8 was a foreshadowing of what would occur from June 19 to July 30 at Petersburg. Following the initial series of attacks on June 15–18, when the Federals merely dented the defenses of Petersburg without achieving a decisive breakthrough, Grant spent several weeks mulling over the next move in his grand tactics. Meanwhile, a siege approach in the form of a large mine was dug by the 48th Pennsylvania at the most narrow spot of no-man's-land, opposite a shallow angle in the Confederate line called Pegram's, or Elliott's, Salient. Grant also issued directions for Meade to begin siege approaches above ground while the mine was being dug, but those approaches were never started before he again lost interest in their possibilities. Eventually, the restless general-in-chief decided to use the Union mine as the centerpiece of a complex offensive, but the result was a miserable failure for Federal arms on July 30, referred to as the battle of the Petersburg Crater. The Federals employed no more offensive mining or siege approaches at Petersburg. Instead, Grant came to rely on efforts to get around Lee's right flank. After many months and several costly offensives, this grand tactic eventually worked.[66]

Grant's restless spirit, his willingness to try any expedient, best explains why he attempted siege approaches at Cold Harbor on June 3 and then canceled them a few days later. If they had proven feasible and held promise of success, he might well have remained longer at Cold Harbor to give them a better try.

10

Holding the Trenches at Cold Harbor, June 7–12

The last five days of the confrontation at Cold Harbor were an interim period during which both armies held their positions while Grant prepared for the move across the James River. It was the most intense period of trench warfare thus far in the histories of the Army of the Potomac and the Army of Northern Virginia. The field entrenchments were the living and fighting environment for the men of both armies. Although work on the siege approaches had stopped, the Federals continued to improve their new lines close to the Confederate works.

In addition to digging in ever deeper, the Yankees had to do something about the wounded and dead left in no-man's-land after the June 3 attack. Some were close enough to the forward position so that daring men could crawl out on their stomachs and drag both the wounded and the dead into the line. The bodies were buried in trenches to the rear, each hole ten to twenty feet long, six feet wide, and three feet deep. Blankets or other cloth were used to cover their faces. When filled, enough dirt was piled on top to raise the surface a foot above ground. In some cases, the dead were covered over as new works were pushed into the area where they lay and the bodies became part of the new parapet. On the sector held by the Eighteenth Corps, a few trenches were dug forward of the line just far enough to reach the wounded, allowing the Federals to bring them in safely.[1]

But there were still hundreds of unburied bodies in the narrow space that separated the two armies. Veterans who had grown hardened to all the other sufferings produced by the campaign could not ignore the smell arising from these corpses. It seemed to settle in the lowest places — the bottom of trenches and shelter pits. No breeze could reach these low areas, yet the sun baked their living occupants and intensified the stench. The smell even drifted some 600 yards to the rear of the Confederate line. By June 6, both Yankees and Rebels arranged informal, local truces to bury a few dead on the Second and Sixth Corps sectors. An Eighteenth Corps division commander sent out detachments of pioneers, screened by skirmishers, for burial duty on the night of June 6. Lee agreed to a general truce to end at 10:00 P.M. that night, but his dispatch to Grant was so delayed that it did not reach the Federals in time. Negotiations continued until everyone consented to set aside two hours on the evening of June 7 to accomplish the task. By that time, 6:00 to 8:00 P.M., there were hardly any wounded still alive between the lines, but George Stannard's brigade of the Eighteenth Corps found seventy-one bodies before its section of the line. They had turned completely black and were covered with maggots and worms; no one could identify any of them. The pioneers dug a trench as the stretcher bearers gathered the bodies. All involved were issued a ration of whiskey to help them through the ordeal.[2]

The Confederates were keen to make sure the Yankees did not take advantage of the burial truce. When a few gunners at a battery near the 8th Maine stood up on the parapet and tried to repair the embrasures of their gun emplacements, "the Johnnies ordered them down at once."[3]

Before and after the truce, the Federals never stopped working on their fortifications. Members of the 12th New Jersey in John Gibbon's division dug a tunnel under their parapet and ran a communication trench from it forward to the skirmish line. This allowed them to relieve the pickets in safety. Gibbon also constructed several covered ways to connect his main line with the rear. Hancock's aides paid close attention to the strength of the works on the main line. They believed that the parapet was too high along three-fourths of the corps front and that it would be "impossible for the troops to fire horizontally over" it. Barlow ordered that banquettes be placed to allow the men to fire properly over them. James A. Beaver had made the parapet of his forward line high with the intention of loopholing it for greater protection from sharpshooters, but he responded to orders from division headquarters and lowered it.[4]

The 20th Massachusetts in the Second Corps occupied a trench deep enough to allow the men to walk upright in it without fear of exposure. It had a banquette so they could fire over the parapet, and shelves were cut into the forward wall of the trench for storing extra cartridges in case of an attack. By June 10, the Massachusetts men added headlogs to the parapet that were made of timbers taken from a nearby house.[5]

Wright's Sixth Corps was close to the Confederate position in many places. The parapets on the sector held by Oliver Edwards's brigade had been made with a base of logs four feet tall, with several feet of dirt thrown over them. Edwards had two lines, thirty yards apart, with skirmish pits another thirty yards in front of the first line. The Confederate skirmishers were as close as fifty yards from the Federal skirmishers. Some parts of the Sixth Corps line had parapets that were configured in a zigzag pattern, "to protect ourselves from a cross fire," according to Wilbur Fisk in Lewis Grant's brigade. Ample covered ways connected the second line with the rear, and the men managed to place some abatis in front of the first line during the night.[6]

Thomas Neill's division, which included Edwards's and Grant's brigades, had a more complex set of defenses than Fisk realized. The division was squeezed in between Ricketts on the right and Russell on the left, just to the north of Cold Harbor Road and opposite Hoke's division. It had a front of 1,000 yards and a depth of at least five lines, according to Hazard Stevens, a member of Neill's staff. Each line was connected by communication trenches, many of which were built in a zigzag pattern. Stevens could count up to twenty lines in some places, but most of them were short, often detached trenches that were not always manned. Men were hit even as far back as the sixth line by bullets that sailed over all the others in front. Stevens called the ground behind Neill's division "a perfect honey comb. The bullets come from every direction but one." Some parts of that "perfect honeycomb" were small pits dug for just one man. The Federals often placed logs and dirt over these small excavations to create a covered burrow, entering through a hole, or they simply dug a rifle pit with a parapet and then "pitched their tents behind it."[7]

Frank Wheaton sent details from his Sixth Corps brigade to help the 50th New York Engineers construct "a small earth-work, pierced for four guns" to his left and behind the skirmish line of Grant's brigade. The work was only 100 yards from the Confederates and "the Bullets Whizzed around our ears like Bees," commented James M. Snook of the engineer regiment. Snook and his comrades often had to jump into the ditches they were digging for protection. They actually spent as much time building a military road to the fort as they did on the work itself, digging it eighteen inches deep and ten feet wide. The engineers piled the dirt onto rails and small tree trunks laid along each side of the covered way to create two parapets. The Federals deployed forty-two engineer troops as well as detailed infantry to work on the covered way. Constantly harassed by Confederate fire, they lost two killed and one wounded on the night of June 9.[8]

The Eighteenth Corps fortified strongly too. The trench was deep enough in Stannard's brigade to permit his men to walk without stooping.

Gunners of the battery near the 8th Maine fashioned coverings made of "heavy hewn planks that would stop musket balls," according to Daniel W. Sawtelle, and used them to cover the same embrasures they had tried to repair during the burial truce on June 7. The mantlets could be flipped out of the way to fire the guns, or they had small openings cut in them for the muzzle to stick through. Any digging that exposed the men to enemy fire was done at night, with other men ready to cover them if the Confederates detected the work and opened fire.[9]

In the Ninth Corps, the regiments earlier designated as acting engineers for each division did a much greater share of work than the other units. The 51st New York was the engineer regiment for Robert Potter's division. When it was told to dig rifle pits for skirmishers, George Washington Whitman devised a clever plan to protect his men. They used empty cracker boxes filled with dirt as temporary breastworks. Two boxes were given to each soldier, providing enough protection for them. Whitman's scheme fell apart only when the Confederates advanced a skirmish line and the regiment to his right fell back, forcing his troops to do likewise.[10]

The 35th Massachusetts, the engineer regiment for Crittenden's division, worked incessantly while the army was at Cold Harbor. It started a redoubt called Fort Fletcher (also known as Battery Fletcher), designed by Burnside's chief engineer, James St. Clair Morton. Located on the far left of the corps line, close to where Willcox's division connected to the Eighteenth Corps and near the Widow Thompson House, the engineers had begun the redoubt on June 5 as soon as Burnside's men filled the hole between Smith and Warren. Fort Fletcher had a square configuration with parapets 8 feet high and 28 feet wide at the base. The ditch was 8 feet deep and 15 feet wide. The fort was asymmetrical. Its front face was 72 feet long but the rear was 160 feet long. The right face measured 83 feet while the left face was 103 feet long. The work was also called "Red Fort" because of its impressive mounds of red clay.

The 35th Massachusetts continued its labors on the night of June 5, when the men dug communication trenches and a road connecting the lines with the rear. They built a bridge near Burnside's headquarters during the daylight hours of June 6, then rested for most of the night. Resuming work at 5:00 A.M. on June 7, they divided into two shifts to complete Fort Fletcher. An advance by Confederate skirmishers, probably the same probe that had stopped Whitman's construction of the skirmish pits, temporarily halted their work. They continued a bit later, adding a stockade to the fort. On June 8, they built a traverse from the right front corner of the work to the center of its rear face, then added a magazine that was six feet deep and twelve feet long, with five feet of protective earth on top of the roof. Capt. Jacob Roemer emplaced three guns of his 34th New York Battery on the night of June 8 and opened fire at noon on June 10, discharging a cannon every five minutes for the next eight hours. During the course of all this labor on the redoubt, the Massachusetts men unearthed several unexploded shells from McClellan's Peninsula campaign. They carefully disposed of them and continued working.

The fort was a departure from the norm at Cold Harbor, where the fieldworks were strong but not elaborate. This redoubt more closely resembled the many works later constructed at Petersburg that were similar to the semipermanent works that ringed Washington, D.C. Fort Fletcher had a log and post revetment, embrasures that were cut halfway down into the revetment, and a raised continuous platform for the three guns. The gunners stretched their shelter tent halves between the cannon to provide cover from the scorching sun.[11]

While the Massachusetts regiment spent much time on this fort, the other units of Burnside's Ninth Corps were nearly as busy improving their own fortifications. "The whole district became a maze of lines of earthworks, running in all directions, and difficult to thread even to us who saw it grow," wrote the historian of the 35th Massachusetts. "The owners of plantations thereabouts must have been astonished when they came to examine their premises after our departure."[12]

As early as June 1, Grant had given orders to fortify his forward depot of supplies at the White House on the Pamunkey River. Capt. George H. Mendell laid out the defenses, but the post commander, Brig. Gen. John J. Abercrombie, made slow progress building them due to a shortage of tools. Designed for a garrison of 1,400 troops, Abercrombie completed the White House defenses by June 10. They consisted of five redoubts mounting sixteen guns and were connected by infantry trenches. Both flanks of the line rested on the Pamunkey, and Abercrombie's troops constructed a short reserve line closer to the landing. They also dug two small redoubts for fifty men each at Cumberland Point, about five miles downstream.[13]

On the Fifth Corps sector at Cold Harbor, artillery chief Charles S. Wainwright was amazed at the extensive fortifying as he rode along the lines on June 9. Wainwright remembered his service in the Peninsula campaign and how McClellan had been publicly criticized for the digging he had done in 1862. "Were all the earth thrown out by his army on the Peninsula including that in front of Yorktown for road, approaches, and everything, made into one mound, and that thrown on this campaign into another, the former would be hardly visible in comparison. Yet Yorktown was a regular siege; the digging done after leaving there would barely make one night's work for this army." Wainwright wondered how history would characterize the Overland campaign. "*Spades* were said to be *trumps* with McClellan; what are they then with Grant?"[14]

This extensive digging was facilitated by the quality of earth at Cold Harbor. "No country could be more favorable for such work," thought Theodore Lyman of Meade's staff. It was easy for the men to scoop the dry, sandy soil with anything—tin plates, bits of board, their hands, "or canteens split in two, when shovels are scarce." The small pine trees were straight and easily chopped down by men experienced with the ax. Their trunks made good revetment for the parapets.[15]

An interesting drawing by Edwin Forbes purports to show Union troops constructing a line of works at some spot on the battlefield on June 1. It probably was not accurate, for it depicts troops working openly without fear of being hit by enemy fire. They built the revetment first by sinking the posts in the ground, then lining up the logs horizontally against them and digging a ditch in front. Forbes produced a neat picture of how earthworks ought to be made in ideal conditions, but there is hardly any sign of a ditch in the surviving earthwork remnants at Cold Harbor today. Most of these works were constructed under less-than-ideal conditions, with enemy troops within rifle range. It was too dangerous to dig a ditch in front of the parapet, even at night.[16]

An authentic relic of trench warfare at Cold Harbor is on display at the visitor's center of the Richmond National Battlefield Park. It is a canteen converted into an entrenching tool by splitting it halfway around from the spout. Both halves were then bent outward to form a *V*, as Lyman mentioned in the above quote. One can easily imagine how effectively it could be used to shovel loose, sandy soil.[17]

It is tempting to assume that this specimen of an improvised tool was used by a Confederate soldier, for the Rebels had a lot of trouble finding suitable entrenching tools at Cold Harbor. In fact, the Confederacy habitually had this difficulty throughout the war. Orders for tools began to filter into the Engineer Bureau at Richmond by May 30, involving modest numbers of spades, shovels, picks, and axes. John Gregg's brigade of Field's division had only three picks and three shovels available one night when it had to dig a new trench, and most of the men were forced to use their bayonets and tin cups.[18]

Digging in at Cold Harbor. The caption of this illustration indicates Federal digging on June 1, 1864, based on a wartime sketch by Edwin Forbes, but it is difficult to pinpoint the location. Note the revetment, the uniformly constructed parapet, the ditch, abatis, and living arrangements. (Johnson and Buel, Battles and Leaders, *4:224)*

But then the requisitions grew in number and size. Alfred L. Rives, filling in for the absent chief engineer, knew that his meager storehouse of tools could not satisfy all of these requests. He queried commanders to find out why they needed them, so he could set priorities, and urged Adj. Gen. Samuel Cooper to issue general orders encouraging field commanders to take special care of what tools they already possessed. Rives bemoaned the "carelessness & extravagance" with which many units used, abused, and lost their implements. He frantically sought new sources, authorizing an agent in Nassau to purchase 10,000 shovels and ship them through the blockade. Rives also contracted with the firm of A. J. Rahm and Company to make tools as fast as possible.[19]

The Federals had a greater supply of implements and they tended to account for them with more care. Hancock paid a lot of attention to this problem throughout the Overland campaign, often issuing circulars to division leaders cautioning them to gather entrenching tools and make sure they were packed in wagons whenever the corps was scheduled to move. Sgt. James M. Snook was in charge of three wagonloads of tools, which included sixty-eight axes, belonging to the Sixth Corps. Mostly their disbursement went smoothly, although Snook recorded that on one occasion soldiers took the tools "by force," refusing to sign receipts. Snook also assigned a detail to sharpen the axes at one point in the campaign. That the Federals took their accounting responsibilities seriously is attested to by William F. Smith, who had to borrow entrenching tools from the Army of the Potomac when his Eighteenth Corps arrived to take part in the Cold Harbor fighting. Smith immediately ordered 3,000 spades or shovels, 3,000 axes, and 600 picks from the quartermaster general of the U.S. Army, and they arrived before his troops were ordered away from Meade in mid-June. Smarting under Meade's frustration at sharing valuable resources with the Eighteenth Corps, Smith took pleasure in informing him that he could return every tool borrowed from the Army of the Potomac.[20]

Engineer officers and troops were assigned as evenly as possible across the front. Lt. Ranald S. Mackenzie and Company A of the U.S. Engineer Battalion were sent to the Second Corps. Mackenzie worked diligently until June 10, when he accepted command of the 2nd Connecticut Heavy Artillery. Lt. Charles W. Howell and Company B of the regular engineers went to the Sixth Corps, while Company C was assigned to the Ninth Corps and Company D to the Eighteenth Corps.[21]

Because of the relative size of the two, the U.S. Engineer Battalion could not offer as much help to the Army of the Potomac as did the 50th New York Engineers, which became the workhorse of Federal engineer units at Cold Harbor. The regiment was distributed along the line, with a company allotted to each division of the Sixth Corps, and various other detachments were given to other units.[22]

Wesley Brainerd's battalion of the 50th remained with Hancock's Second Corps. He agreed to go forward to a detached work some 250 feet ahead of the main line. The work detail had not extended it to right or left, and it was not yet connected to the main line. The only way to get there was to run across the open ground, and Brainerd accompanied an infantry officer who wanted his expert advice on what to do with the little fort. The bullets flew around the two officers as they sprinted ahead. The fort was well protected with a high parapet, and loopholes cut near the top offered a good view of all the ground nearby. This visit took place before the burial truce of June 7, and Brainerd saw dozens of blackened bodies littering the ground. When he had finished his survey and offered his advice, Brainerd steeled his nerves and sprinted back. He and the infantry officer managed to make it without injury.[23]

Most members of the 50th New York Engineers worked in less exposed places. They constructed covered ways, which often were as much as ten feet wide and eighteen inches deep. As when constructing parapets, the diggers laid down rails and poles to serve as the base of the earthen banks along both sides of the road, raising the level of protection for artillery units and men on foot who used the covered way.[24]

The Confederates fortified far less because their line had already been well developed by the time of the June 3 attack. Edward Porter Alexander later complained that the Rebel entrenchments at Cold Harbor had slight defects, especially where units connected with neighbors to right and left. Short gaps existed along the army's line, covered by the fire of Union sharpshooters. Alexander was in charge of Anderson's First Corps artillery and was also given responsibility for Hoke's artillery on June 5. He found that this division had even more gaps in its works than Anderson's corps. A lot of men were needlessly lost while sprinting along the weak portions of the line.[25]

It is unclear why these mistakes were not corrected, for there were more engineer officers on duty with the Army of Northern Virginia at Cold Harbor than previously in the campaign. Four additional engineers reported for duty by June 12. Martin L. Smith was quite busy inspecting the line, supervising the strengthening of works, and laying out additional redoubts. Jedediah Hotchkiss, Early's topographer, was dragged into the trenches to help Smith with this work. Hotchkiss sketched the line near the McGhee House and helped to decide where best to locate a fort. "It was very unpleasant working through the trenches," he reported. "The day was very warm." Hotchkiss also directed a portion of the 1st Confederate Engineers as it worked on another fort near the Stewart House.[26]

The 1st Confederate Engineers laid out lines by the book, stretching lengths of cord with pieces of white cotton cloth tied "a few feet" apart so the cord could be seen at night. A man placed every 20 feet and an engineer officer placed every 100 feet kept the cord straight. This line of soldiers stepped into the darkness while the officer in charge counted off the predetermined number of paces to reach the spot where the new work was to be located. A line of infantrymen then marched forward and lined up along the cord. As soon as they began to dig, the engineers took the cord somewhere else and started the process over again. "By this means the dangerous, irregular salient angles were avoided which came so near proving fatal to us in Spotsylvania," wrote Maj. W. W. Blackford.[27]

Blackford was wrong in assuming that such careful measures were taken at every part of the line, for there certainly were bulges in the Confederate position. None of them were pronounced and therefore offered no dangers like those associated with the Mule Shoe Salient at Spotsylvania. The 1st Engineers constructed a redoubt only 120 yards from the Federals near or at Edgar's Salient on the night of June 10. Lt. Henry Herbert Harris was one of the engineers in charge of this work. His contingent of the 1st Engineers marched to the area after sunset, stacked its arms, and waited for the tools to arrive. As soon as they were in hand, Harris's men approached the rear of the Confederate position through a hollow, crossed a secondary line of works, and marched an additional quarter mile to the first line. Here the redoubt was laid out just behind the trench. They worked all night and rested on June 11, repeating the routine for the next two days. The men were much exposed, but cloudy weather helped to conceal them on the night of June 11. The next night, the moon shone periodically, and Harris had to urge his men to keep down as much as possible. The engineers even altered the planned profile of the fort to "lessen the labor of building." The redoubt was nearly finished when the Cold Harbor phase of the Overland campaign came to an end on the night of June 12.[28]

Because he had to constantly walk along the works on a daily basis, Edward Porter Alexander remembered them as poorly made. He argued that in many places they were only three feet wide and two feet deep, and that the parapet was no more than three feet tall. These dimensions were barely enough to protect the men. Sharpshooters improved their stations by installing loopholes made of logs and sandbags. After the Federals pulled out to cross the James River, Alexander examined their fortifications and was amazed at "how enormous and elaborate they looked in comparison" to the Rebel works. He thought the Yankees had "anticipated attack from every point, except the skies, and fortified against them all." Harris disagreed. Although he found the Yankee fortifications held by Hancock's Second Corps south of Cold Harbor Road "much more numerous" than the Confederate works, they were not as well made. It was one of the differences, he concluded, "between offensive and defensive works."[29]

No matter which side made the better earthworks, there was constant activity at Cold Harbor. The lines were so close that sharpshooters could ply their trade without letup, and artillery boomed at all hours. The continual firing was very much like that of an active siege, in which one side tried to wear down the other. "The air was filled with whistling bullets," noted Brainerd, "yet not a man could be seen, nothing but a dull line of fresh yellowish earth from which during the day ascended a succession of little white clouds of smoke and at night, bright flashes of fire." On Hancock's part of the line, the firing sputtered around the clock. It reached "almost the quality of a battle," according to George D. Bowen of the 12th New Jersey, "and then gradually dropping off to a few shots but it never ceases." The Confederates on the Sixth Corps front had a habit of firing artillery at 9:00 P.M., hoping to disrupt a pullout by the Federals. Orders finally were issued to retaliate if local commanders thought it could be done without unduly exposing their men to return fire. Everyone agreed that it would.[30]

The constant sharpshooting was especially intense on some parts of the line. The Federals were only 125 yards away from Capt. Basil C. Manly's North Carolina Battery, of Col. Henry C. Cabell's Battalion of the First Corps. An unidentified gunner wrote a descriptive letter to Raleigh's *Daily Confederate* about the perils of serving on the line. Federal sharpshooters hit "any thing from the size of a quarter dollar, up to a man," he reported. "Some of our boys put a tin cup on the breastworks yesterday, and in less than a minute they put three holes through it." The Tar Heels retaliated by firing double charges of canister with fuses set at only one second, yet the hail of bullets so damaged a wheel of one Napoleon that it had to be replaced. Artillery rounds then knocked off a piece of the muzzle and broke the trail, forcing Manly to scrap the gun and ask for a replacement. When the piece was pulled to the rear, someone tipped the barrel down and several spent bullets rolled out. Nearly all the spokes on the other guns were also hit and had numerous nicks and gouges to prove it. Even the bronze tubes were nicked with bullet marks.[31]

More than Manly's guns suffered from the incessant fire. A military road leading through the woods up to Manly's position was repeatedly cleared of fallen limbs, shot off the trees by Federal artillery projectiles. Once or twice, the pioneers evacuated the road to escape the falling branches while they worked. On another part of the Confederate line, Robert Stiles noted that a shelter tent pitched behind Lt. Morgan Calloway's Georgia Battery had ninety bullet holes in it. This was in the center of the Confederate position, on Anderson's corps front. Farther south, on John C. Breckinridge's sector, the Federals also were close enough to deliver a constant round of bullets across no-man's-land. "Frequently hats were raised on the points of swords or bayonets," recalled Col. August Forsberg of the 51st Virginia, "and immediately perforated by a bullet. Several of my men paid the penalty of their lives for unnecessary exposure."[32]

Unexplained lulls often occurred during the firing. Brig. Gen. John R. Cooke's North Carolina brigade of Henry Heth's division relieved Alfred Colquitt's Georgia brigade south of Cold Harbor Road after dark on

June 8. The Tar Heels found the Federals unusually quiet the next day. Still, one-third of Cooke's men remained awake all night to be ready for trouble. When it looked like the Yankees were digging a new trench on June 10, orders went out to open fire and disrupt the work. This sparked a renewal of sharpshooting that lasted the rest of that day and the next. Colquitt's men relieved Cooke after dark on June 11, but the Georgians now had to contend with very annoying fire on what had once been a quiet sector of the line. Still, much of this sporadic action did little harm. Along Edwards's brigade line in the Sixth Corps, "fusillades of musketry rattle along the lines at night, inflicting no particular injury on either side, as both are firing from their intrenched positions."[33]

The intense skirmishing and the prolonged stay in the Cold Harbor trenches led Brig. Gen. William N. Pendleton, Lee's chief of artillery, to consider the use of unusual weapons. After seeing a newspaper notice about a "stink-shell," Pendleton asked the army's ordnance chief if some could be brought to the lines. He thought they might be delivered by tilting Napoleon howitzers so as to fire them like mortars. "The question is whether the explosion can be combined with suffocating effect of certain offensive gases, or whether apart from explosion such gases may not be emitted from a continuously burning composition as to render the vicinity of each falling shell intolerable. It seems at least worth a trial." Pendleton also believed that hand grenades would be useful at Cold Harbor, either for repelling a Federal assault or for clearing out a Yankee trench if the Confederates decided to launch an attack of their own. Lt. Col. Briscoe G. Baldwin, Lee's ordnance chief, forwarded the request to Richmond. There were 1,000 hand grenades in stock and another 1,000 were ordered in response to Pendleton's suggestion, but no stink balls were available. The ordnance bureau promised to have some made, but there is no evidence that either the grenades or this early experiment in chemical warfare ever made it to the trenches at Cold Harbor.[34]

The Second Corps had used Coehorn mortars at Cold Harbor to support the June 3 attack. Three days later, Smith requested twelve of the weapons for his Eighteenth Corps, and Meade, who had none available, ordered six to be shipped from the north. At close range, Federal gunners heard the shouts of surprise and pain when one of the shells exploded on target. The high-angled trajectory created a fascinating pyrotechnic display when the weapon was fired at night, for the projectile flew so slowly through the air that its fuse could easily be seen. Meade ordered twenty-two more Coehorns on June 9, and engineer John G. Barnard was so impressed by their usefulness that he urged Grant to ensure that an adequate supply was available.[35]

The Confederates were also impressed. August Forsberg noted that his men in the 51st Virginia paid little attention to artillery fire, as their parapet protected them from its effect, but they could not ignore these little mortars. The "sound of a bomb slowly, as it seems, rising in the air, has a most painful effect," Forsberg commented. "By force of imagination every man expects the bomb to fall right on him, and the anxiety and suspense, before the bomb falls, is intense."[36]

Edward Porter Alexander ordered some Coehorn mortars from the depot at Richmond and, in the meantime, improvised by converting a few howitzers into ersatz mortars. The guns were placed on skids so the tubes could be positioned at a high angle to lob shells into the Union trenches with a small powder charge. This worked well enough, but another mortar improvised by some men near Harris's Mississippi brigade was a failure. They burned out a hole at the end of a log and borrowed shells and powder from a battery. The charge detonated but there was no accuracy in the result, only a great deal of noise. The men stopped when the novelty wore off.[37]

As soon as Alexander's Coehorns arrived, the Confederates opened fire on the evening of June 11. Miles's brigade in Hancock's Second Corps received six to eight rounds, which wounded seven men. "Every few minutes a shell comes screaming over," reported Elisha Hunt Rhodes of the 2nd Rhode Island in the Sixth Corps, "and then we run to our holes. It is amusing as well as dangerous."[38]

Also dangerous was an outbreak of fighting on the far right flank of Meade's army. Potter had refused the right flank of his division, curving two regiments around the head of a branch draining into Matadequin Creek and posting the members of the 48th Pennsylvania as skirmishers on a hill near the Tucker and Bosher houses on the evening of June 5. It was important to hold this hill, because whoever occupied it could rake the rest of Potter's line with artillery fire. On the morning of June 6, Potter expressed his unease at holding the hill with only a skirmish line, suggesting that he push his main line forward and heavily fortify the rise. Before further action could be taken, the ever restless Early, with Lee's approval, probed into this area on the afternoon of June 6 and pushed back Potter's entire skirmish line. A brigade of John B. Gordon's division, perhaps Col. William R. Terry's Virginia unit, drove the 48th Pennsylvania from the hill and planted two batteries on the rise. Fearing that this might be the beginning of a more serious effort to turn Meade's right, Potter pushed his skirmishers forward that evening. They reoccupied a portion of the hill, but the Confederates evacuated the position and the rest of the Federal skirmish line they had earlier occupied, later that night.

Potter once again sent troops to secure the hill near Bosher's on the morning of June 7. By early afternoon, his men had nearly finished an infantry trench and were ready to dig artillery emplacements. The Federals also began to construct a military road leading through the woods toward the hill, and to build a corduroy road through a swampy area leading toward the rise. Before mid-afternoon, Brig. Gen. William Gaston Lewis's North Carolina brigade advanced toward the hill, and the 48th Pennsylvania evacuated the position as the officer in charge had no stomach for sacrificing his men. Potter was displeased, however, for "there was no excuse for not holding it. The surprise seems to have been complete, and shows that some one was to blame." The Ninth Corps had no better division commander than Potter, and he carefully weighed his options for retaking the position. It was too dangerous to attempt a frontal attack, for the rise was "a natural bastion." The Confederates did not honor the flag of truce raised at 6:00 P.M. on the evening of June 7 to allow the Federals to bury their dead. They continued to dig in on the rise, and there was little the Yankees could do to stop them. With Lewis's brigade holding the hill, and supported by another brigade, Potter believed that the Confederates could hold out against seven times the number of troops he had available in his depleted command. He asked that all of Crittenden's division be sent to support his projected counterattack.[39]

Potter began to place twenty field guns at the Bosher House, where they could bombard the hill, and planned a flank attack early on the morning of June 8. Fortunately for his men, dawn revealed that the Confederates had once again evacuated the hill. They apparently were surprised by the new battery Potter had erected during the night and withdrew in such a rush that they left their entrenching tools behind. Potter hurried John I. Curtin's brigade forward to hold the strategic spot, supported by James H. Ledlie's brigade. Burnside supported Potter's earlier suggestion to move his division line forward to incorporate the hill, but Potter now felt the strain. He complained that his command was stretched too thinly; he did not even feel comfortable running guns onto the hill for fear of not being able to protect them. Some of Potter's regiments had been on skirmish duty for forty-eight hours at a stretch, and his "whole force has been at work all night every night since they have been here, and are getting used up." Nevertheless, the division worked hard enough so that the hill was "thoroughly fortified," and by the evening of June 8 Potter felt confident of holding it.[40]

LIFE IN THE TRENCHES

The fortifications along the Cold Harbor lines were the fighting and living environment of the troops. The men were forced to have their meals, catch a few minutes of sleep, and even relieve themselves while using the protective cover of the parapets. All the while they were exposed to the burning sun and the hot, humid atmosphere of coastal Virginia. With the opposing lines so close to each other, everything had to be done with the enemy in mind. It was a cramped, harried existence, made endurable by the knowledge that each man had the opportunity to make life as stressful for the enemy as it was for himself.

The armies transformed the landscape at Cold Harbor, cutting thousands of trees and digging long lines across the countryside. "The whole plain occupied by our army was dug over," noted Surg. George T. Stevens of the 77th New York. "One was reminded, in riding over the plain, of the colonies of prairie dogs with their burrows and mounds." The troops stretched their shelter tent halves across the trenches to provide some protection from the sun. They dug short traverses into the rear of the trench to build fires for cooking. One man in the 12th New Jersey dug a cave and cooked underground, although it must have been a smoky hole indeed.[41]

It was difficult to get water up to the lines. The 12th New Jersey conquered this problem by loading one man with canteens and sending him to the rear. Often one or more of the canteens was hit by sniper fire on the way. The soldiers quickly learned to use the precious liquid only for drinking and postponed bathing indefinitely. Some units dug wells in ravines behind the lines. After going twenty feet, they usually found a thick, clay mud out of which they could squeeze some filthy water. For some men, this was all that was available. Ironically, when it happened to rain, the water problem was reversed. An all-night shower on June 6 turned the trenches into rivers. "Men lying in the ditch were mud all over," recorded Capt. Alexander B. Pattison of the 7th Indiana.[42]

The works were dug with an eye for comfort as well as security. Stannard's brigade of the Eighteenth Corps was on a higher bit of ground, approachable from the rear by a ravine. Stannard placed his quarters in a shelter pit deep enough so he could stand upright under a canvas cover. Cooks prepared rations at the rear and brought them forward through the

Federal bombproofs at Cold Harbor. The caption of this illustration indicates the date as June 3, 1864, and the location as the Second Corps Line, based on a wartime sketch by Edwin Forbes. The main line is in the background, the bombproofs open toward the rear. (Johnson and Buel, Battles and Leaders, *4:219)*

ravine, even though bullets constantly fell around the pit and the head of the ravine. Brigade pioneers hollowed out a shelter pit inside the ravine, measuring five by ten feet, for the medical staff of the 23rd Massachusetts. The pioneers dug down four feet on the deeper side and piled the dirt up on the opposite side to form a parapet. Asst. Surg. James A. Emmerton could stand upright in it without fear of being hit, and shelter tent halves fastened together provided a sunscreen. Emmerton thought it was a good hole, but he constantly smelled a foul odor which made him think they were near a grave from the 1862 Peninsula campaign.[43]

After June 6, soldiers everywhere dug bombproofs by the hundreds, usually at night because they had to expose themselves to get the job done. A typical bombproof was square, six feet tall and four feet wide. Pine logs constituted the revetment of the walls, and poles covered with tree branches offered shelter against the sun if the occupants decided not to cover the roof with dirt. They were comparatively safe but uncomfortable. George D. Bowen found the bombproofs extremely hot and slept very little in them.[44]

The trenches locked the men in their positions at such close ranges that they had to exercise extreme caution. Pvt. William A. Ketcham of the 13th Indiana recalled that "every morning before the cold gray dawn began to think of breaking, we were invariably drawn in line at the works with everything ready to resist an attack and there stood until the broken day would give us full warning of any movement." In the Sixth Corps, regiments rotated out of the front line every twenty-four hours. The troops rested as best they could in the second or third lines and returned to the first in forty-eight hours. On the Second Corps front, where available manpower was stretched to the limit, the 12th New Jersey had no opportunity to rotate out of the front line from June 3 through June 12. Even then, the Jerseymen were given only one day to rest and wash before starting out to cross the James River.[45]

With the opposing lines static and close together, the men often arranged impromptu truces to relieve the stress of trench life by temporarily removing the danger. Officers usually frowned on such undertakings, but they occurred nonetheless. A typical example took place on the Sixth Corps front on June 9. Both sides stopped firing without warning, then a few men slowly exposed themselves to see if it was a trick. When they realized it was safe, everyone stood up and many walked into no-man's-land. They chatted with the enemy while the rest lay atop the parapet to stretch. Col. Thomas D. Johns of the 7th Massachusetts, corps officer of the day, tried to put a stop to it. He walked into no-man's-land and told both Union and Confederate soldiers to go back or he would order the second line to open fire. The men reluctantly did so, but they yelled warnings to each other to "'get back under cover for we are going to shoot.'" Soon the firing resumed, but for a welcome moment there was peace and understanding on a little portion of the Cold Harbor battlefield.[46]

Edward Porter Alexander believed those days at Cold Harbor were among the worst Lee's army ever endured. The flat nature of the landscape provided no cover from enemy fire, except at the bottom of the trenches. "That kept the men crowded together & in constrained positions all day long," he remembered. The works were too small for this, but soldiers could not be spared to widen them or dig covered ways to the rear. The Confederates used "a few natural approaches," such as ravines and hollows, that happened to come up to the rear of the Rebel line, but there were no more than one of these conveniences for every mile. All of the food and ammunition had to be taken up to the line through these natural approaches, and all of the wounded and dead had to be carried out through them. Soldiers passed orders up and down the line by hand.[47]

Robert Stiles eloquently summarized the living conditions at Cold Harbor: "Thousands of men cramped up in a narrow trench, unable to go

Remnants of Confederate works at angle of line, north of Bloody Run, Cold Harbor. (Earl J. Hess)

out, or to get up, or to stretch or to stand, without danger to life and limb; unable to lie down, or to sleep, for lack of room and pressure of peril; night alarms, day attacks, hunger, thirst, supreme weariness, squalor, vermin, filth, disgusting odors everywhere; the weary night succeeded by the yet more weary day; the first glance over the way, at day dawn, bringing the sharpshooter's bullet singing past your ear or smashing through your skull, a man's life often exacted as the price of a cup of water from the spring."[48]

Neither Alexander nor Stiles exaggerated the unpleasant nature of life in the trenches, "cooped up in narrow pits," as Capt. Will Biggs of the 17th North Carolina put it. One-third of the men had to stay awake all night, and everyone prepared for an attack at 3:00 A.M. each morning. "So soon as daylight comes nearly everyone goes to bed again," reported John F. Sale of the 12th Virginia, "or rather, not to bed but to lie in every conceivable position in the trenches. The constant toil and excitement of the past month or so has told with a good deal of effect."[49]

It was bad enough to stay put in one place in the works, but Edward Porter Alexander had to constantly move through them to inspect his battery positions. He was forced to stoop over a great deal and carefully step

Remnants of Confederate trenches, north of Bloody Run, Cold Harbor. (Earl J. Hess)

over hundreds of men who lay or sat at the bottom of the trenches, in both daylight and dark. Ironically, he found it worse during the day, because the soldiers stretched blankets across the trench as a sunscreen. They used bayoneted guns as posts, securing the corners of the blankets in the hammers. This meant that the sunscreen was only three or four feet above the bottom of the trench, and four men crammed beneath it. "Imagine how thick four men with canteens, blankets, & haversacks must lie to one single blanket," Alexander insisted, "conceive that vermin were plentifully distributed in the army, conceive all the nuisances attendant upon great & crowded aggregations of humanity, & conceive that every once in a while a sick or freshly killed or wounded comrade is to be cared for, & you begin to have a mental picture of the Cold Harbor trenches."[50]

Conditions were far better for officers. John Gregg, commander of the Texas and Arkansas brigade in Anderson's corps, had his headquarters in a hole dug 3 feet deep and 4 by 8 feet in dimension. It was located only 20 feet behind the trench, more than enough to distance him from the fetid works, although a small communication trench connected the two excavations. Gregg placed his headquarters at the head of a shallow ravine that stretched 300 yards to the rear and emptied into a small stream. It was safe and easy to walk upright through most of the ravine toward the line, until one reached a point about 50 yards from Gregg's headquarters. Here one's head began to appear above the Confederate parapet, and then he had to crawl the rest of the way on hands and knees.[51]

Federal engineers also found it difficult to do their job along the line, exposed to both the discomforts of the trench and the ever-present danger of enemy sharpshooters. Cpl. Gilbert Thompson of the U.S. Engineer Battalion took two men to survey the Second and Sixth Corps front "with compass and chain." It was "tedious and dangerous work" because the trench was "broken up by traverses and bombproofs." Confederate sharpshooters often fired at the crew, aiming at their hats which appeared just above the parapet. This usually threw a shower of sand into Thompson's face, for the bullets often hit the top of the parapet.[52]

Hancock's Second Corps probably suffered more losses than other units in the Army of the Potomac due to its proximity to the enemy. Gibbon's Second Division alone had 280 casualties from sniping and artillery fire during the period June 3–12. Gibbon ably expressed his men's trials by writing that they were "confined for ten days in narrow trenches with no water to wash with and none to drink except that obtained at the risk of losing life." They were "unable to obey a call of nature or to stand erect without forming targets for hostile bullets, and subjected to the heat and dust of midsummer, which soon produced sickness and vermin." Gibbon concluded that this was "the most trying period of this most trying campaign."[53]

Thomas A. Smyth recorded the discomfort of one of Gibbon's brigade commanders in the Cold Harbor trenches. The night of June 6 was the "most disagreeable one I have spent since I occupied the front line." Initially he could not sleep, and when he finally dozed off Confederate skirmish fire woke him. It continued sporadically all night. Smyth also visited his own sharpshooters at 9:00 P.M., 1:00 A.M., and 3:00 A.M., and inspected the pioneers who were working all night under cover of darkness. He was dozing when another bullet sailed through his tent early on the morning of June 7. "My Head Quarters is not a very pleasant place this morning for nervous young men," he playfully wrote. "I don't think I will be troubled much with visits from the division staff."[54]

Frank Wheaton's brigade in the Sixth Corps constructed works good enough by June 7 so that the men "were tolerably protected against the enemy's artillery fire," but only "by hard and constant labor night and day, and the building of traverses, covered ways, & c." From that point, Neill issued orders to hold the two front lines of his division while bivouacking the rest of the division in the rear "for rest and sanitary purposes." But Wheaton found that even half a mile behind the lines, his men were hit by Confederate mortar fire, "and but little rest, comparatively, was enjoyed while remaining in the vicinity of Cold Harbor."[55]

The crowded living conditions and the constant sniping and artillery fire strained but did not break the morale of Lee's men. Many of them began to yearn for a pitched battle in the open, "for this kind of fighting is almost using us up," reported Will Biggs to his sister in a letter of June 5. After three weeks in the trenches, Biggs's 17th North Carolina was allowed two days of rest in the rear. It was none too soon for Biggs, whose duties as captain of Company A added more stress to his time in the trenches. "I was completely broken down in body & almost in spirit," he admitted. Eighteen men of his company, many hit in the head, had been either killed or wounded since the opening of the spring campaign. Biggs took it all personally. "It almost breaks my heart to see my men fall so fast & sudden," he wrote. "I have seen them all die." Biggs admitted that the death of his brother Arch was the worst to bear. Shot in the temple by a sharpshooter soon after the repulse of the Federal attack on June 3, Arch was dead by the time Will could bend down and cradle him in his arms. His death "completely prostrated me for several days," he informed his sister on June 12, "and I have not recovered from it yet." Arch was "the only *friend* & *comrade* I had in the company. So now I am alone, none to associate or commune with. Since his death I lost much of my interest in the company and were it not for devotion to me, & unwillingness to part, I should most certainly try to get another position, more agreeable to my feelings."[56]

Biggs suffered an unusually severe loss at Cold Harbor. Most of his comrades, on the other hand, managed to hold up well in the trenches, despite the discomfort and fatigue. Morale among Lee's soldiers remained quite high as a rule during the early part of June, and rations actually seemed to increase now that the army remained stationary and close to the Confederate capital. Every other day ample supplies of coffee, onions, sugar, bread, and a pound of meat came up to the 27th North Carolina in Cooke's brigade of Heth's division. Members of the Rockbridge Artillery, a Virginia battery in the Third Corps, had so much to eat that they consented to donate one day's ration out of six to feed the poor people of Richmond. Potatoes, vinegar, bacon, cornmeal, and sometimes sugar or molasses rounded out the bill of fare in the Rebel trenches.[57]

The majority of Confederates at Cold Harbor had no fear of the Yankees or their tactics. "I think that Mr. Grant has got tired a charging our men and has gone to work with the spade," mused Joseph F. Shaner of the Rockbridge Artillery. "[M]aybe he thinks that he can dig in to Richmond as he did at Vicksburg but he has not got gen Pemberton to contend with here but he has got Mas Robert to contend with. he may dig as much as he pleases and when he is done he will find out that he will have to go back to Washington city with what few men that he will have left." There had been a general feeling in Lee's army that Grant's western victories, as Shaner indicated, had been facilitated by poor Confederate generalship. "That he was bold and aggressive, we all knew," remembered Evander M. Law, "but we believed that it was the boldness and aggressiveness that arise from the consciousness of strength." Yet they "were not prepared for the unparalleled stubbornness and tenacity with which he persisted in his attacks under the fearful losses which his army sustained at the Wilderness and at Spotsylvania." Grant's apparently artless movements to Cold Harbor succeeded only because "he relied almost entirely upon the brute force of numbers for success."[58]

Most Confederates seemed to share these assessments of Grant's generalship and personality. They did not fear him because, as Edward Hitchcock McDonald put it, "his obstinacy is accompanied with so much blind fool hardiness as to make him easily to be handled by the cool strategy of 'massa Bob.'" Yet some Rebels recognized that Grant's methods applied Union strength against Lee's weakness. They understood that there was to be no relief from Grant's relentless pressure until they were ground down or until Lee could devise some strategy to convince him to give up, as he had done with all the other commanders of the Yankee army.[59]

Morale on the Union side of the battlefield was subdued but not broken. "The feeling of the troops is good," contended Hazard Stevens, "but nobody sees 'daylight' yet awhile. Our difficulties have just commenced." One of the most upbeat reports came from John Grierson of the 14th New York Heavy Artillery. "I have great confidence in Gen. Grant," he reported home, "the army has settled down to the real issue, namely *get* all we can and *hold* what we get." But Grierson was virtually alone in expressing such confidence in future operations.[60]

Food supplies were adequate. In the Fifth Corps, a lot of hardtack, beef or pork twice a week, and coffee sweetened with sugar was the fare. Now that the army was near the swampy Chickahominy River, more Federals reported sick. Typhoid, malaria, intermittent fever, diarrhea, and dysentery were the chief causes. The exhausted condition of the men made them more susceptible to disease, and the new recruits and draftees who were beginning to arrive in large numbers also were vulnerable to the unhealthy conditions of the Cold Harbor works. Scurvy began to appear in the Ninth Corps, according to one report, prompting the army's commissary to issue beans, dried fruit, and curry as antidotes.[61]

The losses thus far in the Overland campaign deeply impaired the efficiency of the Army of the Potomac. John Gibbon carefully documented the casualties in his Second Corps division. It had lost 3,562 men from May 5 through May 31, but 366 of those losses were suffered by the Fourth Brigade, which had joined his command on May 17. Counting the original members of the division, his losses totaled 3,196, or 47 percent of the total. The large number of casualties was bad enough, Gibbon noted, but the most valuable men tended to be shot first. "These always [had] remained in the ranks and did the fighting and by their example and spirit stimulated the rest. When they were gone the number who served as leaders was fearfully reduced and this, of course, immensely to the detriment of the fighting force of the division."[62]

Hancock's Second Corps suffered most in this regard, primarily due to the bloodletting of May 12 at Spotsylvania. Francis Walker, an officer on the Second Corps staff, recorded Hancock's losses from June 2 through June 12 as 3,510 men. Division commander Francis C. Barlow openly admitted that the losses in his command, and the dampening of morale that resulted, severely limited his ability to perform on the battlefield. "The men feel just at present a great horror and dread of attacking earth-works again," he informed Walker on June 6, "and the unusual loss of officers, which leaves regiments in command of lieutenants, and brigades in command of inexperienced officers, leaves us in a very unfavorable condition for such enterprises." Barlow made it clear that frontal attacks were not an option for the time being. "I think the men are so wearied and worn out by the harassing labors of the past week that they are wanting in the spirit and dash necessary for successful assaults."[63]

Worse than exhaustion, the good men began to develop a creeping feeling that they were not being supported by the replacements. The more recruits and draftees who came to Cold Harbor, the deeper this feeling grew. Frank Wilkeson was a young recruit who saw his first fighting at the Wilderness as an artilleryman in the Second Corps. He first noticed large numbers of draftees and what he called "bounty men" at Cold Harbor, and invariably they were the worst soldiers. They gathered by the hundreds to the rear of the army where they could safely make coffee and pretend that they were on detached duty. "These worthless creatures weakened every battle line they were forced into," he concluded. Knowledge of this could hardly fail to affect the spirit of the army.[64]

PREPARING TO CROSS THE JAMES RIVER

The man most responsible for shaping the course of the campaign had no intention of keeping Meade's army tied down at Cold Harbor. Grant had decided pretty early that siege operations would not be feasible after all. "My idea from the start has been to beat Lee's Army, if possible, North of Richmond," he informed Halleck, "then after destroying his lines of communication North of the James river to transfer the Army to the South side and besiege Lee in Richmond, or follow him South if he should retreat." In a general way, this was an accurate description of the Overland campaign thus far. Grant was persuaded that Lee's adoption of the defensive indicated that he feared the destruction of his army if he dared to attack. This encouraged Grant's sanguine spirit, but it also offered a dilemma. Grant had become convinced that frontal attacks against Lee's fortifications had to be limited. "Without a greater sacrifice of human life than I am willing to make all cannot be accomplished that I had designed outside of the City," he wrote.[65]

If Lee would not come out to meet him and further Union attacks were unprofitable, then Grant had to resort to movement once again. While the cavalry rode west to tear up the Virginia Central Railroad, the Army of the Potomac would cross the James just east of the mouth of the Chickahominy River and cut Lee's supply lines coming from the south and southwest by capturing Petersburg. Grant's grand strategy was sound, but he did not understand the morale of Meade's men. He informed Halleck that the Rebels felt comfortable only when protected by heavy fieldworks, but the Yankees were confident in their ability to fight in the open, whether on the attack or the defense. "All the fight, except defensive and behind breast works, is taken out of Lee's army," Grant wrote a friend. "Unless my next move brings on a battle the balance of the campaign will settle down to a siege."[66]

Lee continued to express frustration at his inability to take the offensive. The Federal works at Cold Harbor were far too strong to offer such an opportunity. "I shall make every effort to strike at him," Lee assured President Davis, "but fear that his usual precautions will prevent unless I

undertake to assault his fortifications which I desire to avoid if possible."
He was more emphatic when addressing his corps commanders:

> The time has arrived, in my opinion, when something more is nec-
> essary than adhering to lines and defensive positions. We shall be
> obliged to go out and prevent the enemy from selecting such positions
> as he chooses. If he is allowed to continue that course we shall at last
> be obliged to take refuge behind the works of Richmond and stand
> a siege, which would be but a work of time. You must be prepared to
> fight him in the field, to prevent him taking positions such as he de-
> sires, and I expect the co-operation of all the corps commanders in the
> course which necessity now will oblige us to pursue.[67]

Conclusion

The Overland campaign witnessed a major shift in the use of field fortifications in the eastern theater. Although fieldworks had always been
a feature of campaigning, the level at which the Army of the Potomac
and the Army of Northern Virginia relied on them was sporadic. During
some campaigns, such as that on the Peninsula, both sides relied fairly
heavily on field defenses. At Second Manassas and Antietam, specially
constructed fieldworks were conspicuous by their absence, whereas soldiers in both armies partially fortified their lines at Fredericksburg, Chancellorsville, and Gettysburg. In some cases, like the Confederate Warwick
Line at Yorktown and Maj. Gen. Joseph Hooker's fortified bridgehead
at Chancellorsville, the fieldworks were impressive examples of military
engineering.

Union and Confederate soldiers both tended to dig in after a sharp
battle had been fought and their enemy was still within striking distance.
The shock of combat drove the officers and men to erect some sort of
artificial defense. This happened after Big Bethel, First Manassas, Fredericksburg, and Gettysburg. At Mine Run, for the first time in its history,
Lee's army constructed a line of fieldworks covering its entire front just
before engaging the enemy. These works were adorned with artillery emplacements, headlogs, traverses, and obstacles in front to trip an attacker.
The strength of these defenses altered the course of the Mine Run campaign, discouraging the Federals from launching a planned offensive and
creating a tactical stalemate in which Union commanders felt they had no
choice but to break contact and retire from the field.[1]

With Grant's introduction of continuous contact in the spring of 1864,
the result was a more intense reliance on field defenses by both armies.
The battle of the Wilderness was the pivot on which this change in grand
tactics took place. Both sides only partially dug in on May 5, and half the
combat that day occurred without the aid of field defenses. Little more
fortifying was done on May 6. Most of the extensive fieldworks that now

adorn the Wilderness battlefield were constructed on the night of May 6 and all day of May 7, after the fighting ended, as both sides expected a renewal of action. Most of these defenses were modest in size and strength. When Grant moved the scene of operations to Spotsylvania, the Confederates fully accepted the utility of digging in before any fighting began. As a result, both armies took a leap into trench warfare. Lee's men built their strongest and most sophisticated line of field fortifications to date, and Grant tried to find a way to crack it open or to outflank it. The Spotsylvania phase of the Overland campaign became bogged down in trench warfare, intensified by the wooded terrain, bad weather, and repeated attacks across the same ground at Laurel Hill and in the area of the Mule Shoe Salient. The near destruction of Lee's army at the salient on May 12 haunted the Confederate commander for weeks after, and the losses suffered here began a decline in the combat effectiveness of the Union Second Corps. All of this occurred because Lee embraced the defensive with heavy fieldworks and Grant became fixated on breaking Lee's army behind its entrenchments. Spotsylvania was a battle ruled by the influence of field fortifications.

Grant ended his attacks at Spotsylvania before he wrecked either his own or Lee's armies and once again moved south, to the North Anna River. Although there were no general attacks here, the North Anna phase of the Overland campaign was similarly dominated by Lee's earthworks. The famous inverted *V* stymied Union offensive hopes just as surely as the Rebel fieldworks had done at Mine Run.

Cold Harbor was for Grant a reversion to the Spotsylvania mode of operations, a series of flawed attacks on various parts of the Confederate line. In addition, there was one poorly planned general assault all along the Rebel line on June 3. No attack came as close as the Second Corps had done on May 12 to simulating a success. Exhausted, the Army of the Potomac entered a new phase of its operations on June 3, seamlessly switching from attacks to something like siege warfare. The Federals dug parallels and started a mine while building extensive works and bombproof shelters behind their position. This was not a siege in the classic sense, for Lee's army could not be cut off from the outside world. But it did represent the employment of certain siege techniques in a field engagement where the opposing lines had become static, impervious to penetration, and difficult to outflank. The same situation applied later outside Petersburg.

Thus the Overland campaign fell into two distinct phases. The first, beginning with May 5 at the Wilderness and extending to the morning of June 3 at Cold Harbor, was characterized by full-scale, traditional attacks on fortified positions. As on May 12 at Spotsylvania, some were massive and bloody affairs, but none produced a decisive victory for the attackers, who were unable to exploit their limited breakthroughs. At the Wilderness, on May 6, John B. Gordon mashed the right end of the Sixth Corps Line because it was inadequately refused and fortified, but he could go no farther. Micah Jenkins's brigade also took a section of the Second Corps works along Brock Road that evening due to a fire that forced the Federals to retire, but the South Carolinians were later driven out before they could exploit their advantage. That was a common failing of three Union attacks that achieved limited penetration of the Confederate line at Spotsylvania — J. H. Hobart Ward's on May 10 at Laurel Hill, Emory Upton's on May 10 at the west face of the Mule Shoe Salient, and Winfield Hancock's at the tip of the salient on May 12. None of these initially promising assaults could acquire more than a tenuous hold on the Confederate works.

In the Bermuda Hundred campaign, Butler's Army of the James occupied a Confederate fieldwork that essentially had been abandoned by the Rebels and was, in turn, driven out of it a couple of days later. At the North Anna, the only Confederate earthwork taken in battle was Henagan's Redoubt, isolated and held by an outnumbered garrison. And at Cold Harbor, there were two limited penetrations of Lee's line. One occurred on June 1, when elements of the Sixth Corps temporarily threw the Confederates into disarray at Bloody Run. On June 3, Second Corps troops temporarily captured a salient held by a battalion of John C. Breckinridge's division. None of these advantages could be pushed to greater levels of success.

Ironically, the first phase of the Overland campaign also witnessed several open field attacks with no fortifications involved. A number of such actions took place on both days at the Wilderness. Later, Ewell's reconnaissance in force on May 19 at Spotsylvania, part of Warren's Fifth Corps fight with Wilcox at Jericho Mills on the south side of the North Anna River, and Early's attack on Warren at Bethesda Church on May 30 at Cold Harbor also took place without earthworks. Several attacks during the Bermuda Hundred campaign were launched against unfortified positions.

The second phase of the Overland campaign started immediately after the failed attack of June 3 and involved less costly methods. The use of siege approaches placed this part of the Cold Harbor battle in the same category of other campaigns such as Sevastopol in the Crimean War of 1854–55, Vicksburg, Port Hudson, and the operations against Battery Wagner on Morris Island in 1863 and Petersburg in 1864.

The transition from the first phase of the Overland campaign, with its dramatic assaults, to the siege approaches of the second phase was not planned by either Grant or Meade. There had been many failed attacks on Confederate fortified positions before June 3; the key difference that day was that the Federals did not fall back when their attack ended. They fell down instead and immediately dug in as close as forty yards from the enemy. This inspired Grant to attempt siege approaches to cover the remaining ground that separated the two armies.

It was a short-lived experiment, however, for Grant soon wearied of the time and effort needed to approach the Confederate works. Moreover, the possibility of successfully conducting these approaches seemed dim. Unlike Vicksburg, Grant had an alternative to siege operations at Cold Harbor. He launched a flanking maneuver, on a grander scale than before, and nearly won a huge advantage over Lee in his attempt to take Petersburg by traditional assaults on June 15–18. With the heartbreaking failure of those attacks, he once again settled into a combination of siege approaches and flanking maneuvers at Petersburg, which stretched into the next ten months. Throughout all of this time, the use of fieldworks dominated operations at Petersburg, as they had done at Spotsylvania, North Anna, and Cold Harbor.

ATTRITION

The extensive use of earthworks contributed to a campaign of attrition that developed during the advance from the Rapidan to the James. But attrition was a double-edged sword: it weakened both armies in different ways. Lee lost 36,000 men, half of his strength, while putting out of action 64,000 Federals. Yet Grant's casualty rate was the same as Lee's. Those Federals shot down on the bloody road from the Wilderness to Petersburg could not be replaced by men of equal quality. Union replacements—never as plentiful as previous historians have thought—were largely inexperienced heavy artillerymen, ineffectual draftees, or poorly motivated bounty men. As the Yankees retained the offensive, Grant's army thus had greater difficulty maintaining its fighting edge than did Lee's.[2]

In fact, the bloody trench warfare of the Overland campaign reduced the operational effectiveness of the Army of the Potomac to a sometimes dangerously low level. The ability to command and control was seriously eroded on the corps and division levels, and there are signs of a refusal to fight among some units at Cold Harbor. The problems associated with exploiting a penetration of a fortified line were never solved. No time was available to rest between engagements, and too many fallen officers were replaced by men who had no chance to learn their jobs before the next fight. Grant fought Meade's army to a frazzle in six weeks of unrelenting pressure.

John Gibbon's division of the Second Corps lost 7,970 men in May and June. That was 72 percent of its total strength. From May 4 to July 31, Gibbon's four brigades went through seventeen commanders; nine of them were killed or wounded. His thirty regiments lost forty commanders as well. The average casualty rate for each division of Meade's army was less than half Gibbon's rate. "The effect of these losses and the general wear and tear upon the efficiency of the troops was, to me, very marked," Gibbon later recalled, "and was the subject of general comment throughout the army. . . . The strain on the human system, both mental and physical, was of the severest."[3]

The entire Second Corps was slightly less affected by the campaign. It lost 20 brigade leaders, 100 regimental commanders, and 17,000 troops. They were the corps's best men as well, unmatched in their depth of experience and loyalty to corps pride. "We cannot replace the officers lost with experienced men," Meade reported, "and there is no time for reorganization or careful selection."[4]

The new recruits were a decidedly inferior lot, according to all veterans of the army. "Some were wounded and some killed," remembered Josiah Fitch Murphey of the 20th Massachusetts, "and we had not had time to even learn their names." Adding so many raw men to a small remnant of exhausted veterans was like "deluging a drop of spirits with a bucket of water," according to Gibbon.[5]

The recruits added much needed bulk to an army that was shorn of 64,000 men in six weeks of fighting, but they could not increase its punching power. The older men who survived the punishing campaign ran out of steam and developed an overwhelming respect for field fortifications. "One thing is certain," reported Hazard Stevens, a Sixth Corps staff officer, "our men are not so ready to charge earth works as they were, so many of the best officers and men have been killed, that the remainder are rather adverse to rushing in blindly." Fifth Corps artillery chief Charles S. Wainwright put it less daintily: "As to getting the men up to assaulting point, I do not believe it possible[;] never has the Army of the Potomac been so demoralized as at this time. . . . Grant has used the army up, and will now have to wait until its morale is restored before he can do anything."[6]

As an officer of the 20th Maine later put it, the "elasticity of the men was gone." The world wars of the twentieth century produced thousands of similarly worn-out soldiers. "I think there is a kind of heroism in the endurance," thought Oliver Wendell Holmes Jr., "in the endurance I was going to say of the men—I tell you many a man has gone crazy since this campaign began from the terrible pressure on mind & body."[7]

Many soldiers bitterly resented that their comrades were sacrificed, and their own lives were imperiled, apparently for nothing. "The feeling here in the army is that we have been absolutely butchered," reported a Ninth Corps officer named Stephen Minot Weld. "In the Second Corps the feeling is so strong that the men say they will not charge any more works." Weld confessed that "it is discouraging" to see so many men who were "time and again recklessly and wickedly placed . . . in slaughter-pens." Incompetent officers, as high as corps and army level in his view, were responsible. "We can't afford to make many more such bloody attacks as we have been doing," he concluded. "The enemy will outnumber us if we do so."[8]

I KNEW IT WAS THE ONLY WAY

The man most responsible for the conduct of the Overland campaign seemed unfazed by the bloodletting, and he seldom acknowledged the depth of disappointment brought on by the many failed attacks. Grant kept whatever emotions the campaign elicited to himself. He left behind scant evidence that he understood how exhausted and dispirited his soldiers had become by mid-June.

Grumble and complain as they might, Grant's soldiers developed a grudging respect for him. Frank Wilkeson, the Second Corps gunner, heard many and loud complaints about the tactics of the Overland campaign. He also heard many men compare Grant to George B. McClellan, the man who created the Army of the Potomac and led it for more than a year. The men had real affection for McClellan but seldom gave him credit for the kind of military talent needed to defeat Lee. They hated Grant's waste of manpower but liked his combative tenacity. They believed that he would eventually win the war with it.[9]

Grant was certainly aware of the comments on his style of generalship. On April 16, 1866, after dining at the home of Senator William Sprague of Rhode Island, he offered his dinner partners some rare thoughts about the bloody campaign that was nearly two years in the past. "My object in war was to exhaust Lee's army," Grant said. "I was obliged to sacrifice men to do it. I have been called a butcher. Well, I never spared men's lives to gain an object; but then I gained it and I knew it was the only way."[10]

Grant may well have been right in asserting that the mode of operations he employed from the Wilderness to Cold Harbor was the "only way" to defeat Lee. The foundation of his method was to seize the strategic and grand tactical initiative and never let it go. This was the primary reason for his concept of continuous contact. The observer should not be fooled by the gory assaults that riveted everyone's attention from Spotsylvania onward—the Overland campaign was at heart a campaign of maneuver. In it, Grant reversed a two-year trend in operations in the east. Lee had saved Richmond in June 1862 by pushing the Army of the Potomac away from the gates of the Confederate capital in the Seven Days campaign. Then he enlarged the theater of operations by driving northward to Second Manassas, some sixty miles north of the city. He further enlarged the theater of operations by invading the border state of Maryland. Defeated in this attempt, he nevertheless maintained the theater of operations along the line of the Rapidan and Rappahannock rivers from October 1862 through May 1864, with another failed attempt to raid Union-held territory during June–July 1863. Whether acting on the defensive or the offensive, Lee had managed to either hold or decisively influence the strategic offensive for two years, and in the process he kept the fighting as far from Richmond as possible.

Grant has never been given full credit for reversing this remarkable Confederate achievement. Many observers branded his Overland campaign as a failure because he did not destroy Lee's army, or they bemoaned the heavy loss of life as a price too high to pay for the incremental advantage Grant gained by the time his army dug in at Cold Harbor. They often noted that McClellan had gotten to this point at the apex of his Peninsula campaign with far fewer casualties in 1862.[11]

But these criticisms were shortsighted. Grant's most significant achievement in the Overland campaign was not in capturing territory, or in positioning his army close to Richmond, or in reducing the fighting strength of the Army of Northern Virginia by 50 percent; rather, it lay in robbing Lee of the opportunity to launch large-scale offensives against the Army of the Potomac. In laying claim to the strategic initiative, Grant won an important physical and emotional victory over Lee, and he did it with fewer losses than his predecessors had suffered in attempting the same goal.

Lee lost 28,500 men in the Seven Days and Second Manassas, the two campaigns that enabled him to seize and keep the strategic initiative in 1862. Federal efforts to wrest it back from him involved 32,200 losses suffered at Fredericksburg, Chancellorsville, and Mine Run—to name the most important offensive battles. The Federals also suffered 50,400 losses in resisting Lee's attempts to expand the theater of operations onto Northern-controlled territory in Maryland (1862) and Pennsylvania (1863). These invasions, or raids, grew out of the fact that Union commanders had lost control of the strategic initiative, and their casualties were a heavy price to pay for that loss.

In other words, McClellan, Burnside, Hooker, and Meade experienced a grand total of 82,600 casualties while dealing with Lee's control of the strategic initiative in the eastern theater over the course of nearly two years. Grant reversed this fundamental condition in six weeks while suffering 64,000 casualties. Most important, he did not give up the strategic initiative and thereby brought the war to an end. The Overland campaign was as much a watershed in the strategic course of the Civil War as the Seven Days. It is ironic that Grant's losses should obscure these facts among observers and even a lot of modern-day historians, for it is difficult to see how the war in the east could have ended any other way.

Field fortifications played a large role in Grant's success, although there is no evidence that he or any other high-ranking commander planned to use them. Middle-ranking commanders and the common soldiers were primarily responsible for their employment, spurred on by the need for protection as both armies remained within striking distance of each other for six weeks of unrelenting contact. The Federals used field defenses to remain within close range of Lee's army without exposing themselves to a surprise counterattack, and to serve as a base from which to extend their reach around Lee's right flank. The Overland drive constituted a superb example of how field fortifications could be used to sustain a long, difficult offensive against a dangerous enemy.

Grant never fully appreciated the role of field defenses in his campaign. He consistently saw Lee's assumption of a defensive posture behind earthworks as a sign that the Rebel commander was morally beaten. He easily believed the testimony of deserters and prisoners of war about the low state of morale among Lee's men. The fact that Grant ordered hastily prepared assaults against strong earthworks also indicates that he did not fully understand the defensive power of field fortifications until after the

Overland campaign ended. On June 21, three days after the depressing failure of Meade's attacks on the Petersburg lines, Grant warned the army commander not to butt his head against Confederate works as he sent the Second and Sixth Corps on an offensive sweep to get around Lee's right flank.[12]

In all of his conversations and public expressions, Grant spoke of the Overland campaign as a contest of wills first and a tactical operation second. Assistant Secretary of War Charles A. Dana, who had gained acceptance into Grant's circle while observing his operations during the Vicksburg and Chattanooga campaigns, believed that Grant respected Lee's military ability as a defensive fighter. The general always praised Lee's handling of his army at Antietam and Fredericksburg. But Grant thought little of Lee as an offensive fighter, believing that he had "recklessly laid himself open to ruin" at Chancellorsville. Grant had to force Lee onto the defensive in 1864, and he had to accept the fact that the Confederates employed heavy fieldworks to aid their defensive efforts. He created an air of unpredictability in launching his attacks, which helped to keep Lee on the defensive. Grant would have preferred to fight Lee in the open, as he consistently told Dana and his superiors in Washington, D.C., but he also knew that he had to fight his opponent wherever Lee chose to stand, even behind heavy fieldworks.[13]

The situation was quite different in Georgia during May and June 1864, although the extensive use of field fortifications was a common theme in both campaigns. "Grant's Battles in Virginia are fearful but necessary," Gen. William T. Sherman wrote to his wife on May 20, as news of Spotsylvania came filtering through the communications network. "Immense slaughter is necessary to prove that our northern armies can & will fight. That once impressed will be an immense moral power." Sherman recognized that Grant could go too far and lose the confidence of his men, but he tried to convince Secretary of War Edwin M. Stanton that the moral force to be gained by a vigorous offensive was worth the loss of life. It would "do more good than to capture Richmond." In fact, Sherman was convinced that "[t]his moral result must precede all mere advantages of strategic movements, and this is what Grant is doing." By mid-June, he was conscious of pressing his opponent in Georgia hard enough to prevent the Confederates from sending reinforcements to Virginia. "In the mean time Grant will give Lee all the fighting he wants until he [is] sick of the word." But by the end of June, after Cold Harbor, even Sherman hesitated at the heavy cost of Grant's operational methods. "[A]t this distance from home," he quietly assured his wife, "we cannot afford the losses of such terrible assaults as Grant has made."[14]

Sherman fully understood the morale advantage that Grant was trying so hard to achieve over Lee. In his memoirs, he discussed how it entered his thinking while planning the march through the Carolinas. "It was to me manifest that the soldiers and people of the South entertained an undue fear of our Western men, and, like children, they had invented such ghostlike stories of our prowess in Georgia, that they were scared by their own inventions. Still, this was a power, and I intended to utilize it." He expressed the psychological dimension of military operations in a way that Grant probably would have supported. "My aim then was, to whip the rebels, to humble their pride, to follow them to their inmost recesses, and make them fear and dread us."[15]

TRENCH WARFARE

The trend toward greater reliance on field fortifications saw full fruit in the Overland campaign. "The pick, the shovel, and the axe did not really come into general use on the Union side until it was forced upon us by seeing what a few hours' work by every man in the enemy's ranks could do towards converting slight natural advantages into wellnigh impregnable positions," remembered Edwin C. Mason, an officer in the Sixth Corps. Pvt. Wilbur Fisk of the Vermont brigade noted that Confederate defensive power was increased at least three times by fieldworks, "and unless we can oblige them to fight us in open field, or, what would be better, make them attack us in our breastworks, they have us to a serious disadvantage."[16]

While the Confederates took the lead in the increased use of and rapidly growing design of field fortifications, with their array of traverses and obstacles, the Federals were forced to follow suit. The 109th New York in Orlando B. Willcox's division of the Ninth Corps initiated the construction of a new earthwork on twelve days of the Overland campaign—on average, about one day out of three. Yankee officers often commented in their official reports that their men were "throwing up an immense number of earth-works," or that "Intrenching, &c., was carried on mostly night and day."[17]

The source of this dependence on fieldworks by both armies has been a topic of debate. Brent Nosworthy has suggested that the high command of the Army of the Potomac might have determined to use them even before the Overland campaign began, but he bases this only on the fact that

Hancock issued an order for his Second Corps to dig in on the evening of May 5 at the Wilderness. Nosworthy also has suggested that a sort of cross-pollination between West and East might have taken place, given that James Longstreet's divisions returned from a long tour of duty in Georgia and Tennessee just before the Wilderness. He further has written that the presence of officers and enlisted men from the Corps of Engineers with the Army of the Potomac might have led to the increased use of field-works, but these officers and enlisted men had served with that army since the beginning of the war.[18]

Most commentators, however, have pointed to the experience of combat and the common soldier's reaction to it as the fertile breeding ground for a desire to seek protection on the battlefield. "Who first introduced into our armies the plan of hasty intrenchments on the field, has never been settled," commented an anonymous writer in the *Army and Navy Journal* in 1868. "So far as we know, it was the work of no general officer, but something instinctive with the men." Most survivors of the Overland campaign would have generally agreed with this assessment. Matthew Venable, a member of Lee's 1st Confederate Engineers, observed that even a flimsy breastwork steadied the nerves of soldiers and "gave men something definite to defend." Venable probably spoke for many combat soldiers when he asserted, "We soon found . . . that Old Mother Earth is the soldier's best friend."[19]

Were field fortifications used too much in Virginia during the spring of 1864? Historian Paddy Griffith thinks so. "Improved weaponry did not force the armies to dig fortifications," Griffith has written, "but fashion and book-learning did. Once the fieldworks had been dug they became symbols of specific tactical qualities—firepower and protection—which Civil War soldiers had decided were most important. As the fortification principle was extended, the alternative tactics of mobility and shock fell proportionately into disrepute."[20]

Griffith discounts the physical advantages offered by fortifications; he believes that any earthwork could have been climbed if few defenders manned it. The real deterrent, in Griffith's view, lay in the fire delivered by defenders. He suggests that a good unit lying prone behind undulations in the ground could hold its position as easily as if stationed behind earthworks. All that was needed was to clear a field of fire before a position, or at most to hastily throw up slight defenses. Griffith is convinced that fieldworks were overused in the Civil War, which caused an unnecessary fear among soldiers about taking the offensive. The presence of fieldworks on the enemy's side of the battlefield was often used as an excuse for not attacking. Thus the widespread use of field fortifications "helped to defer military decisions—and thereby made the war longer and costlier than it might otherwise have been."[21]

There is some support for this view in the writings of a few veterans of the Overland campaign. Robert Stiles of the Richmond Howitzers noted after the war that fighting from behind earthworks had a "tendency to demoralize the men." He often saw troops refuse to expose themselves to fire across the parapet, shooting with their musket barrels at such a high angle that there was no possibility of hitting anyone. Stiles claimed that some infantry officers became so exasperated at their men's tendency to dig in at every halt in the march that they issued orders against it. Yet Stiles recognized that all his comments applied mostly to weak soldiers. "It is fair to say that, after a while, the better men of the army, at least, learned to use without abusing the vantage ground of earth-works."[22]

More than mere fashion, or habit, led to the employment of field fortifications on the battlefield. Soldiers on all levels—the rank and file and their officers alike—reacted in logical ways when they received orders to dig in, or when they took it upon themselves without orders to seek protection. The presence of the rifle musket was not the real reason that fieldworks came into vogue in 1864, and it is wrong to assume that ditches, parapets, traverses, and abatis offered no physical impediment to an attacking line, even if they were poorly defended. The key was to have soldiers man an earthwork who could deliver fire on an attacker while enjoying a great degree of protection from return fire. A combination of firepower and artificial construction enabled a defender to increase the defensive power of a position. Griffith also fails to note that field fortifications were used for offensive as well as defensive purposes.

The use of field fortifications evolved during the Civil War not due to some irrational fear, but due to a real and potent threat: the continued presence of an enemy army within striking distance. Their use was a rational and logical response to that threat. The discussion should not be centered on whether it was wise to use them, but on how they were used by each side. Defending or attacking fieldworks became a major feature of military operations in Virginia by the spring of 1864, and there was more to come. The Army of the Potomac, the Army of the James, and the Army of Northern Virginia were on the threshold of their long campaign around Petersburg, where they would seemingly be bogged down in the most sophisticated trench systems yet dug in military history.

Appendix
The Design and Construction of Field Fortifications in the Overland Campaign

The battlefields of the Overland campaign are graced with some of the best remnants of field fortifications that were built during the Civil War. In fact, the remnants at Spotsylvania and in the Cold Harbor Unit of the Richmond National Battlefield are the most important in the eastern theater. In quantity and detail of construction, they are also better than the remnants on western battlefields, except for those at Kennesaw Mountain National Battlefield. In the east, only the remnants of the Warwick Line at Yorktown, those to be found at Fredericksburg, and those on the Chancellorsville battlefield come close to the remnants at Spotsylvania and Cold Harbor as important historical resources.

This appendix makes use of insights gained by thorough examination of the fortification remnants at the Wilderness, Spotsylvania, North Anna, and Cold Harbor. It is an attempt to record most remnants of fieldworks in the Overland campaign, and to explain details of design, construction, and use. A thorough engineering perspective on Civil War field fortifications takes into account not just the physical dimensions of the work itself, but where it is sited to achieve command over its target without dead space (or ground in front that is not covered by defending fire). The physical dimensions of the work (the height, thickness, and shape of the parapet as well as the protection afforded the defender) are important in defining a work as strong or weak, but engineers had to consider all factors in the surrounding landscape, including the presence of tree cover that could obscure the position in the eyes of the attacker while not obstructing the defender's fire. All of these factors taken together defined whether a position, not just an earthwork, was strong or weak. In the case of the Confederate Mule Shoe Salient at Spotsylvania, for example, the earthwork was impressively strong but the position in relation to the landscape was not. In fact, the Confederates lavished so much labor on the earthworks there precisely because the position was weak.[1]

Most of the Union and Confederate works built on the Wilderness battlefield seem to have survived the passage of more than 140 years, probably because the thicket protected them from farmers who normally tried to reclaim battlefields as soon as possible after the war ended. Many of these remnants played a role in the fighting on May 5–6, but the visitor must assume that their current appearance is a faded representation of what the earthworks looked like by the evening of May 7. Most are simple earthworks, occupied for no more than three days, that display comparatively few embellishments such as traverses, in contrast to the entrenchments at Spotsylvania. They more closely approximate the fieldworks used at Chancellorsville a year earlier than they foreshadow what was to come during the Overland campaign.

Confederate Fortifications

Ewell's Line North of Orange Turnpike

Ewell's Second Corps of Lee's army was the first unit to dig in at the Wilderness on the morning of May 5, immediately after arriving on the battlefield. The entire corps constructed a trench line north as well as south of Orange Turnpike, one of two major roads across the battlefield. Ewell's men held this line against several Union advances and launched some limited counterattacks from it, in addition to one significant effort to roll up the Union right flank on the evening of May 6. They strengthened and improved the works for three days, evacuating them on May 8.

Ewell's Line on the west side of Saunders's Field has three small traverses located about thirty yards north of Orange Turnpike. They are placed inside the trench about twenty yards from each other. Two of them are simply knobs of natural earth protruding from the front wall of the trench.

As Ewell's men extended this line 175 yards north of the road, they noticed that the ground in front rose slightly higher, so they built a forward line leading off from the original work to that higher elevation. For 40 yards, the Confederates had two lines of defense here. The forward line crosses a gully and abruptly ends, but it is continued about 75 yards farther forward.

Here, at this gap, begins another line built by Gordon's men after their flank attack on the evening of May 6. Conducted by Gordon's Georgia brigade against Seymour's and Shaler's Union brigades, this attack mangled

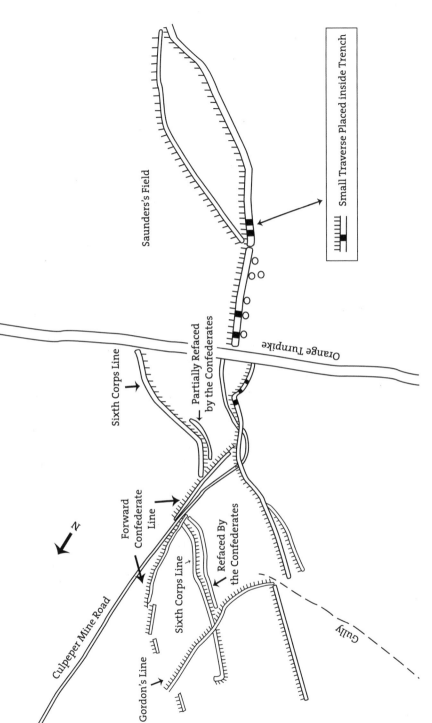

Small Traverse Placed inside Trench

Saunders's Field

Orange Turnpike

Sixth Corps Line

Partially Refaced by the Confederates

N

Forward Confederate Line

Culpeper Mine Road

Sixth Corps Line

Refaced By the Confederates

Gordon's Line

Gully

Ewell's Line at the Wilderness, May 5–7, 1864 (based on field visit, 1991) and pushed back the Union right flank some distance until Neill's brigade stopped it. Although unsuccessful at rolling up the Federals, Gordon came into possession of a few hundred yards of Union trench. Somewhere along this captured Federal line, observant Rebels noticed that corpses had been incorporated into the parapet. Gordon's men dug a connecting line at a right angle to Ewell's Line, crossing the captured Federal line of fieldworks and facing southeast to secure the ground they had taken from Seymour and Shaler. Gordon's Line has no traverses.

The Federal Sixth Corps Line, opposite Ewell's left, was built like the Confederate fieldwork. Before Gordon's attack on the evening of May 6, Sedgwick's extreme right was refused for about three yards, not enough to offer real protection against the surprise Rebel attack. Three yards from the end of the line a traverse was placed inside the trench, but there are no other traverses or gun emplacements on the line. Like Ewell's work, there is only intermittent ditching in front of the parapet.

After Gordon's men captured this section of the Sixth Corps Line and threw up the work already described, the Sixth Corps fell back from the position where Neill's brigade had stopped Gordon. The Confederates then moved forward a quarter of a mile and built another line roughly parallel to Gordon's Line along a small trace called Culpeper Mine Road. Constructed hastily on May 7, this line has an intermittent trench but no ditches or artillery emplacements. Two small traverses were placed in the trench. The left flank ends abruptly at a ravine, but short segments of trench were dug to the left rear of this line, en echelon, nearly back to the left end of Gordon's Line a quarter of a mile to the rear. The right wing of this forward Confederate line continues until it connects with Ewell's Line. Again, there are no traverses or gun emplacements here.

The Confederates reworked the quarter-mile stretch of the Sixth Corps works between Gordon's Line, which was built on the evening of May 6, and the forward line made on May 7. The Rebels dug a trench on the outside of the Union parapet and used the dirt to widen it. There is a small traverse placed inside the newly dug trench about ten yards short of Culpeper Mine Road. The Federal line that lay south of Culpeper Mine Road was partially reworked by the Confederates. The Rebels refaced only thirty yards of its northern end.[2]

Ewell's Line South of Orange Turnpike

South of Orange Turnpike, the Confederate works are similar to those north of the road. There are actually two lines here. One was built just before the fighting started on May 5. The other, placed a bit forward of the original line to take advantage of slightly higher ground, was constructed sometime after the start of the battle. There is also a line of detached rifle pits, each one about three yards wide, stretching for seventy-five yards south of the turnpike. The original Confederate line was placed immediately in front of these holes, indicating that the pits were the first field fortifications dug by Ewell's corps early on the morning of May 5, undoubtedly by skirmishers.

The forward line branches off from the rear line about 75 yards south of the turnpike and occupies ground about four feet higher than the rear line. At most, the two lines are separated by 40 yards. Some 400 yards south of the turnpike, the right end of the forward line joins the rear line. There is no evidence of ditches or artillery emplacements along either line, and there are two traverses inside the trench of the rear line close to the turnpike. Most of Ewell's Line from this area south to the Chewning Farm is intact, but there is no evidence of traverses, ditches, or gun emplacements.

A handful of postwar photographs reveal that the works along Ewell's front were held up by log revetments. Horizontal rows of logs were supported by vertical posts, which often were buttressed by slanting posts angled with one end on the ground and the other affixed to the top of the vertical supports. One photograph shows what might have been an emplacement for a single field gun, with traverses made of logs instead of dirt placed at a right angle to the parapet. That would explain why there are no visible remnants of artillery emplacements today.[3]

Hill's Line

Whereas Ewell's Line displays no gun emplacements and few indications of unique construction, A. P. Hill's Line west of Widow Tapp's Field has these features. Hill's men devoted little attention to fortifying while under fire, but they worked hard on the afternoon of May 6. Assigned to extend Lee's position north of Orange Plank Road, up to a point near Chewning Farm, they built a line studded with gun emplacements and graced with quirky design features. It started at the west side of the large open field, mostly facing north, and eventually curved to align with Ewell's Line.

The line begins with a single infantry trench that extends fifty yards west of Widow Tapp's Field. Then a one-gun emplacement, with a semicircular parapet and a six-foot-wide gap separating it from the infantry

Legend:

Traverse	
Small Traverse Placed inside Trench	
Eroded One-Gun Emplacement Placed inside Trench	
Larger One-Gun Emplacement with Semicircular Design	

Widow Tapp's Field

N

Hill's Line at the Wilderness, May 6, 1864 (based on field visit, 1995) parapet, was dug. The emplacement is open to the rear. Two more similar gun emplacements were made just to the left of the first one. For the next several hundred yards, there are many short traverses, often so small that they are fitted into the trench. Several artillery emplacements were positioned next to these traverses, although the emplacements tend to be so eroded that it is difficult to tell if all traverses had a field gun next to them. There are other emplacements that obviously have no traverses at all. Most of the traversed emplacements are about twenty yards apart. The gun positions are simply a level space dug inside the trench directly behind the parapet. Although the parapet and trench tend to be well preserved, there is no evidence of a ditch except in front of one artillery emplacement on the far right.

This unique line, more complex than any other on the battlefield, is well preserved for 500 yards before it disappears. Marcus B. Toney of the 1st Tennessee in Heth's division recalled that his comrades used bayonets and tin plates to build this line on the afternoon of May 6.[4]

Perry-Perrin-Perry Line

Another Confederate work dug on the afternoon and evening of May 6 is fairly well preserved. Located north of Orange Plank Road, three of Longstreet's and Hill's brigades constructed it to block Burnside's advance south. Law's Alabama brigade of the First Corps, led by Col. William F. Perry; Perrin's Alabama brigade of the Third Corps, led by Brig. Gen. Abner Perrin; and Perry's Florida brigade of the Third Corps, led by Brig. Gen. Edward A. Perry, offered the names of their commanders to this line. The position held, although the Federals briefly captured a portion of the line. The work was strengthened in the evening but evacuated by May 7. About fifty yards of the line remains. There is a trench and a parapet but no ditch. Several small traverses are fitted into the trench; one is simply a knob of earth (sometimes termed a balk) left on the rear wall of the trench.[5]

Longstreet's Line

Longstreet's corps dug in on the evening of May 6, following its failed attack on Hancock's Brock Road Line. North of Plank Road, elements of the First Corps built a good parapet at the eastern edge of Widow Tapp's Field. There is no ditch, but seven bays for infantry were created by placing small traverses inside the trench just north of Plank Road. The bays are about ten feet wide. There are no remnants of artillery emplacements on this line. The continuation of Longstreet's Line south of the road is some distance farther east of Widow Tapp's Field. It also appears to have no gun emplacements or traverses, although the work is poorly preserved in the median of an entrance road to a housing development.[6]

Federal Fortifications

The remnants of Union earthworks on the Wilderness battlefield show that they were made much the same way as the Confederates constructed their works. The Sixth Corps Line north of Orange Turnpike has already been discussed. Much of it was so altered by the Confederates that the line belonged as much to Ewell's men as to Sedgwick's.

McCandless's Line

The Fifth Corps works south of the turnpike, however, show only slight differences in design. Col. William McCandless's Pennsylvania brigade of Crawford's division constructed a line south of Saunders's Field on May 6. It is on the military crest of a gentle slope along a branch of Wilderness Run. There are two small traverses inside the trench, but no ditch or artillery emplacements.

Leonard-Baxter Line

To the east, and running along the south side of Orange Turnpike, Col. Samuel H. Leonard's brigade and Brig. Gen. Henry Baxter's brigade of Robinson's division constructed a line on the afternoon of May 5. It consists of a parapet, heavier than most at the Wilderness, and a trench but no ditch. Several thick traverses, about fifteen to twenty yards apart, were placed behind the right end of this line to protect men from fire coming from the west. These are the traverses built by Gilbert Thompson and other members of the U.S. Engineer Battalion on the evening of May 6. At three yards long, the traverses extend to the rear and thereby offered more protection than the small traverses that were fitted into the trench. But these traverses exist only for about 100 yards along the right wing of the Leonard-Baxter Line, which is about 375 yards in total length.

Fifth Corps Line and Wainwright's Lunettes

Running south, perpendicular to the Leonard-Baxter Line, is the work that Griffin's division started on the morning of May 5. It later was manned and improved by Bartlett's brigade and Brig. Gen. Romeyn B. Ayres's brigade of Griffin's division, and by Col. Andrew W. Denison's brigade of

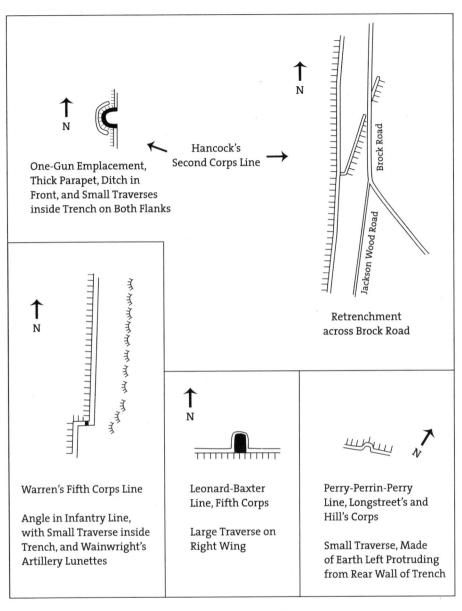

One-Gun Emplacement,
Thick Parapet, Ditch in
Front, and Small Traverses
inside Trench on Both Flanks

Hancock's
Second Corps Line

Brock Road

Jackson Wood Road

Retrenchment
across Brock Road

Warren's Fifth Corps Line

Angle in Infantry Line,
with Small Traverse inside
Trench, and Wainwright's
Artillery Lunettes

Leonard-Baxter
Line, Fifth Corps

Large Traverse on
Right Wing

Perry-Perrin-Perry
Line, Longstreet's and
Hill's Corps

Small Traverse, Made
of Earth Left Protruding
from Rear Wall of Trench

*Details of Union and Confederate Fortifications at the Wilderness, May 5–7, 1864
(based on field visit, 1995)*

Robinson's division. The right flank begins at the turnpike. The line is straight and has a good parapet and two small traverses inside the trench, but no ditch. About 100 yards south of the turnpike, atop the first significant rise of ground, is a huge traverse stretching east for 40 yards to the rear of the line. Another such traverse lies 20 yards farther south, but this one extends west for 75 yards forward of the line. Whereas the eastern traverse was dug on both sides, the western traverse has a ditch on the north side but not on the south.

Atop the next rise of ground south of these two traverses lies a peculiar dogleg, or angle, in the line. The line protrudes forward for ten yards, then redirects south. Behind this section of the infantry line are a series of artillery lunettes constructed under the supervision of Col. Charles S. Wainwright, Fifth Corps artillery chief, on May 6. They are all one-gun emplacements with semicircular parapets and a ditch in front. The guns rested on natural earth—there was no digging to sink them. The lunette on the far left is only twenty yards behind the dogleg in the infantry line. Each of the next three are about three yards to the right and rear of the one to its left, while the remaining eight are in a straight line. Farther south from the dogleg and Wainwright's lunettes, the infantry line continues across the wide valley of Wilderness Run.

Second Corps Line

The Second Corps Line along Brock Road is probably the most famous on the Wilderness battlefield because of the sharp fight and resulting fire that took place on the evening of May 6. Most of the line along the western edge of the road is preserved. It was constructed in much the same way as other fieldworks on the battlefield; there is a good trench and parapet, but mostly no ditch. A large traverse was placed inside the trench at one spot, and at least two artillery emplacements are well preserved. Both were configured for one gun and were made by bulging the parapet forward and digging a ditch in front to strengthen it. Hancock's men added flank protection for the guns by locating traverses in the trench on both sides of the emplacement.

The Federals looked after the safety of their flank, conscious of the fact that the Second Corps was the leftmost unit of Meade's army. They built a retrenchment a little more than a mile south of the junction of Brock Road and Orange Plank Road. Brock Road curves eastward here, but the line continued south along another road, today called Jackson Wood Road or Jackson Trail because it had been used by Stonewall Jackson during his flank march the year before at the battle of Chancellorsville. Exactly opposite the intersection, Hancock's men dug a line due east for three yards, then angled it to the northeast for fifty yards until it crossed Brock Road. The retrenchment continued on the other side for some distance. Although the retrenchment had no artillery emplacements, it effectively covered any Rebel approach from the south along Brock Road. The main line continued along Jackson Wood Road south of the retrenchment.

The Second Corps Line continues to hug the west edge of Brock Road north of its junction with Orange Plank Road. Two traverses, placed inside the trench, are located just north of Plank Road. A forward position built by Hancock's men was located about thirty yards in front of it. Remnants of this forward line exist for about twenty yards north and south of Plank Road. Another small traverse was placed inside the trench in this forward line just north of the roadway.[7]

A sketch of the Second Corps works along Brock Road, made on the morning of May 7, shows that the revetment consisted of logs and posts, like that of other lines on the battlefield. Hancock's men erected their shelter tents behind the work as the dense thicket in front helped to shield them from the Rebels.[8]

SPOTSYLVANIA

Most of the fortifications on the Spotsylvania battlefield were constructed and improved over a long period of time. The earliest entrenchments were built on May 8, and the armies occupied the Spotsylvania line until about May 22. This makes it difficult to know precisely what state the works were in at any given time. One must assume that what is there today represents the combined efforts of two weeks' labor by more than 100,000 men of both armies.

Confederate Fortifications

The extensive remnants of Confederate fortifications demonstrate that the Army of Northern Virginia built the most sophisticated fieldwork system of its history to date. The six-mile-long line is not uniformly preserved; most of the remnants cluster along the outline, base, and shoulders of the Mule Shoe Salient. The slight remnants at Laurel Hill indicate little in the way of ditching before the parapet, but there are extensive remains of traverses at the salient. This giant bulge in Lee's Line, which encompassed two miles of the Confederate position, was a challenging fortification project because of its great curve.

Doles's Salient (Part of the Mule Shoe Salient)

Doles's Salient is fairly well preserved and has slight remnants of traverses that are three to six feet long and about six feet apart. In addition to the important secondary line, which is well preserved, the forward line at Doles's Salient also had two parapets for about fifty yards, one a few yards behind the other. There are small traverses inside the trench of both the secondary and forward line. The ground rises to a slight crest of two to three feet between the secondary and forward lines. A fortified Confederate skirmish line in front of Doles's Salient, constructed after the Federal evacuation of this area, consists of a small trench and parapet but no ditch.

West Angle and East Angle (Mule Shoe Salient)

From Doles's Salient to the West Angle and East Angle there are few remnants of traverses, but enough to show that they were placed at intervals of three to twenty yards. Most of the traverses are short and join the parapet perpendicularly, but some of them join it at a slanting angle. There is at least one clear example of an enclosed bay between the West and East Angles, but only two clear signs of traverses between the East Angle and the Apex.

Apex (Mule Shoe Salient)

Whereas the west side and tip of the Mule Shoe Salient is only moderately well preserved, the east side shows the complexity of this fortified bulge more clearly. It was also thoroughly reworked by the Federals after May 12 and thus is probably the best example of Confederate and Union field fortifications coexisting side by side in the entire war. From the East Angle to the Apex, the Federals constructed a curved line to the rear of the Confederate work, placed on the southern side of the shallow crest of the ridge. The Confederate main line was placed on the northern side to allow infantrymen to fire into the arm of the ravine that came close to the Apex. The Federals dug a ditch in front of their curved line, which is no more than about thirty yards behind the Rebel work.

The Confederates had dug an extension from the Apex toward the east to better fire into the arm of the ravine. It has forty-two intact traverses that are three to twelve feet long and about one to ten yards apart. Some of them are curved a great deal. The Federals left most of this line intact after May 12, except to enclose the ends of the first six traverses to form bays. They also built their own extension from this line toward the south-

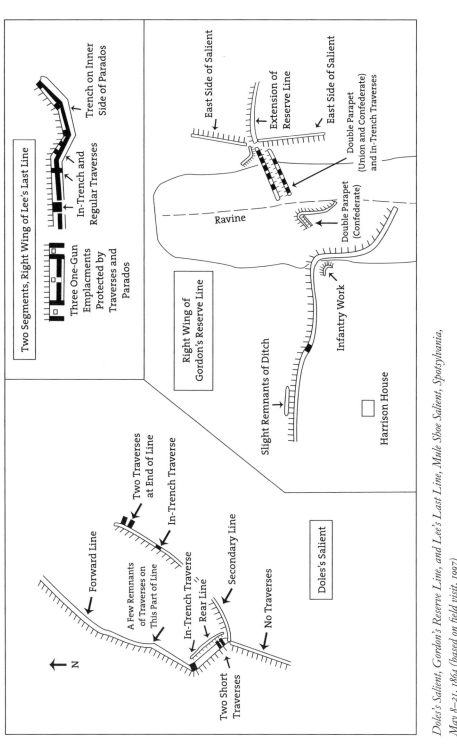

Doles's Salient, Gordon's Reserve Line, and Lee's Last Line, Mule Shoe Salient, Spotsylvania, May 8–21, 1864 (based on field visit, 1997)

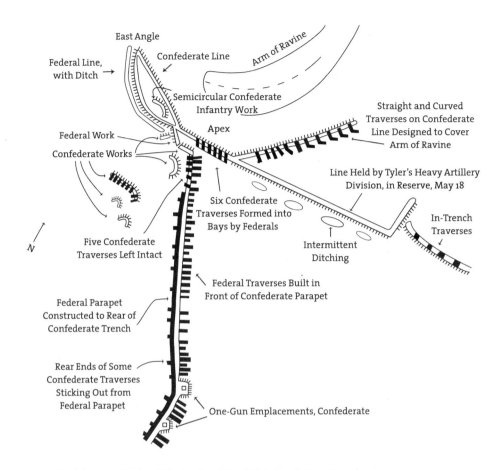

Confederate and Federal Works, East Side of Mule Shoe Salient, Spotsylvania, May 8–21, 1864 (based on field visit, 1997)

east, with intermittent ditching. There is a right angle in this line and a continuation from that right angle that includes some in-trench traverses. Tyler's Heavy Artillery division was stationed behind this line on May 18 while waiting in reserve to support Hancock's attack on Lee's Last Line.

The Federals also left intact five small detached works built by the Confederates behind the Apex. One of them has eight traverses. These detached works are as much as forty yards behind the Apex and on ground that is about two feet lower.

Ewell's men had dug many traverses behind the parapet of the east side of the salient, but the Federals retained only the first five nearest the Apex. They thoroughly redug the interior of the Confederate work from there down to near the point where Gordon's Reserve Line joins this face, widening the trench, making it continuous, and even cutting into most of the traverses. The Yankees left the ends of some Confederate traverses sticking out from the front of a new parapet they dug to the rear of the Rebel trench. Two one-gun Confederate emplacements, which had been incorporated into the Rebel parapet, were left intact. But the Federals transformed the front of the Confederate parapet with fifty-one traverses covering the 500 yards from the Apex to Gordon's Reserve Line. They are from three to ten feet long and mostly cover infantrymen, although a few seem designed for artillery. There seems to be a two-gun emplacement, with a small traverse between the two platforms, at one such spot.

When journalist John T. Trowbridge visited Spotsylvania in the summer of 1865, he was amazed by the mixture of Union and Confederate works along the east side of the Mule Shoe Salient. Trowbridge wrote of "a strange medley of intrenchments, which it would have required an engineer to unravel and understand. Here Grant's works had been pushed up against Lee's, swallowing them as one wave swallows another."[9]

Gordon's Reserve Line (Mule Shoe Salient)

Gordon's Reserve Line is poorly preserved, but the right wing offers an interesting look at how it was joined to the east side of the salient. Remnants of an extension of the Reserve Line continue for at least 100 yards east of the salient's east face. Immediately to the west of the east face, the Confederates had to take the Reserve Line across a large ravine. From the top of the ravine slope, the line curved to the right rear until it reached the bottom of the drain, with a small, semicircular infantry work behind the angle. Also, the Confederates placed a short, curved line forward of this refused segment of the Reserve Line to better cover the ravine. The line that stretches from the ravine bottom to the east face was reworked by the Federals so that it now has two trenches and parapets. Both trenches have several small traverses. The right wing of Gordon's Reserve Line has no artillery emplacements and only intermittent ditching.

Lee's Last Line (Mule Shoe Salient)

Lee's Last Line, hastily dug on May 12 and greatly improved over the following days, is a fascinating complex of fieldworks. The configuration of the extreme left makes little sense on first impression and probably resulted from the desperate circumstances under which it was built. It connected to the west side of the base of the Mule Shoe Salient where the Confederates had dug a series of long zigzags, some with in-trench traverses and others with regular traverses. The initial line started across the base of the salient near Brock Road, but it was abandoned after about 75 yards in favor of angling the line forward in stages. The first angled line stretches forward, with both regular and in-trench traverses, for about 200 yards to the trace of a wood road. The end of the trench is flared out a bit to serve as a flank protection without refusing the line. Then another line was started about 15 yards forward; it continued to the right a couple of hundred yards to a ravine, where two detached works 75 yards to the right and rear of the east end of this line helped to cover the ravine. Another line was built forward from this line, just to the right of the wood road. It too has a combination of regular and in-trench traverses with a one-gun emplacement thrown in for good measure. This line has an angled extension toward the northeast that eventually will continue the line all across the base of the salient. One sees on this angled line not only a one-gun emplacement, but also some holes dug just behind the line to serve as shelter. They probably are the remnants of bombproofs.

The right wing of Lee's Last Line was heavily reinforced by the construction of a parados, a parapet protecting the rear of the position. The trench was widened and a second trench was dug just behind the parados to get sufficient fill dirt. The parados is very thick and almost as high as the parapet itself. Small traverses were placed inside the forward trench to create bays, and regular traverses extend rearward from the parapet through the parados, indicating that they were dug before the parados was constructed. Additionally, there is at least one large, square traverse built so that space exists all around it, allowing men to pass through the parados to the rear of the line. Gun positions were incorporated into this feature as well. One was placed inside the widened trench, with extra space created by cutting through the parados to allow the gun to be brought into and out of position. The parados stretches for at least fifty yards along the line.

Theodore Lyman, who visited Spotsylvania on April 13, 1866, described the right end of Lee's Last Line. It was "a curiosity of fortification. The high parapet was not only traversed as often as every ten or twelve feet, but was inclosed in the rear, so that the line was divided into a series of square pens, with banks of earth heavily riveted with oak logs. From space to space was what looked like a wooden camp chimney, but in truth was an elevated post for sharpshooters with a little loophole in front. I never saw any like them."[10]

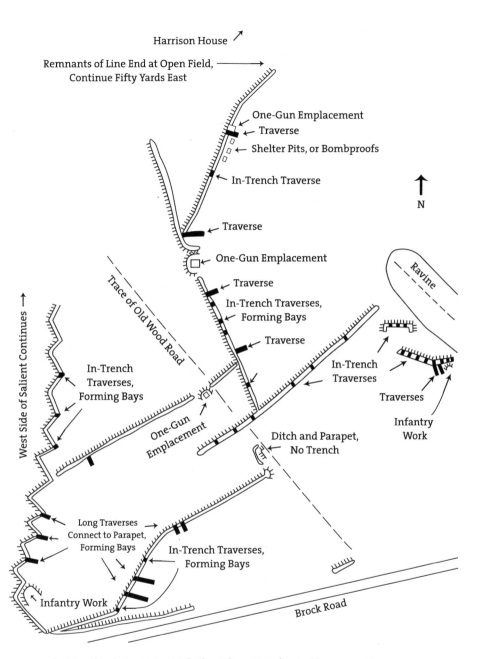

Harrison House

Remnants of Line End at Open Field,
Continue Fifty Yards East

One-Gun Emplacement
← Traverse

← Shelter Pits, or Bombproofs

← In-Trench Traverse

← Traverse

N

← One-Gun Emplacement

Ravine

← Traverse

In-Trench Traverses,
← Forming Bays

Trace of Old Wood Road

← Traverse

In-Trench
Traverses

In-Trench
Traverses,
Forming Bays

Traverses

One-Gun
Emplacement

Infantry
Work

West Side of Salient Continues →

Ditch and Parapet,
No Trench

Long Traverses
Connect to Parapet,
Forming Bays

In-Trench Traverses,
Forming Bays

Infantry Work

Brock Road

Left Wing of Lee's Last Line, Mule Shoe Salient, Spotsylvania, May 12–21, 1864
(based on field visit, 1997)

Heth's Salient

Although not as large or famous as the Mule Shoe Salient, Heth's Salient is well preserved and offers the best opportunity to see an undisturbed fieldwork built at relative leisure and occupied for most of the Spotsylvania phase of the campaign. It is a large work. The forward line coming south curves eastward to form the north face of the salient, with many traverses along the way. Some connect to the parapet while others connect only to the trench. It is possible that the former were built when the parapet was constructed and the latter were added on later. There are two one-gun emplacements on the north face, positioned to fire into the flank of any Federals who attacked Confederate positions north of the salient. A number of shelter pits, or bombproofs, lie close to the line. Some of these shelter pits are actually trenches two to four yards long. All are positioned about two feet behind the trench. The collection of shelter pits stretches for about fifty yards.

The east face of Heth's Salient crosses a wide and deep ravine that bisects the entire position. A number of traverses, some connecting to the parapet and some to the trench, exist on this face. The south side of Heth's Salient, about 200 yards long, has many traverses, especially along the eastern stretch of the face. Many of these traverses turn at right angles to enclose the rear of several adjoining traverses and form bays. From west to east, these features start with six bays, followed by three short and unenclosed traverses. Then there are four bays and three unenclosed traverses. The largest collection of enclosed traverses makes nine bays in a row. This method of enclosing bays is unique. A sally port twenty yards wide exists at the southwest corner of the salient.

The west face is straight and forms the base of the bulge, providing for defense in depth. It has several in-trench traverses and a curious circular hole some fifteen feet deep and fifteen yards wide, protected by its own parapet, forward of but attached to the west face. It probably was a magazine or a very deep bombproof. The west face of Heth's Salient is about 700 yards from Brock Road. The continuation of the Third Corps Line south of the salient is no longer intact, but one can emerge from the heavy tree cover that protects the salient to see that it is located on significantly high ground. A good view across the open fields to the south illustrates the wisdom of providing for ample protection of this spot.

The line at the base also crossed the ravine that bisected the salient, but not continuously. The left end of the west face is angled forward to better allow infantrymen to fire into the ravine, but it ends partway down the

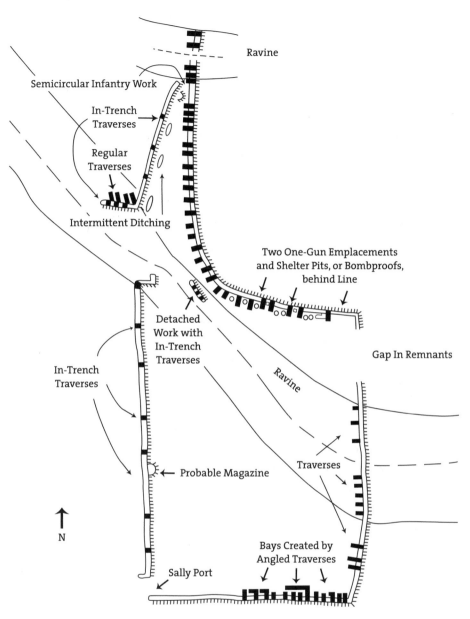

Heth's Salient, Spotsylvania, May 10–21, 1864 (based on field visit, 1997)

slope. On the other side, the line commences partway up the slope. This line, too, is refused and has several in-trench and regular traverses and intermittent ditching. The line stretches for 200 yards until its left ends 15 yards from the forward line.

There is surprisingly little ditching along the Confederate works at Spotsylvania, perhaps the result of the close proximity of Union troops. Whatever the Rebels failed to do in front of their parapet, they more than made up for behind it. The Spotsylvania works are marvelous examples of field fortifications crafted by men who had come to respect the defensive power of earthworks. There are innovative design features and clever adaptations to the subtle inequalities of the ground. The Army of Northern Virginia's reliance on fieldworks had come to full fruition.[11]

Federal Fortifications

As the attacking party, the Federals did not consistently build a large, complex system of earthworks at Spotsylvania. There are a few eroded remnants along the Fifth Corps position north of Spindle Field that show the line to have been quite simple, with intermittent ditching and a few traverses at curves and artillery emplacements. A segment of line that stretches along Grant Drive east of Brock Road is moderately well preserved. It has a detached one-gun emplacement to the rear and curves to conform to the military crest of an irregular bit of ground. A traverse stretches forward of the line at a right angle.

Galleries on Sixth Corps Line

Yet, north of Grant Drive and east of this line, Sixth Corps troops constructed two complex galleries on a steep slope. The first, located west of a wide ravine, consists of four detached infantry works in a row. Collectively, they are on ground that ascends twelve feet in about thirty yards. East of the ravine, a line begins with a one-gun emplacement and then climbs fifteen feet in about thirty yards. The Federals constructed ten traverses along this part of the line to shelter infantrymen, digging a ditch in front. The main line continued from this unusual construction for at least 350 yards and then was refused. To the rear and on top of the rise of ground, Union soldiers dug twelve one-gun emplacements to support the attack on May 12. Three detached infantry lines also straddle the ravine to the right of the emplacements, and a communication trench connects the forward work with the rear areas. It is a rather unusual way to fortify a steep slope.[12]

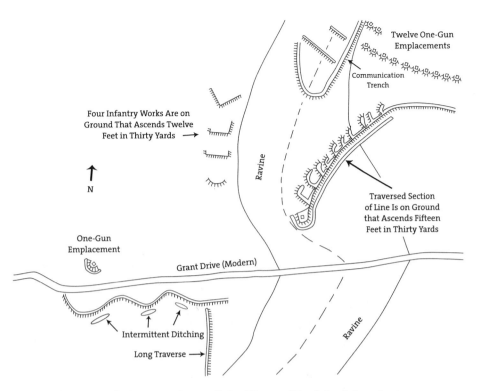

Galleries on Sixth Corps Line, between Shelton House and Brock Road, Spotsylvania, May 8–21, 1864 (based on field visit, 1997)

Second and Sixth Corps Works near Landrum House

The Sixth Corps dug a line from the captured West Angle of the Mule Shoe Salient on May 12. It was abandoned—unfinished—the next day, but the remnant is well preserved, at least near the angle. It is very straight and consists of a parapet dug on both sides, forming both a trench and a ditch. Hancock's men also dug works near the Landrum House after May 12. Eight one-gun emplacements with ditches lie near the house site, protected in front by a semicircular infantry work. A straight infantry line stretches off to the right, constructed by Hancock's reserves on May 12, and a short, detached infantry work lay partway between this line and the tip of the salient. The house was located 550 yards from the Confederate works; the gun emplacements and a straight infantry line were placed on a slight ridge bordering the north side of the ravine that separated it from the salient. In fact, the crest of the ridge lies between the gun emplacements and the infantry line, and rises about two feet higher than either fortification.[13]

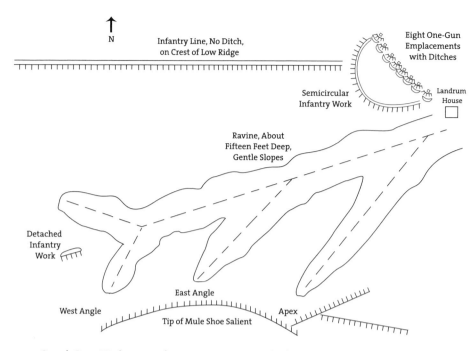

Second Corps Works at Landrum House, opposite Mule Shoe Salient, Spotsylvania,
May 12–21, 1864 (based on field visit, 1997)

Potter's Division Line and Ninth Corps Salient

The Ninth Corps remnants are extensive and complex, probably because this area remained undeveloped after the war. A portion of Potter's
Division Line south of Heth's Salient exhibits defense in depth. The Federals built three detached infantry works behind the forward line. Two
were long lines with a traverse attached to each one. There is also a two-
gun emplacement with a short curtain attached to the left. Nearby, an
emplacement for eleven guns was made by snaking a parapet in curves
to form semicircular protection for each piece, and a traverse was placed
in the middle of this unique design. Whereas the forward line here has
intermittent ditching, the infantry works usually do not. The artillery emplacements, however, always have ditches. This complex of rear defensive
works was built to face south, overlooking a ravine that bisected the forward line.[14]

South of this area the Ninth Corps Line bent at nearly a ninety-degree
angle to head east. The salient formed was in the shape of a curved infantry line with several traverses added for protection. A communication
trench stretched to the rear, and five detached infantry works provided

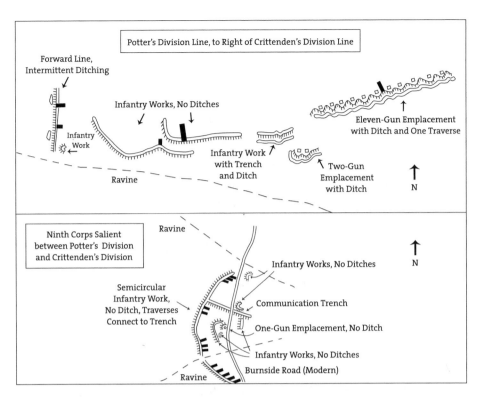

Potter's Division Line, to Right of Crittenden's Division Line

Forward Line,
Intermittent Ditching

Infantry Works, No Ditches

Eleven-Gun Emplacement
with Ditch and One Traverse

Infantry
Work

Infantry Work
with Trench
and Ditch

Two-Gun
Emplacement
with Ditch

Ravine

N

Ninth Corps Salient
between Potter's Division
and Crittenden's Division

Ravine

Infantry Works, No Ditches

N

Semicircular
Infantry Work,
No Ditch, Traverses
Connect to Trench

Communication Trench

One-Gun Emplacement, No Ditch

Infantry Works, No Ditches

Burnside Road (Modern)

Ravine

*Potter's Division Line and Ninth Corps Salient, Spotsylvania, May 10–21, 1864
(based on field visit, 1997)*

secondary defenses inside the salient. There is also a one-gun emplacement here. There are no ditches, and the traverses all connect to the trench rather than to the parapet.

Crittenden's Division Line

Farther east, Crittenden's Division Line has a complex set of works behind a series of artillery emplacements along the forward line. The ground here is regularly intersected by ravines that segment the line and give a different character to each section. One section has ten traverses of varied length attached to the parapet, but there are no visible remnants of artillery platforms at these gun positions. There are seventeen detached infantry lines of all lengths and shapes arrayed to the rear, mostly at right angles to the forward line and located just a few yards to the rear. Three of these have traverses. There are also two one-gun emplacements well to the rear with two circular holes next to them, probably the remnants of magazines,

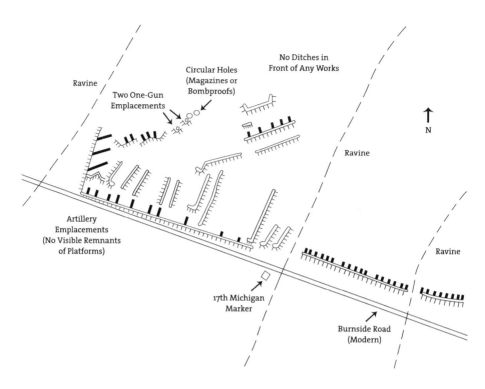

Crittenden's Division Line, between Ninth Corps Salient and Willcox's Division Line, Spotsylvania, May 10–21, 1864 (based on field visit, 1997)

bombproofs, or protection for limber chests. The right flank of this segment of the line is well refused, with three traverses and one infantry line
attached to the refused line. To the left, across the next ravine, the forward
line has seventeen short traverses three to six yards long attached to the
parapet but no rear defense works. The next segment on the other side of
the ravine has nine traverses. There are no ditches along the forward line
or in front of any rear defense works.[15]

Federal "Bay Battery" and Willcox's Division Line

Farther to the left, Willcox's division held a part of the Ninth Corps
Line that angled southward again. The Federals defended both sides of a
wide ravine by constructing a large semicircular infantry work with five
short traverses and one long traverse inside it. To the left, on the ravine
slope, they developed two short infantry lines. On the opposite ravine
slope, two one-gun emplacements with ditches and a longer infantry line
with three long and three short traverses appeared. Consistent with most

of the Ninth Corps forward line, there were no ditches in front of the infantry works.

Between this segment of Willcox's Line and Fredericksburg Road lies a large work for infantry and artillery, called the "Bay Battery" by modern researchers. It occupies an angle as the Federal line jogs eastward again. Two heavy parapets, one behind the other, climb up from the bottom of a ravine and head south. Both of them have a ditch for most of their length, and each has five traverses located on the part of the parapet that climbs the ravine slope. Fewer traverses are located on top of the higher ground, outside the ravine. The ends of these two parapets are connected by the forward line as it heads east. This forward line has six long traverses which constitute the artillery emplacements, even though there are no visible remnants of platforms. The Bay Battery is a simple yet strong artillery position at a strategic angle in the line. It is unusual that there is almost no trench on the inside of any parapet at this location.[16]

The Federal fortifications at Spotsylvania are less well known than the Confederate works, but they show that the Army of the Potomac also had learned how to construct effective protection in the field. The long days spent near Spotsylvania gave the Yankees opportunities to build sometimes unusual configurations and incorporate defense in depth. Often the latter seems more the result of an individual desire to make additional shelters to the rear than the result of a concerted plan. There is no evidence that any of the Union works were as stoutly built with heavy traverses as the Mule Shoe Salient, but then there was less need of such construction along the Union line because none of these works were ever attacked.

Several historic photographs and line drawings depict the works at Spotsylvania. One that portrays the Rebel works at Laurel Hill shows a palisade of sharpened tree trunks sticking almost horizontally in front of the parapet. In fact, it appears that the butts of the pales are secured in the ditch of the work. The other images document the heavy log revetments and a one-gun emplacement along a line of parapet, perhaps one of the two situated along the east side of the Mule Shoe Salient.[17]

NORTH ANNA RIVER

Although no major attack occurred during the North Anna phase of the Overland campaign, the earthworks that Lee's army constructed are justifiably famous. Occupied for no more than four days, they forced Grant to cancel any hope of attack and plan another flanking movement. In this, they duplicated the effect of Lee's strong earthworks during the

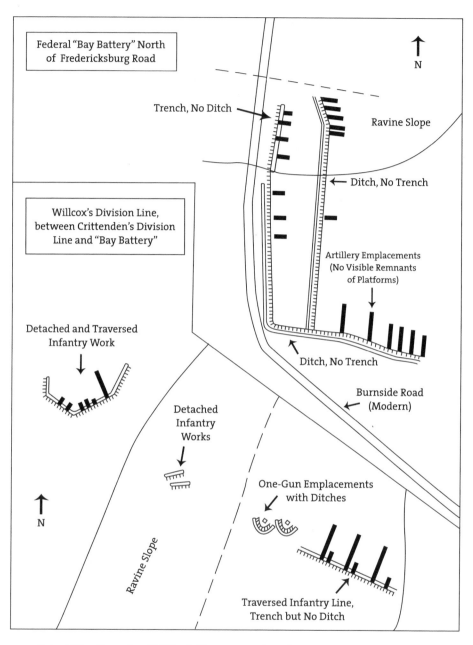

Federal "Bay Battery" and Willcox's Division Line, Spotsylvania, May 10–21, 1864 (based on field visit, 1997)

Mine Run campaign the previous December. The central portion of Lee's entrenchments at the North Anna River, those leading up to the apex of the inverted *V*, are extremely well preserved. They show these works to be among the best-constructed temporary fortifications of the war.

Confederate Fortifications

The section of line occupied by Sanders's and Harris's brigades on May 23, the aiming point of Ledlie's abortive attack, has several small works just to the rear of the main line. They consist of semicircular trenches and parapets, some big enough for one or two men while others are large enough for ten men. These probably were fortified command posts for regimental and brigade leaders. Some are as much as fifty yards behind the line. There is also a large in-trench traverse here and two one-gun emplacements with traverses on both sides and the platform dug into the trench.

As one walks farther toward the apex, the traverses become more and more numerous. They all connect to the parapet, which has little ditching in front. The traverses range from three to twelve feet long, and they tend to angle away from the apex the closer one walks to that point. The traverses are often spaced only two feet apart, but sometimes as much as fifteen yards separate them. At one stretch of the line there are no traverses for at least thirty yards. There is just one gun emplacement along this stretch of line near the apex, and it is situated just to the left of a traverse.

Two lines stretch eastward from the apex; one of them — the main line — is located atop the river bluff, and the other — a forward line — is placed on a shelf of land midway between the bluff and the river bank. Both lines, held by Wright's Georgia brigade of Mahone's division, cross Ox Ford Road and are interrupted by a ravine 600 yards east of the apex. Wright's main line has no ditch, but its simple trench and parapet closely follow the edge of the bluff. It is situated on ground about thirty feet above the intermediate shelf and about sixty feet above the level of the river. The slope in front of both lines is very steep. Wright's men placed very few traverses on their main line, and there are just one or two in-trench traverses. A few one-gun emplacements similar to those on the Sanders-Harris part of the line can be seen. One other is constructed differently. The parapet of the main line bulges forward to accommodate it, but there are still two traverses to protect the flanks and the platform is dug into the trench as well. Wright's forward line on the shelf is constructed in much the same way.[18]

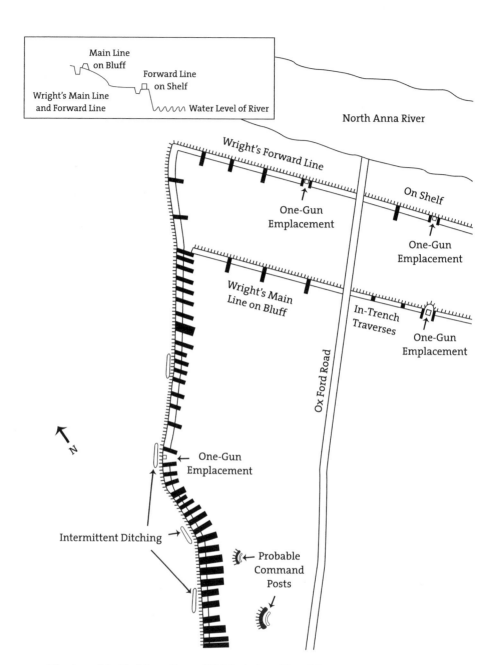

Main Line
on Bluff

Forward Line
on Shelf

Wright's Main Line
and Forward Line

Water Level of River

North Anna River

Wright's Forward Line

On Shelf

One-Gun
Emplacement

One-Gun
Emplacement

Wright's Main
Line on Bluff

In-Trench
Traverses

One-Gun
Emplacement

Ox Ford Road

One-Gun
Emplacement

N

Intermittent Ditching

Probable
Command
Posts

The Apex of the Confederate Inverted V, *North Anna River, May 23–27, 1864
(based on field visit, 1996)*

Federal Fortifications

Little is left of the Federal fortifications at North Anna, but two photographs by Timothy O'Sullivan, both taken on May 25, show how Hancock's and Willcox's men converted the Confederate works in and around Henagan's Redoubt for their own use. The first photograph displays the work of Second Corps troops who placed an additional parapet to close the rear of the redoubt. They revetted it with horizontal logs and vertical posts up to the bottom of the embrasure, then packed about three feet of dirt on top of that without a revetment. A gap was left in this top layer of earth to form the embrasure. At least one traverse as high as the revetment was built for one of the gun emplacements.

The other photograph is unique. It shows Willcox's men lounging in a section of Confederate trench converted to face south and overlooking the North Anna River. They have spread shelter tents over poles placed across the trench to provide shelter from the sun, and some men sit atop the rear wall of the trench. Bayoneted muskets are stuck into the ground so the men do not have to lean several of them together into a pyramid or lay them on the ground. This is one of the few images that document how soldiers lived in trenches during the Civil War.[19]

COLD HARBOR

Most Union and Confederate works at Cold Harbor have long since disappeared, but an important segment is well preserved in the Cold Harbor Unit of the Richmond National Battlefield Park. Although small in comparison to the total volume of works constructed here, the Cold Harbor Unit protects the most singular set of Civil War fieldworks we have. It is a key sector of the battlefield, encompassing both sides of Bloody Run where the Sixth Corps attacked on June 1. The unit holds multiple lines of trenches on both the Union and Confederate sides of the battlefield, showcasing defense in depth. It also includes the deadly space of no-man's-land. These works were dug during June 1–4; many of those on the Union side were thrown together after the failed attack of June 3. Thus they are characterized by hasty construction, odd configuration, and uncoordinated placement of short lines of works. In short, the remnants are a student's dream come true, an authentic portrayal of a hasty fortification system dug under fire and occupied for more than a week of tough campaigning.

The remnants can be divided into quadrants: the Confederate works south and north of Bloody Run constitute two sections, while the Federal

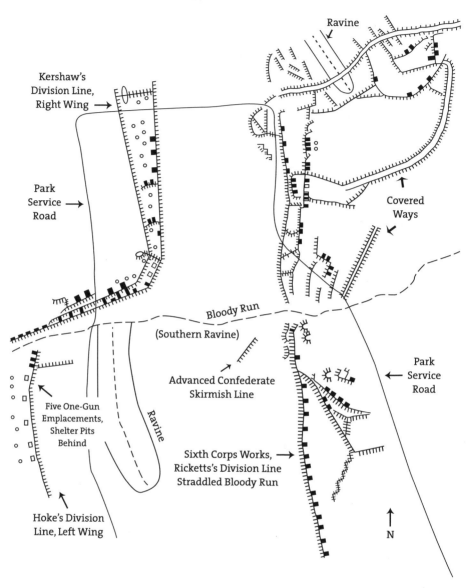

Union and Confederate Works, Cold Harbor Unit, Richmond National Battlefield Park,
June 1–12, 1864 (based on field visit, 1996)

Sixth Corps works north and south of the stream are the other two. The Union works are more complex and confusing because most were dug under fire after the June 3 attack.

Confederate Fortifications

Hoke's division held the line south of Bloody Run. The works have no ditch or traverses, but the trench and parapet are quite large. Five one-gun artillery emplacements are preserved here, with the platform dug inside the trench and partially into the rear wall. Also, many circular holes are located two to four yards behind the line. These bombproofs tend to be clustered in groups. Four larger holes are positioned twenty to thirty yards behind the line just south of Bloody Run, and probably are the remnants of shelters used by brigade officers and staff. Only when the trench runs down the slope of Bloody Run did the Confederates build traverses on this portion of the line. They also dug a traverse extending forward of the main line, facing north, about thirty yards down from the natural crest of the ravine slope. This traverse has no ditch either, but it has two in-trench traverses.

Kershaw's Works North of Bloody Run

The Confederate works north of Bloody Run were held by Kershaw's division. The line runs west to east along the natural crest of the ravine slope until two angles force it to turn north. This southward-facing line is heavily fortified in depth and has a big parapet. Traverses three to six yards long are placed about every three yards, and there is some ditching in front of the main line. A few in-trench traverses also appear on the main line. The Confederates dug a second line about thirty yards from the start of the main line and placed it only six yards behind the front trench. A third line was started nearly fifty yards from the start of the second line and also located only six yards behind the second one. This third line is short, although it has three sizable traverses. A bombproof for a higher-ranking officer is located a few yards behind the third line and connected to it with a communication trench.

Only the first and second lines stretch all the way to the first angle that begins to take the Confederate works north once again. The traverses are spaced a bit farther apart as they near the angle (up to eight yards separate them) and there are a number of circular holes just behind the second line. Only one artillery emplacement is located on this stretch of the trench sys-

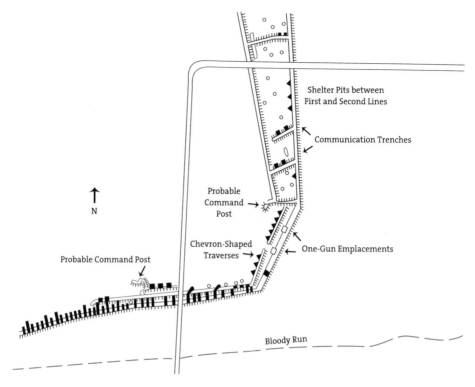

N

Shelter Pits between
First and Second Lines

Communication Trenches

Probable
Command →
Post

Chevron-Shaped
Traverses →

One-Gun Emplacements

Probable Command Post

Bloody Run

Kershaw's Works North of Bloody Run, Cold Harbor Unit, Richmond National Battlefield Park, June 1–12, 1864 (based on field visit, 1996)

tem. It is for one gun and appears ten yards from the angle. The platform is cut into the trench of the first line, but the parapet of the second line is also cut through to give the piece and its gunners access to the rear.

The first and second angles are about seventy yards apart and redirect the line northward once again. There is a ditch in front of the first line between the two angles and a one-gun emplacement in the first angle and another in the second angle. Two more are positioned between. These emplacements have only minimal traversing. Between the two angles, the second line begins to drift farther to the rear of the first line. At the first angle, it is only two yards behind, but at the second angle, it is twelve yards to the rear. Also, the second line has oddly shaped traverses, forming triangles, spaced only two to six yards apart from each other. Several shelter holes are scattered just behind the second line, which has no ditch, but the Confederates cut a passageway through the parapet and trench so that gun crews could easily take their weapons up to the first line.

The continuation of the Rebel line from the second angle northward to the boundary of the Cold Harbor Unit is only about 133 yards long. The forward line has a ditch in front but fewer traverses, which are spaced from 5 to 12 yards apart. The second line is 12 yards to the rear of the first line at the second angle, but it drifts to a point at least 22 yards to the rear close to the northern boundary of the unit. Four communication trenches connect the two lines, two of them have traverses extending from them to the north, and one does not go all the way to the second line. There are many circular holes, big enough for two to ten men, located between the two lines, and a command post is situated behind the second line near the second angle. Like the other command post behind the third line along the ravine slope, this one is connected to the works with a communication trench.

Federal Fortifications

The Federal fortifications inside the Cold Harbor Unit are not in such orderly layers as the Confederate works. They were improvised over time in successive bouts of digging and thus are not connected by order or system, although taken as a whole they do form a formidable defensive feature. If Lee had assaulted these works, his men would have floundered in the maze of trenches.

Sixth Corps Works North of Bloody Run (Northern Section)

North of Bloody Run, and just south of the northern boundary of the Cold Harbor Unit, the Sixth Corps works have a relatively simple first line. In fact, it might be a parallel dug after the June 3 attack, for it is straight and has traverses but no ditch. There is a forward extension, semicircular in design and connected to the first line by a communication trench, to encompass a bit of ground three feet higher than the rest. This certainly was dug after the June 3 attack. There is also a detached line, dug in a zigzag fashion, to shield the left flank of this extended work.

The second line is stronger and more elaborate than the first. It has numerous traverses, most of which connect to the parapet, but some do not. There also is intermittent ditching and many holes to the rear of the line. An infantry bay was formed by connecting the ends of two traverses. The Federals constructed a four-gun artillery emplacement on the second line, which bulges forward and has a good ditch and three traverses for flank protection. The second line also has adequate flank protection on the right, with a series of detached infantry trenches. Two large covered ways

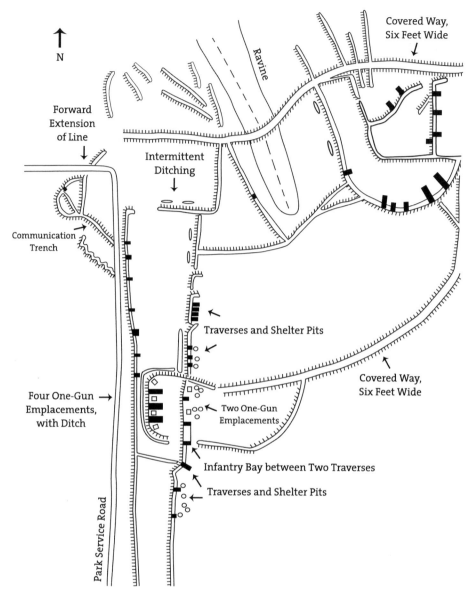

N

Covered Way,
Six Feet Wide

Ravine

Forward
Extension
of Line

Intermittent
Ditching

Communication
Trench

Traverses and Shelter Pits

Four One-Gun
Emplacements,
with Ditch

Covered Way,
Six Feet Wide

Two One-Gun
Emplacements

Infantry Bay between Two Traverses

Traverses and Shelter Pits

Park Service Road

Sixth Corps Works North of Bloody Run (Northern Section), Cold Harbor Unit, Richmond National Battlefield Park, June 1–12, 1864 (based on field visit, 1996) connect the second line to the rear. A large, semicircular complex faces west and south to the rear of the second line's right flank. It consists of two main semicircular lines, a couple of in-trench traverses in the first one, and regular traverses on both lines. There is only intermittent ditching in this complex.

Sixth Corps Works North of Bloody Run (Southern Section)

Farther south, but still north of Bloody Run, the Union lines look quite different but retain some of the same characteristics. Communication trenches connect the first and second lines, but the first line continues to be lighter and simpler than the second one. More traverses and numerous shelter holes are located on the rear line. One of the biggest bombproofs in the Cold Harbor Unit is located just behind the second line on the northern slope of Bloody Run, with a cluster of smaller shelter holes around it. Here, near the ravine, the Federals constructed several short lines behind the second line. The third line has a sharp angle at the crest of the ravine slope to allow for defense in two directions, with strong traverses to protect the flanks of any troops in this section of the line. There are two additional, shorter lines here too, making five altogether. The remnants of a covered way, six feet wide, comes from the northeast toward the rear of the fifth line.

Sixth Corps Works South of Bloody Run

South of Bloody Run, the Sixth Corps troops did not duplicate the configuration of the works north of the stream. They did not continue the third, fourth, or fifth lines, and the forward line has a great number of traverses. The first Federal line here is a long stretch of the Confederate skirmish line captured either on June 1 or 3, and reversed, so there is a ditch (the former Confederate trench) in front of it. The Federals also dug two semicircular detached works just behind the line in the ravine, as well as some forward lines in front of this section. There are lots of shelter pits in the area, but defense in depth is not so deep or well organized here as it is north of the run. The second line angles backward from the first and has fewer traverses. A third line angles back from the second, also with few traverses. Two detached works to the rear of the third line, one semicircular and the other rectangular, apparently did not contain artillery emplacements and may well have been command posts for brigade or division leaders. Two communication trenches, one configured in a zigzag

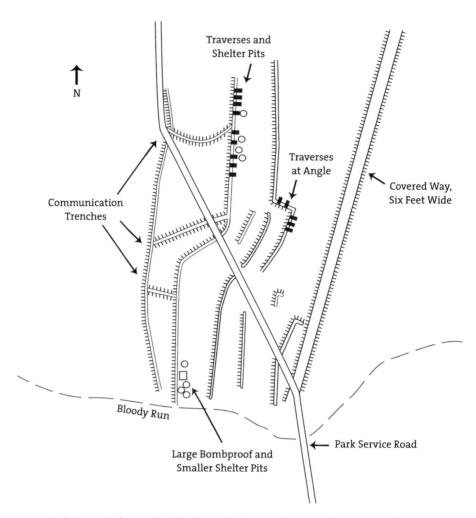

Sixth Corps Works North of Bloody Run (Southern Section), Cold Harbor Unit, Richmond National Battlefield Park, June 1–12, 1864 (based on field visit, 1996)

pattern, are located in this area. One can easily see the spot where Federals and Confederates met south of Bloody Run; between the lines there are remnants of works for both Yankee and Rebel skirmishers.[20]

Outside the Cold Harbor Unit, there is little for the student to easily see. A twenty-yard section of some Fifth Corps works remains accessible near the location of Bethesda Church, but the works are very poorly preserved. Another twenty-yard section of a Confederate trench remains on the south side of Totopotomoy Creek near Highway 606. This fragment

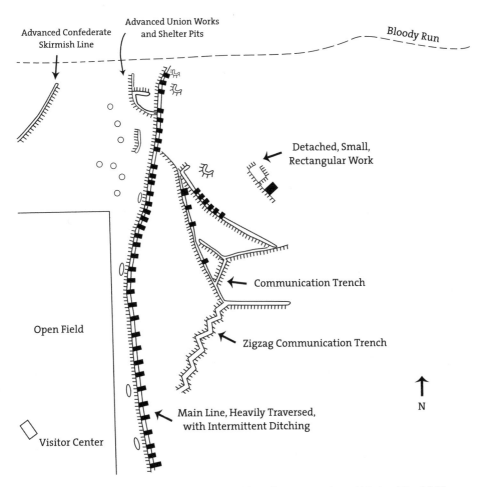

Advanced Confederate
Skirmish Line

Advanced Union Works
and Shelter Pits

Bloody Run

Detached, Small,
Rectangular Work

Communication Trench

Zigzag Communication Trench

Open Field

N

Main Line, Heavily Traversed,
with Intermittent Ditching

Visitor Center

Sixth Corps Works South of Bloody Run, Cold Harbor Unit, Richmond National Battlefield Park, June 1–12, 1864 (based on field visit, 1996)

consists of a straight parapet with no remaining ditch or trench. It is located on the crest of the creek valley. There are other fragments on the sprawling battlefield of Cold Harbor, but they are on private land and not easily accessible. Likewise, the battle is not well documented by historic photographs. One such image, taken by photographer J. Reekie in April 1865, purports to show works on the battlefield. Upon closer examination, it seems to depict the work of local farmers who are pulling fence rails out of the fortifications and stacking them up to dry. There are no signs of earthworks in the photograph.[21]

Notes

ABBREVIATIONS

BHL-UM   University of Michigan, Bentley Historical Library, Ann Arbor

DPA   Delaware Public Archives, Dover

ECU   East Carolina University, East Carolina Manuscript Collection, Greenville, N.C.

FB   Fredericksburg Battlefield, Fredericksburg, Va.

ID-ISL   Indiana Division, Indiana State Library, Indianapolis

IHS   Indiana Historical Society, Indianapolis

KCL   Knox College Library, Galesburg, Ill.

LC   Library of Congress, Manuscript Division, Washington, D.C.

LOV   Library of Virginia, Richmond

Mary-HS   Maryland Historical Society, Baltimore

MC   Museum of the Confederacy, Richmond, Va.

MCL-DU   Medical Center Library, Duke University, Durham, N.C.

NARA   National Archives and Records Administration, Washington, D.C.

NCDAH   North Carolina Division of Archives and History, Raleigh

N-YHS   New-York Historical Society, New York, N.Y.

OR   *The War of the Rebellion: A Compilation of the Official Records of the Union and Confederate Armies.* 70 vols. in 128. Washington, D.C.: Government Printing Office, 1880–1901. Unless otherwise noted, all citations are to series 1.

OR Atlas   *The Official Military Atlas of the Civil War.* New York: Fairfax Press, 1983.

PHMC   Pennsylvania Historical and Museum Commission, Harrisburg

RNB   Richmond National Battlefield, Richmond, Va.

SCL-DU   Special Collections Library, Duke University, Durham, N.C.

SHC-UNC   Southern Historical Collection, University of North Carolina, Chapel Hill

UO   University of Oregon, Eugene

USAMHI   U.S. Army Military History Institute, Carlisle Barracks, Pa.

UVA	University of Virginia, Special Collections, Charlottesville
VBHS-UR	University of Richmond, Virginia Baptist Historical Society, Richmond
VHS	Virginia Historical Society, Richmond
WLU	Washington and Lee University, Special Collections, Lexington, Va.

PREFACE

1   Gordon C. Rhea's series of books on the Wilderness, Spotsylvania, North Anna, and Cold Harbor, all of which are cited in the notes and bibliography of this study, contain the best analysis of the grand tactics of the Overland campaign. See also Mark Grimsley's survey of the campaign, *And Keep Moving On.*

2   Hess, *Field Armies and Fortifications*, xi–xviii, 308–14.

3   Ibid., 9, 78–84, 122–24, 189–93, 222–33, 293–99.

4   Ibid., 311–12, 388n.

5   The standard description of the grand tactics of the Atlanta campaign is in Castel, *Decision in the West.*

6   Swinton, *Campaigns of the Army of the Potomac*, 489.

7   Ulysses S. Grant to Henry W. Halleck, May 11, 1864, in Simon, *Papers of Ulysses S. Grant*, 10:423; Dana, *Recollections*, 210, 214–15; Sherman, *Memoirs*, 2:254; Adams, *Fighting for Defeat*, 155–61.

CHAPTER 1

1   Warner, *Generals in Blue*, 117–18, 510; Abbott, "Corps of Engineers," 125; J. C. Woodruff to Lorenzo Thomas, April 23, 1864, Letters Sent by the Chief of Engineers, M1113, RG77, NARA.

2   Hagerman, *American Civil War*, 237.

3   "James Chatham Duane"; James C. Duane to R. Jones, August 27, 1848, Duane to Samuel Cooper, June 10, 1856, Duane to Lorenzo Thomas, July 2, 1863, Duane to R. C. Drum, October 12, 1886, in Duane personnel file, Letters Received by the Commission Branch of the Adjutant General's Office, M1064, RG94, NARA; Joseph G. Totten to Truman Seymour, January 29, 1863, Letters Sent by the Chief of Engineers, M1113, RG77, NARA.

4   Abbott, "Cyrus Ballou Comstock," 218–19; James Harrison Wilson, *Under the Old Flag*, 1:445.

5   McAndrews, "George Gillespie."

6   Cullum, *Biographical Register*, 2:437–38; Hagerman, "From Jomini to Dennis Hart Mahan," 211; Special Orders No. 178, Adjutant General's Office, War Department, May 16, 1864, *OR* 36(2):827.

7   George H. Mendell to James C. Duane, August 5, 1864, *OR* 36(1):317.

8   Cullum, *Biographical Register*, 2:812–13; Pleasants and Straley, *Inferno at Peters-burg*, 49.

9   "Michie, Peter Smith."

10   Wagner, "Michler, Nathaniel"; Shiman, "Army Engineers," 41–42; "Brief Synopsis of the Services Performed by Bvt Colonel Michler U.S.A. during the War," enclosed in Nathaniel Michler to C. H. Morgan, April 10, 1866, Michler to E. D. Townsend, August 25, 1866, B. A. Clements to Adjutant General, U.S. Army, July 25, 1881, Michler to Lorenzo Thomas, December 8, 1864, "Military History of Nathaniel Michler," in Michler personnel file, Letters Received by the Commission Branch of the Adjutant General's Office, M1064, RG94, NARA.

11   Nathaniel Michler to Seth Williams, October 20, 1864, *OR* 36(1):292–95. For information on the use of maps in the Overland campaign, see Gouverneur K. Warren to Andrew A. Humphreys, May 31, 1864, and Humphreys to Warren, May 31, 1864, *OR* 36(3):391–92.

12   Lyman, "Usefulness of the Maps." Warren agreed with Lyman — see Warren to Humphreys, May 26, 1864, *OR* 36(3):219.

13   *OR Atlas*, pl. 55, no. 4.

14   Hess, *Field Armies and Fortifications*, 12; record of events, 15th New York Engineers, *Supplement to the Official Records*, 43(2):210; record of events, 1st New York Engineers, *Supplement to the Official Records*, 42(2):400.

15   Thompson, *Engineer Battalion*, 56; Malles, *Bridge Building in Wartime*, 27, 344n; descriptive book, Company E, 50th New York Engineers, Ira Spaulding service record, 50th New York Engineers, RG94, NARA.

16   Malles, *Bridge Building in Wartime*, xv–xvi, 22, 251–53.

17   Ira Spaulding to James C. Duane, August 30, 1864, *OR* 36(1):304; Special Orders No. 92, Headquarters, Army of the Potomac, April 9, 1864, *OR* 51(1):1155; Leverett E. Seymour to brother, April 29, 1864, Seymour Letters, N-YHS; Thompson, *Engineer Battalion*, 56–70.

18   *History of the Thirty-fifth Regiment*, 241; George Washington Whitman to mother, June 18, 1864, in Loving, *Civil War Letters of George Washington Whitman*, 120.

19   *History of the Thirty-fifth Regiment*, 241–42.

20   Katcher, *Building the Victory*, 56–57, 60; Andrew Jackson Crossley to Sam, May 19, 1864, Bradbury Papers, SCL-DU; Shiman, "Army Engineers," 47; Constant Luce to R. A. Hutchins, August 8, 1864, *OR* 36(1):958–59; record of events, Company B, 50th New York Engineers, *Supplement to the Official Records*, 44(2):117–18.

21   Shiman, "Army Engineers," 38–39; John R. Brooke to Assistant Adjutant General, First Division, Second Corps, November 1, 1865, and George W. Getty to C. A. Whittier, October 13, 1864, *OR* 36(1):407, 678; James W. Forsyth to David McM. Gregg, May 16, 1864, *OR* 36(2):827; Rufus Ingalls to Simon F.

Barstow, February 26, 1864, *OR* 33:596. Warren wanted his Fifth Corps pioneers to always stay with their parent brigades unless detailed for a very good reason, as well as to be available for use as infantry "if needed." Circular, Headquarters, Fifth Corps, May 16, 1864, *OR* 36(2):821.

22 Gallagher, *Fighting for the Confederacy*, 370.

23 Steven B. Rhodes, "Jeremy Gilmer," 5–6, 9–10, 16–17, 25–26, 36, 53–92, 94–95, 98, 101–3, 144, 146, 156–58; Denson, "Corps of Engineers," 415; General Orders No. 90, Adjutant and Inspector General's Office, June 26, 1863, *OR*, ser. 4, 2:609–10; James L. Nichols, *Confederate Engineers*, 25.

24 Harry L. Jackson, *First Regiment Engineer Troops*, 13, 29; Warner, *Generals in Gray*, 179.

25 Warner, *Generals in Gray*, 282–83.

26 Rose, *Colours of the Gray*, 27, 35; Circular, Headquarters, Army of Northern Virginia, May 3, 1864, *OR* 36(2):944.

27 Martin L. Smith to Alexander R. Lawton, June 4, 1864, Lawton Papers, SHC-UNC.

28 James L. Nichols, *Confederate Engineers*, 87–88; Jedediah Hotchkiss Journal, May 9–June 3, 1864, in McDonald, *Make Me a Map of the Valley*, 201–2, 205–6, 208–10; Jedediah Hotchkiss Journal, May 23, June 11, 1864, in *Supplement to the Official Records*, 6:527, 531.

29 Harry L. Jackson, *First Regiment Engineer Troops*, 3–5, 10–13, 15–27, 30; Denson, "Corps of Engineers," 412–13, 426; Steven B. Rhodes, "Jeremy Gilmer," 169–70; James L. Nichols, *Confederate Engineers*, 93–95; Talcott, "Reminiscences of the Confederate Engineer Service," 258.

30 Blackford Commonplace Book, 2, MC; Harry L. Jackson, *First Regiment Engineer Troops*, 35–43; Talcott, "Reminiscences of the Confederate Engineer Service," 260, 262, 264; Gordon Memoirs, 136–43, WLU.

31 Robert E. L. Krick, *Staff Officers in Gray*, 279; muster cards and T. M. R. Talcott to Samuel Cooper, April 13, 1863, with Robert E. Lee endorsement, in Talcott service record, 1st Confederate Engineers, M258, RG109, NARA.

32 Jeremy Gilmer to James A. Seddon, July 25, 1863, Alfred L. Rives endorsement on T. M. R. Talcott letter dated December 14, 1863, Rives to Talcott, January 5, 1864, Rives endorsement, March 11, 1864, on Talcott letter dated March 9, 1864, Rives to Lee, April 1, 1864, and Rives to Seddon, April 1, 1864, Letters and Telegrams Sent by the Engineer Bureau of the Confederate War Department, M628, RG109, NARA; record of events, Companies C, D, F, 1st Confederate Engineers, M258, RG109, NARA; Talcott to Rives, March 9, 1864, and Rives to Samuel Cooper, April 12, 1864, in Talcott service record, 1st Confederate Engineers, M258, RG109, NARA; Harry L. Jackson, *First Regiment Engineer Troops*, 11; Blackford Commonplace Book, 2, MC.

33 Harry L. Jackson, *First Regiment Engineer Troops*, 13, 15–27, 29–30; Rives endorsement on T. M. R. Talcott letter, October 16, 1863, Letters and Telegrams

Sent by the Engineer Bureau of the Confederate War Department, M628, RG109, NARA.

34 Daniel, "H. H. Harris' Civil War Diary," 1840–47.

35 Warner, *Generals in Blue*, 176, 241, 316, 359, 462, 541, 548, 575; Warner, *Generals in Gray*, 22, 180.

36 Winfield S. Hancock to Assistant Adjutant General, Army of the Potomac, February [n.d.], 1865, *OR* 36(1):319; Warner, *Generals in Blue*, 203.

37 Hess, *Field Armies and Fortifications*, 25; Kennedy, *Civil War Battlefield Guide*, 281, 284, 288, 292.

CHAPTER 2

1 Ulysses S. Grant to Benjamin F. Butler, April 19, 1864, and Grant to George G. Meade, April 9, 17, 1864, in Simon, *Papers of Ulysses S. Grant*, 10:327, 274, 309.

2 Rhea, *Battle of the Wilderness*, 34, 62–63, 81–82, 92–93, 434.

3 Winters, *Battling the Elements*, 101; Francis A. Walker, *History of the Second Army Corps*, 417; Milton Myers Journal, 7, FB; field visit to the Wilderness, July 13, 1995.

4 Richard S. Ewell to Walter H. Taylor, March 20, 1865, *OR* 36(1):1070; Rhea, *Battle of the Wilderness*, 105, 123–26.

5 Ewell to Taylor, March 20, 1865, *OR* 36(1):1070; Rhea, *Battle of the Wilderness*, 137, 142–43, 156, 161, 163, 166, 171; A. J. Buckles speech, September 17, 1912, Marsh Papers, ID-ISL.

6 Rhea, *Battle of the Wilderness*, 176, 180–83.

7 Ibid., 62, 133–35, 190.

8 Winfield S. Hancock to Assistant Adjutant General, Army of the Potomac, February [n.d.], 1865: Michael W. Burns to James H. Lockwood, August 9, 1864, *OR* 36(1):319, 503; Rhea, *Battle of the Wilderness*, 190–208; Hancock to Assistant Adjutant General, Army of the Potomac, February [n.d.], 1865, *OR* 36(1):319; Robert S. Robertson Diary, May 5, 1864, in Walker and Walker, "Diary of the War," pt. 3, 162; Josiah F. Murphey reminiscences, in Miller and Mooney, *Civil War*, 98; John Gibbon to Mama, May 7, 1863, Gibbon Papers, Mary-HS.

9 Rhea, *Battle of the Wilderness*, 190–91, 194–206, 225, 234, 237–38.

10 Ibid., 245; William W. Smith, "The Wilderness and Spotsylvania," Daniel Papers, UVA.

11 Truman Seymour to Horatio G. Wright, August 12, 1864, *OR* 36(1):728.

12 William W. Smith, "The Wilderness and Spotsylvania," in Daniel Papers, SCL-DU; Buck, *With the Old Confeds*, 104; Rhea, *Battle of the Wilderness*, 246–48.

13 Seymour to Wright, August 12, 1864, *OR* 36(1):728; Rhea, *Battle of the Wilderness*, 264, 270, 272, 275–82.

14   Cadmus M. Wilcox to unidentified, November 16, 1864, in *Supplement to the Official Records*, 6:716; Rhea, *Battle of the Wilderness*, 285–86, 289, 291, 293–94.

15   William T. Poague memoir, in Cockrell, *Gunner with Stonewall*, 89; Rhea, *Battle of the Wilderness*, 294.

16   Lewis A. Grant to Peter T. Washburn, August 27, 1864, *OR* 36(1):699; Rhea, *Battle of the Wilderness*, 300–301, 311, 315.

17   Rhea, *Battle of the Wilderness*, 351, 354–56, 359, 366–70.

18   Hancock to Assistant Adjutant General, Army of the Potomac, February [n.d.], 1865, *OR* 36(1):323; Rhea, *Battle of the Wilderness*, 363–64; Webb, "Through the Wilderness," 157n, 160.

19   Rhea, *Battle of the Wilderness*, 324, 326, 328–31, 337, 375, 380, 383, 385–86, 399–401.

20   Henry G. Elder to John W. Hofmann, September 22, 1872, Hancock Papers, SCL-DU; James C. Stephens, "The Battle of the Wilderness," 32, Stephens Papers, IHS; Law, "From the Wilderness to Cold Harbor," 124; Rhea, *Battle of the Wilderness*, 389–90, 392.

21   Francis A. Walker, *History of the Second Army Corps*, 432; Rhea, *Battle of the Wilderness*, 393.

22   Hancock to Assistant Adjutant General, Army of the Potomac, February [n.d.], 1865, Michael W. Burns to James H. Lockwood, August 9, 1864, and Edwin B. Dow to U. D. Eddy, August 7, 1864, *OR* 36(1):324, 504, 514; Rhea, *Battle of the Wilderness*, 394; Samuel Clear Diary, May 6, 1864, and Daniel Chisholm to father, May 19, 1864, in Menge and Shimrak, *Civil War Notebook of Daniel Chisholm*, 13, 113; Hancock to Assistant Adjutant General, Army of the Potomac, February [n.d.], 1865, *OR* 36(1):324.

23   Josiah F. Murphey reminiscences, in Miller and Mooney, *Civil War*, 99; Jonah F. Dyer Diary, May 7, 1864, Chesson, *Journal of a Civil War Surgeon*, 148; Hancock to Andrew A. Humphreys, May 6, 1864, 7:15 P.M., *OR* 36(2):447; James C. Stephens, "The Battle of the Wilderness," 38, Stephens Papers, IHS; Rhea, *Battle of the Wilderness*, 394–95.

24   Charles S. Wainwright Journal, May, 6, 1864, in Nevins, *Diary of Battle*, 353; Rhea, *Battle of the Wilderness*, 318.

25   Rhea, *Battle of the Wilderness*, 317–20, 322–24.

26   William W. Smith to John W. Daniel, October 17, 1905, Daniel Papers, SCL-DU; Rhea, *Battle of the Wilderness*, 322–23.

27   Seymour to Wright, August 12, 1864, *OR* 36(1):729; Humphreys to Gouverneur K. Warren and John Sedgwick, May 6, 1864, 10:35 A.M., *OR* 36(2):451–52; Rhea, *Battle of the Wilderness*, 342.

28   Ira Spaulding to James C. Duane, August 30, 1864, *OR* 36(1):307; George H. Mendell to Duane, August 5, 1864, *OR* 36(1):317; Nathaniel Michler to Seth Williams, October 20, 1864, *OR* 36(1):296; Warren to Humphreys, May 6, 1864, 11:00 A.M., *OR* 36(2):452; record of events, Company K, 50th New York

Engineers, *Supplement to the Official Records*, 44(2):192; Thompson, *Engineer Battalion*, 56–57.

29   Humphreys to Warren, May 6, 1864, Sedgwick to Humphreys, May 6, 1864, 11:30 A.M., and Circular, First Division, Sixth Corps, May 6, 1864, 11:00 A.M., *OR* 36(2):455, 459–60; Snook Diary, May 6, 1864, Mary-HS; John W. Horn to J. A. Gump, September 14, 1864, *OR* 36(1):736–37.

30   Sedgwick to Humphreys, May 6, 1864, *OR* 36(2):460; Seymour to Wright, August 12, 1864, *OR* 36(1):729.

31   Seymour to Wright, August 12, 1864, *OR* 36(1):729; Snook Diary, May 6, 1864, Mary-HS; Rhea, *Battle of the Wilderness*, 404–5, 416, 422–23.

32   Richard S. Ewell to Walter H. Taylor, March 20, 1865, *OR* 36(1):1071; Bradwell, "Gordon's Ga. Brigade in the Wilderness," 642; Joseph McMurran Diary, May 7, 1864, LOV.

33   Thompson, *Engineer Battalion*, 57–58; Thompson Journal, 251–52, LC; George H. Mendell to James C. Duane, August 5, 1864, *OR* 36(1):317.

34   Ira Spaulding to James C. Duane, August 30, 1864, *OR* 36(1):307.

35   Humphreys to Warren, May 6, 1864, 11:30 P.M., and Cyrus B. Comstock to Ambrose E. Burnside, May 7, 1864, 7:30 A.M., *OR* 36(2):455, 511; Ira Spaulding to James C. Duane, August 30, 1864: Edwin Evans to [John D. Bertolette], n.d., *OR* 36(1):307, 961.

36   Charles S. Venable, "General Lee in the Wilderness Campaign," 240–41; John Gibbon to Mama, May 7, 1864, Gibbon Papers, Mary-HS; Winne Journal, May 8, 1864, Trent Collection, MCL-DU; Rhea, *Battle of the Wilderness*, 27, 51.

37   John Gibbon to Mama, May 7, 1864, Gibbon Papers, Mary-HS.

38   Caldwell, *History of a Brigade of South Carolinians*, 131. Even though he accepts the traditional interpretation about the tactical value to Lee of meeting Grant in the Wilderness, Gordon Rhea admits that lack of effective coordination hampered Union attacks at the Wilderness as much, or more, than did the effect of vegetation. Rhea, *Battle of the Wilderness*, 271.

39   Rhea, *Battle of the Wilderness*, 435, 440; Stewart, *Camp, March and Battlefield*, 384.

40   Hagerman, *American Civil War*, 255.

41   Charles W. Trueheart to father, June 27, 1864, in Williams, *Rebel Brothers*, 94.

42   Ulysses S. Grant to George G. Meade, May 5, 1864, in Simon, *Papers of Ulysses S. Grant*, 10:399.

43   Rhea, *Battle of the Wilderness*, 434–35.

CHAPTER 3

1   Rhea, *Battles for Spotsylvania Court House*, 14, 17–21, 28, 37–38, 42–43, 46–47, 53, 55–56, 59, 61–65; Hagerman, *American Civil War*, 257.

2   Manuscript map of area around Todd's Tavern, May 8, 1864, G185, Map Collection, RG77, NARA; Winfield S. Hancock to Assistant Adjutant General,

Army of the Potomac, February [n.d.], 1865, and Second Corps Headquarters Journal, May 8, 1864, *OR* 36(1):329, 355; Rhea, *Battles for Spotsylvania Court House*, 74–82, 86.

3   Robert K. Krick, "Insurmountable Barrier," 81; Richard S. Ewell to Walter H. Taylor, March 20, 1865, *OR* 36(1):1071; Rhea, *Battles for Spotsylvania Court House*, 87–90.

4   Robert K. Krick, "Insurmountable Barrier," 82; Gallagher, *Fighting for the Confederacy*, 372; Ewell to Taylor, March 20, 1865, *OR* 36(1):1072.

5   Gallagher, *Fighting for the Confederacy*, 372; William Cary Maupin to John W. Daniel, August 5, 1905, Daniel Papers, UVA; Terry L. Jones, *Civil War Memoirs of Captain William J. Seymour*, 119–120; James A. Walker, "Letter," 232–33; Carter, "Letter," 239.

6   Francis A. Walker to Gershom Mott, May 9, 1864, 12:15 P.M., and Hancock to [Andrew A. Humphreys], May 10, 1864, 6:40 and 7:00 A.M., *OR* 36(2):571–72, 599; Rhea, *Battles for Spotsylvania Court House*, 101–14; Thompson, *Engineer Battalion*, 58; Thompson Journal, 254, LC.

7   Martin T. McMahon to Horatio G. Wright, May 9, 1864, *OR* 36(2):579; Rhea, *Battles for Spotsylvania Court House*, 94; Caldwell, *History of a Brigade of South Carolinians*, 139; William T. Poague memoir, in Cockrell, *Gunner with Stonewall*, 91; Roberts, "Diary," 68; John Bratton to not stated, January 1, 1865, and James R. Hagood to A. C. Sorrel, December 20, 1864, *OR* 36(1):1066, 1069.

8   Nathaniel Michler to Seth Williams, October 20, 1864, *OR* 36(1):297; Thompson, *Engineer Battalion*, 60; Myers Journal, May 9–10, 1864, FB.

9   Rhea, *Battles for Spotsylvania Court House*, 130–31.

10 Hancock to Assistant Adjutant General, Army of the Potomac, September 21, 1865, *OR* 36(1): 331–32.

11 Ibid., 331; Rhea, *Battles for Spotsylvania Court House*, 134–40; Hess, *Lee's Tar Heels*, 219–21.

12 Thompson Journal, 256, LC.

13 Hancock to Assistant Adjutant General, Army of the Potomac, September 21, 1865, and John Gibbon to Septimius Carncross, November 7, 1864, *OR* 36(1):334, 430; Thompson Journal, 256, LC; Rhea, *Battles for Spotsylvania Court House*, 142–43, 146–49.

14 P. Regis de Trobriand to J. P. Finkelmeier, October 20, 1864, *OR* 36(1):470; Orlando B. Willcox to [Ambrose E. Burnside], May [10], 1864, 6:30 and 7:15 P.M., *OR* 36(2):614; Rhea, *Battles for Spotsylvania Court House*, 149–50, 177–81, 184–85.

15 Michler to Williams, October 20, 1864, and Emory Upton to Henry R. Dalton, September 1, 1864, *OR* 36(1):297, 667; Oliver Wendell Holmes Jr. Diary, May 10, 1864, in Mark DeWolfe Howe, *Touched with Fire*, 112; Rhea, *Battles for Spotsylvania Court House*, 163–64. Col. J. Catlett Gibson of the 49th Virginia in John Pegram's brigade later recalled that the short secondary

line immediately behind Doles's Salient was poorly made. He claimed that the trench was only knee-deep and two feet wide, and that the parapet was only eight inches tall. The dirt was "grayish white." Gibson called the line "a quadrilateral from our main line of works, silly planned and executed." Gibson and Smith, "Battle of Spotsylvania," 206.

16 Wright to Mott, May 10, 1864, and Mott to Wright, May 10, 1864, 2:05 P.M., *OR* 36(2):603; Upton to Dalton, September 1, 1864, *OR* 36(1):667; Rhea, *Battles for Spotsylvania Court House*, 122, 164–66.

17 Upton to Dalton, September 1, 1864, *OR* 36(1):668.

18 Upton to Dalton, September 1, 1864, William N. Pendleton to Taylor, February 28, 1865, and Ewell to Taylor, March 20, 1865, *OR* 36(1):668, 1043, 1072; Rhea, *Battles for Spotsylvania Court House*, 168–76.

19 Lee to Ewell, May 10, 1864, 8:15 P.M., *OR* 36(2):983.

20 Rhea, *Battles for Spotsylvania Court House*, 185–87.

21 Toney, "Reminiscences of the Wilderness," 89.

22 Caldwell, *History of a Brigade of South Carolinians*, 140; Bryan Grimes to wife, May 11, 1864, in Gallagher, *Extracts of Letters of Major-General Bryan Grimes*, 51.

23 Morrison, *Memoirs of Henry Heth*, 186–87.

24 Circular, Headquarters, Army of the Potomac, May 11, 1864, 7:30 A.M., *OR* 36(2):630; Warren to Samuel W. Crawford and Lysander Cutler, May 11, 1864, 3:00 P.M., and Wright to Williams, May 11, 1864, 9:15 A.M., *OR* 36(2):639–41.

25 Grant to Meade, May 11, 1864, 3:00 P.M., *OR* 36(2):629; Rhea, *Battles for Spotsylvania Court House*, 214–15, 217, 224; Francis A. Walker, *History of the Second Army Corps*, 467–68; Hancock to Assistant Adjutant General, Army of the Potomac, September 21, 1865, *OR* 36(1):335.

26 Rhea, *Battles for Spotsylvania Court House*, 221–23; Francis A. Walker, *History of the Second Army Corps*, 468.

27 Black, "Reminiscences of the Bloody Angle," 423–25.

28 Circular, Headquarters, Second Corps, May 11, 1864, *OR* 36(2):635; John Haley Journal, May 12, 1864, in Silliker, *Rebel Yell and the Yankee Hurrah*, 155.

29 Gallagher, *Fighting for the Confederacy*, 374–75; Rhea, *Battles for Spotsylvania Court House*, 219–20, 225–26.

30 Purifoy, "Jeff Davis Artillery at Bloody Angle," 222–23; Carter, "Letter," 240; Rhea, *Battles for Spotsylvania Court House*, 226–27.

31 Edward C. Jackson, "Bloody Angle," 260; Tyler, *Recollections of the Civil War*, 176.

32 Tyler, *Recollections of the Civil War*, 176; Cadwallader Jones, "Tree Cut Down by Bullets"; Green, "From the Wilderness to Spotsylvania," 100; Randolph Barton memoir, in Colt, *Defend the Valley*, 314; Clark, "From the Rapidan to Petersburg," 382; Rhea, *Battles for Spotsylvania Court House*, 150. The parapet on other parts of the Confederate line at Spotsylvania apparently was not as

thick as at the Mule Shoe Salient. Lt. Dent Burroughs of George V. Moody's Louisiana battery, in Lt. Col. Frank Huger's battalion of the First Corps, was killed on May 12 when a Federal artillery round "passed through the parapet." William N. Pendleton to Walter H. Taylor, February 28, 1865, *OR* 36(1):1045.

33 James A. Walker, "Letter," 233–34. For modern color photographs of the landscape in front of the salient line, see "General's Tour: The Battles at Spotsylvania Court House," 53–56.

CHAPTER 4

1 Winfield S. Hancock to Assistant Adjutant General, Army of the Potomac, September 21, 1865, *OR* 36(1):335; Rhea, *Battles for Spotsylvania Court House*, 229–32, 235, 237. A Sixth Corps survivor of the battle recalled substantial abatis fronting a portion of the west side of the salient. He described it as fifteen yards deep, consisting of "entire trees interlaced with smaller timber and heavy limbs from the trunks used in the construction of the breastwork. . . . Its height and width and solidity made it a formidable obstacle." Mason, "Through the Wilderness to the Bloody Angle," 305.

2 Green, "From the Wilderness to Spotsylvania," 99; Robert McAllister to Gershom Mott, January 24, 1882, in James I. Robertson, *Civil War Letters of General Robert McAllister*, 418; Hancock to Assistant Adjutant General, Army of the Potomac, September 21, 1865, and John R. Brooke to Assistant Adjutant General, First Division, Second Corps, November 1, 1865, *OR* 36(1):335, 409–10; Edward C. Jackson, "Bloody Angle," 260; George A. Bowen, "Diary of Captain George D. Bowen," 184.

3 Robert S. Robertson Diary, May 12, 1864, in Walker and Walker, "Diary of the War," pt. 4, 182; Rhea, *Battles for Spotsylvania Court House*, 235; James A. Walker, "Letter," 235–36; Carter, "Letter," 240–41.

4 Stephen D. Ramseur to Major Peyton, August 10, 1864, *OR* 36(1):1082; Rhea, *Battles for Spotsylvania Court House*, 240, 255–57.

5 Rhea, *Battles for Spotsylvania Court House*, 242, 311–12.

6 Barlow, "Capture of the Salient," 254; Francis A. Walker, *History of the Second Army Corps*, 471; Green, "From the Wilderness to Spotsylvania," 101; John Haley Journal, May 12, 1864, in Silliker, *Rebel Yell and the Yankee Hurrah*, 156; Edward C. Jackson, "Bloody Angle," 261; Rhea, *Battles for Spotsylvania Court House*, 242.

7 Robert S. Robertson Diary, May 12, 1864, in Walker and Walker, "Diary of the War," pt. 4, 183; George A. Bowen, "Diary of Captain George D. Bowen," 184; Rhea, *Battles for Spotsylvania Court House*, 246.

8 Robert S. Robertson Diary, May 12, 1864, in Walker and Walker, "Diary of the War," pt. 4, 183; Edward C. Jackson, "Bloody Angle," 261.

9 Ambrose E. Burnside to Seth Williams, November 26, 1864, and Robert B. Potter to Lewis Richmond, August 1, 1864, *OR* 36(1):909–10, 928; Rhea, *Battles*

for *Spotsylvania Court House*, 248, 250, 252–55; Francis A. Walker, *History of the Second Army Corps*, 472.

10 Gambrell, "Fighting at Spottsylvania C.H."; Rhea, *Battles for Spotsylvania Court House*, 266–70.

11 Cadwallader Jones, "Tree Cut Down by Bullets"; Rhea, *Battles for Spotsylvania Court House*, 267, 274. Ewell claimed that his men managed to retake two-thirds of the works they lost in the morning. Richard S. Ewell to Walter H. Taylor, March 20, 1865, *OR* 36(1):1073.

12 Rhea, *Battles for Spotsylvania Court House*, 290.

13 Francis A. Walker, *History of the Second Army Corps*, 471; Barlow, "Capture of the Salient," 254–55; Rhea, *Battles for Spotsylvania Court House*, 260–62, 264. Grant later disputed Barlow's claim that his brigade had disrupted Barlow's division, maintaining that the Second Corps unit already was in disorder when he arrived. Grant, "Review of Major-General Barlow's Paper," 266.

14 Grant, "Review of Major-General Barlow's Paper," 267; Robert S. Robertson Diary, May 12, 1864, Walker and Walker, "Diary of the War," pt. 4, 185; Rhea, *Battles for Spotsylvania Court House*, 272–73.

15 Rhea, *Battles for Spotsylvania Court House*, 274–77, 280–81.

16 Ibid., 291.

17 George G. Meade to Gouverneur K. Warren, May 12, 1864, 8:00 A.M., Warren to Meade, May 12, 1864, Warren to Andrew A. Humphreys, May 12, 1864, 9:10 A.M., Humphreys to Warren, May 12, 1864, 9:30 A.M., Warren to Samuel W. Crawford and Charles Griffin, May 12, 1864, 9:30 A.M., Wright to Humphreys, May 12, 1864, 5:10 P.M., and Meade to Wright, May 12, 1864, 6:15 P.M., *OR* 36(2):662–63, 668–69, 674–75; Rufus R. Dawes to J. D. Wood, August 7, 1864, *OR* 36(1):620; Rhea, *Battles for Spotsylvania Court House*, 277, 294, 296, 298–300, 302–6.

18 David Holt reminiscences, in Cockrell and Ballard, *Mississippi Rebel in the Army of Northern Virginia*, 256.

19 Caldwell, *History of a Brigade of South Carolinians*, 142–43; Berry Benson reminiscences, in Benson, *Berry Benson's Civil War Book*, 76; unidentified soldier of the 1st South Carolina, quoted in Power, *Lee's Miserables*, 32.

20 John Haley journal, May 12, 1864, in Silliker, *Rebel Yell and the Yankee Hurrah*, 156; Mason, "Through the Wilderness to the Bloody Angle," 305; Tyler, *Recollections of the Civil War*, 191–94; James L. Bowen, "General Edwards's Brigade," 177.

21 Galloway, "Hand-to-Hand Fighting at Spotsylvania," 174.

22 Ibid., 173; Charles Harvey Brewster to Mary, May 13, 1864, in Blight, *When This Cruel War Is Over*, 296.

23 Berry Benson reminiscences, in Benson, *Berry Benson's Civil War Book*, 75–76; George A. Bowen, "Diary of Captain George D. Bowen," 185; Grant, "Review of Major-General Barlow's Paper," 269; Robert S. Robertson Diary,

May 12, 1864, in Walker and Walker, "Diary of the War," pt. 4, 184; Galloway, "Hand-to-Hand Fighting at Spotsylvania," 170.

24 Tyler, *Recollections of the Civil War*, 192–93.

25 Cadwallader Jones, "Tree Cut Down By Bullets."

26 Galloway, "Hand-to-Hand Fighting at Spotsylvania," 173; Rhea, *Battles for Spotsylvania Court House*, 280; David Holt reminiscences, in Cockrell and Ballard, *Mississippi Rebel in the Army of Northern Virginia*, 261.

27 Hancock to Assistant Adjutant General, Army of the Potomac, September 21, 1865, *OR* 36(1):336; Rhea, *Battles for Spotsylvania Court House*, 277–79; Galloway, "Hand-to-Hand Fighting at Spotsylvania," 171–72.

28 Rhea, *Battles for Spotsylvania Court House*, 291. The Army of the Potomac had forty Coehorn mortars by the end of the Overland campaign, distributed among the 1st Connecticut Heavy Artillery, the 4th and 15th New York Heavy Artillery, and Henry L. Abbott's Siege Train. Lord, "Coehorn Mortar," 18.

29 Galloway, "Hand-to-Hand Fighting at Spotsylvania," 173; Berry Benson reminiscences, in Benson, *Berry Benson's Civil War Book*, 75.

30 Nathan Church to not stated, October 21, 1864, *OR* 36(1):373–74.

31 Cadwallader Jones, "Tree Cut Down by Bullets."

32 Caldwell, *History of a Brigade of South Carolinians*, 145.

33 Galloway, "Hand-to-Hand Fighting at Spotsylvania," 173; Emory Upton to G. Norton Galloway, August 31, 1878, in Michie, *Life and Letters of Emory Upton*, 112; Daniel M. Holt to wife, May 16, 1864, in Greiner, Coryell, and Smither, *Surgeon's Civil War*, 190.

34 Brown, *Colonel at Gettysburg and Spotsylvania*, 259; Cadwallader Jones, "Tree Cut Down by Bullets"; Emory Upton to G. Norton Galloway, August 31, 1878, in Michie, *Life and Letters of Emory Upton*, 112. The stump of the twenty-two-inch tree was later preserved by local residents and stored in a smokehouse at Spotsylvania. Nelson Miles and Maj. Nathan Church of the 26th Michigan found it when they visited the battlefield on May 10, 1865. Miles gave it to the War Department, which later donated it to the Smithsonian Institution. The stump, with its delicately frayed end, was put on display at the Centennial Exposition at Philadelphia in 1876 and the Columbian Exposition in Chicago in 1893 before being placed on permanent exhibit at the National Museum of American History in Washington, D.C., in the 1920s. Brown, *Colonel at Gettysburg and Spotsylvania*, 261. For a modern color photograph of the stump, see Kernan, "The Object at Hand," 24.

35 Casler, *Four Years in the Stonewall Brigade*, 213.

36 Ewell to Taylor, March 20, 1865, *OR* 36(1):1073; Rhea, *Battles for Spotsylvania Court House*, 306; Berry Benson reminiscences, in Benson, *Berry Benson's Civil War Book*, 76; Tyler, *Recollections of the Civil War*, 195.

37 Humphreys to Hancock, May 12, 1864, 8:00 and 9:20 P.M., Circular, Headquarters, Second Corps, May 12, 1864, and Humphreys to Warren, May 12,

1864, 7:50 P.M., *OR* 36(2):660–61, 666; Percy Daniels to E. C. Mauran, June 3, 1864, and William B. Reynolds to Peter T. Washburn, May 20, 1864, *OR* 36(1):931, 936.

38 John Haley journal, May 12, 1864, in Silliker, *Rebel Yell and the Yankee Hurrah*, 156–57.

CHAPTER 5

1 Tyler, *Recollections of the Civil War*, 195–96; Oliver Wendell Holmes Jr., diary, May 12–13, 1864, in Mark DeWolfe Howe, *Touched with Fire*, 116–17; Charles Harvey Brewster to Mary, May 13, 1864, in Blight, *When This Cruel War Is Over*, 296; Second Corps Headquarters Journal, May 13, 1864, and J. William Hofmann to C. McClellan, August 10, 1864, *OR* 36(1):360, 626.

2 Galloway, "Hand-to-Hand Fighting at Spotsylvania," 174.

3 Robert A. Guyton to sister, May 19, 1864, Guyton and Heaslet Papers, SCL-DU; Rhea, *Battles for Spotsylvania Court House*, 308–12; Rhea, *To the North Anna River*, 24–25.

4 Robert K. Krick, "Insurmountable Barrier," 87, 106; Rhea, *Battles for Spotsylvania Court House*, 313.

5 Edward Johnson to Richard S. Ewell, August 16, 1864, *OR* 36(1):1080; Edward P. Alexander memoir, in Gallagher, *Fighting for the Confederacy*, 376.

6 Hancock to Humphreys, May 13, 1864, *OR* 36(2):707.

7 Nathaniel Michler to Seth Williams, October 20, 1864, William S. Tilton to Assistant Adjutant General, Second Brigade, First Division, Fifth Corps, August 8, 1864, Emory Upton to Henry R. Dalton, September 1, 1864, and Diary of First Corps, May 14, 1864, *OR* 36(1):298, 562, 669–70, 1057; Hancock to Humphreys, May 13, 1864, and Fitzhugh Birney to William Blaisdell, May 14, 1864, *OR* 36(2):707, 755; Rhea, *To the North Anna River*, 33, 72–74, 76–90; Abner R. Small reminiscences, in Small, *Road to Richmond*, 142. Russell's division continued to fortify on May 16 by slashing trees in front of its line. Wright to Humphreys, May 16, 1864, *OR* 36(2):822.

8 Fitzhugh Birney to Gershom Mott, May 15, 1864, 4:40 P.M., Ambrose E. Burnside to George G. Meade, May 15, 1864, 12:45 [P.M.], Orville E. Babcock to Burnside, May 15, 1864, Ulysses S. Grant to Burnside, May 15, 1864, 3:05 P.M., Burnside to Grant, May 15, 1864, 3:20 P.M., David B. Birney to Burnside, May 15, 1864, Meade to Burnside, May 15, 1864, 4:40 P.M., and Burnside to John A. Rawlins, May 16, 1864, 9:50 A.M., *OR* 36(2):785, 795–96, 826; Rhea, *To the North Anna River*, 98, 100, 114–15.

9 Nathaniel Michler to Seth Williams, October 20, 1864, *OR* 36(1):298; Circular, Headquarters Second Army Corps, May 16, 1864, *OR* 36(2):814.

10 Gorman Diary, 2, NCDAH; Daniel M. Holt to wife, May 16, 1864, in Greiner, Coryell, and Smither, *Surgeon's Civil War*, 190.

11 Caldwell, *History of a Brigade of South Carolinians*, 150.

12 Circular, Headquarters, Second Corps, May 18, 1864, 1:00 A.M., *OR* 36(2):870–71.

13 Ewell to Walter H. Taylor, March 20, 1865, *OR* 36(1):1073; Circular, Headquarters, Second Corps, May 18, 1864, 1:00 A.M., *OR* 36(2):870–71; Rhea, *To the North Anna River*, 127–29, 131–32, 134–36; Francis A. Walker, *History of the Second Army Corps*, 485; Rhea, *Battles for Spotsylvania Court House*, 310.

14 Rhea, *To the North Anna River*, 139–42.

15 Hancock to Williams, May 18, 1864, 6:50 A.M., *OR* 36(2):868; Frank Wheaton to Charles Mundee, September 1, 1864, *OR* 36(1):685.

16 Myers Journal, 27, FB; Francis C. Barlow to mother, May 18, 1864, Samito, *"Fear Was Not in Him,"* 197; Robert S. Robertson to parents, May 18, 1864, Robertson Letters, FB; Francis A. Walker, *History of the Second Army Corps*, 485–86; Hancock to Assistant Adjutant General, Army of the Potomac, September 21, 1865, Second Corps Headquarters Journal, May 18, 1864, John R. Brooke to Assistant Adjutant General, First Division, Second Corps, November 1, 1865, John Gibbon to Septimius Carncross, November 7, 1864, and Frank Wheaton to Charles Mundee, September 1, 1864, *OR* 36(1):338, 362, 410, 431, 685–86; Hancock to Humphreys, May 18, 1864, 5:40 A.M., Hancock to Williams, May 18, 1864, 6:50 A.M., Humphreys to Hancock, May 18, 1864, 8:45 A.M., and Warren to Humphreys, May 18, 1864, *OR* 36(2):867–69, 876; Rhea, *To the North Anna River*, 142–54.

17 George G. Meade to wife, May 19, 1864, in Meade, *Life and Letters*, 2:197.

18 Snook Diary, May 20–21, 1864, Mary-HS; Rhea, *To the North Anna River*, 159–60. Wheaton's brigade found the terrain "covered with small pine and brush" when it assumed its new position on the Union left. The men slashed it and dug a trench. Frank Wheaton to Charles Mundee, September 1, 1864, *OR* 36(1):686.

19 Diary of First Corps, May 19, 1864, *OR* 36(1):1058; ibid., 166–68, 170–85, 187–88. The battlefield of May 19 appears today much as it did in 1864. One can see across the expansive, open fields from Highway 208, the old Fredericksburg Road. Field visit, June 25, 1997.

20 Theodore Lyman to wife, May 18, 1864, in Agassiz, *Meade's Headquarters*, 99–100.

21 Jordan, *Some Events and Incidents during the Civil War*, 77; Caldwell, *History of a Brigade of South Carolinians*, 139.

22 William T. Poague memoir, in Cockrell, *Gunner with Stonewall*, 93.

23 Hagerman, *American Civil War*, 258–59; Joseph F. Shaner to parents, May 7, 1864, Shaner Correspondence, WLU.

24 Lyons Diary, May 8–17, 1864, SHC-UNC.

25 Arthur T. Chapin diary, May 21, 1864, in Longacre, "From the Wilderness to Cold Harbor in the Union Artillery," 209. The Confederates also relied

on close cooperation between infantry and artillery officers in strengthening their defenses. All of Lee's top artillery commanders and his chief engineer consulted on how best to hold the area where Massaponax Church Road crossed the Confederate line. William N. Pendleton to Edward Porter Alexander, May 18, 1864, 9:00 P.M., *OR* 36(2):1020.

26 Elisha Hunt Rhodes diary, May 20, 1864, in Robert Hunt Rhodes, *All for the Union*, 154.

27 Rhea, *Battles for Spotsylvania Court House*, 312–19.

28 Charles S. Venable, "General Lee in the Wilderness Campaign," 244; Rhea, *Battles for Spotsylvania Court House*, 319, 324.

29 Daniel M. Holt diary, May 10–11, 1864, in Greiner, Coryell, and Smither, *Surgeon's Civil War*, 186.

30 Robert McAllister to Ellen and family, May 11, 1864, in James I. Robertson, *Civil War Letters of General Robert McAllister*, 417.

31 John S. Jones, "From North Anna to Cold Harbor," 156; Reardon, "A Hard Road to Travel," 176–79, 181–82, 185–90, 196.

32 Ulysses S. Grant to Henry W. Halleck, May 8, 1864, Grant to Halleck, May 10, 1864, Grant to Edwin M. Stanton and to Halleck, May 11, 1864, Grant to Julia, May 13, 1864, and Grant to Halleck, May 16, 1864, in Simon, *Papers of Ulysses S. Grant*, 10:411, 418–19, 422–23, 443–44, 451–52.

33 Robert E. Lee to Jefferson Davis, May 9, 1864, in Freeman, *Lee's Dispatches*, 176; Lee to Davis, May 18, 1864, ibid., 183–84.

34 Thomas J. Linebarger to family, May 15, 1864, Linebarger Snuggs Papers, SHC-UNC.

CHAPTER 6

1 Warner, *Generals in Blue*, 60–61.

2 Ibid., 176–77; Quincy A. Gillmore to John W. Shaffer, May 22, 1864, *OR* 36(3):105.

3 Warner, *Generals in Blue*, 462–64.

4 Longacre, *Army of Amateurs*, 36–39, 63; William Glenn Robertson, *Back Door to Richmond*, 31.

5 Smith, "Butler's Attack on Drewry's Bluff," 207–8.

6 Benjamin F. Butler to Edwin M. Stanton, May 7, 1864, and Gillmore to Butler, May 7, 1864, *OR* 36(2):517, 519; William Glenn Robertson, *Back Door to Richmond*, 57, 59, 61, 65, 69–72, 79, 83, 86, 89, 91; Longacre, *Army of Amateurs*, 73–78; Valentine C. Randolph diary, May 7, 1864, in Roe, *Civil War Soldier's Diary*, 202.

7 Harris M. Plaisted to Edward W. Smith, May 11, 1864, *OR* 36(2):75–76; William Glenn Robertson, *Back Door to Richmond*, 107, 109, 112–13, 119–21, 123, 127, 139–40; Longacre, *Army of Amateurs*, 79–84.

8 William F. Smith to John W. Shaffer, June 7, 1864, *OR* 36(2):115; William Glenn Robertson, *Back Door to Richmond*, 143, 147–48; Smith, "Butler's Attack on Drewry's Bluff," 209.

9 Seth M. Barton to Theodore O. Chestney, May 7, 1864, and Robert F. Hoke to Braxton Bragg, May 13, 1864, *OR* 36(2):973, 999; William Glenn Robertson, *Back Door to Richmond*, 148.

10 Gillmore to Shaffer, May 25, 1864, Alfred H. Terry to Edward W. Smith, May 17, 1864, and Butler to Stanton, May 14, 1864, *OR* 36(2):37, 41, 771.

11 Gillmore to Shaffer, May 25, 1864, Terry to Smith, May 17, 1864, Smith to Shaffer, June 7, 1864, and Butler to Stanton, May 14, 1864, *OR* 36(2):37, 42, 115, 771.

12 William T. H. Brooks to Assistant Adjutant General, Eighteenth Corps, May 25, 1864, Frederick F. Wead to C. H. Lawrence, May 22, 1864, Butler to Gillmore, May 14, 1864, 3:00 P.M., and Israel R. Sealy to John W. Turner, May 14, 1864, *OR* 36(2):127, 131, 773–74.

13 Butler to [William F.] Smith, May 14, 1864, Smith to Butler, May 14, 1864, and Gillmore to Butler, May 15, 1864, *OR* 36(2):776, 804–5; William Glenn Robertson, *Back Door to Richmond*, 150, 154–55, 170.

14 Hiram Burnham to Theodore Read, May 22, 1864, and Godfrey Weitzel to Nicolas Bowen, May 22, 23, 1864, *OR* 36(2):135, 150, 152; William Glenn Robertson, *Back Door to Richmond*, 175–76; Smith, "Butler's Attack on Drewry's Bluff," 210; Bruce, "General Butler's Bermuda Hundred Campaign," 329; Schiller, "Beast in a Bottle," 20.

15 Burnham to Read, May 22, 1864, and Weitzel to Bowen, May 23, 1864, *OR* 36(2):135, 152; Bruce, "General Butler's Bermuda Hundred Campaign," 329; William Glenn Robertson, *Back Door to Richmond*, 175–76.

16 Winslow P. Spofford to Charles B. Amory, May 24, 1864. James O'Neill to W. H. Abel, May 24, 1864, and Francis U. Farquhar to Gillmore, May 15, 1864, *OR* 36(2):82–83, 159, 804.

17 Beauregard, "Defense of Drewry's Bluff," 197–99; William Glenn Robertson, *Back Door to Richmond*, 149–51, 153.

18 Beauregard, "Defense of Drewry's Bluff," 200; William Glenn Robertson, *Back Door to Richmond*, 171.

19 *Drewry's Bluff*, RNB Park Brochure; field visit to Fort Darling, August 29, 1995. The fort is very well preserved. See also superb period photographs and modern color photographs of works at and around Fort Darling in Davis and Wiley, *Photographic History of the Civil War*, 2:1087, 1089–90, and in "General's Tour: The Bermuda Hundred Campaign," 57–59. See also a Civil War image of Fort Darling and a view of the same spot, taken in the 1930s, in 1939 World's Fair Photograph Collection, LOV.

20 Field visit to Inner Line, August 29, 1995.

21 Field visit to Fort Stevens, August 29, 1995. See also a modern color photograph of Fort Stevens in "General's Tour: The Bermuda Hundred Campaign," 57.

22 Field visit to Outer Line, August 29, 1995.

23 Compton, "About the Battle at Drury's Bluff"; Seay, "Vivid Story of Drury's Bluff Battle"; William Glenn Robertson, *Back Door to Richmond*, 182–87.

24 J. H. Neil reminiscences, *News and Herald*, May 25, 1910; Witherspoon, "Battle of Drewry's Bluff"; William Glenn Robertson, *Back Door to Richmond*, 189–90.

25 Weitzel to Bowen, May 22, 23, 1864, R. H. Keeble to Bushrod R. Johnson, May 22, 1864, and William N. James to R. E. Foote, May 22, 1864, *OR* 36(2):150, 152, 247, 249; Witherspoon, "Battle of Drewry's Bluff"; Curtis, "About the Battle of Drewry's Bluff"; William Glenn Robertson, *Back Door to Richmond*, 190–91.

26 William Glenn Robertson, *Back Door to Richmond*, 192–93.

27 Ibid., 198–206, 209–15.

28 Ibid., 143, 217; Longacre, *Army of Amateurs*, 100, 104.

29 William Glenn Robertson, *Back Door to Richmond*, 218–19; Loehr, *War History*, 49. Harris had to call on Walter H. Stevens for half a dozen carpenters to build gun platforms at Battery Dantzler. Alfred L. Rives to W. H. Stevens, May 25, 1864, Letters and Telegrams Sent by the Engineer Bureau of the Confederate War Department, M628, RG109, NARA.

30 Stephen Elliott Jr. to R. E. Foote, June 2, 1864, *OR* 36(2):265–66; *Bermuda Hundred Campaign in Chesterfield County*, 23; Hagood, *Memoirs of the War of Secession*, 250–51; field visit to Fort Clifton, August 29, 1995. See a modern color photograph of Fort Clifton in "General's Tour: The Bermuda Hundred Campaign," 55.

31 G. T. Beauregard to Jefferson Davis, May 21, 1864, *OR* 36(3):181; Hagood, *Memoirs of the War of Secession*, 252; William Glenn Robertson, *Back Door to Richmond*, 221–22.

32 Special Orders No. 11, Headquarters, Department of North Carolina and Southern Virginia, May 23, 1864, *OR* 36(3):827; Circular, Department of North Carolina and Southern Virginia, May 24, 1864, D. H. Hill Papers, NCDAH; William Glenn Robertson, *Back Door to Richmond*, 224.

33 Beauregard to Davis, May 21, 1864, John M. Richardson to D. H. Hill, May 26, 1864, Beauregard to Hill, May 26, 1864, Special Orders No. 15, Headquarters, Department of North Carolina and Southern Virginia, May 29, 1864, and P. R. Page to Hill, June 2, 1864, *OR* 36(3):818, 835, 849, 869.

34 Gillmore to Butler, May 17, 1864, Bowen to William T. H. Brooks and Godfrey Weitzel, May 17, 1864, Butler to [not given], May 18, 1864, 3:00 P.M., Francis U. Farquhar to Gillmore, May 18, 1864, Edward W. Smith to

Alfred H. Terry, May 18, 1864, and Adelbert Ames to Edward W. Smith, May 19, 1864, *OR* 36(2):860–62, 899–900, 902, 937; Valentine C. Randolph diary, May 18–20, 22–23, 1864, in Roe, *Civil War Soldier's Diary*, 208–9.

35 Cooke Diary, May 17, 1864, VHS; Edward W. Serrell to Edward W. Smith, May 20, 1864, *OR* 36(3):35.

36 Butler to Smith and Weitzel, May 19, 1864, *OR* 36(2):937; Circular, Department of Virginia and North Carolina, May 20, 1864, General Orders No. 65, May 20, 1864, Gillmore to Butler, May 20, 1864, and General Orders No. 67, Department of Virginia and North Carolina, May 22, 1864, *OR* 36(3):32, 34, 104; Warner, *Generals in Blue*, 548–49.

37 Weitzel to Gillmore, May 20, 1864, *OR* 36(3):38–39.

38 Bowen to Brooks, May 22, 1864, *OR* 36(2):109; Butler to Gillmore, May 20, 1864, 10:50 and 11:00 P.M., Gillmore to Butler, May 20, 1864, Edward W. Serrell to Gillmore, May 20, 1864, Gillmore to Butler, May 21, 1864, Weitzel to Gillmore, May 21, 1864, General Orders No. 21, Headquarters, Eighteenth Corps, May 21, 1864, Weitzel to Gillmore, May 22, 1864, Smith to Weitzel, May 22, 1864, Serrell to Capt. Israel R. Sealy, May 23, 1864, and Frederick E. Graef to Gillmore, May 28, 1864, *OR* 36(3):38, 69–71, 74, 105–6, 108, 142, 283–84.

39 Henry L. Abbot to Edward W. Smith, May 31, 1864, General Orders No. 7, Headquarters, Tenth Corps, June 1, 1864, and Henry J. Hunt to Abbott, June 10, 1864, *OR* 36(3):419, 474, 741; Richard Delafield to W. P. Trowbridge, May 31, 1864, Letters Sent by the Chief of Engineers, M1113, RG77, NARA.

40 *Bermuda Hundred Campaign in Chesterfield County*, 12, 22; Weitzel and Michie manuscript map of Union line at Bermuda Hundred, G158, Map Collection, RG77, NARA; Richard Delafield to Edwin M. Stanton, October 30, 1865, *OR*, ser. 3, 5:183; Valentine C. Randolph diary, May 31, 1864, in Roe, *Civil War Soldier's Diary*, 214.

41 Beauregard, "Defense of Drewry's Bluff," 204–5; William Glenn Robertson, *Back Door to Richmond*, 222, 237.

42 Grant to Montgomery C. Meigs and John G. Barnard, May 21, 1864, and Halleck to Butler, May 26, 1864, *OR* 36(3):68–69, 234; Longacre, *Army of Amateurs*, 111–22; William Glenn Robertson, *Back Door to Richmond*, 235, 237.

43 Gillmore to Weitzel, May 30, 1864, Weitzel to Gillmore, June 1, 1864, and endorsement by Gillmore, Gillmore to Butler, June 3, 1864, General Orders No. 8, Headquarters, Tenth Corps, June 3, 1864, Gillmore to Weitzel, June 11, 1864, and Weitzel to Gillmore, June 11, 1864, *OR* 36(3):370, 474, 566–68, 756.

44 Weitzel to Gillmore, June 1, 1864, Butler to C. E. Fuller, June 2, 1864, Fuller to Butler, June 2, 1864, and Gillmore to Alfred H. Terry, Turner, Kautz, June 3, 1864, *OR* 36(3):473, 515, 568; Valentine C. Randolph diary, June 7, 1864, in Roe, *Civil War Soldier's Diary*, 219.

45 Grant borrowed the phrase from Barnard, who used it when reporting to Grant after his and Meigs's inspection of Butler's situation. Grant regretted using the phrase because he felt that it was unjust to Butler. Grant, *Personal Memoirs*, 2:493–94; "Controversy: Was Butler 'Bottled Up'?"

CHAPTER 7

1 Ulysses S. Grant to George G. Meade, May 18, 1864, *OR* 36(2):865; Rhea, *To the North Anna River*, 155–57, 192, 194–95, 197–98.

2 Meade to Grant, May 20, 1864, 10:30 A.M., Andrew A. Humphreys to Horatio G. Wright, May 20, 1864, 9:30 A.M., 1:20 P.M., and 5:20 P.M., Wright to Humphreys, May 20, 1864, 1:10 P.M., Grant to Ambrose E. Burnside, May 20, 1864, Burnside to Grant, May 20, 1864, 7:30 P.M., Horace Porter to Burnside, May 20, 9:00 P.M., Wright to Humphreys, May 21, 1864, 8:10 and 8:25 A.M., and David R. Larned to Thomas L. Crittenden, May 21, 1864, 7:00 A.M., *OR* 36(3):5, 16–17, 19, 61–62, 65; Smith Diary, May 21, 1864, Mary-HS; Rhea, *To the North Anna River*, 212, 216, 220–23, 225, 228–30.

3 Second Corps Headquarters Journal, May 21, 1864, and John Coonan to William A. LaMotte, August 9, 1864, *OR* 36(1):363, 466; Francis A. Walker, *History of the Second Army Corps*, 491–92; Jonah F. Dyer diary, May 22, 1864, in Chesson, *Journal of a Civil War Surgeon*, 158; Rhea, *To the North Anna River*, 238–40. I visited Milford Station on August 10, 1996, but could find no easily accessible remnants of the Second Corps fieldworks.

4 Record of events, Companies A, C, and E, 1st Confederate Engineers, M258, RG109, NARA; Rhea, *To the North Anna River*, 241–53.

5 Rhea, *To the North Anna River*, 258–59, 261–63.

6 Smith Diary, May 22, 1864, Mary-HS; Robert E. Lee to Jefferson Davis, May 22, 1864, in Freeman, *Lee's Dispatches*, 192; Rhea, *To the North Anna River*, 265–67.

7 Rhea, *To the North Anna River*, 266.

8 Grant and Meade endorsements on Hancock to Williams, May 23, 1864, *OR* 36(3):119; Rhea, *To the North Anna River*, 279, 283, 288; Hagerman, *American Civil War*, 261; field visit to North Anna River, August 10, 1996.

9 Rhea, *To the North Anna River*, 298–303, 324. Field visit, August 10, 1996. Henagan's Redoubt and some of the connecting lines are intact but not publicly accessible. Communication from David Lowe to author, November 15, 2005.

10 William B. White to L. C. Bartlett, August [n.d.], 1864, *OR* 36(1):577; Dunlop, *Lee's Sharpshooters*, 80–81; *OR Atlas*, pl. 55; Rhea, *To the North Anna River*, 290–94, 304–19.

11 Gallagher, *Fighting for the Confederacy*, 389; Rhea, *To the North Anna River*, 320, 323, 372.

12　Martin L. Smith to Sarah, May 29, 1864, Schoff Collection, BHL-UM; Jedediah Hotchkiss journal, May 23, 1864, in McDonald, *Make Me a Map of the Valley*, 207; Rhea, *To the North Anna River*, 323–24.

13　Rhea, *To the North Anna River*, 326, 328–29, 331–36.

14　Ibid., 337–39, 341.

15　Ibid., 335–36, 342–49, 352, 354.

16　Francis A. Walker, *History of the Second Army Corps*, 496.

17　William H. Moody to editor of unidentified newspaper, May 29, 1864, FB; First Corps Headquarters Journal, May 24, 1864, *OR* 36(1):1058.

18　Wesley Brainerd reminiscences, in Malles, *Bridge Building in Wartime*, 225–27; Rhea, *To the North Anna River*, 349.

19　Frassanito, *Grant and Lee*, 128, 130. An illustration based on this Timothy O'Sullivan photograph is in Law, "From the Wilderness to Cold Harbor," 137. The other image depicting engineer troops making a road is of the Volunteer Engineer Brigade during the Peninsula campaign. See Hess, *Field Armies and Fortifications*, 108.

20　Gouverneur K. Warren to Meade, May 25, 1864, *OR* 36(3):191–92; Rhea, *To the North Anna River*, 357–59.

21　Thomas J. Linebarger to E. Ann, May 25, 1864, Linebarger Snuggs Papers, SHC-UNC; James S. Wingard to brother, May 25, 1864, Simon P. Wingard Papers, SCL-DU; Joab Goodson to Nannie, May 30, 1864, in Hoole, "Letters of Captain Joab Goodson," 223; Charles S. Venable, "General Lee in the Wilderness Campaign," 244; Smith Diary, May 25–27, 1864, Mary-HS; Charles Marshall to Richard H. Anderson, May 26, 1864, *OR* 36(3):834.

22　Miller, *North Anna Campaign*, 5–6.

23　Ibid., 139; Wilkeson, *Recollections of a Private Soldier*, 120–23.

24　Grant to Halleck, May 26, 1864, in Simon, *Papers of Ulysses S. Grant*, 10:491.

25　Edward A. Wild to Solon A. Carter, May 25, 1864, *OR* 36(2):270–71; Rhea, *To the North Anna River*, 362–67.

26　Circular, Headquarters, Second Corps, May 26, 1864, *OR* 36(3):215; Rhea, *To the North Anna River*, 361–62.

27　Wesley Brainerd reminiscences, in Malles, *Bridge Building in Wartime*, 227–30; Rhea, *To the North Anna River*, 367.

CHAPTER 8

1　Nathaniel Michler to Seth Williams, October 20, 1864, R. A. Brown to G. H. Caldwell, August 9, 1864, John Coonan to William A. LaMotte, August 9, 1864, P. Regis de Trobriand to J. P. Finkelmeier, October 20, 1864, Robert McAllister to William J. Rusling, n.d., Philip Sheridan to John A. Rawlins, May 13, 1865, and David McM. Gregg to C. Kingsbury Jr., July 7, 1864, *OR* 36(1):300, 380, 466, 472, 495, 793, 854; Henry W. Halleck to Benjamin F. Butler, May 26, 1864, and Circular, Headquarters, Second Corps, May 28, 1864, *OR* 36(3):234, 269; Thompson Journal, 273, LC; Thompson, *Engineer Battalion*, 63–64; Beaver Papers, May 28, 1864, PHMC; Howell, "Historical Example of Forcing a River Crossing," 754–56; Rhea, *Cold Harbor*, 32–41, 46, 61–89. There is a modern color photograph of the crossing at Nelson's Bridge in "Grant and Lee, 1864," 13.

2 Nevins, *Diary of Battle*, 389–90.

3 Elisha Hunt Rhodes diary, May 28, 1864, in Robert Hunt Rhodes, *All for the Union*, 155; entry of May 28, 1864, in George A. Bowen, "Diary of Captain George D. Bowen," 189.

4 Andrew A. Humphreys to Ambrose E. Burnside, May 28, 1864, 9:45 P.M., *OR* 36(3):271–71; Rhea, *Cold Harbor*, 94–95.

5 Robert S. Robertson Diary, May 29, 1864, in Walker and Walker, "Diary of the War," pt. 4, 198–99; Rhea, *Cold Harbor*, 97, 102–3. There are modern color photographs of the Shelton House and of nearby Totopotomoy Creek in "Grant and Lee, 1864," 16–17.

6 Smith Diary, May 29, 1864, Mary-HS.

7 John F. Sale diary, May 29, 1864, Sale Papers, LOV.

8 Rhea, *Cold Harbor*, 124, 130, 132–33, 137, 139–40, 142–46, 148, 153, 156–57.

9 Robert S. Robertson diary, May 30, 1864, in Walker and Walker, "Diary of the War," pt. 4, 200; R. A. Brown to G. H. Caldwell, August 9, 1864, *OR* 36(1):380.

10 Hancock to Assistant Adjutant General, Army of the Potomac, September 21, 1865, Second Corps Headquarters Journal, May 29, 1864, and John C. Tidball to not stated, July 1, 1864, *OR* 36(1):343, 365, 511; Hancock to Williams, May 29, 1864, 9:00 P.M., Charles H. Morgan to David B. Birney, May 29, 1864, Hancock to Williams, May 30, 1864, 9:00 A.M., and Tidball to Francis A. Walker, May 30, 1864, *OR* 36(3):296–97, 300, 326, 331–32.

11 Robert S. Robertson Diary, May 31, 1864, in Walker and Walker, "Diary of the War," pt. 4, 202, and James A. Beaver diary, May 30–31, 1864, Beaver Papers, PHMC.

12 Morton, "Incidents of the Skirmish," 47; Joab Goodson to Nannie, May 30, 1864, in Hoole, "Letters of Captain Joab Goodson," 223.

13 Romeyn B. Ayres to Charles Griffin, May 31, 1864, Lysander Cutler to Capt. Marvin, May 31, 1864, 8:40 A.M., and Burnside to Humphreys, May 31, 1864, 2:25, 5:20, and 8:00 P.M., *OR* 36(3):394, 398, 406–8; Rhea, *Cold Harbor*, 163–73.

14 Humphreys to Hancock, May 31, 1864, 10:45 A.M., Hancock to Meade, May 31, 1864, 1:00 P.M., Wright to Hancock, May 31, 1864, 3:00 P.M., Hancock to Humphreys, May 31, 1864, 6:50 and 11:00 P.M., Humphreys to Hancock, May 31, 1864, 11:20 and 11:35 P.M., Circular, Headquarters, Second Corps, May 31, 1864, 11:00 and 11:50 P.M., Francis C. Barlow to Francis A. Walker, May 31,

1864, 7:10 A.M., Walker to Barlow, May 31, 1864, 10:30 P.M., Wright to Humphreys, May 31, 1864, received 9:30 A.M., sent 9:05 A.M., 1:15 and 2:10 P.M., and Meade to Wright, May 31, 1864, 9:45 P.M., *OR* 36(3):380–86, 399, 401–2, 404; Rhea, *Cold Harbor*, 163–73.

15 Gallagher, *Fighting for the Confederacy*, 400; Rhea, *Cold Harbor*, 211.

16 Sheridan to Rawlins, May 13, 1866, Alfred T. A. Torbert to James W. Forsyth, July 4, 1864, George A. Custer to A. E. Dana, July 4, 1864, and Wesley Merritt to Dana, June 26, 1864, *OR* 36(1):794, 805, 822, 848; Meade to Wright, May 31, 1864, 9:45 P.M., *OR* 36(3):404; Rhea, *Cold Harbor*, 182, 185, 188, 191.

17 Wright to Humphreys, June 1, 1864, 9:00 A.M. and 2:10 P.M., *OR* 36(3):454–55; Rhea, *Cold Harbor*, 196, 213, 227.

18 Sheridan to Humphreys, June 1, 1864, Sheridan to Rawlins, May 13, 1866, and Torbert to Forsyth, July 4, 1864, *OR* 36(1):783, 794, 806; Sheridan to Humphreys, June 1, 1864, 9:00 A.M., *OR* 36(3):470; Rhea, *Cold Harbor*, 197–98.

19 Gallagher, *Fighting for the Confederacy*, 400; Rhea, *Cold Harbor*, 202–3.

20 Meade to William F. Smith, June 1, 1864, noon, *OR* 36(3):466; Hagood, *Memoirs of the War of Secession*, 258; Rhea, *Cold Harbor*, 207, 213, 227, 229–33.

21 Rhea, *Cold Harbor*, 234–37.

22 Emory Upton to Henry R. Dalton, September 1, 1864, *OR* 36(1):671; Best, *History of the 121st New York*, 156; Rhea, *Cold Harbor*, 242.

23 Rhea, *Cold Harbor*, 243–46.

24 Smith to Meade, June 2, 1864, Smith to Chief of Staff, Army of the Potomac, August 9, 1864, Guy V. Henry to Theodore Read, June 10, 1864, Itinerary of First Brigade, Third Division, Eighteenth Corps, June 1, 1864, and Zina H. Robinson to Charles Devens, June 27, 1864, *OR* 36(1):996, 1000, 1012, 1018–20; William T. H. Brooks to not stated, n.d., 1864, *OR* 51(1):1248; Rhea, *Cold Harbor*, 247–52; Furgurson, *Not War but Murder*, 103–4.

25 William N. Pendleton to Walter H. Taylor, February 28, 1865, *OR* 36(1):1049; Wright to Humphreys, June 1, 1864, 9:30 P.M., *OR* 36(3):457; Rhea, *Cold Harbor*, 153–54, 164–65; Furgurson, *Not War but Murder*, 107–9.

26 Meade to Hancock, June 1, 1864, 10:00 A.M., Hancock to Williams, June 1, 1864, 12:30 P.M., Joshua T. Owen to John M. Norvell, June 1, 1864, 11:15 A.M., and John F. Hartranft to Orlando B. Willcox, June 1, 1864, 10:00 A.M., *OR* 36(3):435, 437, 445, 465; Hess, *Lee's Tar Heels*, 226–28; Rhea, *Cold Harbor*, 207, 211–12, 256, 259, 266.

27 Hancock to Williams, June 1, 1864, 12:30 P.M., *OR* 36(3):437.

28 Meade to Wright, June 1, 1864, 10:10 P.M., Grant to Meade, June 2, 1864, 2:00 P.M., Humphreys to Hancock, Wright, and Smith, June 2, 1864, 1:30 P.M., and Hancock to Humphreys, June 2, 1864, *OR* 36(3):457–58, 478, 481–82; Rhea, *Cold Harbor*, 262, 279–80, 283, 285–86, 289–91.

29 Warren to Burnside, June 2, 1864, 7:00 A.M., *OR* 36(3):499.

30 Williams to Burnside, June 1, 1864, 8:00 P.M., Burnside to Humphreys, June 1, 1864, 9:25 P.M., Meade to Burnside, June 1, 1864, 9:40 P.M., Warren to Meade, June 2, 1864, and Warren to Burnside, June 2, 1864, 7:00 A.M., *OR* 36(3):462–63, 493, 499; Rhea, *Cold Harbor*, 282–83, 286, 296–98, 302–5.

31 Hess, *Lee's Tar Heels*, 229–30; Rhea, *Cold Harbor*, 300, 305–6.

32 Keating, *Carnival of Blood*, 117; George M. Edgar to Col. Johnston, July 24, 1902, Edgar Collection, SHC-UNC; Morton, "Incidents of the Skirmish," 55; Rhea, *Cold Harbor*, 292.

33 George M. Edgar, "When Grant Advanced against a Wall: Reminiscences of the Battle of Cold Harbor," 6, and Edgar to Col. Johnston, July 24, 1902, Edgar Collection, SHC-UNC; Rhea, *Cold Harbor*, 292–93.

34 George M. Edgar to Col. Johnston, July 24, 1902, Edgar Collection, SHC-UNC.

35 Rhea, *Cold Harbor*, 293.

36 James P. Simms to J. M. Goggin, December [n.d.], 1864, *OR* 36(1):1064; Gallagher, *Fighting for the Confederacy*, 401, 405; Laine and Penny, *Law's Alabama Brigade*, 270; Rhea, *Cold Harbor*, 308.

37 William N. Pendleton to Walter H. Taylor, February 28, 1865, *OR* 36(1):1049; Law, "From the Wilderness to Cold Harbor," 138–39; Stiles, *Four Years under Marse Robert*, 276; Gallagher, *Fighting for the Confederacy*, 405; Laine and Penny, *Law's Alabama Brigade*, 270; Rhea, *Cold Harbor*, 308.

38 G. W. Nichols, *Soldier's Story of His Regiment*, 164; Rhea, *Cold Harbor*, 311.

39 Rhea, *Cold Harbor*, 307, 309.

40 Billings, *History of the Tenth Massachusetts Battery*, 199–200.

41 Thompson, *Engineer Battalion*, 64; Best, *History of the 121st New York*, 157; Greenleaf T. Stevens to E. N. Whittier, September 16, 1864, *OR* 36(1):761; Rhea, *Cold Harbor*, 310.

42 Map of the Battlefields of the Totopotomoy and Bethesda Church, G182, Map Collection, RG77, NARA; Rhea, *Cold Harbor*, 309.

43 Hagood, *Memoirs of the War of Secession*, 257; John F. Sale diary, June 2, 1864, Sale Papers, LOV.

CHAPTER 9

1 Rhea, *Cold Harbor*, 312–16.

2 Thomas A. Smyth to A. H. Embler, August 29, 1864, and John Byrne to William A. LaMotte, August 7, 1864, *OR* 36(1):452, 463; entry of June 3, 1864, in George A. Bowen, "Diary of Captain George D. Bowen," 190; Rhea, *Cold Harbor*, 331–37.

3 Hancock to Assistant Adjutant General, Army of the Potomac, September 21, 1865, *OR* 36(1):345; "Grant and Lee, 1864," 52; Henry Richard Swan to Abbie, June 4, 1864, *Civil War Times Illustrated* Collection, USAMHI; Rhea, *Cold Har-*

bor, 338–40; [Sketch of action near Cold Harbor, Va.], G134, Map Collection, RG77, NARA. A photograph taken in 1887 shows the flat terrain over which the Second Corps attacked on June 3. See "Blunt Collection of Cold Harbor Photographs," 47.

4 DuBois, "Cold Harbor Salient," 277; Keating, *Carnival of Blood*, 118, 126; George M. Edgar to Col. Johnston, July 24, 1902, Edgar Collection, SHC-UNC; Rhea, *Cold Harbor*, 319–22.

5 Keating, *Carnival of Blood*, 120; DuBois, "Cold Harbor Salient," 277; George M. Edgar to Col. Johnston, July 24, 1902, Edgar Collection, SHC-UNC; Rhea, *Cold Harbor*, 323.

6 Hancock to Assistant Adjutant General, Army of the Potomac, September 21, 1865, *OR* 36(1):345; DuBois, "Cold Harbor Salient," 278; Rhea, *Cold Harbor*, 324–25.

7 Rhea, *Cold Harbor*, 325–26.

8 Hancock to Assistant Adjutant General, Army of the Potomac, September 21, 1865, Second Corps Headquarters Journal, June 3, 1864, *OR* 36(1):345, 366; Rhea, *Cold Harbor*, 326–27; Keating, *Carnival of Blood*, 123, 127; James A. Beaver diary, June 3, 1864, Beaver Papers, PHMC.

9 Keating, *Carnival of Blood*, 131; Rhea, *Cold Harbor*, 329.

10 John C. Tidball to not stated, July 1, 1864, and Edwin B. Dow to U. D. Eddy, August 7, 1864, *OR* 36(1):512, 515; Hancock to Meade, June 3, 1864, 8:25 A.M., Francis C. Barlow to Francis A. Walker, June 3, 1864, noon, and Hancock to Humphreys, June 3, 1864, 12:45 P.M., *OR* 36(3):531, 533.

11 George W. Getty to C. A. Whittier, October 13, 1864, J. Warren Keifer to Andrew J. Smith, November 1, 1864, Otho H. Binkley to John A. Gump, September 7, 1864, and Augustin N. Parsons to Acting Assistant Adjutant General, Artillery Brigade, Sixth Corps, August 30, 1864, *OR* 36(1):680, 735, 744, 764; Rhea, *Cold Harbor*, 343, 345–46.

12 William F. Smith to Chief of Staff, Army of the Potomac, August 9, 1864, *OR* 36(1):1002; William T. H. Brooks to Assistant Adjutant General, Eighteenth Corps, June [n.d.], 1864, John H. Martindale to Nicholas Bowen, July 1, 1864, and George J. Stannard to W. H. Abel, June 20, 1864, *OR* 51(1):1249, 1254, 1261–62; Laine and Penny, *Law's Alabama Brigade*, 271–72, 274; Law, "From the Wilderness to Cold Harbor," 139–40; Rhea, *Cold Harbor*, 348–57.

13 Rhea, *Cold Harbor*, 358.

14 Burnside to Seth Williams, November 26, 1864, Robert B. Potter to Lewis Richmond, August 1, 1864, and Orlando B. Willcox to J. C. Youngman, September 13, 1864, *OR* 36(1):914, 930, 942; Humphreys to Warren, June 2, 1864, Potter to Burnside, June 3, 1864, and Willcox to P. M. Lydig, October 29, 1864, *OR* 36(3):494, 551, 946; Rhea, *Cold Harbor*, 369–72; Hopkins, *Seventh Regiment Rhode Island*, 184.

15 John F. Hartranft to John D. Bertolette, October 25, 1864, and Albert B.

Twitchell to Robert A. Hutchins, August 8, 1864, *OR* 36(1):952, 983; Willcox to Lydig, October 29, 1864, *OR* 36(3):946.

16 Smith, "Eighteenth Corps at Cold Harbor," 227; Rhea, *Cold Harbor*, 375–76; Furgurson, *Not War but Murder*, 165–67.

17 Nathaniel Michler to Seth Williams, October 20, 1864, *OR* 36(1):301–2.

18 Grant to Meade, June 3, 1864, in Simon, *Papers of Ulysses S. Grant*, 11:13; Grant to Meade, June 3, 1864, 12:30 P.M., *OR* 36(3):526; Rhea, *Cold Harbor*, 378–79.

19 Unnumbered Orders, Headquarters, Army of the Potomac, June 3, 1864, 1:30 P.M., and Willcox to Lydig, October 29, 1864, *OR* 36(3):528–29, 946.

20 Rhea, *Cold Harbor*, 359, 362.

21 Malles, *Bridge Building in Wartime*, 234–36.

22 Entry of June 3, 1864, in George A. Bowen, "Diary of Captain George D. Bowen," 190; Henry Richard Swan to Abbie, June 4, 1864, *Civil War Times Illustrated* Collection, USAMHI.

23 John S. Jones, "From North Anna to Cold Harbor," 155; William Houghton to father, May 31, 1864, Houghton Papers, IHS.

24 Andrew Glaser to brother, May 31, 1864, Charles W. Glaser Papers, SCL-DU.

25 Meade to unidentified correspondent, June 6, 1864, in Meade, *Life and Letters*, 2:201.

26 Ropes, "Battle of Cold Harbor," 351–55.

27 Theodore Lyman to wife, June 3, 1864, in Agassiz, *Meade's Headquarters*, 144, 147; Hagerman, *American Civil War*, 263.

28 Wright to Humphreys, June 3, 1864, 6:45 P.M., *OR* 36(3):545–46.

29 Meade to Grant, June 3, 1863, 5:45 P.M., and John Gibbon to Francis A. Walker, June 3, 1863, *OR* 36(3):526, 534.

30 Hancock to Assistant Adjutant General, Army of the Potomac, September 21, 1865, Gibbon to Septimius Carncross, November 7, 1864, Edwin B. Dow to U. D. Eddy, August 7, 1864, John B. Vande Wiele to [Eddy], October 20, 1864, and Frank Wheaton to Charles Mundee, September 1, 1864, *OR* 36(1):345, 433, 516, 526, 689.

31 Daniel W. Sawtelle reminiscences, in Buckingham, *All's for the Best*, 99–102; Griffin A. Stedman to W. H. Abel, June 10, 1864, *OR* 51(1):1265.

32 James F. Brown to H. J. Morse, September 3, 1864, and Josiah Pickett to William Schouler, December 16, 1864, *OR* 36(1):1014, 1016.

33 Thompson, *Engineer Battalion*, 64, 66.

34 William Nelson Pendleton to Walter H. Taylor, February 28, 1865, *OR* 36(1):1050; Charles Marshall to John C. Breckinridge, June 3, 1864, 10:00 A.M., *OR* 36(3):870.

35 John G. Hall to father, June 3, 1864, W. P. Hall Collection, NCDAH; LeGrand James Wilson, *Confederate Soldier*, 177; Laine and Penny, *Law's Alabama Brigade*, 276.

36 [Tucker], "Some Florida Heroes," 363–64; Barlow to Walker, June 3, 1864, and Smyth to Embler, August 29, 1864, *OR* 36(1):369, 452.

37 William B. Greene to mother, June 6, 1864, and diary entry, June 3, 1864, Hastings, *Letters from a Sharpshooter*, 218.

38 James A. Beaver diary, June 4, 1864, Beaver Papers, PHMC; Haines, *History of the Men of Co. F*, 67; entry of June 3, 1864, in George A. Bowen, "Diary of Captain George D. Bowen," 191–92.

39 Wheaton to Mundee, September 1, 1864, *OR* 36(1):689–90; Wright to Humphreys, June 5, 1864, *OR* 36(3):616.

40 Thompson, *Engineer Battalion*, 66–67; Stedman to Abel, June 10, 1864, *OR* 51(1):1265; General Orders No. 19, First Division, Ninth Division, June 5, 1864, and Special Orders and Circulars, Second Brigade, First Division, Ninth Corps, June–September 1864, RG393, NARA.

41 Smyth to Embler, August 29, 1864, and James H. Wood to Assistant Adjutant General, Artillery Brigade, Second Corps, July 1, 1864, *OR* 36(1):452, 528; Grant to Meade, June 4, 1864, 8:20 P.M., Meade to Grant, June 4, 1864, 8:30 P.M., with Grant's endorsement, Circular, Headquarters, Army of the Potomac, June 4, 1864, 9:40 P.M., Wright to Hancock, June 4, 1864, Hancock to Wright, June 4, 1864, 10:50 P.M., Hancock to Humphreys, June 4, 1864, and June 4, 10:45 P.M., C. H. Morgan to John Tidball, June 4, 1864, and Wright to Humphreys, June 4, 1864, 11:38 P.M., *OR* 36(3):570–71, 573–74, 582.

42 Furgurson, *Not War but Murder*, 185–86; Hess, *Lee's Tar Heels*, 231.

43 Itinerary of Third Division, Second Corps, June 3–4, 1864, and Potter to Lewis Richmond, August 1, 1864, *OR* 36(1):468, 930; Circular, Headquarters, Ninth Corps, June 4, 1864, Humphreys to Warren, June 5, 1864, 11:45 A.M. and 1:30 P.M., Burnside to Humphreys, June 5, 1864, 1:30 A.M., and Humphreys to Sheridan, June 5, 1864, 8:30 A.M., *OR* 36(3):587, 610–11, 617, 628.

44 Potter to Richmond, August 1, 1864, *OR* 36(1):930; Circular, Headquarters, Second Corps, June 4, 1864, Humphreys to Warren and Burnside, June 4, 1864, 7 P.M., Wright to James B. Ricketts, June 4, 1864, 6:30 P.M., Humphreys to Warren, June 5, 1864, 4:20 P.M., Burnside to Warren, June 5, 1864, 7:05 P.M., Burnside to Orlando B. Willcox, June 5, 1864, 3:30 [A.M.], Willcox to Burnside, June 5, 1864, midnight, Humphreys to Burnside, June 5, 1864, 10:50 A.M., Burnside to Humphreys, June 5, 1864, 4:30 P.M., Humphreys to Burnside, June 5, 1864, 5:15 and 7:35 P.M., Humphreys to Ferrero, June 5, 1864, 7:30 P.M., Burnside to Smith, June 5, 1864, Warren to Humphreys, June 6, 1864, 4:30 A.M., and unnumbered Special Orders, Headquarters, Fifth Corps, June 6, 1864, *OR* 36(3):574, 578, 583, 612–13, 619–24, 650–51.

45 Nevins, *Diary of Battle*, 406.

46 Jonah F. Dyer journal, June 4, 1864, in Chesson, *Journal of a Civil War Surgeon*, 165; Warren to Humphreys, June 4, 1864, *OR* 36(3):578; Nevins, *Diary of Battle*, 406.

47 Andrew Jackson Crossley to Samuel Bradbury, June 6, 1864, Bradbury Papers, SCL-DU; Turtle, "History of the Engineer Battalion," 8.

48 Barlow to Walker, June 6, 1864, *OR* 36(3):646; Turtle, "History of the Engineer Battalion," 8; Barlow to Walker, June 7, 1864, *OR* 36(3):673; Thompson Journal, 276, LC.

49 Barlow to Walker, June 6, 7, 1864, and Hancock to Williams, June 7, 1864, 9:10 A.M., *OR* 36(3):646, 671, 673; Turtle, "History of the Engineer Battalion," 8; James A. Beaver diary, June 5–6, 1864, Beaver Papers, PHMC; Thompson, *Engineer Battalion*, 66–67.

50 Barlow to Walker, June 7, 1864, *OR* 36(3):672–73; Thompson, *Engineer Battalion*, 67; Blackford, "Memoirs," 436, LOV.

51 Theodore G. Ellis to H. J. Morse, August 9, 1864, and John Ramsey to not stated, November 28, 1864, *OR* 36(1):458, 461; Hancock to Williams, June 5, 1864, 7:45 A.M., *OR* 36(3):603.

52 Circular, Headquarters, Army of the Potomac, June 6, 1:30 P.M., Circular, Headquarters, Second Corps, June 6, 1864, and Gibbon to Walker, June 6, 7, 1864, *OR* 36(3):640, 645–47, 673.

53 Itinerary of Third Division, Second Corps, June 5–6, 1864, *OR* 36(1):468; Charles H. Morgan to David B. Birney, June 7, 1864, 9:00 A.M., and Hancock to Williams, June 7, 1864, 9:10 A.M., *OR* 36(3):671.

54 George W. Getty to C. A. Whittier, October 13, 1864, and J. Warren Keifer to Andrew J. Smith, November 1, 1864, *OR* 36(1):680, 735; Wright to Humphreys, June 6, 1864, 9:30 A.M., and June 7, 1864, 8:30 A.M., *OR* 36(3):652, 678.

55 Smith to Humphreys, June 7, 1864, *OR* 36(3):687; Stedman to Abel, June 10, 1864, *OR* 51(1):1265.

56 Burnside to Meade, June 5, 1864, 2:00 A.M. and 10:25 [A.M.], James St. Clair Morton to Orlando B. Willcox, June 6, 1864, Burnside to Humphreys, June 7, 1864, 9:00 A.M., and Willcox to Burnside, June 7, 1864, 3:00 P.M., *OR* 36(3):617–18, 659, 680, 686–87.

57 Duane, *Manual for Engineer Troops*, 147.

58 Halleck to Grant, May 31, 1864, and Special Orders Nos. 28 and 31, Headquarters, U.S. Armies, June 5 and 9, 1864, in Simon, *Papers of Ulysses S. Grant*, 11:31n; John G. Barnard to Grant, June 6, 1864, *OR* 36(3):637.

59 Meade to Wright, June 6, 1864, Circular, Headquarters, Sixth Corps, June 6, 1864, Wright to Meade, June 6, 1864, Barlow to Walker, June 6, 1864, and Gibbon to Walker, June 6, 1864, *OR* 36(3):652–53, 646–48.

60 Hancock to Williams, June 6, 1864, 3:20 P.M., and Smith to Meade, June 6, 1864, 11:25 A.M., *OR* 36(3):642–43, 660.

61 Wesley Brainerd memoirs, in Malles, *Bridge Building in Wartime*, 237; Ira Spaulding to James C. Duane, August 30, 1864, *OR* 36(1):315; Alex Chisholm to father, June 8, 1864, in Menge and Shimrak, *Civil War Notebook of Daniel*

Chisholm, 118; Robert McAllister to Ellen and family, June 6, 1864, in James I. Robertson, *Civil War Letters of General Robert McAllister*, 434; Elisha Hunt Rhodes diary, June 7, 1864, in Robert Hunt Rhodes, *All for the Union*, 160.

62 John F. Sale diary, June 4, 8, 1864, Sale Papers, LOV; Thomas Jackson Strayhorn to sister, June 12, 1864, in Wagstaff, "Letters of Thomas Jackson Strayhorn," 316.

63 Grant to Halleck, June 5, 1864, in Simon, *Papers of Ulysses S. Grant*, 11:19–20; Smith to Meade, June 6, 1864, 11:25 A.M., Grant to Butler, June 6, 1864, and Circular, Headquarters, Army of the Potomac, June 7, 1864, *OR* 36(3):660, 662, 669.

64 Williams to Hancock, June 7, 1864, *OR* 36(3):672; Thompson, *Engineer Battalion*, 67; James A. Beaver diary, June 9, 1864, Beaver Papers, PHMC.

65 Jonah F. Dyer diary, June 4, 1864, in Chesson, *Journal of a Civil War Surgeon*, 169; Pat Brady, who is working on a study of the Cold Harbor phase of the Overland campaign, does not believe that Grant was serious about pushing the siege approaches. Notes and communication courtesy of Pat Brady (hereafter referred to as Pat Brady notes).

66 Grant to Meade, July 5, 8, 11, 1864, in Simon, *Papers of Ulysses S. Grant*, 11:173, 193–94, 218; Grant to Meade, July 25, 1864, *OR* 40(3):438.

CHAPTER 10

1 Josiah F. Murphey "reminiscences," in Miller and Mooney, *Civil War*, 106–7; Smith, "Eighteenth Corps at Cold Harbor," 228.

2 Aaron F. Stevens to C. A. Clark, June 10, 1864, *OR* 36(1):1012; Hancock to Humphreys, [June 6, 1864], note in letter book of Headquarters, Armies of the United States, June 6, 1864, Circular, Headquarters, Army of the Potomac, June 7, 1864, Wright to Meade, June 7, 1864, Smith to Meade, June 7, 1864, and Smith to Williams, June 9, 1864, *OR* 36(3):643, 666, 669, 679, 687–88, 715; David Holt reminiscences, in Cockrell and Ballard, *Mississippi Rebel in the Army of Northern Virginia*, 277; Hagood, *Memoirs of the War of Secession*, 262.

3 Daniel W. Sawtelle reminiscences, in Buckingham, *All's for the Best*, 102–3.

4 Haines, *History of the Men of Co. F*, 68; Francis A. Walker, *History of the Second Army Corps*, 517; Circular, Headquarters, Second Corps, and endorsement by John Hancock, June 7, 1864, and James A. Beaver to Hancock, June 7, 1864, *OR* 36(3):672–73.

5 Josiah F. Murphey memoirs, in Miller and Mooney, *Civil War*, 108.

6 Charles Harvey Brewster to Mattie, June 11, 1864, in Blight, *When This Cruel War Is Over*, 314–15; Wilbur Fisk to editor of *The Green Mountain Freeman*, June 11, 1864, in Rosenblatt and Rosenblatt, *Hard Marching Every Day*, 225–26.

7 Hazard Stevens to mother, June 6, 1864, Stevens to aunt, June 7, 1864, Isaac Stevens Papers, UO; Joseph K. Taylor to father, June 11, 1864, in Murphy,

Civil War Letters, 195. Lewis Grant's Vermont brigade of Neill's division had seven successive lines, whereas Benjamin F. Smith's brigade of Ricketts's division had only four. Lewis A. Grant to Peter T. Washburn, September 6, 1864, William H. Ball to John A. Gump, September 10, 1864, and Otho H. Binkley to Gump, September 7, 1864, *OR* 36(1):709, 744, 747. One member of the 50th New York Engineers counted fourteen successive lines on parts of the Cold Harbor battlefield. Clarke Baum to wife, June 11, 1864, Baum Letters, RNB.

8   Frank Wheaton to Charles Mundee, September 1, 1864, *OR* 36(1):690; Snook Diary, June 4–10, 1864, Mary-HS.

9   Emmerton, *Record of the Twenty-third Regiment*, 214; Daniel W. Sawtelle reminiscences, in Buckingham, *All's for the Best*, 101; John Morton to brother, June 10, 1864, Civil War Miscellaneous Collection, USAMHI.

10 George Washington Whitman to mother, June 18, 1864, in Loving, *Civil War Letters of George Washington Whitman*, 121.

11 *History of the Thirty-fifth Regiment*, 246–49; Humphreys to Burnside, June 6, 1864, Burnside to Humphreys, June 6, 1864, James St. Clair Morton to Orlando B. Willcox, June 6, 1864, and Willcox to Burnside, June 10, 1864, 7:30 and 10:30 A.M., *OR* 36(3):655–56, 659, 734–35; Pat Brady notes; drawing of Fort Fletcher in Francis W. Knowles Diary, June 9, 1864, ECU; field sketches of Fort Fletcher by Pvt. Andrew McCallum in Scott, *Forgotten Valor*, after p. 532.

12 *History of the Thirty-fifth Regiment*, 249.

13 Grant to John J. Abercrombie, June 1, 1864, Abercrombie to Halleck, June 2, 1864, Williams to Edward Schriver, June 8, 1864, Williams to George H. Mendell, June 10, 1864, and Schriver to Williams, June 10, 1864, *OR* 36(3):471–72, 512, 695, 722–23.

14 Nevins, *Diary of Battle*, 412.

15 Theodore Lyman to wife, June 3, 1864, in Agassiz, *Meade's Headquarters*, 143.

16 A copy of Edwin Forbes's drawing of Federals constructing works at Cold Harbor is on display at the visitor's center of the Richmond National Battlefield Park. A similar drawing is in Smith, "Eighteenth Corps at Cold Harbor," 224.

17 The canteen that had been converted into an entrenching tool is on display at the visitor's center of the Richmond National Battlefield Park.

18 Thomas R. Price to George P. Mcmurdo, May 30, June 4, 1864, Letters and Telegrams Sent by the Engineer Bureau of the Confederate War Department, M628, RG109, NARA; J. B. Polley to Nellie, July 6, 1864, in Polley, *A Soldier's Letters*, 244–45.

19 Alfred L. Rives to T. T. L. Snead, June 7, 1864, Rives to Samuel Cooper, June 7, 1864, Rives to L. Heyliger, June 11, 1864, Rives to James A. Seddon, June

17, 1864, and Rives to David B. Harris, June 18, 1864, Letters and Telegrams Sent by the Engineer Bureau of the Confederate War Department, M628, RG109, NARA.

20 Orders, Headquarters, Second Corps, May 23, 1864, Circular, Headquarters, Second Corps, May 26, 1864, W. W. Van Ness to Montgomery C. Meigs, May 27, 1864, and Smith to Humphreys, June 5, 1864, *OR* 36(3):123, 215, 265, 626; Circular, Headquarters, Second Corps, May 16, 1864, *OR* 36(2):814; Snook Diary, May 3, 7, 8, 13, 14, 19, 20, 1864, Mary-HS; Richard Delafield to chief engineer, Eighteenth Corps, May 28, 1864, Letters Sent by the Chief of Engineers, M1113, RG77, NARA.

21 Michler to Williams, October 20, 1864, *OR* 36(1):302; Turtle, "History of the Engineer Battalion," 8.

22 Ira S. Spaulding to James C. Duane, August 30, 1864, *OR* 36(1):314.

23 Wesley Brainerd memoirs, in Malles, *Bridge Building in Wartime*, 237–39.

24 Snook Diary, June 7, 1864, Mary-HS.

25 Gallagher, *Fighting for the Confederacy*, 410, 412.

26 Smith Diary, June 4–12, 1864, Mary-HS; Jedediah Hotchkiss journal, June 9–11, 1864, in McDonald, *Make Me a Map of the Valley*, 210.

27 Blackford, *War Years with Jeb Stuart*, 257–58. The 1st Confederate Engineers also opened several crossings of the Chickahominy River to the rear of Lee's army for logistical purposes. Blackford, "Memoirs," 433, LOV.

28 Harry L. Jackson, *First Regiment Engineer Troops*, 47–48; Harris Diary, June 10–13, 1864, VBHS-UR.

29 Gallagher, *Fighting for the Confederacy*, 308, 408; Harris Diary, June 13, 1864, VBHS-UR; Cold Harbor map, G443, vol. 1, pp. 13, 21, Map Collection, RG77, NARA.

30 Elisha Hunt Rhodes diary, June 8, 1864, in Robert Hunt Rhodes, *All for the Union*, 160; Malles, *Bridge Building in Wartime*, 236; entry of ca. June 4, 1864, in George A. Bowen, "Diary of Captain George D. Bowen," 193; McMahon, "Cold Harbor," 219–20.

31 Unidentified member of Manly's battery to editor, June 6, 1864, *Daily Confederate*, June 10, 1864; Stiles, *Four Years under Marse Robert*, 302. Stiles noted (p. 303) that the damaged artillery piece became a relic. Parts of it were hung on display in Richmond and Dr. Gaines, who owned the farm at Gaines's Mill, kept the first damaged wheel at his house. "I saw it there a few years later," Stiles wrote. "The hub and tire had actually fallen apart."

32 Stiles, *Four Years under Marse Robert*, 301–2; Forsberg Memoir, 27, WLU.

33 Mullen Diary, June 8–11, 1864, MC; Oliver Edwards to Henry R. Dalton, August 31, 1864, *OR* 36(1):674.

34 William N. Pendleton to Briscoe G. Baldwin, June 10, 1864, with endorsements by Baldwin and W. LeRoy Brown, *OR* 36(3):888–89.

35 Malles, *Bridge Building in Wartime*, 239–40; Smith to Humphreys, June 6,

1864, Meade to Smith, June 6, 1864, and Halleck to Grant, June 9, 1864, *OR* 36(3):660, 709; John G. Barnard to Grant, June 6, 1864, in Simon, *Papers of Ulysses S. Grant*, 11:31n. There is a good illustration of Coehorn mortars in action at Cold Harbor in Grant, "General Grant on the Wilderness Campaign," 148.

36 Forsberg Memoir, 27, WLU.

37 Gallagher, *Fighting for the Confederacy*, 413; David Holt reminiscences, in Cockrell and Ballard, *Mississippi Rebel in the Army of Northern Virginia*, 280.

38 Nelson A. Miles to John Hancock, June 11, 1864, *OR* 36(3):749; Elisha H. Rhodes diary, June 7, 1864, in Robert Hunt Rhodes, *All for the Union*, 160.

39 Robert B. Potter to Burnside, June 7, 1864, 3:30 P.M., and June 8, 1864, 12:30 A.M., *OR* 36(3):686, 699.

40 Robert B. Potter to Lewis Richmond, August 1, 1864, *OR* 36(1):931; Burnside to Humphreys, June 6, 1864, 1:00 and 5:10 P.M., Potter to Burnside, June 6, 1864, 9:00 A.M. and 9:35 P.M., Potter to Burnside, June 7, 1864, 12:45 and 3:30 P.M., Burnside to Humphreys, June 7, 8, 1864, and Potter to Burnside, June 8, 1864, 12:30 A.M., 6:30 A.M., 5:00 P.M., *OR* 36(3):654–55, 657, 659, 680, 685–86, 698–99, 700–701; Pat Brady notes.

41 Stevens, *Three Years in the Sixth Corps*, 354–55; Edmund J. Cleveland diary, June 6, 1864, in Cleveland, "Second Battle of Cold Harbor," 32; Haines, *History of the Men of Co. F*, 68.

42 Entry of ca. June 4, 1864, in George A. Bowen, "Diary of Captain George D. Bowen," 193–94; Josiah F. Murphey memoirs, June 4, 1864, in Miller and Mooney, *Civil War*, 106; Pattison Diary, June 6, 1864, IHS.

43 Emmerton, *Record of the Twenty-third Regiment*, 210–11, 213.

44 Entries of June 6, 8, 1864, in George A. Bowen, "Diary of Captain George D. Bowen," 193–94; Charles H. Brewster to Mattie, June 11, 1864, in Blight, *When This Cruel War Is Over*, 314–15. For an illustration of bombproofs at Cold Harbor, see McMahon, "Cold Harbor," 219.

45 William A. Ketcham reminiscences, 22, John Lewis Ketcham Papers, IHS; Tyler, *Recollections of the Civil War*, 214–15; entry of June 12, 1864, in George A. Bowen, "Diary of Captain George D. Bowen," 195.

46 Clarke Baum to wife, June 11, 1864, Baum Letters, RNB.

47 Gallagher, *Fighting for the Confederacy*, 408–9.

48 Stiles, *Four Years under Marse Robert*, 290.

49 Will Biggs to sister, June 5, 1864, Asa Biggs Papers, SCL-DU; John F. Sale diary, June 9, 1864, Sale Papers, LOV.

50 Gallagher, *Fighting for the Confederacy*, 409–10.

51 Ibid., 411–12.

52 Thompson, *Engineer Battalion*, 66–67, 67n.

53 Second Corps Headquarters Journal, June 6, 1864, and John Gibbon to Septimius Carncross, November 7, 1864, *OR* 36(1):368, 434.

54 Smyth Diary, June 6–7, 1864, DPA.

55 Frank Wheaton to Charles Mundee, September 1, 1864, *OR* 36(1):690.

56 Will Biggs to sister, June 5, 12, 1864, Asa Biggs Papers, SCL-DU.

57 Power, *Lee's Miserables*, 72–78; Strayhorn to sister, June 12, 1864, in Wagstaff, "Letters of Thomas Jackson Strayhorn," 317; Joseph F. Shaner to sisters, June 12, 1864, Shaner Correspondence, WLU; T. James Linebarger to sister, June 7, 1864, Linebarger Snuggs Papers, SHC-UNC.

58 Joseph F. Shaner to sisters, June 12, 1864, Shaner Correspondence, WLU; T. James Linebarger to sister, June 7, 1864, Linebarger Snuggs Papers, SHC-UNC; Law, "From the Wilderness to Cold Harbor," 142.

59 Edward Hitchcock McDonald to Marshall McDonald, June 5, 1864, Marshall McDonald Papers, SCL-DU; Eggleston, "Notes on Cold Harbor," 230–31.

60 Hazard Stevens to aunt, June 7, 1864, Isaac Stevens Papers, UO; John Grierson to sister, June 10, 1864, John Grierson Papers, KCL.

61 Winne Journal, June 14, 1864, Trent Collection, MCL-DU.

62 Gibbon, *Personal Recollections*, 227.

63 Francis A. Walker, *History of the Second Army Corps*, 521; Francis C. Barlow to Francis A. Walker, June 6, 1864, *OR* 36(3):647.

64 Wilkeson, *Recollections of a Private Soldier*, 187–89.

65 Grant to Halleck, June 5, 1864, in Simon, *Papers of Ulysses S. Grant*, 11:19.

66 Grant to Halleck, June 5, 1864, Grant to Butler, June 6, 1864, and Grant to Elihu B. Washburn, June 9, 1864, ibid., 11:20, 23, 32.

67 Robert E. Lee to Jefferson Davis, June 6, 1864, in Freeman, *Lee's Dispatches*, 219–20; Lee to A. P. Hill, June [n.d.], 1864, *OR* 40(2):702–3.

CONCLUSION

1 Hess, *Field Armies and Fortifications*, 308–14.

2 McPherson, *Ordeal by Fire*, 426, 429; Miller, *North Anna Campaign*, 6.

3 Gibbon, *Personal Recollections*, 227–28.

4 Francis A. Walker, *History of the Second Army Corps*, 556; Wilkeson, *Recollections of a Private Soldier*, 191–92; George G. Meade to unidentified, June 24, 1864, in Meade, *Life and Letters*, 2:207.

5 Josiah F. Murphey memoirs, in Miller and Mooney, *Civil War*, 109; Gibbon, *Personal Recollections*, 230.

6 Hazard Stevens to mother, June 28, 1864, Stevens Papers, LC; Charles S. Wainwright journal, June 19, 30, 1864, in Nevins, *Diary of Battle*, 426, 431.

7 Ellis Spear reminiscences, in Spear et al., *Civil War Recollections*, 125; Oliver Wendell Holmes Jr. to parents, June 24, 1864, in Mark DeWolfe Howe, *Touched with Fire*, 149–50.

8 Stephen Minot Weld to father, June 21, 1864, in Weld, *War Diary and Letters*, 318. Many historians have written of a Cold Harbor syndrome, defined as "a

reluctance to make head-on assaults against trenches" in McPherson, *Ordeal by Fire*, 426. There is some validity to this concept, but, as other historians have already noted, it did not prevent the Army of the Potomac from pushing forward. No matter how reluctant Grant's men were to attack entrenched positions, the vast majority of them more or less obeyed the orders to do so even as they grumbled and complained. See Rhea, *Cold Harbor*, 268, and Thomas J. Howe, *Wasted Valor*, 60.

9 Wilkeson, *Recollections of a Private Soldier*, 191–92.

10 Henry Yates Thompson diary, April 16, 1866, in Chancellor, *An Englishman in the American Civil War*, 4.

11 Swinton, *Campaigns of the Army of the Potomac*, 489–96.

12 Feis, *Grant's Secret Service*, 217; Grant to Meade, June 21, 1864, in Simon, *Papers of Ulysses S. Grant*, 11:103.

13 Dana, *Recollections*, 214–15. Dana repeated Grant's argument that the Confederates were morally beaten by the time of the confrontations at the North Anna and Cold Harbor, based on their consistent defensive stands behind earthworks. He defended the decision to launch a general attack on June 3 and pointed out that Union commanders in the east had lost 143,925 men from May 24, 1861, through May 4, 1864, whereas Grant's losses totaled 124,390 from May 4, 1864, to the end of the war. Ibid., 204, 206, 209–11. Interestingly, a few of Grant's soldiers also believed this line of interpretation. Joseph K. Taylor of the 37th Massachusetts wrote, "Lee has lost his prestige of success and fights solely on the defensive." Taylor to father, June 28, 1864, in Murphy, *Civil War Letters*, 200.

14 William T. Sherman to Ellen, May 20, June 12, 30, 1864, in Simpson and Berlin, *Sherman's Civil War*, 638, 647, 660; Sherman to Edwin M. Stanton, May 23, 1864, *OR* 38(4):294.

15 Sherman, *Memoirs*, 2:249, 254.

16 Mason, "Recollections of the Mine Run Campaign," 330; Wilbur Fisk to the *Green Mountain Freeman*, July 11, 1864, in Rosenblatt and Rosenblatt, *Hard Marching Every Day*, 237.

17 John Smith to P. W. Black, June 4, 1864, Richard Moroney to William H. Courtney, December 27, 1864, and Edwin Evans to [John D. Bertolette], n.d., *OR* 36(1):393–94, 961–63.

18 Nosworthy, *Bloody Crucible of Courage*, 535–38.

19 "Field Entrenchments," 184; Matthew Walton Venable, *Eighty Years After*, 52–53.

20 Griffith, *Battle Tactics of the Civil War*, 189.

21 Ibid., 128–30, 132–34.

22 Stiles, *Four Years under Marse Robert*, 347.

APPENDIX

1   The discussion of a comprehensive engineering perspective that considers terrain in relation to the physical dimensions of an earthwork comes from David Lowe, who has shared his views with me on numerous occasions, most recently in a communication dated November 15, 2005.

2   Gilbert Thompson, an enlisted man in the U.S. Engineer Battalion, helped to map the Wilderness battlefield in 1866 and reported the works along and to the north of Orange Turnpike well preserved. Thompson Journal, unpaginated note, LC. For the published map that resulted from this survey, see *OR Atlas*, pl. 96, no. 1. Also, the *Atlas* map at pl. 55, no. 1, vividly depicts Gordon's two lines as they intersect the battered Sixth Corps Line north of Orange Turnpike.

3   Rhea, *Battle of the Wilderness*, photograph section following 208; Davis and Wiley, *Photographic History of the Civil War*, 2:626, 628.

4   Toney, "Reminiscences of the Wilderness," 89.

5   "General's Tour: The Battle of the Wilderness, Part II," 58, identifies this as a remnant of a work made by Burnside's Ninth Corps, but I believe it faces north and northwest rather than south. Most earthwork remnants at the Wilderness have no ditch in front, and the excavation here is on the south side of the parapet.

6   Field visit to the Wilderness, July 12–14, 1995.

7   Ibid., July 12–13, 1995.

8   Law, "From the Wilderness to Cold Harbor," 127. See also a good illustration of Union troops constructing field fortifications at the Wilderness in Webb, "Through the Wilderness," 156.

9   Trowbridge, *Desolate South*, 81.

10 Theodore Lyman quoted in Shreve, "Operations of the Army of the Potomac," 295, and Peirson, "Operations of the Army of the Potomac," 237.

11 Field visit, June 24–26, 1997.

12 David Lowe has seen the 350-yard extension of the Federal main line at the galleries and described it in a communication to me dated November 15, 2005.

13 Communication from David Lowe to author, November 15, 2005. Theodore Lyman saw the Federal line that had been constructed from the West Angle on his visit in April 1866. Peirson, "Operations of the Army of the Potomac," 238.

14 Lyman thought the Confederate main line that crossed Fredericksburg Road 200 yards east of Spotsylvania Court House was "a simple one." But the Federal works 700 to 800 yards east of it were "much more complex, as they come in by successive approaches from the crest above the Ny to this point." Quoted in Peirson, "Operations of the Army of the Potomac," 236.

15 Communication from David Lowe to author, November 15, 2005.

16　Field visit, June 24–25, 1997.

17　Rhea, *Battles for Spotsylvania Court House*, 150; Davis and Wiley, *Photographic History of the Civil War*, 2:635; Law, "From the Wilderness to Cold Harbor," 133.

18　Field visit to North Anna River, August 10, 1996.

19　Frassanito, *Grant and Lee*, 136–37. An illustration based on Timothy O'Sullivan's photograph of Willcox's troops in their trench appears in Law, "From the Wilderness to Cold Harbor," 135.

20　Field visits, August 10, November 1, 1996. For modern color photographs of the remnants and of no-man's-land, see "Grant and Lee, 1864," 56.

21　Field visit to Cold Harbor, November 1, 1996; Davis and Wiley, *Photographic History of the Civil War*, 2:674. David Lowe has seen the well-preserved Fort Fletcher as well as segments of the Second Corps works and opposing Confederate defenses on private property. Communication from Lowe to author, November 15, 2005. There is a good 1930s image of the Confederate works in the Cold Harbor Unit in the 1939 World's Fair Photograph Collection, LOV.

Bibliography

ARCHIVAL SOURCES

Delaware Public Archives, Dover
      Thomas A. Smyth Diary
Duke University, Medical Center Library, Durham, North Carolina
      Josiah Trent Collection
           Charles Knickerbocker Winne Journal
Duke University, Special Collections Library, Durham, North Carolina
      Asa Biggs Papers
      Samuel Bradbury Papers
      Charles W. Glaser Papers
      Robert A. Guyton and J. B. Heaslet Papers
      Winfeld Scott Hancock Papers
      Marshall McDonald Papers
      Simon P. Wingard Papers
East Carolina University, East Carolina Manuscript Collection, Greenville,
   North Carolina
      Francis W. Knowles Diary
Fredericksburg Battlefield, Fredericksburg, Virginia
      William H. Moody Letter
      Milton Myers Journal
      R. S. Robertson Letters
Indiana Historical Society, Indianapolis
      William Houghton Papers
      John Lewis Ketcham Papers
      Alexander B. Pattison Diary
      James C. Stephens Papers
Indiana State Library, Indiana Division, Indianapolis
      Henry C. Marsh Papers
Knox College Library, Galesburg, Illinois
      John Grierson Papers
Library of Congress, Manuscript Division, Washington, D.C.
      Hazard Stevens Papers

Gilbert Thompson Journal

Library of Virginia, Richmond
    1939 World's Fair Photograph Collection
    W. W. Blackford, "Memoirs: First and Last, or Battles in Virginia"
    Joseph McMurran Diary
    John F. Sale Papers

Maryland Historical Society, Baltimore
    John Gibbon Papers
    Martin L. Smith Diary
    James M. Snook Diary

Museum of the Confederacy, Richmond, Virginia
    William W. Blackford Commonplace Book
    Joseph Mullen Jr. Diary

National Archives and Records Administration, Washington, D.C.
    RG77 Records of the Office of the Chief of Engineers
        Map Collection
        M1113 Letters Sent by the Chief of Engineers, 1812–1869
    RG94 Records of the Adjutant General's Office
        Compiled Service Records of Volunteer Union Soldiers Who Served in
            Organizations from the State of New York
        M1064 Letters Received by the Commission Branch of the Adjutant
            General's Office, 1863–1870
    RG109 War Department Collection of Confederate Records
        M258 Compiled Service Records of Confederate Soldiers Who Served
            in Organizations Raised Directly by the Confederate Government
        M628 Letters and Telegrams Sent by the Engineer Bureau of the
            Confederate War Department, 1861–1864

New-York Historical Society, New York, New York
    Leverett E. Seymour Letters

North Carolina Division of Archives and History, Raleigh
    John C. Gorman Diary
    W. P. Hall Collection
    D. H. Hill Papers

Pennsylvania Historical and Museum Commission, Harrisburg
    James A. Beaver Papers

Richmond National Battlefield, Richmond, Virginia
    Clarke Baum Letters

University of Michigan, Bentley Historical Library, Ann Arbor
    James S. Schoff Collection

University of North Carolina, Southern Historical Collection, Chapel Hill
    George M. Edgar Collection
    Alexander R. Lawton Papers

Anne Linebarger Snuggs Papers

Jacob Lyons Diary

University of Oregon, Special Collections, Eugene

Isaac Stevens Papers

University of Richmond, Virginia Baptist Historical Society, Richmond, Virginia

Henry Herbert Harris Diary

University of Virginia, Special Collections, Charlottesville

John Warwick Daniel Papers

U.S. Army Military History Institute, Carlisle Barracks, Pennsylvania

Civil War Miscellaneous Collection

John Morton Letters

Civil War Times Illustrated Collection

Henry Richard Swan Correspondence

Virginia Historical Society, Richmond

Giles Buckner Cooke Diary

Washington and Lee University, Special Collections, Lexington, Virginia

August Forsberg Memoir

William Alexander Gordon Memoirs

Joseph F. Shaner Correspondence

NEWSPAPERS

Daily Confederate (Raleigh, North Carolina)

News and Herald (Winnsboro, S.C.)

BOOKS, ARTICLES, AND BROCHURES

Abbott, Henry L. "The Corps of Engineers." In *The Army of the United States*, edited by Theo F. Rodenbough and William L. Haskin, 111–25. New York: Argonaut Press, 1966.

————. "Cyrus Ballou Comstock." In *Professional Memoirs, Corps of Engineers, United States Army and Engineer Department at Large* 7 (1916): 218–22.

Adams, Michael C. C. *Fighting for Defeat: Union Military Failure in the East, 1861–1865*. Lincoln: University of Nebraska Press, 1992.

Agassiz, George R., ed. *Meade's Headquarters, 1863–1865: Letters of Colonel Theodore Lyman from the Wilderness to Appomattox*. Boston: Atlantic Monthly Press, 1922.

Barlow, Francis Channing. "Capture of the Salient, May 12, 1864." In *The Wilderness Campaign, May–June 1864: Papers of the Military Historical Society of Massachusetts*, 245–62. Vol. 4. Boston: Cadet Armory, 1905.

Beauregard, G. T. "The Defense of Drewry's Bluff." In *Battles and Leaders of the Civil War*, edited by Robert Underwood Johnson and Clarence Clough Buel, 4:195–205. New York: Thomas Yoseloff, 1956.

Beers, Henry Putney. *The Confederacy: A Guide to the Archives of the Government of the Confederate States of America.* Washington, D.C.: National Archives and Records Administration, 1986.

Benson, Susan Williams, ed. *Berry Benson's Civil War Book: Memoirs of a Confederate Scout and Sharpshooter.* Athens: University of Georgia Press, 1992.

The Bermuda Hundred Campaign in Chesterfield County, Virginia. Chesterfield, Va.: Chesterfield Office of News and Public Information, 1993.

Best, Isaac O. *History of the 121st New York State Infantry.* Chicago: W. B. Conkey, 1921.

Billings, John D. *The History of the Tenth Massachusetts Battery of Light Artillery in the War of the Rebellion.* Boston: Hall and Whiting, 1881.

Black, John D. "Reminiscences of the Bloody Angle." *Glimpses of the Nation's Struggle, Fourth Series: Papers Read Before the Minnesota Commandery of the Military Order of the Loyal Legion of the United States, 1892–1897.* St. Paul: H. L. Collins, 1898: 420–436.

Blackford, W. W. *War Years with Jeb Stuart.* New York: Charles Scribner's Sons, 1945.

Blight, David W., ed. *When This Cruel War Is Over: The Civil War Letters of Charles Harvey Brewster.* Amherst: University of Massachusetts Press, 1992.

"The Blunt Collection of Cold Harbor Photographs." *Blue & Gray* 11 (1993): 47–49.

Bowen, George A., ed. "The Diary of Captain George D. Bowen, 12th Regiment New Jersey Volunteers." *Valley Forge Journal* 2 (1985): 176–231.

Bowen, James L. "General Edwards's Brigade at the Bloody Angle." In *Battles and Leaders of the Civil War,* edited by Robert Underwood Johnson and Clarence Clough Buel, 4:177. New York: Thomas Yoseloff, 1956.

Bradwell, I. G. "Gordon's Ga. Brigade in the Wilderness." *Confederate Veteran* 16 (1908): 641–42.

Brown, Varina D. *A Colonel at Gettysburg and Spotsylvania.* Columbia, S.C.: State Co., 1931.

Bruce, George A. "General Butler's Bermuda Hundred Campaign." In *Operations on the Atlantic Coast, 1861–1865: Virginia, 1862, 1864, Vicksburg: Papers of the Military Historical Society of Massachusetts,* 9:303–45. Boston: Cadet Armory, 1912.

Buck, Samuel D. *With the Old Confeds: Actual Experiences of a Captain in the Line.* Baltimore: H. E. Houck, 1925.

Buckingham, Peter H., ed. *All's for the Best: The Civil War Reminiscences and Letters of Daniel W. Sawtelle.* Knoxville: University of Tennessee Press, 2001.

Caldwell, J. F. J. *The History of a Brigade of South Carolinians Known First as "Gregg's," and Subsequently as "McGowan's Brigade."* Philadelphia: King and Baird, 1866.

Carter, Thomas H. "Letter." *Southern Historical Society Papers* 21 (1893): 239–42.

Casler, John O. *Four Years in the Stonewall Brigade.* Dayton, Ohio: Morningside Bookshop, 1971.

Castel, Albert. *Decision in the West: The Atlanta Campaign of 1864.* Lawrence: University Press of Kansas, 1992.

Chancellor, Sir Christopher, ed. *An Englishman in the American Civil War: The Diaries of Henry Yates Thompson, 1863.* New York: New York University Press, 1971.

Chesson, Michael B., ed. *J. Franklin Dyer: The Journal of a Civil War Surgeon.* Lincoln: University of Nebraska Press, 2003.

Clark, George. "From the Rapidan to Petersburg: Wilcox's Alabama Brigade in That Memorable Campaign." *Confederate Veteran* 17 (1909): 381–82.

Cleveland, Edmund J., Jr., ed. "The Second Battle of Cold Harbor." *Proceedings of the New Jersey Historical Society* 66 (1948): 25–37.

Cockrell, Monroe F., ed. *Gunner with Stonewall: Reminiscences of William Thomas Poague.* Jackson, Tenn.: McCowat-Mercer, 1957.

Cockrell, Thomas D., and Michael B. Ballard, eds. *A Mississippi Rebel in the Army of Northern Virginia: The Civil War Memoirs of Private David Holt.* Baton Rouge: Louisiana State University Press, 1995.

Colt, Margaretta Barton. *Defend the Valley: A Shenandoah Family in the Civil War.* New York: Orion Books, 1994.

Compton, E. F. "About the Battle at Drury's Bluff." *Confederate Veteran* 12 (1904): 123.

"Controversy: Was Butler 'Bottled Up'?" *Blue & Gray* 7 (1989): 27–29.

Cullum, George W. *Biographical Register of the Officers and Graduates of the U.S. Military Academy at West Point, N.Y.* 3 vols. Boston: Houghton Mifflin, 1891.

Curtis, J. H. "About the Battle of Drewry's Bluff." *Confederate Veteran* 3 (1895): 347.

Dana, Charles A. *Recollections of the Civil War with the Leaders at Washington and in the Field in the Sixties.* New York: D. Appleton, 1902.

Daniel, W. Harrison, ed. "H. H. Harris' Civil War Diary (1863–1865), Part II." *Virginia Baptist Register*, no. 36 (1997): 1840–61.

Davis, William C., and Bell I. Wiley, eds. *Photographic History of the Civil War.* 2 vols. New York: Black Dog and Leventhal, 1994.

Denson, C. B. "The Corps of Engineers and Engineer Troops." In *Histories of the Several Regiments and Battalions from North Carolina in the Great War, 1861–'65*, edited by Walter Clark, 4:409–32. Goldsboro: Nash Brothers, 1901.

Drewry's Bluff. Richmond National Battlefield Park brochure.

Duane, J. C. *Manual for Engineer Troops.* New York: D. Van Nostrand, 1862.

DuBois, A. "Cold Harbor Salient." *Southern Historical Society Papers* 30 (1902): 276–79.

Dunlop, W. S. *Lee's Sharpshooters; Or, The Forefront of Battle.* Dayton, Ohio: Morningside Bookshop, 1982.

Eggleston, George Cary. "Notes on Cold Harbor." In *Battles and Leaders of the Civil War*, edited by Robert Underwood Johnson and Clarence Clough Buel, 4:230–32. New York: Thomas Yoseloff, 1956.

Emmerton, James A. *A Record of the Twenty-third Regiment Mass. Vol. Infantry in the War of the Rebellion, 1861–1865*. Boston: William Ware, 1886.

Feis, William B. *Grant's Secret Service: The Intelligence War from Belmont to Appomattox*. Lincoln: University of Nebraska Press, 2002.

"Field Entrenchments." *Army and Navy Journal* (November 7, 1868): 184–85.

Frassanito, William A. *Grant and Lee: The Virginia Campaigns, 1864–1865*. New York: Charles Scribner's Sons, 1983.

Freeman, Douglas Southall, ed. *Lee's Dispatches: Unpublished Letters of General Robert E. Lee, C.S.A. to Jefferson Davis and the War Department of the Confederate States of America, 1862–1865*. New York: G. P. Putnam's Sons, 1957.

Furgurson, Ernest B. *Not War but Murder: Cold Harbor, 1864*. New York: Alfred A. Knopf, 2000.

Gallagher, Gary W., ed. *Extracts of Letters of Major-General Bryan Grimes to His Wife*. Wilmington, N.C.: Broadfoot Publishing, 1986.

———, ed. *Fighting for the Confederacy: The Personal Recollections of General Edward Porter Alexander*. Chapel Hill: University of North Carolina Press, 1989.

Galloway, G. Norton. "Hand-to-Hand Fighting at Spotsylvania." In *Battles and Leaders of the Civil War*, edited by Robert Underwood Johnson and Clarence Clough Buel, 4:170–74. New York: Thomas Yoseloff, 1956.

Gambrell, Robert. "Fighting at Spottsylvania C.H." *Confederate Veteran* 17 (1909): 225.

"The General's Tour: The Battle of the Wilderness, Part I, The Fighting on May 5, 1864." *Blue & Gray* 12 (1995): 53–63.

"The General's Tour: The Battle of the Wilderness, Part II, The Fighting on May 6, 1864." *Blue & Gray* 12 (1995): 50–64.

"The General's Tour: The Battles at Spotsylvania Court House Virginia, May 8–21, 1864." *Blue & Gray* 1 (1984): 35–57.

"The General's Tour: The Bermuda Hundred Campaign." *Blue & Gray* 7 (1989): 51–59, 61–62.

Gibbon, John. *Personal Recollections of the Civil War*. New York: G. P. Putnam's Sons, 1928.

Gibson, J. Catlett, and William W. Smith. "The Battle of Spotsylvania Courthouse, May 12, 1864." *Southern Historical Society Papers* 32 (1904): 200–215.

"Grant and Lee, 1864: From the North Anna to the Crossing of the James." *Blue & Gray* 11 (1993): 10–22, 44–46, 50–54, 56–58.

Grant, Lewis A. "Review of Major-General Barlow's Paper on the Capture of the Salient at Spottsylvania, May 12, 1864." In *The Wilderness Campaign, May–June 1864: Papers of the Military Historical Society of Massachusetts*, 4:265–71. Boston: Cadet Armory, 1905.

Grant, Ulysses S. "General Grant on the Wilderness Campaign." In *Battles and Leaders of the Civil War*, edited by Robert Underwood Johnson and Clarence Clough Buel, 4:145–51. New York: Thomas Yoseloff, 1956.

————. *Personal Memoirs of U. S. Grant*, 2 vols. New York: Viking, 1990.

Green, William H. "From the Wilderness to Spotsylvania." In *War Papers Read before the Commandery of the State of Maine, Military Order of the Loyal Legion of the United States*, 2:91–104. Portland, Maine: Lefavor-Tower, 1902.

Greiner, James M., Janet L. Coryell, and James R. Smither, eds. *A Surgeon's Civil War: The Letters and Diary of Daniel M. Holt, M.D.* Kent, Ohio: Kent State University Press, 1994.

Griffith, Paddy. *Battle Tactics of the Civil War.* New Haven, Conn.: Yale University Press, 1987.

Grimsley, Mark. *And Keep Moving On: The Virginia Campaign, May–June 1864.* Lincoln: University of Nebraska Press, 2002.

A Guide to Civil War Maps in the National Archives. Washington, D.C.: National Archives and Records Administration, 1986.

Hagerman, Edward. *The American Civil War and the Origins of Modern Warfare: Ideas, Organization, and Field Command.* Bloomington: Indiana University Press, 1988.

————. "From Jomini to Dennis Hart Mahan: The Evolution of Trench Warfare and the American Civil War." *Civil War History* 13 (1967): 197–220.

Hagood, Johnson. *Memoirs of the War of Secession: From the Original Manuscripts of Johnson Hagood.* Columbia, S.C.: State Co., 1910.

Haines, William P. *History of the Men of Co. F, with Descriptions of the Marches and Battles of the 12th New Jersey Vols.* Mickelton, N.J.: N.p., 1897.

Hastings, William H., transcriber. *Letters from a Sharpshooter: The Civil War Letters of Private William B. Greene, Co. G, 2nd United States Sharpshooters (Berdan's), Army of the Potomac, 1861–1865.* Belleville, Wis.: Historic Publications, 1993.

Hess, Earl J. *Field Armies and Fortifications in the Civil War: The Eastern Campaigns, 1861–1864.* Chapel Hill: University of North Carolina Press, 2005.

————. *Lee's Tar Heels: The Pettigrew-Kirkland-MacRae Brigade.* Chapel Hill: University of North Carolina Press, 2002.

Hicks, Roger W., and Frances E. Schultz. *Battlefields of the Civil War.* Topsfield, Mass.: Salem House, 1989.

History of the Thirty-fifth Regiment Massachusetts Volunteers, 1862–1865. Boston: Mills, Knight, 1884.

Hoole, W. Stanley, ed. "The Letters of Captain Joab Goodson, 1862–1864, Part II." *Alabama Review* 10 (July 1957): 215–31.

Hopkins, William P. *The Seventh Regiment Rhode Island Volunteers in the Civil War, 1862–1865.* Providence, R.I.: Snow and Farnham, 1903.

Howard, James McH. "Brig. Gen. Walter H. Stevens." *Confederate Veteran* 30 (1922): 249–50.

Howe, Mark DeWolfe, ed. *Touched with Fire: Civil War Letters and Diary of Oliver Wendell Holmes, Jr., 1861–1864.* Cambridge: Harvard University Press, 1946.

Howe, Thomas J. *Wasted Valor: The Petersburg Campaign, June 15–18, 1864.* Lynchburg, Va.: H. E. Howard, 1988.

Howell, R. P., Jr. "An Historical Example of Forcing a River Crossing: The Federal Cavalry at the Pamunkey River, Va., May 27, 1864." In *Professional Memoirs, Corps of Engineers, United States Army and Engineer Department at Large* 7 (1915): 753–57.

Jackson, Edward C. "The Bloody Angle." In *Civil War Sketches and Incidents: Papers Read by Companions of the Commandery of the State of Nebraska, Military Order of the Loyal Legion of the United States*, 1:258–62. Omaha: Commandery, 1902.

Jackson, Harry L. *First Regiment Engineer Troops, P.A.C.S.: Robert E. Lee's Combat Engineers*. Louisa, Va.: R. A. E. Design and Publishing, 1998.

"James Chatham Duane." In *Professional Memoirs, Corps of Engineers, United States Army and Engineer Department at Large* 4 (1912): 407–8.

Jones, Cadwallader. "Tree Cut Down by Bullets." *Confederate Veteran* 34 (1926): 8.

Jones, John S. "From North Anna to Cold Harbor." In *Sketches of War History, 1861–1865: Papers Prepared for the Ohio Commandery of the Military Order of the Loyal Legion of the United States, 1890–1896*, 4:147–58. Cincinnati: Robert Clarke, 1896.

Jones, Terry L., ed. *The Civil War Memoirs of Captain William J. Seymour: Reminiscences of a Louisiana Tiger*. Baton Rouge: Louisiana State University Press, 1991.

Jordan, William C. *Some Events and Incidents during the Civil War*. Montgomery, Ala.: Paragon Press, 1909.

Katcher, Philip, ed. *Building the Victory: The Order Book of the Volunteer Engineer Brigade, Army of the Potomac, October 1863–May 1865*. Shippensburg, Pa.: White Mane, 1998.

Keating, Robert. *Carnival of Blood: The Civil War Ordeal of the Seventh New York Heavy Artillery*. Baltimore: Butternut and Blue, 1998.

Kennedy, Frances H., ed. *The Civil War Battlefield Guide*. 2nd ed. Boston: Houghton Mifflin, 1998.

Kernan, Michael. "The Object at Hand." *Smithsonian* 20 (May 1989): 24–28.

Krick, Robert E. L. *Staff Officers in Gray: A Biographical Register of the Staff Officers in the Army of Northern Virginia*. Chapel Hill: University of North Carolina Press, 2003.

Krick, Robert K. "An Insurmountable Barrier between the Army and Ruin: The Confederate Experience at Spotsylvania's Bloody Angle." In *The Spotsylvania Campaign*, edited by Gary W. Gallagher, 80–126. Chapel Hill: University of North Carolina Press, 1998.

Laine, J. Gary, and Morris M. Penny. *Law's Alabama Brigade in the War between the Union and the Confederacy*. Shippensburg, Pa.: White Mane, 1996.

Law, E. M. "From the Wilderness to Cold Harbor." In *Battles and Leaders of the Civil War*, edited by Robert Underwood Johnson and Clarence Clough Buel, 4:118–44. New York: Thomas Yoseloff, 1956.

Loehr, Charles T. *War History of the Old First Virginia Infantry Regiment*. Richmond: William Ellis Jones, 1884.

Longacre, Edward G. *Army of Amateurs: General Benjamin F. Butler and the Army of the James, 1863–1865.* Mechanicsburg, Pa.: Stackpole Books, 1997.

——, ed. "From the Wilderness to Cold Harbor in the Union Artillery." *Manuscripts* 35 (1983): 202–13.

Lord, Francis A. "The Coehorn Mortar." *Civil War Times Illustrated* 5, no. 5 (August 1966): 18–19.

Loving, Jerome M., ed. *Civil War Letters of George Washington Whitman.* Durham, N.C.: Duke University Press, 1975.

Lyman, Theodore. "Usefulness of the Maps Furnished to Staff of the Army of the Potomac Previous to the Campaign of May 1864." In *The Wilderness Campaign, May–June 1864: Papers of the Military Historical Society of Massachusetts,* 4:79–80. Boston: Cadet Armory, 1905.

Malles, Ed, ed. *Bridge Building in Wartime: Colonel Wesley Brainerd's Memoir of the 50th New York Volunteer Engineers.* Knoxville: University of Tennessee Press, 1997.

Mason, Edwin C. "Recollections of the Mine Run Campaign." In *Glimpses of the Nation's Struggle.* 1st ser. *A Series of Papers Read before the Minnesota Commandery of the Military Order of the Loyal Legion of the United States,* 308–36. St. Paul: St. Paul Book, 1887.

——. "Through the Wilderness to the Bloody Angle at Spotsylvania Court House." In *Glimpses of the Nation's Struggle.* 4th ser. *A Series of Papers Read before the Minnesota Commandery of the Military Order of the Loyal Legion of the United States, 1892–1897,* 281–312. St. Paul: H. L. Collins, 1898.

McAndrews, Eugene V. "George Gillespie and the Medal of Honor." *Military Engineer* 61 (September–October 1969): 334–35.

McDonald, Archie P., ed. *Make Me a Map of the Valley: The Civil War Journal of Stonewall Jackson's Topographer.* Dallas: Southern Methodist University Press, 1973.

McMahon, Martin T. "Cold Harbor." In *Battles and Leaders of the Civil War,* edited by Robert Underwood Johnson and Clarence Clough Buel, 4:213–20. New York: Thomas Yoseloff, 1956.

McPherson, James. *Ordeal by Fire: The Civil War and Reconstruction.* 3rd ed. New York: McGraw-Hill, 2001.

Meade, George, ed. *The Life and Letters of George Gordon Meade.* 2 vols. New York: Charles Scribner's Sons, 1913.

Menge, W. Springer, and J. August Shimrak, eds. *The Civil War Notebook of Daniel Chisholm: A Chronicle of Daily Life in the Union Army, 1864–1865.* New York: Ballantine Books, 1989.

Michie, Peter S. *The Life and Letters of Emory Upton.* New York: D. Appleton, 1885.

"Michie, Peter Smith." *Dictionary of American Biography,* 12:597–98. New York: Charles Scribner's Sons, 1933.

Miller, J. Michael. *The North Anna Campaign: "Even to Hell Itself," May 21–26, 1864.* Lynchburg, Va.: H. E. Howard, 1989.

Miller, Richard F., and Robert F. Mooney, eds. *The Civil War: The Nantucket Experience, Including the Memoirs of Josiah Fitch Murphey*. Nantucket, Mass.: Wesco, 1994.

Moore, J. H. "Archer's Tennesseans at Spottsylvania." In *Camp-Fire Sketches and Battle-Field Echoes*, 311–13. Springfield, Mass.: King, Richardson, 1889.

Morrison, James L., Jr., ed. *The Memoirs of Henry Heth*. Westport, Conn.: Greenwood Press, 1974.

Morton, T. C. "Incidents of the Skirmish at Totopotomoy Creek, Hanover County, Virginia, May 30, 1864." *Southern Historical Society Papers* 16 (1888): 47–56.

Munden, Kenneth W., and Henry Putney Beers. *The Union: A Guide to Federal Archives Relating to the Civil War*. Washington, D.C.: National Archives and Records Administration, 1986.

Murphy, Kevin C., ed. *The Civil War Letters of Joseph K. Taylor of the Thirty-seventh Massachusetts Volunteer Infantry*. Lewiston, Maine: Edwin Mellen Press, 1998.

Neil, J. H. Reminiscences, *The News and Herald* (Winnsboro, S.C.), May 25, 1910.

Nevins, Allan, ed. *A Diary of Battle: The Personal Journals of Colonel Charles S. Wainwright, 1861–1865*. New York: Harcourt, Brace, World, 1962.

Nichols, G. W. *A Soldier's Story of His Regiment*. Kennesaw, Georgia: Continental Book Company, 1961.

Nichols, James L. *Confederate Engineers*. Tuscaloosa, Ala.: Confederate Publishing, 1957.

Nosworthy, Brent. *The Bloody Crucible of Courage: Fighting Methods and Combat Experience of the Civil War*. New York: Carroll and Graf, 2003.

The Official Military Atlas of the Civil War. New York: Fairfax Press, 1983.

Peirson, Charles Lawrence. "The Operations of the Army of the Potomac, May 7–11, 1864." In *The Wilderness Campaign, May–June 1864: Papers of the Military Historical Society of Massachusetts*, 4:207–40. Boston: Cadet Armory, 1905.

Pleasants, Henry, Jr., and George H. Straley. *Inferno at Petersburg*. Philadelphia: Chilton Co., 1961.

Polley, J. B. *A Soldier's Letters to Charming Nellie*. New York: Neale, 1908.

Power, J. Tracy. *Lee's Miserables: Life in the Army of Northern Virginia from the Wilderness to Appomattox*. Chapel Hill: University of North Carolina Press, 1998.

Purifoy, John. "The Jeff Davis Artillery at Bloody Angle." *Confederate Veteran* 24 (1916): 222–24.

Reardon, Carol. "A Hard Road to Travel: The Impact of Continuous Operations on the Army of the Potomac and the Army of Northern Virginia in May 1864." In *The Spotsylvania Campaign*, edited by Gary W. Gallagher, 170–202. Chapel Hill: University of North Carolina Press, 1998.

Rhea, Gordon C. *The Battle of the Wilderness, May 5–6, 1864*. Baton Rouge: Louisiana State University Press, 1994.

————. *The Battles for Spotsylvania Court House and the Road to Yellow Tavern, May 7–12, 1864*. Baton Rouge: Louisiana State University Press, 1997.

————. *Cold Harbor: Grant and Lee, May 26–June 3, 1864*. Baton Rouge: Louisiana State University Press, 2002.

————. *To the North Anna River: Grant and Lee, May 13–25, 1864*. Baton Rouge: Louisiana State University Press, 2000.

Rhodes, Robert Hunt, ed. *All for the Union: The Civil War Diary and Letters of Elisha Hunt Rhodes*. New York: Orion Books, 1991.

Rhodes, Steven B. "Jeremy Gilmer and the Confederate Engineers." M.A. thesis, Virginia Polytechnic Institute and State University, 1983.

Roberts, James Walter. "Diary." *Florida Historical Quarterly* 11 (1932): 58–75.

Robertson, James I., Jr., ed. *The Civil War Letters of General Robert McAllister*. New Brunswick, N.J.: Rutgers University Press, 1965.

Robertson, William Glenn. *Back Door to Richmond: The Bermuda Hundred Campaign, April–June 1864*. Newark: University of Delaware Press, 1987.

Roe, David D., ed. *A Civil War Soldier's Diary: Valentine C. Randolph, 39th Illinois Regiment*. DeKalb: Northern Illinois University Press, 2006.

Ropes, John C. "The Battle of Cold Harbor." In *The Wilderness Campaign, May–June 1864: Papers of the Military Historical Society of Massachusetts*, 4:343–62. Boston: Cadet Armory, 1905.

Rose, Rebecca Ansell. *Colours of the Gray: An Illustrated Index of Wartime Flags from the Museum of the Confederacy's Collection*. Richmond: Museum of the Confederacy, 1998.

Rosenblatt, Emil, and Ruth Rosenblatt, eds. *Hard Marching Every Day: The Civil War Letters of Private Wilbur Fisk, 1861–1865*. Lawrence: University Press of Kansas, 1992.

Roth, Dave, and Greg Mertz. "The General's Tour: Upton's Attack at Spotsylvania, C.H., Va., May 10, 1864." *Blue & Gray* 18 (Summer 2001): 54–65.

Samito, Christian G., ed. *"Fear Was Not in Him": The Civil War Letters of Major General Francis C. Barlow, U.S.A.* New York: Fordham University Press, 2004.

Schiller, Herbert M. "Beast in a Bottle: The Bermuda Hundred Campaign, May 1864." *Blue & Gray* 7 (1989): 8–26.

Scott, Robert Garth, ed. *Forgotten Valor: The Memoirs, Journals, and Civil War Letters of Orlando B. Willcox*. Kent, Ohio: Kent State University Press, 1999.

Seay, W. M. "Vivid Story of Drury's Bluff Battle." *Confederate Veteran* 12 (1904): 229.

Sherman, William T. *Memoirs of General William T. Sherman*. 2 vols. New York: D. Appleton, 1875.

Shiman, Philip L. "Army Engineers in the War for the Union, 1861–1865." Courtesy of the author.

Shreve, William P. "The Operations of the Army of the Potomac, May 13–June 2,

1864." In *The Wilderness Campaign, May–June 1864: Papers of the Military Historical Society of Massachusetts*, 4:291–318. Boston: Cadet Armory, 1905.

Silliker, Ruth L., ed. *The Rebel Yell and the Yankee Hurrah: The Civil War Journal of a Maine Volunteer*. Camden, Maine: Down East Books, 1985.

Simon, John Y., ed. *The Papers of Ulysses S. Grant*. 26 vols. Carbondale: Southern Illinois University Press, 1967–2003.

Simpson, Brooks D., and Jean V. Berlin, eds. *Sherman's Civil War: Selected Correspondence of William T. Sherman, 1860–1865*. Chapel Hill: University of North Carolina Press, 1999.

Small, Harold A., ed. *The Road to Richmond: The Civil War Memoirs of Major Abner R. Small of the Sixteenth Maine Volunteers*. New York: Fordham University Press, 2000.

Smith, William Farrar. "Butler's Attack on Drewry's Bluff." In *Battles and Leaders of the Civil War*, edited by Robert Underwood Johnson and Clarence Clough Buel, 4:206–12. New York: Thomas Yoseloff, 1956.

———. "The Eighteenth Corps at Cold Harbor." In *Battles and Leaders of the Civil War*, edited by Robert Underwood Johnson and Clarence Clough Buel, 4:221–30. New York: Thomas Yoseloff, 1956.

Spear, Abbott, et al., eds. *The Civil War Recollections of General Ellis Spear*. Orono: University of Maine Press, 1997.

Stevens, George T. *Three Years in the Sixth Corps*. Albany, N.Y.: S. R. Gray, 1866.

Stewart, A. M. *Camp, March and Battlefield; Or, Three Years and a Half with the Army of the Potomac*. Philadelphia: James B. Rodgers, 1865.

Stiles, Robert. *Four Years under Marse Robert*. New York: Neale, 1904.

Supplement to the Official Records of the Union and Confederate Armies. 100 vols. Wilmington, N.C.: Broadfoot Publishing, 1993–2000.

Swinton, William. *Campaigns of the Army of the Potomac: A Critical History of Operations in Virginia, Maryland, and Pennsylvania from the Commencement to the Close of the War, 1861–65*. New York: Charles B. Richardson, 1866.

Talcott, T. M. R. "Reminiscences of the Confederate Engineer Service." In *The Photographic History of the Civil War*, edited by Francis Trevelyan Miller, 5:256–70. New York: Review of Reviews, 1911.

Thienel, Phillip M. *Mr. Lincoln's Bridge Builders: The Right Hand of American Genius*. Shippensburg, Pa.: White Mane, 2000.

Thompson, Gilbert. *The Engineer Battalion in the Civil War*. Washington, D.C.: Press of the Engineer School, 1910.

Toney, Marcus B. "Reminiscences of the Wilderness." *Confederate Veteran* 3 (1895): 89–90.

Trowbridge, John T. *The Desolate South, 1865–1866*. Freeport, N.Y.: Books for Libraries, 1970.

Trudeau, Noah Andre. "The Walls of 1864." *MHQ: Quarterly Journal of Military History* 11 (1994): 23–31.

[Tucker, James F.]. "Some Florida Heroes." *Confederate Veteran* 11 (1903): 363–65.

Turtle, Thomas. "History of the Engineer Battalion." *Printed Papers of the Essayons Club of the Corps of Engineers* 1 (1868–72): 1–9.

Tyler, Mason Whiting. *Recollections of the Civil War, with Many Original Diary Entries and Letters Written from the Seat of War, and with Annotated References.* New York: G. P. Putnam's Sons, 1912.

Venable, Charles S. "General Lee in the Wilderness Campaign." In *Battles and Leaders of the Civil War,* edited by Robert Underwood Johnson and Clarence Clough Buel, 4:240–46. New York: Thomas Yoseloff, 1956.

Venable, Matthew Walton. *Eighty Years After; Or, Grandpa's Story.* Charleston, W.Va.: Hood-Hiserman-Brodhag, 1929.

Wagner, Frank. "Michler, Nathaniel." In *The New Handbook of Texas,* 4:703–4. Austin: Texas State Historical Association, 1996.

Wagstaff, Henry McGilbert, ed. "Letters of Thomas Jackson Strayhorn." *North Carolina Historical Review* 13 (1936): 311–34.

Walker, Charles N., and Rosemary Walker, eds. "Diary of the War, by Robt. S. Robertson." Pts. 3, 4. *Old Fort News* 28 (1965): 119–74.

Walker, Francis A. *History of the Second Army Corps in the Army of the Potomac.* New York: Charles Scribner's Sons, 1887.

Walker, James A. "Letter." *Southern Historical Society Papers* 21 (1893): 231–38.

Warner, Ezra J. *Generals in Blue: Lives of the Union Commanders.* Baton Rouge: Louisiana State University Press, 1964.

———. *Generals in Gray: Lives of the Confederate Commanders.* Baton Rouge: Louisiana State University Press, 1959.

The War of the Rebellion: A Compilation of the Official Records of the Union and Confederate Armies. 70 vols. in 128. Washington, D.C.: U.S. Government Printing Office, 1880–1901.

Webb, Alexander S. "Through the Wilderness." In *Battles and Leaders of the Civil War,* edited by Robert Underwood Johnson and Clarence Clough Buel, 4:152–69. New York: Thomas Yoseloff, 1956.

Weld, Stephen Minot. *War Diary and Letters of Stephen Minot Weld.* 2nd ed. Boston: Massachusetts Historical Society, 1979.

Wilkeson, Frank. *Recollections of a Private Soldier in the Army of the Potomac.* New York: G. P. Putnam's Sons, 1893.

Williams, Edward B., ed. *Rebel Brothers: The Civil War Letters of the Truehearts.* College Station: Texas A & M University Press, 1995.

Wilson, James Harrison. *Under the Old Flag.* 2 vols. New York: D. Appleton, 1912.

Wilson, LeGrand James. *The Confederate Soldier.* Memphis: N.p., 1973.

Winters, Harold A. *Battling the Elements: Weather and Terrain in the Conduct of War.* Baltimore: Johns Hopkins University Press, 1998.

Witherspoon, J. M. "The Battle of Drewry's Bluff." *Confederate Veteran* 3 (1895): 229.

Index

Bradwell, Isaac, 38

Bragg, Gen. Braxton, 108

Brainerd, Col. Wesley, 8–10, 133, 136–37, 163, 175, 186, 188

Bridge building, 133, 136–37

Brooke, Col. John R., 34, 51, 65

Brown, Col. Hiram, 60

Bryan, Sgt. P. N., 167

Buck, Capt. Samuel D., 27

Bull Run, first battle of, xiv

Burns, Lt. Col. Michael W., 25

Burnside, Maj. Gen. Ambrose E., 3–4, 10, 28, 48, 54, 143, 170, 174

Burroughs, Lt. Dent, 264 (n. 32)

Butler, Maj. Gen. Benjamin F., xiii, 4, 19, 99–100, 104, 106–7, 112, 115

Cabell, Col. Henry C., 153, 189

Caldwell, J. F. J., 41, 92

Calloway, Lt. Morgan, 189

Carpenter, Lt. Col. E. P., 117

Carroll, Col. Samuel S., 30

Casler, John O., 82

Chancellorsville, battle of, xiii, xv, 20, 40–42

Chapin, Arthur T., 93

Church, Maj. Nathan, 266 (n. 34)

Clear, Samuel, 34

Clingman, Brig. Gen. Thomas L., 114, 147–49

Coehorn mortars, 79, 159, 190–91, 266 (n. 28), 285 (n. 35)

Cold Harbor, battle of, xvi; field fortifications at, 140, 142, 144, 155–62, 164–68, 183–84, 187–88, 193–99, 205–8, 217, 245–53, 283 (n. 16), 286–87 (n. 8), 289 (nn. 20–21)

Colquitt, Alfred, 189–90

Comstock, Cyrus B., 2–3, 60, 162

Confederate troops

1st Engineers, 14–16, 121, 187–88, 215, 284 (n. 27)

2nd Engineers, 14

3rd Engineers, 14

4th Engineers, 14

Connecticut troops

1st Heavy Artillery, 116, 266 (n. 28)

14th Infantry, 30, 172

21st Infantry, 166

Cooke, Brig. Gen. John R., 28, 30, 189–90, 199

Corps of Engineers (C.S.), 12

Corps of Engineers (U.S.), 1, 4, 17

Corps of Topographical Engineers (U.S.), 4

Crater, battle of the, 177

Curtis, Capt. J. H., 111

Dana, Charles A., 213, 287 (n. 13)

Daniel, Brig. Gen. Junius, 22, 57–58, 67

Dantzler, Col. Olin M., 113

Davis, Jefferson, 1, 108

Delafield, Brig. Gen. Richard, 1, 116–17

Doles, Brig. Gen. George, 55, 57

Drake, Col. Jeremiah C., 117

Drewry, Col. Augustus H., 108

Drewry's Bluff Line, 104–6, 108–10, 118

Duane, Maj. James Chatham, 2, 6–7, 10, 36, 52, 87, 139

DuBois, Pvt. Augustus, 158

Dyer, Surg. Jonah F., 176

Edgar, Col. George M., 151–52, 158

Edwards, Col. Oliver, 72, 76, 78, 82, 180, 190

Elliott, Brig. Gen. Stephen, 114

Ellis, Col. Theodore G., 172

Ellis, Maj. William, 76

Emmerton, Surg. James A., 194

Engineer Bureau (C.S.), 12, 14, 184–85

Engineer officers, 1–7, 12–14

Perry, Brig. Gen. Edward A., 33

Perry, Col. William F., 33

Petersburg: campaign of, xvii–xviii, 4, 177; town of, 18

Pioneers, 11–12, 15–16, 61, 180, 258 (n. 21)

Plaisted, Col. Harris M., 104

Pleasants, Lt. Col. Henry, 4

Poague, Lt. Col. William T., 30, 49, 92

Potter, Brig. Gen. Robert B., 33, 54, 191–93

Ramseur, Stephen D., 57, 67

Ransom, Maj. Gen. Robert, 108

Reardon, Carol, 96

Reekie, J., 253

Rhea, Gordon C., 34, 84, 129, 132, 261 (n. 38)

Rhode Island troops
  2nd Infantry, 93
  7th Infantry, 82

Rhodes, Elisha Hunt, 93, 191

Rice, Brig. Gen. James C., 28

Richmond, 18; defenses of, 19–20

Ricketts, Brig. Gen. James B., 27

Rives, Col. Alfred L., 13–14, 185

Robertson, Robert S., 69, 90, 142

Robinson, Brig. Gen. John C., 27–28

Roemer, Capt. Jacob, 183

Russell, Brig. Gen. David A., 55

Sale, John F., 154, 175–76, 196

Sawtelle, Daniel W., 165–66, 182

Scales, Brig. Gen. Alfred M., 28

Seddon, James A., 14, 16

Sedgwick, Maj. Gen. John, 28, 35–37, 49

Serrell, Lt. Col. Edward W., 8, 114, 116

Seymour, Brig. Gen. Truman, 27–28, 35, 37–38

Shaler, Brig. Gen. Alexander, 37–38

Shaner, Joseph F., 93, 200

Sheridan, Maj. Gen. Philip, 3

Sherman, Maj. Gen. William T., xv, 1, 7, 213–14

Sieges, xvi, 19–20, 188, 207–8; approaches to, 162, 168–78; mining and, 171–72, 177; use of sap roller in, 172, 174, 177

Sleeper, Capt. J. Henry, 153

Smith, Maj. Gen. Martin Luther, 13, 32, 47, 122, 124, 128–29, 134, 141

Smith, Maj. Gen. William F., 17, 100, 102, 104–6, 111–12, 114, 116, 145–47, 162, 176, 186

Smith, Lt. Col. William Proctor, 13

Smith, William W., 27, 35

Smyth, Col. Thomas A., 51, 198

Snook, Sgt. James M., 37–38, 181, 185

Sorrel, G. Moxley, 32, 40

South Carolina troops
  2nd Infantry, 124
  3rd Battalion Infantry, 124
  3rd Infantry, 124
  7th Battalion Infantry, 110
  7th Infantry, 124–25
  12th Infantry, 80
  20th Infantry, 153
  22nd Infantry, 113

Spaulding, Lt. Col. Ira, 8–10, 39

Spofford, Col. Winslow P., 107

Spotsylvania, battle of, xv, 213, 268 (n. 19); field fortifications at, 45–98, 205–7, 217, 227–42, 288 (n. 14); Heth's Salient at, 58–59, 73, 234–36; Mule Shoe Salient at, 47–48, 54–58, 65–85, 124, 152, 163, 187, 217, 228–33, 263–64 (n. 32), 264 (n. 1), 266 (n. 34), 288 (nn. 12–13)

Sprague, William, 210

Steuart, Brig. Gen. George H., 57, 65, 68

Stevens, Surg. George T., 193

Stevens, Capt. Greenleaf T., 154

Stevens, Hazard, 181, 200, 209
Stevens, Col. Walter H., 107–8, 271
    (n. 29)
Stewart, Chap. A. M., 41
Stiles, Robert, 153, 189, 195, 216, 284
    (n. 31)
Stink-shells, 190
Stuart, Maj. Gen. J. E. B., 15
Swan, Henry Richard, 163
Swinton, William, xvi

Talcott, Andrew, 15
Talcott, Col. Thomas M. R., 15–16, 172
Taylor, Joseph K., 287 (n. 13)
Tennessee troops
    17th Infantry, 111
    23rd Infantry, 111
    25th Infantry, 111
Terry, Brig. Gen. Alfred H., 105
Terry, Col. William R., 119, 191
Thompson, Ord. Sgt. Buck, 35
Thompson, Gilbert, 52, 198, 224, 288
    (n. 2)
Tidball, Col. John C., 143
Toney, Marcus B., 58
Tools, 12, 37, 48–49, 87, 114, 143, 184–
    86, 283 (n. 17)
Totten, Brig. Gen. Joseph G., 1
Trees, 18, 20, 34, 39–41, 48, 50, 80–81,
    268 (n. 19)
Trench warfare, xvii, 43, 91–98, 193–
    202
Trowbridge, John T., 231
Trueheart, Charles W., 41
Turnbull, Capt. Charles N., 52
Turner, John W., 118
Twitchell, Capt. Albert B., 161
Tyler, Mason Whiting, 78, 83

United States troops
    Battery C, 5th Artillery, 78

Engineer Battalion, 4, 7–8, 36,
    38–39, 49–52, 153–54, 166, 168–69,
    171, 176, 186, 198, 224, 288 (n. 2)
    14th Infantry, 164
    2nd Sharpshooters, 167
Upton, Col. Emory, 54–58, 72, 76, 86,
    94, 147

Venable, Charles S., 39
Venable, Matthew, 215
Vicksburg campaign, 43, 162, 176, 200
Virginia Forces, 15
Virginia troops
    Rockbridge Artillery, 200
    1st Infantry, 112
    12th Infantry, 154, 196
    26th Battalion Infantry, 151, 158
    28th Infantry, 149
    49th Infantry, 27, 262–63 (n. 15)
    51st Infantry, 189, 191
Volunteer Engineer Brigade, 7–9, 11

Wadsworth, Brig. Gen. James S., 22,
    28, 30, 33
Wainwright, Col. Charles S., 35, 140,
    170, 183–84, 209–10, 226
Walker, Francis A., 132, 201
Walker, Brig. Gen. James A., 48, 57,
    65, 67
Walker, Capt. John, 104
Ward, Brig. Gen. J. H. Hobart, 54
Warren, Maj. Gen. Gouverneur K.,
    16–17, 258 (n. 21); at Cold Harbor,
    140, 142, 146–47, 150; at North
    Anna, 126–27; at Spotsylvania,
    45, 52, 59, 74, 87; at the Wilder-
    ness, 22, 27, 36–37, 39
Weather, 18, 74, 85–86
Weitzel, Brig. Gen. Godfrey, 17, 106,
    111, 115–16, 118
Weld, Stephen Minot, 210

West Point, U.S. Military Academy
at, 1
Wheaton, Frank, 198–99
Whiting, Maj. Gen. William H. C.,
112, 198
Whitman, George Washington, 10, 182
Wilcox, Maj. Gen. Cadmus M., 26, 28,
41, 49, 54, 69
Wild, Brig. Gen. Edward A., 136
Wilderness, battle of the, xiii–xv, 19–
43, 288 (n. 2); Brock Road Line
at, 25–27, 33–35, 42; field fortifi-
cations at, 41–43, 205–6, 217–27,
288 (nn. 5, 8)
Wilkeson, Frank, 96, 135, 201–2, 210
Willcox, Brig. Gen. Orlando B., 33,
161, 174
Wilson's Wharf, battle of, 136
Wisconsin troops
36th Infantry, 149, 156
Witcher, Col. William, 65, 84
Wright, Maj. Gen. Horatio G., 16–17,
23, 37; at Cold Harbor, 145, 165,
169, 174; at Spotsylvania, 49, 59